Women's Organizing and Public Policy in Canada and Sweden

The authors of this volume examine women's organizing and public policy in two northern welfare states, Canada and Sweden. They analyse and compare the gender implications of some key areas of public policy and examine strategic interventions organized by women to challenge and reconstruct these policies. The contributors seek to understand the constraints and possibilities provided by the institutional, political, and discursive contexts in both Sweden and Canada, at the same time as they endeavour to make women's agency visible. The volume is arranged in three sections: domestic policy (childcare, health, education, violence, and sexuality, around which women have organized extensively); vehicles for organizing (the state, political parties, and unions highlight the contexts within which women organize and the struggles around representation in particular); and challenges to the boundaries of "nation" (immigration and regional integration through the European Union and the North American Free Trade Agreement).

Women's Organizing and Public Policy in Canada and Sweden

Edited by
LINDA BRISKIN and
MONA ELIASSON

McGill-Queen's University Press
Montreal & Kingston · London · Ithaca

ISBN 0-7735-1855-X (cloth)
ISBN 0-7735-1891-6 (paper)

Legal deposit third quarter 1999
Bibliothèque nationale du Québec

Printed in Canada on acid-free paper

This book has been published with the help of a grant from the Swedish Council for Research in the Humanities and Social Sciences.

McGill-Queen's University Press acknowledges the financial support of the Government of Canada through the Book Publishing Industry Development Program for its activities. We also acknowledge the support of the Canada Council for the Arts for our publishing program.

Canadian Cataloguing in Publication Data

Main entry under title:
Women's organizing and public policy
in Canada and Sweden
Includes bibliographical references and index.
ISBN 0-7735-1855-X (bound) –
ISBN 0-7735-1891-6 (pbk.)
1. Women – Social networks – Canada. 2. Women – Social networks – Sweden. 3. Women – Government policy – Canada. 4. Women – Government policy – Sweden. 5. Women – Canada – Social conditions. 6. Women – Sweden – Social conditions.
I. Briskin, Linda, 1949– II. Eliasson, Mona
HQ1233.W662 1999 305.4'0971 C99-900234-1

Typeset in ITC Sabon 10/12 with Gill Sans Condensed display by Caractéra inc., Quebec City

Contents

Preface: Collaboration and Comparison

LINDA BRISKIN AND MONA ELIASSON

With the support of various granting agencies in Canada and Sweden, eighteen feminist researchers from the two countries came together in Canada in August 1994 and in Sweden in August the following year. Their goal was to analyse and compare the gender implications of some key areas of public policy and to examine strategic interventions organized by women to challenge and reconstruct these policies. In most cases, the researchers were paired, one from each country, on the basis of shared expertise.[1] They addressed the following policy areas – trade and regional integration, immigration, health, education, violence, sexuality, and childcare – and considered the vehicles for women's organizing – trade unions, political parties, and the state. This choice of issues was meant to balance a focus on conventional areas of policy study, such as health, education, and childcare, with relatively new concerns, such as regional integration, and those that have traditionally been less visible, such as immigration, sexuality, and violence against women. Our interest in highlighting women's organizing explains the chapters on unions, political parties, and the state. This collection of ten in-depth articles emerged out of the collaboration.

A number of threads, some serendipitous and some substantive, led to this project. Part of the story relates to the Swedish Canadian Academic Foundation (SCAF). In June 1991 a cooperative agreement was signed which created a formal network among eight Canadian and Swedish universities to promote research, seminars, and academic exchanges. The coordinating agency, under the auspices of the Swedish ambassador to Canada, was located at York University. Linda Briskin heard about this network in its fledging stages and made proposals to develop specific links between the women's studies programs at the participating Canadian universities and the women's *fora* at Swedish universities. She also began to undertake research on women's organizing in Sweden to complement her ongoing study of such organizing in Canada. Mona Eliasson spent the 1992–93 academic year at York under the auspices of the exchange program between York and Uppsala universities. She taught psychology and worked on her book about male violence against women.

The two of us met in the summer of 1992. At SCAF's conference in November 1992, held at York University, we recommended that the foundation endorse a gender-sensitive approach in its own organization and policies which would ensure the participation and fair representation of women in all SCAF programs, gender awareness in its program topics, the gender-fair distribution of resources, and proactive publicizing of programs to women faculty membres and students in both countries. Frankly, little interest was shown in this proposal, and we turned to developing a joint research project on our own (with some financial support from the Canadian section of SCAF).

Briskin was also inspired to organize this project because of her experiences doing research on women's organizing in Sweden. Over a three-year period, she had spent eight months in that country interviewing women who were organizing in unions, political parties, the university, and the community. In the course of this research, she became increasingly sensitive to the problems of comparative research and the complexities and pitfalls of writing about a country not her own. Surprisingly, the problems evidenced in Western women's research on women in developing countries and noted by many researchers (e.g., Mohanty, 1991) were also relevant to researching an advanced industrialized country similar to Canada. Comparable issues arose – about privileging the observer's perspective and about ethnocentrizing.

Briskin notes, with some dismay, that early on she missed the critical significance of women's organizing in Swedish political parties because she read "parties" (which in Canada have rarely, if ever, been a vehicle for an equity agenda) through Canadian feminist eyes; further, she over-identified "women's organizing" with separate and autonomous structures, an approach that made it harder to understand the role of Swedish women in advancing their own interests.

Given the positive profile of Sweden in progressive North American circles, she also had very high expectations and thus a complicated time making sense of Sweden's surprisingly patriarchal interpersonal culture. Yet she also set Canada up as a standard against which she measured Sweden, despite her original concern that she would do the reverse. Even self-consciously constructing her work as a comparison with Canada in order to make visible her reference points did not seem sufficient to overcome the patterns of privileging. Recognizing these problems, however, became the impetus to organize a project to help develop alternative strategies for undertaking such work.

Ensuring that expert voices from both countries were proactively engaged in developing comparative analyses through an ongoing dialogue seemed central to any alternative. Such dialogues could problematize researcher assumptions, engage with diverse appropriations of conceptual tools, and interrupt the almost inevitable privileging of one perspective – that of the outsider.

The key goals, then, that informed the project design were to highlight the impact of women's organizing on public policy in both countries and to develop a language for understanding policy and political practice across countries and cultures. Fulfilling these goals turned out to be considerably more complex than we had imagined. For many in the project, this comparative work became a vehicle to illuminate unarticulated assumptions about their own countries. Wuokko Knocke reflected, "It is unavoidable that one learns *both* about one's own and about the other country."[2] Sue Findlay commented, "Through my partnership, I found that the exploration of Sweden's 'passion for equality' sharpened my understanding of the limits that liberal democracies like Canada pose to the struggle for equality and how much more vulnerable we are to the conservatizing forces of global capitalism."

In some ways, the project created the conditions for auto-ethnography through the study of *another* society, that is, by using "cross cultural distancing," not to study that society, but to make deeper sense of one's own, to study one's own society as "other," to make it exotic. Colleen Lundy remarked, "The opportunity to work with a Swedish colleague and to learn of different approaches to the same area of concern encouraged me to step back and look at the organizing strategies around violence against women in Canada with renewed clarity. As one of the project members said, "We had the opportunity 'to go away and come back home again.'"

For many the undertaking challenged assumptions that they had about the "other" country and their own. Rebecca Coulter commented: "As a Canadian who from childhood had heard about the wonders of Swedish social democracy and who somehow was led to believe that Canada and Sweden were very similar, I entered our comparative project assuming that it would be easy to write a joint paper because our two countries were essentially the same. I very quickly learned that this was not so ... We struggled for a long time to understand how our two countries could end up with very similar kinds of educational policies with respect to gender and yet arrive at them in quite different ways and through different vehicles."

The issue of competitive evaluations that Briskin found in her own research on Sweden also impacted on the project. Lena Wängnerud commented: "At the beginning, the Canadians and the Swedes had a tendency to think that their own country was 'best' on gender equality and more advanced in women's organizing. Over time, a more modest approach developed. We have something to teach them; they have something to teach us." Mona Eliasson noted: "At the beginning, it was all too easy to do all comparisons in competitive terms – 'Who's best?' Over time, I discovered that one needs to know a lot about another country in order to see the nuances. Without this, you tend to look at achievements in terms of whether they exist in your own country or not."

This project also allowed us to do comparative work without over-relying on potentially problematic secondary sources that can multiply errors. For example, when Rita Liljeström (1984: 662) described how two hundred Swedish women academics "convened to open Sweden's first women's university at Umeå" in 1982, she was describing the first interdisciplinary women's studies conference, which was named "Women's University" to challenge the limits of the ordinary university. Using Liljeström as a source, Gisela Kaplan (1992: 71), in her study of contemporary western European feminism, states, "Since 1982, there has been a women's university in Umeå."

The project also offered us the opportunity to work across disciplines. The team of researchers included sociologists, historians, psychologists, geographers, political scientists, social workers, and those trained in interdisciplinary programs. Roxana Ng noted: "The most valuable aspect of the process is the learning I achieved – about Sweden (obviously) and Canada (surprisingly), and about myself (how my thinking and way of working is so deeply shaped by my training as a sociologist, my experience as a minority woman and in feminist organizing). I can now put myself in a larger framework – thinking beyond my immediate experience and beyond the boundaries in which I have been trained." Lena Gonäs reflected on working with a political scientist: "It has been fascinating to work very intensively with a scientist from another discipline. As a geographer, I am more interested in patterns and variations than in details, so I had to go back to all the sources, looking for the precision requested by my partner."

Finally, the project assumed the value of collaboration – a widely supported strategy among feminist scholars – and tried to bring it into the arena of comparative research. For some participants, it was the cooperation built into the heart of the project's structure which attracted them to it: "Before we met, each of us had accumulated much experience working as activists in social movements in our respective countries. It was our belief in collaboration, in the power of collective thought and practice, that shaped our commitment to this comparative project" (Ross and Landström).

Nonetheless, working across language, culture, concept, and organization of academic life was a considerable challenge.[3]

What can one say about writing with a new colleague across an ocean. It is an exercise that stretches one's creativity and flexibility. The physical and intellectual distances ask one to think carefully about the meanings of terms and ideas, and to question those assumptions that one believes are shared. It is an important test of one's ability to think and write clearly and to exchange ideas openly. (Georgina Feldberg)

It was striking how the same concepts had very different meanings, risking misunderstandings if not clarified in the course of work. (Wuokko Knocke)

Language posed certain interesting problems as we tried, for example, to explain to one another what words like "equality" and "equity" meant in each of our cultures. (Rebecca Coulter)

I learned quite a bit about writing. I was astounded at how many assumptions go into the way a sentence is structured. For example, I would begin a sentence with a subordinate clause beginning with "Although ..." and realize that I was assuming all sorts of things about Sweden that may not be true. (Barbara Cameron)

Not unexpectedly, problems around language and concepts were the most complex; certainly, they operated on at least two levels. As these comments from project participants suggest, we had an ongoing struggle with the need to make concepts transparent and with the meanings accorded such terms as "labour market," the "state," the "community," "civil society," "equality," "feminism," and the "family." Even "volunteerism," a concept that seems quite straightforward, has, as Feldberg and Carlsson found, a specific meaning in each country. Traditionally in Sweden it is expected that necessary services will be provided and paid for by the state. Swedish unions have strongly opposed turning over what could be regular paid jobs to unpaid volunteers. In Canada, by contrast, volunteerism is encouraged as a civic duty.

Perhaps no concept needed more deconstruction than "women's organizing," around which the whole project was framed. As the introduction, "Mapping Women's Organizing in Sweden and Canada," demonstrates, it quickly became clear that such a formulation was more appropriate to a Canadian context. Yet it also challenged the

Swedish participants to make visible sites of women's organizing independent of political parties, and the Canadians to disaggregate women's organizing from feminism.

Struggling with the conceptual apparatus of women's organizing also helped us to avoid some of the problematic interpretations of Swedish "feminism" that have been made by those from outside the country. For example, the situation in Sweden has been described with the catchy phrase "feminism without feminists" (Gelb, 1989) and a frequent claim that the country has no women's movement (e.g., Charles, 1993). Closer examination, such as that undertaken in this book, which interrogates the language of "feminism" and the "women's movement," presents a different and considerably more nuanced analysis.

In addition to complex conceptual tangles, the use of English in the project was a subtle and not-so-subtle form of domination, undoubtedly privileging those with English as a first language, putting the Québécois and Swedish participants at a disadvantage, and making a fully equal partnership impossible. Not surprisingly, the problems of "speaking" in another language converge with the connotative issues, generating layered levels of translation and complication.[4] Inga Wernersson commented: "This experience made me aware of the unequal relations between a 'big' and a 'small' language/culture group. It is not so much the pure technical aspects of language that are important but the cultural and ideological connotations embedded in it. Those 'things' are not translatable. The implication is that it is almost impossible to communicate in English the more specifically Swedish aspects."

In the final analysis, however, despite the differences in academic schedules and work habits and the demanding and time-consuming discussions, this method of working rewarded us with far broader views and a deeper comprehension of our two countries than we could have anticipated. It is hoped that this volume will now make a contribution to deepening the understanding of Canada and Sweden, to the elaboration of feminist comparative research methodologies, and to the development of desperately needed strategies to respond to the disturbing patterns of restructuring that are undermining equality gains in both countries.

NOTES

Since this book is in English, we have alphabetized names in the bibliographies and index according to English practice. Thus names beginning with Å appear in sequence with other names beginning with an unaccented A. We apologize to Swedish readers, who will expect to find these names in a separate section at the end of the alphabet. This is just another example of the complexities of crossing language boundaries.

1 Despite the methodological emphasis on joint authorship, two of the articles in this book are not co-authored. Rianne Mahon is in the enviable position of doing research on both Canada and Sweden over many decades and is completely fluent in Swedish. Given this unique background, we felt that she would make an important contribution to the book. As noted in the introduction to her piece on the unions, Briskin's article was also written without a collaborator. Because of unforeseen circumstances, her partner was unable to continue in the project. However, Briskin did do extensive research in Sweden on four extended visits between 1992 and 1995, during which she conducted in-depth interviews with about forty trade unionists, community activists, feminist researchers, political party activists, and state officials which complements her ongoing research on women in Canadian unions. She also had the benefit of working extensively with the team of researchers involved in this book.
2 All comments from participants quoted in this preface were in response to a request for written feedback about their experiences working on the project.
3 Coulter made an interesting comment: "Approaches to research are different in Canada and Sweden. The Canadians always seemed overburdened and rushed, and for them research often seemed to be something they would 'fit in' around other commitments and obligations. Research and its benefits to the thoughtful development of social policy seemed to be more valued in the Swedish context."
4 Surprisingly, there were also significant technical difficulties using and relying on electronic communication and shared computer diskettes. In this era of information technology, many of the teams were surprised by the difficulties that they faced in "translating" material so it could be read by computers in both countries.

REFERENCES

Charles, Nickie. (1993). *Gender Divisions and Social Change.* Hemel Hempstead: Harvester Wheatsheaf.
Gelb, Joyce. (1989). Sweden: Feminism without feminists? In *Feminism and Politics.* Berkeley: University of California Press.
Kaplan, Gisela. (1992). *Contemporary Western European Feminism.* New York: Allen & Unwin.

Liljeström, Rita. (1994). Sweden: Similarity, singularity, and sisterhood. In Robin Morgan (ed.), *Sisterhood Is Global.* Garden City, NY: Anchor Books.

Mohanty, Chandra. (1991). Under Western eyes: Feminist scholarship and colonial discourses. In Chandra Mohanty, Ann Russo, and Lourdes Torres (eds.), *Third World Women and the Politics of Feminism.* Bloomington: Indiana University Press.

Acknowledgments

We would like to thank the Social Sciences and Humanities Research Council of Canada, the Scandinavian Canadian Academic Exchange, the National Institute of Public Health (in Sweden), the Swedish Council for Planning and Co-ordination of Research, the Swedish Council for Social Research, and the Swedish Council for Research in the Humanities and Social Sciences for financial support for this project.

Contributors

CHRISTINA BERGQVIST is a political scientist. She finished her PhD thesis, "Mäns makt och kvinnors intressen" (The power of men and the interests of women) in 1994. Since then she has been teaching and doing research in the Department of Government, Uppsala University, and has been a visiting scholar at the Department of Political Economy, Carleton University. She also has a research position at Arbetslivein-stitutet in Stockholm. Her current research is about the meaning of women's inclusion in political decision-making positions for the formulation of Swedish welfare policies.

LINDA BRISKIN is an associate professor in the Division of Social Science at York University. She has co-edited *Women Challenging Unions: Feminism, Democracy and Militancy* (1993), co-authored *Feminist Organizing for Change: The Contemporary Women's Movement in Canada* (1988), co-edited *Union Sisters: Women in the Labour Movement* (1985), and co-authored *The Day the Fairies Went on Strike* a book for children (1981). She has an activist and scholarly interest in change-making strategies of women in the union movement, in the community-based women's movement, and in the classroom.

BARBARA CAMERON is an associate professor and chair of Political Science at York University's Atkinson College. The main focus of her research is economic restructuring and state policy, particularly the implications for women's equality. She has published articles on gender and free trade, the North American Free Trade Agreement and new reproductive technologies, new frameworks for labour-market regulation, and training policy. She also researches and publishes on the subject of social rights and Canada's ongoing constitutional crisis.

Cameron is currently engaged in research projects on the growth of precarious employment in Canada and the gender implications of innovations in Canadian labour-market training programs.

MARIANNE CARLSSON has a PhD in psychology and is an associate professor at the Centre for Caring Sciences at Uppsala University. She teaches at the bachelor of science, master of science, and doctoral levels. Her research mainly concerns health and quality of life for women with breast cancer.

REBECCA PRIEGERT COULTER is an associate professor and the associate dean of the Faculty of Education at the University of Western Ontario. Her areas of research specialization are the history of childhood and youth in Canada and gender and education. She is interested in gender relations in teaching and has published research on feminist teachers and on male elementary schoolteachers. Coulter is currently doing research on adolescent males and masculinities, on the development of gender-equity policies and schooling in Canada, and on women and educational restructuring.

MONA ELIASSON received her PhD in experimental psychology in 1976. She has since switched to feminist research and is currently involved in work dealing with women's strategies in environments of extreme male domination, such as violent private relationships, and with women in academic careers. Her publications cover both areas. Eliasson has appointments at the Centre for Feminist Research and the Department of Psychology, Uppsala University.

GEORGINA FELDBERG is an associate professor of social science at York University. She is the director of the York University Centre for Health Studies and the academic director of the National Network on Environments and Women's Health, a federally funded centre of excellence. Her research explores the historical development of women's health movements in North America, and she is currently writing a book entitled *Defining Women's Health: Community and Elite Initiatives*.

SUE FINDLAY is a political scientist living in Toronto. She has worked as an "insider" (for the New Democratic Party, the federal bureaucracy, and the Canadian Advisory Council on the Status of Women) and as an "outsider" in a variety of feminist groups in Ottawa, Toronto, and Vancouver. Her experience shapes her ongoing exploration of the practices the feminists have used to lobby the Canadian state and to represent women's interests since the 1960s. Her articles pertinent to this volume include contributions to *Feminism and Political Economy* (1987), *And Still We Rise* (1993), and *Women and the Canadian Welfare State: Challenges and Change* (1997).

LENA GONÄS is adjunct professor in economic geography and deputy director of the unit for Labour Market and Industrial Relations at the National Institute for Working Life (NIWL) in Stockholm. Her research has focused on restructuring in the manufacturing and public sectors, labour-market policies, and gender relations. She is currently writing a book on new labour-market patterns and changing gender relations entitled *Restructuring the Welfare State*. In 1997 NIWL started a multidisciplinary research program on labour-market segregation and women's health, which she co-directs with Åsa Kilbom, the professor of ergonomics at the institute.

WUOKKO KNOCKE, a sociologist, has been working as a senior researcher at the Swedish Centre for Working Life (now the National Institute for Working Life) since 1979. Her research focuses on the work life and labour-market situation of immigrants, with a concentration on issues related to gender, class, and ethnicity. She has also theorized the processes and mechanisms that lead to the marginalization of female and male immigrants in the world of work and to their exclusion from the labour market. She has published extensively in these areas.

CATHARINA LANDSTRÖM received her PhD in the theory of science at Göteborg University in 1998 with the thesis "Everyday actor-network: Locals and globals in molecular biology." She has since worked as a research associate in the Research Policy Group at the Tema Institute, Linköping University. She has been an active member in Riksförbundet för Sexuellt Likaberättigande (RFSL) since 1985.

COLLEEN LUNDY is an associate professor in the School of Social Work at Carleton University. Her research, writing, and practice have focused on violence in women's lives, whether in personal relationships, on university campuses, or in urban settings. She has also published work on alcohol and other drug dependence among women and is co-editor of *Women's Use of Alcohol and Other Drugs in Canada* (1996).

RIANNE MAHON is a professor at Carleton's School of Public Administration. She has written numerous articles on the political economy of Canada and Sweden. She is co-editor, with Jane Jenson, of *Production, Space, Identity: Political Economy Faces the 21st Century* (1993) and *The Challenge of Restructuring: North American Unions Respond* (1993). Mahon has also co-edited, with Wallace Clement, a volume on Sweden – *Swedish Social Democracy: A Model in Transition* (1994). Her contribution to this volume, however, represents the first time that she has tried to weave the stories together.

CHANTAL MAILLÉ is associate professor and chair of the Simone de Beauvoir Institute and the Women's Studies Programmes at Concordia University. Her recent work has focused on Quebec women and nationalism, the women's movement, and women and social policies. She is the author of *Les Québécoises et la conquête du pouvoir politique* (1990) and *Primed for Power: Women in Canadian Politics* (1990), and the co-author of *Sexes et militantisme* (1989), *Et si l'amour ne suffisait pas ... Femmes, famille et adultes dépendants* (1991), and *Travail et soins aux proches dépendants* (1993).

ROXANA NG has been active in the immigrant women's and feminist movements in Canada since the mid-seventies, shortly after she immigrated from Hong Kong. Her activism forms the underpinning of her scholarship, which is concerned with understanding how relations of gender, race, and class are expressed in people's daily experiences. In addition to numerous articles and reports, she has published two books on community-state relations, entitled *The Politics of Community Services: Immigrant Women, Class and State* (1998, 1996) and *Community Organization and the Canadian State* (1990, with J. Muller and Gillian Walker). She teaches at the Ontario Institute for Studies in Education.

BECKI ROSS is a member of the Anthropology/Sociology Department and the Women's Studies Program at the University of British Columbia. Her teaching and research interests include lesbian and gay history, feminist theory, social movements, qualitative methodology, and the sociology of sexualities. She wrote *The House That Jill Built: A Lesbian Nation in Formation* (1995) and the chapter "'It's merely designed for sexual arousal': Interrogating the indefensibility of lesbian smut" in *Bad Attitude/s on Trial: Feminism, Pornography and the Butler Decision* (1997), by Brenda Cossman, Shannon Bell, Lise Gotell, and Becki Ross. A long-time activist in the women's movement, queer politics, and anti-racist struggles, she is currently researching the socio-cultural history of erotic entertainement (burlesque, go-go, and strip-tease) in post-war Vancouver.

LENA WÄNGNERUD is a political scientist. She finished her PhD thesis, "Politikens andra sida: Om kvinnorepresentation i Sveriges riksdag" (The second face of democracy: Women's representation in the Swedish Parliament), in 1998. She is now teaching and doing research at the Department of Political Science, Göteborg University. Her current work is a comparative study on how women have reached top positions of power in Denmark, Norway, and Sweden.

INGA WERNERSSON is an associate professor (docent) in the Department of Education and Educational Research, Göteborg University. She has been working on different research projects on gender and education since the mid-seventies. The main themes have been the perception of gender and gender differences in classroom interaction patterns. Her current research concerns the relations between gendered patterns in classroom interaction and the outcome of schooling in terms of both self-concept and achievement. Another project is a comparative study of how female students in different countries perceive research education and research as an occupation.

Women's Organizing and Public Policy in Canada and Sweden

Mapping Women's Organizing in Sweden and Canada: Some Thematic Considerations

LINDA BRISKIN

ABSTRACT

In this introduction, social-movement theory helps situate some of the themes about organizing that weave through the volume. The chapter begins by problematizing the complex interplay between feminisms and women's organizing and between movement and organization. The second part, on "mapping" women's organizing, examines the limits and possibilities provided by the "political opportunity structure" and highlights the significance of welfare-state regimes in Sweden and Canada. It considers the relationship of inside-outside organizing and rejects any abstract hierarchy of strategies. Finally, this section explores differences in the discursive terrains around class/gender and equality/difference.

The third part of the chapter assesses the effects of women's organizing in both countries, applying the criteria of success used by social-movement scholars. It considers the traditional category of political and policy outcomes but also takes up mobilization and cultural outcomes. As well, it notes the importance of shifts in the discursive field of politics and in the identification of women as a legitimate constituency. The conclusion looks at the impact of restructuring, the globalization of capital, and the growing permeability of national boundaries on women's organizing. It considers five arenas of strategic significance: discursive struggle, re-visioning the state, workplace control, coalitions and alliances, and a new internationalism.

Documenting and analysing women's organizing at this historical conjuncture is critical, and not only because of the threat posed by restructuring and globalization to the gains that women have made. The ideology of neo-liberalism, which promotes a market-driven reality as the only alternative, also undermines belief in the potential for political agency. In such a deeply pessimistic and demobilizing environment, documenting the persistence and success of women's organizing is part of asserting agency, and it provides strategic optimism during these harsh times.

This collection of articles examines women's organizing and public policy in two northern welfare states, Sweden and Canada. Sweden has a well-deserved reputation for taking seriously the challenges of the double day. In policy and in practice it has developed innovative programs to accommodate and ease the tensions between work and family life (Lewis and Åstrom, 1992). As a result, Sweden has provided a model for feminist activists and scholars. Too often interest in Canada has been eclipsed by a focus on the dominant English-speaking countries – the United States and Britain – but this collection suggests that much can be learned from the Canadian experience, about grassroots organizing in particular. The long-standing commitment to some form of the welfare state, currently facing serious challenge in both countries, and the strikingly different patterns of feminist organizing and policy practices provide a provocative context through which to deepen our understanding of the process of making change by and for women.

This book seeks to understand the constraints and possibilities provided by the institutional, political, and discursive contexts in both Sweden and Canada, at the same time as making women's agency visible. So it looks, for example, at how different state forms have influenced women's organizing. But it also addresses the impact of women's organizing on framing and implementing public policy, on reconstituting discourse, and on the practices of unions, political parties, and the state. It explores the strategies that women have used to organize themselves as a vocal and politicized constituency. In so doing, it stretches definitions of organizing and of political practice, politicizes the social and the private, and expands conceptions of agency for each country. The project of comparison allows the mechanisms at work in each society to emerge more clearly, challenging what is often taken for granted in each context. This volume, however, goes beyond a comparison of Sweden and Canada to make visible women's organizing across the boundaries of policy areas and institutions *within* each country.

Despite aiming for thematic continuity around policy and practice, the collection has as its goal the highlighting of a multifaceted complexity rather than seamless generalities that flatten the textures of each society. Neither Canada nor Sweden is a fixed reference point: for example, liberal democracy versus social democracy, pluralist versus corporatist. In each country a multiplicity of competing views and practices coexist; hegemonic practices are constantly being challenged not only from the margins but from internal contradictions within dominant discourses and institutions. Furthermore, each society is in tremendous flux, facing the demands of globalization and economic and political restructuring.

The volume is arranged in three sections: domestic policy (childcare, health, education, violence, and sexuality, around which women have organized extensively); vehicles for organizing (the state, political parties, and unions highlight the contexts within which women organize and the struggles around representation in particular); and challenges to the boundaries of "nation" (immigration and regional integration through the European Union [EU] and the North American Free Trade Agreement [NAFTA]).

In order to avoid homogenizing voices, this introduction does not attempt to summarize the articles; rather, the authors speak for themselves in their texts and also in the abstracts that precede them. Here, social-movement theory helps to situate some of the general themes about organizing that weave through the volume. The discussion opens with a consideration of the relationships among "feminisms," "women's movements," "organizing," and "organizations." The second part, "Mapping Women's Organizing," examines the limits and possibilities provided by what is called the "political opportunity structure," the relationship of inside-outside organizing, and the discursive terrain around equality/difference and class/gender. The third part assesses the effects of women's organizing. In the conclusion, this chapter considers the impact of restructuring and globalization on women's organizing and the strategic importance of building national and international alliances and coalitions.

FEMINISMS, MOVEMENTS, ORGANIZING, AND ORGANIZATIONS

It is a methodological truism that the way in which research is framed influences both what is revealed and what is concealed. The choice to focus on women's "organizing" rather than on the women's movement, feminist organizing, or women's organizations allows the relationships among various sorts of organizing, between women's movements and women's organizations, and between feminisms and women's organizing to emerge. Such an approach highlights both institutional and community-based organizing and rejects polarizing them. It is taken as a given that women's organizing in both Sweden and Canada is heterogeneous and that a multiplicity of organizations and feminisms exist.

Self-consciously structuring this text around women's organizing rather than feminist organizing avoids reductionism and allows the relationship between women's organizing and feminisms as ideologies, as strategies, as analyses, as organizing practices, as visionary alternatives, and as complex self-identifications and identities to be problematized. Such an approach resists reifying feminisms. They emerge, then, not as abstract criteria or boundary markers against which women's organizing is assessed, but as a fluid, contextually located set of meanings and practices. Feminism is a site of struggle, a moment of resistance, an organizing tool; it helps produce communities of interest but also patterns of exclusion.

In a generic way, feminisms challenge gender-based inequity and thus can make visible the common problems that women face. Given the complex diversity of class, race, ethnicity, ability, and sexuality operating in most contexts, however, this trajectory towards gender commonality can be strategically mobilizing or fragmenting. Moreover, not one but multiple feminisms struggle for place, bringing different approaches, for example, to prioritizing issues, to representation, to working with diversities among women, to the practice of leadership, to organizational process, to strategies of separate, self, and autonomous organizing, and to alliances and coalitions.

This approach opens up space to study the range of women's organizing that is explicitly anti-feminist or not overtly or openly identified with feminism (such as nationalist organizing).[1] Although it is beyond the scope of this book to make more than passing reference to nationalist and anti-feminist organizing, disaggregating feminisms and women's organizing is particularly relevant to comparisons between Sweden and Canada, since in the former the convergence of feminism with women's organizing has been considerably weaker than in the latter. The self-identification as feminist, and the labelling of organizing practices, strategies, and solutions as feminist, is more contested in Sweden than in Canada. Problematizing rather than assuming a connection, especially cross-culturally, thus facilitates an important debate about the relationship of feminisms to women's organizing.

The women's movement has a shifting, amoeba-like character; it is, and has always been, politically, ideologically, and strategically diverse, although this diversity takes different forms in Sweden and Canada. Although one aspect of "movement" is the organizations that it produces, the women's movement cannot be reduced to its organizational expressions, nor should the meaning of "movement" be filtered primarily through specific organizational identifications. It is equally reflected in women's consciousness of themselves as a constituency and in public support for a wide range of women's concerns. As this volume demonstrates, the relationship of movement to organization is configured differently in Sweden and Canada.

Women's movement organizations are not necessarily structured in any particular way. Some focus on single issues such as childcare, reproductive rights, or pay equity. Some have a wide-ranging political program. Many are regionally specific; some organize federally, nationally, or institutionally (for example, in universities and government ministries); others are located in small communities. Some organize around legislative issues; some provide services; others focus on organizing women as a constituency inside institutions such as unions and political parties (e.g., the women's committee of the New Democratic Party [NDP] in Canada or the women's organization of the Social Democratic Party [SAP] in Sweden). The membership of some organizations is heterogeneous; others are more homogeneous, with specific constituencies such as immigrant women, lesbians, women of colour, business and professional women, or women in trades. All are shaped by the historical context and the political, economic, and social conditions that they face.

Some use traditional methods of organizing themselves; others have developed unconventional structures and strategies. Suzanne Staggenborg (1995: 343) notes that "the main distinction ... is between organizations that are 'collectivist' or 'participatory' and those that are 'bureaucratic' or 'hierarchical.'" She explores, as others have, the reasons why collectivist organizations have difficulty surviving; but rather than concluding that traditional organizational forms are superior, she considers the contribution of each: "an informal, decentralized structure makes organizational maintenance difficult but tends to encourage strategic and tactical innovation, whereas a formalized and centralized structure promotes maintenance while narrowing strategic choices" (343).

Myra Ferree and Patricia Martin in *Feminist Organizations* (1995) focus on the "intersection of feminism as a social movement with organizations as entities that mobilize and co-ordinate collective action" (13). But they emphasize that feminist organizations are not "static outcome[s] of mobilization efforts" but a "continuing process of organizing to produce social transformations that benefit women" (14). They argue against "prejudging one type of feminist organizational strategy as more central or effective than another," and they conclude that "different organizational forms (such as grassroots and participatory service-delivery, mass-membership mobilization for lobbying or demonstrations, expertise-centred educational efforts, and identity-oriented, culture-building work) all play important and distinctive roles" (10).

MAPPING WOMEN'S ORGANIZING

What I call "mapping" situates women's organizing in relation to social, political, and economic conditions. It highlights the links among and the tensions between multiple sites of organizing, recognizing the degree to which conditions in one context affect possibilities in another. It addresses discursive terrain and struggle. Mapping works with relationships and connections, in contrast to approaches that isolate aspects of women's organizing – for example, studying women's organizing in political parties but not its relationship to community-based organizing. The purpose of mapping, however, is not to provide a complete or coherent picture of each society, represent a found world, or produce a map in the traditional sense. Rather, it resists the somewhat inevitable tendency, especially in a comparative text, to produce "ideal types" in order to contrast, in this case, "Sweden" and "Canada" and set up a binary between the two. Instead of a seamless picture of each country, what emerges is a "map" of contradictions, tensions, and interrelationships.

Mapping complicates the lens through which we read the local and the particular. It provides a graphic reminder that women's organizing in each country is not homogeneous – certainly not across issues or sites, or even around particular issues – but always reflects different political positions, strategies, and organizational locations. For example, in this volume Feldberg and Carlsson identify the multiple positions and strategies of women organizing around health: from those who seek to expand the presence and influence of women within traditional medicine to those who struggle for alternative and oppositional health structures and practices. They also demonstrate the permeable boundaries shaping the defining and organizing around policy areas. For example, to understand women's health organizing, it is necessary to explore organizing for employment and fair wages, environmental protection, and social justice. Reading across the articles in this volume helps to illuminate this sometimes invisible network of strategic and analytic connections.

Mapping both emphasizes and makes significant the fact that different assessments emerge, depending on the positioning of the issues and the authors. Thus some chapters in this book focus on the success of women's organizing in Sweden (e.g., Bergqvist and Findlay and Mahon), while others analyse the gaps and the problems (e.g., Eliasson and Lundy). Trying to make sense of the apparent contradictions deepens our understanding of Swedish political life. Mapping also uncovers corresponding themes in different organizing sites. For example, in both countries, issues of visibility and invisibility infuse the organizing of immigrant women and lesbians (see Knocke and Ng and Ross and

Landström respectively), although the meaning of such struggles is not necessarily the same for each group.

Mapping is interested in highlighting strategic and political relationships. In this way it takes up the call by Burstein, Einwohner, and Hollander (1995) to focus on "bargaining," thereby directing attention to "the interdependence of movement and target" (280) and emphasizing "interactions among movement organizations, the organizations whose behaviour they are trying to change, and relevant actors in the broader environment" (277). Bargaining focuses on instrumental organizing with a direct target and goal, but it also assumes that *relationship* is central to understanding social movements.

Mapping also puts relational realities at the centre of what needs to be understood, but encompasses those less instrumental and contradictory relationships among and between sites of organizing and vehicles for and agents of change, many of which are not proactive or self-conscious, some of which can lead to alliances, and some of which increase confrontation. Such relationships are always significant, if not always visible or proactively mobilized. Both their absence and their presence have an impact.

In their discussion of immigration, Knocke and Ng stress that official policy measures shape and limit the form and content of immigrant women's organizing; concomitantly, women's organizing impacts on policy. However, it is also the case that organizing in one arena limits and facilitates organizing in another. And this process is not always self-conscious, intentional, or without contradiction. Knocke and Ng point to the dialectical relationships among diverse groups of women, and how their struggles with each other and with the larger society inform and transform their practices. They argue that in Canada the early second-wave feminist movement had a significant, but indirect influence on the configuration of intergroup organizing among immigrant women. Although "not attentive to the special needs of immigrant women, their struggle created a social climate for women from diverse backgrounds to speak about their oppression as housewives, as immigrants, as workers." Far from having a stabilizing effect, this process "led to divisions within the feminist movement," but it also "contributed to new theorization and creative alliances." It is this complex relationship between various interventions, organizing strategies, and political practices – indeed, gains and losses – that the text as a whole reveals.

Political Opportunity Structures

Social-movement theorists and those who study women's organizing seek to understand the constraints and possibilities provided by institutional, political, and discursive contexts, and to specify the constellation of factors that affect the emergence and success of social movements. J. Craig Jenkins and Bert Klandermans (1995b) focus on the four-way interaction among citizens, social movements, the political representation system, and the state, and like many scholars in this tradition, they identify "the political opportunity structure" as central to the emergence and development of social movements. "[O]pportunities are primarily structured by the organization of the state, the cohesion and alignment among political elites, and the structure, ideology and composition of political parties" (4). These "afford opportunities for mobilization and set limits on the effectiveness of social movement strategies" (7).[2] In keeping with this approach, Mahon, paraphrasing Marx, notes in this volume that women have had to organize in circumstances not of their own choosing. Analysing the political opportunities afforded in each country, then, is a central theme in this volume. Such a consideration is balanced, however, by highlighting women's agency and by recognizing the construction of political opportunities where there were few or none. For example, Coulter and Wernersson note the "strategic use of the state" in relation to equity in schools.[3] They point out that women's organizing strategies have been particularly effective when they utilize and expand upon existing discourses and when they are seen to meet or match other types of policy objectives; for example, in the attempts to attract more girls and women into science. They conclude that women working for gender equity in schools have consciously appropriated the discourse around education for global competitiveness as an integral part of strategy to draw attention to gender inequality.

Comparisons between political opportunity structures in Sweden and Canada help to uncover "both a national logic and an institutional logic" (Katzenstein, 1987: 4) and in particular highlight the significance of welfare-state regimes. The distinctive features of the Canadian and Swedish welfare-state regimes reflect differences in the political forces that shaped them. The impetus for the modern Canadian welfare state arose from working-class struggles of the late 1930s and the Second World War period. The greatest expansion took place in the 1960s under the combined pressure of the NDP, a moderate social democratic party with formal links to the labour movement, and a growing progressive nationalism in Quebec. The design of social programs has been very strongly shaped by national (Quebec/Canada) and regional considerations centring on Atlantic Canada. In general, the country's political system, particularly federalism and a single-member plurality electoral system, favours political interests that are regionally based rather than those that are evenly dispersed geographically, such as class and gender. Canada's labour movement is highly decentralized, and the central trade union federation politically weak. It is not involved in the negotiation of collective agreements and has no institutionalized role in economic decision-making. Historically, the country's strongest political parties have had solid regional bases of support; the NDP has been in office in three provinces but never at the federal level, and has virtually no support in Quebec.

In contrast, Sweden's welfare state came into being as a result of an economically and politically powerful labour movement. Swedish politics have been organized primarily on the basis of class and have been dominated by centralized and influential organizations of workers and employers. There are strong links, including overlaps in leadership, between the largest trade union federation (LO) and the SAP. Between 1938 and 1990 wages were set through centralized bargaining between the LO and the employers' organization (SAF). In what has often been referred to as a corporatist system, state economic and social policies have been developed through negotiations between the LO, the SAF, and the government; class-based organization are directly represented on state boards, agencies, and commissions.[4]

In comparing the two countries in this volume, Cameron and Gonäs emphasize that, although women organize differently in various welfare-state regimes, there is a common basis for political mobilization of women across regimes, given the gendered organization of production and their greater responsibility for both the public and private reproductive labour of society. This fact helps to explain why similar issues emerge in both countries despite some dramatic differences in welfare-state regimes and in women's organizing strategies.

Traditionally, the Swedish state has been seen as woman-friendly – both responsive to women's concerns and responsible for addressing them (Lewis and Åstrom, 1992; Eduards, 1988). Friendly state policies and the rapid increase in women's formal political representation have appropriately oriented much of Swedish women's organizing to the state and to the political parties closely tied to it, a point stressed by many of the contributors to this volume.[5] Bergqvist and Findlay argue that in Sweden women worked almost exclusively as insiders in the 1970s and 1980s, using political parties as a basis for organizing for women's equality.[6]

Given the privilege accorded the party system, it is not surprising that elected women parliamentarians and women's sections and organizations of the political parties have been central agents and vehicles for taking up women's concerns. For example, Eliasson and Lundy note that, in the 1990s, proposals for change to Swedish state policy regarding violence against women emanated mainly from women in political parties. Women's sections of Swedish political parties led the way in getting the government to admit that sexual violence is a form of male oppression and reflects gender inequity.

It is also not surprising that in Sweden women's constituency organizing (concerned with women's interests) is primarily found inside political parties. Most of the parties (although not the Left Party or the Moderates) have large women's organizations (see Maillé and Wängnerud). Although there are many other long-standing women's organizations, few of them focus specifically on women's rights, with the major exception of the Swedish Organization of Emergency Shelters for Battered Women (SOES) and perhaps the Fredrika Bremer Association.[7] There is less tendency, then, in Sweden to have separate organizing inside of institutions, such as women's committees in unions (see Briskin), or autonomous organizing outside political parties and in the "community" (what Knocke and Ng refer to as "independent" organizing).

Swedish women recognize that state responsiveness is not without contradiction: issues raised by women are often taken over by the state and solutions reshaped and managed in ways that might not have been foreseen and are not always in women's best interests (Eliasson, I, 1993; and Sangregorio, I, 1993).[8] And organizational interventions by women from outside the state and political parties are often subverted. "Political parties in Sweden have been remarkably efficient in co-opting both extra-parliamentary ideas and activists. The Social Democratic strategy is to minimize the room for alternative organizations by incorporating women and women's demands into traditional political institutions. This 'state feminism' gives women material benefits but drains the women's movement of force" (Eduards, 1988: 15).[9]

As a result, many of the new women's networks in Sweden, which are breaking the pattern of party dominance, proactively emphasize their *informal* structure and rarely take the form of building ongoing umbrella organizations. Reluctance to formalize structures reflects concerns about co-optation of women's organizing and presents an explicit challenge to the heavily institutionalized and formalized hierarchical and bureaucratic practices of parties, unions, and the state.[10]

The party monopoly over Sweden's political agenda has also made it more difficult to see the organizing that has occurred outside the party system. This book breaks new ground by naming multiple sites of women's organizing and shifting attention away from the traditional arena of political parties. For example, Ross and Landström explore lesbian organizing inside the key homosexual organization (RFSL), Eliasson and Lundy discuss women's organizing in and through SOES, Feldberg and Carlsson focus on women's health organizations, Knocke and Ng consider organizing in immigrant organizations, and Briskin examines women's strategies in the unions.

Women's organizing in both countries has necessarily focused on making demands on the state, but in Canada women have had limited representation in Parliament, in the bureaucracy, and in the decision-making arenas of political parties. Eliasson and Lundy note that women activists around the issue of violence have been less likely to have their concerns represented by elected women or to find them on agendas of political parties. As a result, women have traditionally organized themselves as "outsiders" (Bergqvist and Findlay). They have built a network of feminist groups to lobby elected politicians and to organize women as a constituency.

Canadian feminist views about the efficacy of focusing on the state have shifted dramatically since the release of the report of the Royal Commission on the Status of Women almost three decades ago, most of whose recommendations are yet to implemented. The views that the Canadian state was a "positive utility which could be successfully influenced" (Vickers, 1991: 78) and "that the women's movement must tailor its strategies to work with the state in a collaborative and consultative manner (Findlay, 1988: 7) have gradually been replaced by a conviction that the state is indifferent, if not actively hostile, to women's needs.[11] Knocke and Ng note that in Sweden the state's receptivity has led to collaboration between immigrant women's groups and the government; in Canada such relations have been contentious and confrontational. These authors also examine the role of the Canadian state in attempting to co-opt, in some ways successfully, the National Organization of Immigrant and Visible Minority Women of Canada.[12] Nevertheless, despite a view of the state as antagonistic and unresponsive, Canadian feminisms have continued to make demands on it.

In Canada the lack of representation and responsiveness, the sharper separation of state and civil society, and the relative weakness of both the union movement and social democracy (in the form of the NDP) have provided a strong impetus and more space for *autonomous*, community-based movements. In contrast to Sweden, there is a plethora of women's rights organizations. The National Action Committee on the Status of Women/Comité Canadien d'Action sur le Statut de la Femme (NAC), a binational (includes Quebec), bilingual umbrella organization that celebrated its twenty-fifth anniversary in 1997, has over six hundred member groups, which collectively represent more than three million Canadian women. In addition to autonomous organizing, an increasingly legitimatized tradition of separate organizing has developed inside institutions such as unions, professional associations, government ministries, and school boards. Canadian women's considerably more limited access to formal institutional vehicles has encouraged formalization of somewhat marginal structures, and these present quite a contrast to the informal Swedish networks.[13]

Inside-Outside Organizing

Mapping provides a new view of the long-standing strategic and theoretical debate about the effect on movement success of incorporating women's organizing into mainstream institutions. Some have argued for the importance of "outsider" status and various forms of separate and autonomous organizing;[14] others have emphasized that such incorporation does not necessarily lead to co-optation and deradicalization.[15]

Ferree and Martin (1995) challenge the common-sense view that radicalism is reduced by the institutionalization of feminist organizations (which they define as "the development of regular and routinized relationships with other organizations"). They point out that such organizations may continue to be agents of change. These associations "question authority, produce new elites, call into question dominant societal values, claim resources on behalf of women and provide space and resources for feminists to live out altered visions of their lives" (6). Importantly, the authors note that "activists wander back and forth between organizational expressions of feminism ... In its penetration of and interconnection with the realities of women's daily lives, the contemporary women's movement differs from the feminist movements that preceded it and from many other late twentieth century social movements" (18).

Mapping rejects any abstract hierarchy of strategies that identifies some as better (or more feminist) on principle – for example, the "by definition" assumption of the radical outside and the co-opted inside. Rather than such programmatic judgments, it suggests contextual assessments of strategy that go beyond the simple pluralism of accepting multiple forms of organizing.[16] Such assessments recognize, of course, that material conditions limit strategic possibilities, but also that strategies in one sector have an impact on the possibilities in another.

In particular, mapping emphasizes the interconnections and relationships between "insider" and "outsider" organizing, making visible the impact of each on the organizing capacity of the other. Dahlerup (1986: 14–15) argues in favour of being outside but understands the complex relationships between inside and outside: "the strength of being outside ... rests on a broad definition of political influence and on ... an understanding of the actual interaction of those 'outside' and those 'inside' ... The interaction between the challenging movement and those working inside the political system is crucial to the strength of being outside ... [B]eing outside is probably a condition of radical new thinking; but this redefinition must be absorbed by some inside the system in order for the movement to influence public policy."

Bergqvist's and Findlay's article suggests that because women were on the "inside" of the Swedish state (both a cause of their success and a reflection of it), there was less pressure on them to organize outside it. Maillé and Wängnerud look at how autonomous (outside) organizing in both countries influenced the practices of representation inside political parties; Mahon discusses the instrumental role of the Swedish Group 222 in shaping early sex-role policy in that country from the outside.

Above, Sweden has been characterized generally as a system where women work from the inside (in part because of better representation), and Canada as a system where they work from the outside. The discussion here goes beyond these generalizations and shifts attention to relationships between inside and outside organizing *in each country*, and it speaks to the tension between representation and constituency organizing by women both inside and outside institutional contexts.

Barbara Pocock (1996: 181) takes up this issue in her writing about women's organizing inside and outside the unions in Australia: "What seems clear from this 'inside/outside' play, however, is that the latter (those on the outside) make space for the former ... the radical claims of those outside accelerate the impulse towards change and give the appearance of 'reason' to the demands of those on the inside." She argues that "the space for women is consequently narrowed," with a decrease in pressure from the outside (what others might see as a result of institutionalization). Pocock also emphasizes the growing importance of women's separate organizations within unions and the continuing need to foster "external organisation amongst feminists activists to facilitate the 'outside voice,' its claims and its capacity to create internal space for women in unions."

Her argument parallels what happened in Sweden when women's representation decreased in the 1991 election. Despite the historic reliance on inside organizing, this event shifted the balance between the inside and the outside. The Support Stockings, a relatively informal group of women from across the political spectrum, organized effectively from the outside. They threatened to set up a women's party if the established parties did not ensure better parliamentary representation of women in the next election (Bergqvist and Findlay and Maillé and Wängnerud in this volume; see also Stark, 1997). This pressure from the outside increased the authority of the demands of women from all political parties for greater numbers of women on their party lists.[17] And in the 1994 election the proportion of women elected rose to 44 per cent.

Insider-outsider organizing may lay the foundation for alliances and coalitions. For example, in Sweden the support of elected women from across the political spectrum for university-based women's studies research helped to build informal alliances between women in the universities and in political parties. In some instances, however, outsider activities subvert the goals of those inside institutions, or vice versa. Organizing from the inside can also destabilize institutions and create new possibilities for successful pressure from both the inside and the outside. Mapping speaks to this complexity.

It also recognizes that, at a certain level, all feminist practice is engaged in a struggle with outside and inside strategies. In an earlier work on this subject (1989: 93–4; also Adamson, Briskin, and McPhail, 1988), I argued for Canada:

> All feminist practice struggles with two poles of attraction- disengagement and mainstreaming. Disengagement which operates from a critique of the system and a standpoint outside of it, and a desire therefore, to create alternative structures and ideologies can provide a vision of social transformation. Mainstreaming operates from a desire to reach out to the majority of the population with popular and practical feminist solutions to particular issues, and therefore relates directly and interacts with major social institutions, such as the family, the work place, the educational system and the state.
>
> Both mainstreaming and disengagement are necessary to the feminist vision. The goal for feminist practice is the maintenance of an effective tension between the two; the dilemma is the tendency for feminist practice to be pulled towards one or other pole. This dilemma is complicated by the fact that each of these poles carries with it a strategic risk. Disengagement can easily lead to marginalization and invisibility; mainstreaming to co-optation ... The map of practice therefore is shaped by the pulls of disengagement and mainstreaming, and by the dilemmas posed by each: marginalization and invisibility on the one hand and co-optation and institutionalization on the other. The task for feminists is to maintain a complex strategic interplay between disengagement and mainstreaming.

Inside institutions – for example, organizing union women's committees – women face a similar dilemma: what I have characterized as the tension between autonomy and integration. As with mainstreaming and disengagement, it is not a choice between one or the other, but rather a struggle to find a balance between always conflicting, but related, needs.

The success of women's separate organizing in unions depends upon maintaining a balance between the degree of autonomy from the structures and practices of the labour movement, on the one hand, and the degree of integration into those structures, on the other. Too little integration and the separate organizing is marginalized; too much integration and the radical edge is necessarily softened. Relatively successful integration produces the level of legitimacy necessary to ensure access to adequate resources. The autonomy axis provides the foundation for a strong voice about women's concerns and the context for building alliances between the movement of union women and the community-based women's movement. To the extent that separate organizing is successful, the autonomy axis can become an additional source of legitimacy. (Briskin, 1993: 101–2)

This discussion of mainstreaming and disengagement and of autonomy and integration stresses complex and often contradictory relationships rather than binaries. An always shifting context defines what constitutes the inside and the outside. The relatively friendly Swedish state has produced a stronger convergence between state and civil society than is expected or accepted in Canada. If the state *is* civil society, what constitutes the "outside"? In such a context, the women's organizations of Swedish political parties, then, may well be described as "outside"; in Canada they would definitely be seen as "inside." With the cutbacks to Swedish welfare programs, Mahon points out, civil society is being reinserted into Swedish discourse by neo-liberals who look to voluntary work and family to supplement the market. In such a context, outside and inside are being unsettled and redefined, as are the organizing strategies of Swedish women.

Inside and outside and autonomous and separate must be understood in relational and contextual, rather than abstract, terms. Always the question needs to be asked: separate from or outside what? The inside is always defined in part by the outside, and vice versa; one is always implicated in the other; and the two are in constant play with each other.

Indeed, mapping problematizes the binary of inside and outside itself. This observation is parallel to the argument made by Joan Scott (1990) regarding the binary of equality and difference:

Here a binary opposition has been created to offer a choice to feminists, of either endorsing "equality" or its presumed antithesis "difference." *In fact, the antithesis itself hides the interdependence of the two terms*, for equality is not the elimination of difference, and difference does not preclude equality. (138; emphasis added)

> When equality and difference are paired dichotomously, they structure an impossible choice. If one opts for equality, one is forced to accept the notion that difference is antithetical to it. If one opts for difference, one admits that equality is unattainable ... How then do we recognize and use notions of sexual difference and yet make arguments for equality? The only response is a double one: the unmasking of the power relationship constructed by posing equality as the antithesis of difference and the refusal of its consequent dichotomous construction of political choices. (142).

Like Scott, I would argue that the antithesis of insiders and outsiders and of community-based and institutional organizing "hides the interdependence" of the two and produces strategic confusion. Rejecting the binary helps us to better understand women's organizing and may reveal new strategic possibilities.

Discursive Terrain, Discursive Struggle

Two discursive tensions – equality/difference and class/gender – provide important reference points for understanding women's organizing and public policy in Sweden and Canada. Women's organizing has shaped the meanings of these discourses and been shaped by the struggle over them. As Scott (1990) suggests, one side of each binary is always implicated in the other.

Swedish political life in the last half-century has been dominated not only by social democracy and a belief in the possibilities of social engineering through state initiatives but also by a consensus-seeking, collectivist, and cooperative ideology. Collectivism has been linked to a strong discourse of reducing class disparities (through, for example, solidaristic wage bargaining),[18] regional differences,[19] and sex inequality – what Bergqvist and Findlay call a "passion for equality." Discourses on equality of the sexes emphasize common interests between, and the same possibilities and options for, women and men (expressed in social policy that encourages and supports them having both family and work responsibilities).[20] This social paradigm has rendered the change-making process more visible and less threatening and has supported changes that have, sometimes indirectly, helped women.

The emphasis on common interests is often expressed in gender-neutral policies, which focus, not on women's issues, women's rights, or discrimination against women, but on the family and the labour market. These policies have eased tensions between waged and unwaged work and between the household and the workplace (Lewis and Åstrom, 1992) and help to explain some of the Swedish successes. They have been part of a larger social debate with employers and the state about organizing and managing the labour market. For example, Cameron and Gonäs argue that accomplishments in Sweden were achieved through policies of full employment that encouraged women's participation in the labour market (see also Ruggie, 1987 and 1988). In their analysis of equity in schooling practices, Coulter and Wernersson suggest that, while women argued for these programs on the basis of fairness and social justice, widespread support was more likely generated because of identified needs in the labour market and the economy.

The gender-neutral approach has forced men to participate in certain discussions and the state to examine men's role, and it has prevented the marginalization of certain family issues. By and large, Swedish women have seen advantages to this approach and have supported "cooperation" between women and men (Eduards, 1991; Gelb, 1989). However, calls for "equality for all," which have supported arguments, for example, that men share responsibility for parenting and childcare, are assumed to speak equally to the needs of women and men, and have often been made without taking account of the patterns of gender discrimination and privilege that make such structural reorganization difficult. Not surprisingly, Swedish women still carry out the bulk of the childcare.

This discourse of common interests has also made voices on the margins (e.g., those of immigrant women and lesbians), difference, and conflict more threatening.[21] In fact, the emphasis on common interests may help to explain the reluctance of the Swedish state to address the disparities in power and privilege accorded women and men and to deal with those issues that reflect the conflicts between women and men (e.g., sexual harassment and other forms of violence against women). It may also explain the resistance to women organizing as a constituency in separate and autonomous structures and the weakness of feminist discourses. Widespread discomfort with labelling oneself a feminist reflects common-sense understandings of feminism as gender conflict and man-hating, and fears that feminism will polarize women and men (see Eliasson and Lundy).

In the Canadian context, gender-neutral approaches have usually worked against the specificities of women's concerns, hidden the practices that privilege men, and made it difficult to talk about power imbalances and conflicts of interest, and in contrast to Sweden, such approaches have rarely supported class or cross-class solidarity. In Canada common interests are increasingly rejected as a basis for strategy or public policy. Actively identifying and challenging practices of male privilege, women have called for policy and legislative initiatives which take account of the differences in power and resources between women and men and among women, and which support affirmative action and autonomous organizing (Adamson, Briskin, and McPhail, 1988; Briskin and McDermott, 1993).

Particular politics of gender neutrality can only be understood in relation to specific historical contexts; such conjunctural analysis reveals the extent to which gender neutrality is about class solidarity and/or about gender discrimination. Bergqvist's and Findlay's account of the development of gender-neutral policies in Sweden is an important reminder of the significance of context. They point out that the strong turn towards gender neutrality in the 1970s reflected a radical shift from a more traditional view of gender relations based on the male-breadwinner model.

It would be naive to suggest that in Canada women have won the right to call themselves feminists without risks and costs. The very successes of the feminist movement have brought out a strong, although minority, right-wing anti-feminist voice. The association of "feminist" with man-hating militance is no longer so strong; now it is perhaps the very legitimacy of feminism that is seen to be threatening. Significantly, Kim Campbell, the first, but short-lived, woman prime minister of Canada and a member of the right wing of the Progressive Conservative Party, calls herself a feminist. The greater legitimacy of the label is connected to the widespread presence of women's studies (degree-granting programs in every university), the success of NAC in claiming a media presence as a feminist voice for Canadian women, and the fact that the gains made by women are more clearly attributed to feminist organizing than to state responsiveness.[22]

Uneasiness with feminism in Sweden is also about class-gender discourse. The labour movement (LO and SAP) continues to struggle with long-standing orthodox class-informed critiques of feminism, which equate it with bourgeois movements, the needs of middle-class women, threats to class solidarity, and aggressive individualism – although these views are now shifting.[23]

In a fascinating account of organizing around the European Union in Sweden, Cameron and Gonäs make visible how this class-gender tension is expressed organizationally and strategically. The Yes forces, representing corporate interests, recognized the importance of women to the outcome of the vote. They adopted a strategy of mobilizing women from the professional and business classes through women's organizations linked to other Yes groups. The No women participated in the campaign through mixed-gender organizations formed within unions, SAP, and the Left Party. They attempted to bring together discourses of class and social reproduction. However, in the last month of the campaign, the No women recognized the need to organize a women's network to respond to the massive publicity campaign directed at women from the Yes side. One cannot help but wonder if the No side might have won – they lost by only about 1 per cent – had they targeted women as a constituency earlier in the campaign. This example highlights the problems with an abstract hierarchy of strategies, expressed, in this case, as an a priori assumption that constituency organizing among women works against class solidarity. Certainly, the experiences in the Canadian union movement demonstrate the opposite (see Briskin in this volume).

Furthermore, the politics of the Canadian women's movement are not overly individualistic, inspired, in part, by an *autonomous* and activist socialist-feminist politic and a class perspective.[24] In the women's movement, socialist-feminist practice has helped to facilitate a recognition of diversity and differences in power among women; to redefine the issues relevant to women to include, for example, free trade; to encourage a strategy of participatory mass action; and to build active alliances in the trade union movement and among other progressive forces which have reinforced a class-informed politic (Briskin, 1990b and 1989; Egan and Yanz, 1983).[25] In Canada class and gender concerns are not necessarily seen as oppositional, and both find a place in the women's movement. In Sweden feminism has often been defined in opposition to class politics.

Gender-neutral policy approaches in that country and the emphasis on common interests are currently being challenged by both a recognition of women's specific concerns and a new individualism. Mahon (1996: 552) points to the "cultural shift from a 'society-centred' to a more individualistic perspective in which the different and shifting interests of individuals take priority over the interests associated with traditional identities like family, region, class and even nation." Recent attacks on the welfare state that affect women disproportionately have also underscored some limits to a gender-neutral approach, highlighting the specificity of women's experiences and acknowledging the differences between women and men (Eduards, 1992). In the current conservative context of economic restructuring and welfare-state cutbacks, however, such a focus on "women" has sometimes been mobilized to support essentialist beliefs in biological difference.[26] Coulter and Wernersson, for example, note the impact of this essentialism in school policy, where there is an increased focus on direct biological explanations of the behaviour of boys and girls, including the belief in an innate male need to express aggression. Furthermore, a shift towards a discourse of gender differences may weaken cross-class solidarity and "the alliance of wage earners." For example, claims for pay equity among professionals (i.e., reducing disparities between women and men of the same class) may increase the pay differentials between women of different classes (see Mahon).

Discourses on equality and difference in Sweden are influenced by the relatively homogeneous population. "Struggles over gender issues in the Nordic countries are less encumbered by the social cleavages of diverse ancestry, strong regional splits, and unevenly developed trade unions characteristic of North America. Both classes and sexes find the social cleavages of ancestry and region to complicate their respective cultures in North America" (Clement and Myles, 1994: 236). The presence of a growing immigrant community is beginning to shift public perceptions, provoking racism and simultaneously increasing the tolerance of difference and the recognition of Sweden as a diverse society (Eduards, I, 1994).[27]

The importance of diversity in the Canadian context cannot be overestimated – racial and ethnic diversity, regional diversity, language diversity, all of which are framed within the context of debates about Quebec as a distinct society and about the right of First Nations peoples to self-government. In fact, in Canada "equity" has a difference-sensitive meaning in legal terms (from the important Abella Commission on Equality in Employment in 1984). As Coulter and Wernersson note, it is used to acknowledge that sometimes equality means ignoring differences and treating women and men the same, and sometimes it means recognizing differences and treating women and men differently. Equity, then, refers to what is fair under the circumstances (also called substantive equality).

In the women's movement, the theme of "unity in diversity" has replaced what is now considered an outdated and racist conception of "sisterhood." Focusing on differences *among* women has been a vehicle, not always successful, to promote solidarity among women across class divides, and across differences based on race, ethnicity, sexuality, ability, and political ideology. In Sweden the weak feminist discourse, consensus-seeking strategies, the discomfort with difference, the relative homogeneity of the population, and the strength of social democracy have converged to make discussions of identity politics (differences among women) – and indeed, of ideological differences *among* feminists – less relevant. In Canada, then, "difference" itself is privileged, reducing the space for essentialist discourses, creating room for competing political perspectives, *and* causing difficulty in developing unified strategies.

Many of the articles in this volume highlight the contrast in discourses about equality/difference in the two countries. Mahon notes that in Sweden, as policies of universality (the same for all) around the provision of childcare are threatened by state restructuring, individual choice (e.g., to stay home with a child) is being constructed as a respect for difference. She notes that in Canada, by contrast, women organizing around childcare have often called for a kind of "comprehensive" universality that recognizes a diversity of needs – of First Nations people, of the disabled, or of those living in rural areas.

Ross and Landström explore how differences in the discourse of diversity affect lesbian organizing in the two countries. They contrast the highly developed and sophisticated discourse of "diversity" in Canada, which supports identity-based lesbian groups, with the discourse of "normalization" in Sweden, where lesbians have emphasized the sameness of lesbians of different backgrounds, and the main gay and lesbian organization the sameness of all homosexuals.

In Canada there is a tension in the operation of difference: hierarchial ordering of power produces discrimination based on class, race, and gender; simultaneously, there is a recognition of multiplicity and diversity. In Sweden tension occurs in the operation of equality: an emphasis on common interests produces less hierarchical ordering of power (e.g., rights of homosexuals enshrined in laws; high representation of women in Parliament; encouragement for women and men both to work and to parent); simultaneously, there is less regard for socially constituted and significant differences. In both countries women have successfully negotiated and challenged the discursive terrain of equality/difference. Although the trajectory has not been the same, in each there has been a recuperation of difference – in Canada differences among women and in Sweden those between women and men.

ASSESSING THE IMPACT OF WOMEN'S ORGANIZING

In both countries, although not with equal success, women's organizing has had wide-ranging effects (many of which are currently under threat). It has struggled for the development and implementation of new policies to alleviate discrimination in a variety of areas: inequalities in pay; access to non-traditional jobs; promotional barriers; the burden of the double day, especially around childcare and housework; reproductive rights and sexual freedom and choices; gender discrimination in educational access, curriculum, and teaching practices; systemic violence against women in public and private spaces; systemic racism that affects women immigrants; and so on. It has addressed inequitable or ineffective representation; the invisibility of oppositional images of diverse groups of women, including women of colour, lesbians, and immigrant and working-class women; the lack of organizational democracy in unions and state bureaucracies; and discriminatory workplace practices. It has raised concerns about the dangers in the breakdown of national standards as a result of free trade and regional integration treaties. Undoubtedly, the self-organization of women as a constituency and public consciousness about their issues have increased dramatically. Women's organizing has been instrumental in naming and renaming women's concerns and changing the parameters of what should be included in public policy (often making the personal public and political).

The gains that women have made can be identified – changes wrought in policy, institutional practices, representation, public consciousness, and self-organization. The role of women's organizing in effecting such gains can be hypothesized. But there is some difficulty, as others have noted,[28] in reliably assessing the impact of such organizing. This book attempts to address this problem by examining and evaluating women's organizing in specific domestic and political arenas.

Clearly, women's organizing cannot be given full credit for the many changes in the last three decades. However, the problem has generally been that its role in breaking the silence about issues such as violence, in pressuring governments to pass legislation and increase funding, and in changing social consciousness has been invisible. A rich literature in recent years has begun to redress this neglect; it is hoped this book will also make a contribution.

Despite the difficulties of making firm assessments, the criteria of social-movement success used by scholars support the conclusion that women's organizing has had a remarkable impact. Much analysis has focused on the traditional areas of changes in law and social policy. Gamson (1990) identified two aspects of success: "the acceptance of a challenging group by its antagonists as a valid representative of a legitimate set of interests, and the winning of new advantages for the group's beneficiary" (quoted in Burstein et al., 1995: 282).[29] This volume identifies numerous instances of such "new advantages." It also speaks to the uneven history of movement legitimacy in each country. A high point in legitimacy for the Canadian women's movement was the nationally televised debate on women's issues by the leaders of the three main political parties during the 1984 federal election (see Maille and Wängnerud); in Sweden it was the success of the Support Stockings, described above, in influencing the 1994 election. The conditions under which social acceptance of both women's concerns and women's organizing is enhanced or undermined and the attempts to use such acceptance to split radical portions of the movement from more traditional sectors deserve more attention from scholars interested in charting patterns of legitimacy.

Staggenborg (1995: 341) expands Gamson's definitions of success to take more account of what has been central to *women's* organizing. To the traditional category of political and policy outcomes (substantive changes through the political system), she adds mobilization outcomes, that is, "organizational successes and the ability to carry out political action," and cultural outcomes: "changes in social norms, behaviours, and ways of thinking among a public that extends beyond movement constituents or beneficiaries, as well as the creation of a collective consciousness among groups such as women."[30]

Groups that are unsuccessful in terms of policy outcomes "may be effective as the centres of movement communities and as originators of cultural changes" (353). Staggenborg notes that the cultural achievements of the women's movement "include the creation of alternative institutions that serve as movement community centres, pools of activists who remain involved in movement activities, models of collective action that are employed by subsequent activists, and ideologies that continue to attract adherents" (353).

What is called "new social-movement theory" (NSMT) pays special attention to what Staggenborg terms "cultural outcomes," but it uses a less instrumental model. William Carroll (1992b: 7) talks about social movements "as emergent forms of praxis with the potential to transform both everyday life and larger institutional practices ... NSMs are viewed as instances of cultural and political praxis though which new identities are formed, new ways of life tested, and new forms of community prefigured."

NSMT often "emphasizes the capacity of new movements to reshape the discursive terrain of politics in distinctive and potentially radical ways" (8). Jane Jenson (1987: 65) focuses on what she calls the "universe of political discourse," which

> comprises beliefs about the way politics should be conducted, the boundaries of political discussion, and the kinds of conflicts resolvable through political processes. In the vast array of tensions, differences and inequalities characteristic of any society, only some are treated as "political" ... The universe of political discourse functions at any single point in time by setting boundaries to political action and by limiting the range of actors that are accorded the status of legitimate participants, the range of issues considered to be included in the realm of meaningful political debate, the policy alternatives feasible for implementation, and the alliance strategies available for achieving change ... Ultimately, its major impact is to inhibit or encourage the formation of new collective identities and/or the reinforcement of older ones. Within a given universe of political discourse, only certain kinds of collective identities can

be forged; for more to be done, the universe itself must be challenged and changed.

Jenson concludes that "the fundamental contribution of the modern women's movement was its ability to alter the universe of political discourse" (64) and to introduce a new collective actor – women – onto the political scene. This outcome implies both the recognition of women as a legitimate constituency and the articulation of a set of women's demands. Such articulation and redefinition of issues and subsequent changes in public consciousness have shifted the discursive field, altering understandings of what is both possible and necessary. In both Canada and Sweden, organizing women as a viable voice and a politicized (if not homogeneous) constituency has been of central importance.

The articles collected here highlight the significance of these shifts. For example, Cameron and Gonäs point out that, as a result of women's organizing around free trade in Canada, it was recognized as a women's issue not only by the women's movement but also by the government; furthermore, the government identified women as a key constituency in its fight for public opinion. Bergqvist and Findlay argue that in both countries women played an active role in defining the barriers to women's equality and the models that governments could use to promote such equality. Briskin describes the redefinition of what constitutes union issues in the Canadian context to include childcare, abortion, sexual harassment, pay equity, affirmative action, and employment equity. She points out that the gendering of issues has prompted a subtle move from an identification of a women's platform to a recognition of the gender implications in all issues. Ross and Landström predict continuing discursive scuffles in both countries about what it means to be lesbian and to conceive and rear children outside hetero-normative contexts. In so doing, they actively challenge the coherence of "women" as a political actor and introduce other political subjects.

A focus on certain kinds of outcomes – those that are quantifiable, recognizable, and easily identified, such as a new piece of legislation or an increase in number of women elected to Parliaments – privileges the relationship between the women's movement and the state. Looking beyond structural and policy change makes manifest some of the effects of women's organizing that can otherwise be obscured. Indeed, to understand women's organizing and its impact, we must both focus on the state and go well beyond it.

NSMT concentrates on the perhaps more complex processes of social change that rest on discursive change. These include, for example, Melucci's notion of disorganizing consent (see Carroll, 1992b: 10) and

Jenson's of challenging the universe of political discourse. It also focuses on the development of new social actors and collective consciousness (in this case, women as a discursive, organizational, and strategic constituency); on the establishment of organizations and new strategic innovations; and on the "destabilization of the gender order" through local and daily resistance (Threlfall, 1997: 302). NSMT politicizes much that is personal and private, and concomitantly constitutes a refusal to "reduce the 'political' to exclusively state-centred practices" (Carroll, 1992b: 16). It turns attention to the impacts on the local and the everyday.

Turning away from the state and focusing on the discursive and the local resonates with Foucauldian understandings of power, which see it as dynamic and fluid, with no fixed sum of power in any given context; conditional, not absolute; situational, contextual, and relational, so negotiated continually; and circulating, not static. This approach rejects the binary of those with and those without power, and it resists reifying the lived experience of both oppression and discrimination. Michel Foucault rejects certain basic assumptions of what he refers to as the "juridico-discursive model of power." In contrast to the notion that power is possessed by individuals or classes, a Foucauldian perspective implies that it is "exercised rather than possessed ... [T]hinking of power as a possession has led to a preoccupation with questions of legitimacy, consent and rights. (Who should possess power? When has power overstepped its limits?) ... For the notion that power is a possession Foucault substitutes a relational model of power as exercised. [He] focus[es] on power relations themselves, rather than on the subjects related (Sovereign-subject, bourgeois-proletarian)" (Sawicki, 1986: 26).

Foucault also rejects the view that power flows from a centralized source (such as the state) or from top to bottom (from the king to the subjects).

> Foucault thinks that focusing on power as possession has led to location of power in a centralized source. For example, the Marxist location of power in a class has obscured an entire network of power relations that invests the body, sexuality, family, kinship, knowledge, technology ... Foucault expands the domain of the political to include a heterogeneous ensemble of power relations operating at the micro-level of society. The practical implication of his model is that resistance must be carried out in local struggles against the many forms of power exercised at the everyday level of social relations. (ibid., 28)[31]

If "resistance must be carried out in local struggles," local impacts must also be more fully assessed. Taking up the Foucauldian view, however, does not mean privileging the local over the larger structural forces at work. Rather, it calls for a solid recognition of both and highlights the need to understand better the impact of the local, often undocumented, organizing by women, not just on the local context but on structural and discursive realities, a topic taken up in the final section of this chapter.

STRATEGIC RESPONSES TO GLOBALIZATION AND RESTRUCTURING

Major changes in social, political, and economic organization are negatively impacting on women and minority workers in all Western countries. Driving the changes are the globalization of capital and increase in corporate rule and the growing permeability of national boundaries as a result of regional integration through NAFTA and the EU. Workplace restructuring has meant increased calls for labour flexibility and competitive wage bargaining across national boundaries; the creation of more non-standard, part-time, part-year service work; and the shift to homework, offshore production, and contracting out. The dismantling and redefinition of the welfare state is expressed in decreased funding to services such as health, education, and support programs – programs on which women depend and where they have often worked. The concomitant decommodification of elder care, health care, and childcare places an increased burden on women in families, and it is reconstructing the meanings of public and private. The combination of decommodification, which increases unpaid labour, and casualization of work, which often forces women to work in many part-time jobs for longer hours, seriously undermines the possibilities of equity. New claims for radical individualism are weakening citizenship rights and the tolerance for making special claims on the basis of difference or systematic discrimination (Brodie, 1995: 57).

Gender is undoubtedly implicated in all these changes, although they impact unevenly on particular groups of women. For example, Knocke and Ng point out that state policies regarding immigration and settlement are in flux because of globalization; and furthermore, that the contraction of the welfare state in both Sweden and Canada is producing new forms of marginalization for immigrant women. Restructuring is actually magnifying differences among women. Increasing competition among workers is a central thrust of workplace and capital reorganization, exacerbating inequalities and reducing the push towards equity; further, the dismantling of universal social programs is undermining the basis for cross-class alliances.

Cameron and Gonäs point out that the increasing dichotomy between national responsibility for social reproduction and regional or corporate responsibility for production is especially problematic for women. On the one hand, social services are a condition of their social equality; on the other, the capacity of national states to deliver these services depends on economic policies that are increasingly determined at regional levels outside their control.

Despite differences in the two countries, these disturbing patterns cross national boundaries and gravely subvert equality gains, especially in Canada. At both a strategic and an analytic level, equity and restructuring cannot be separated. These transformations are changing women's lives dramatically, bringing out new contradictions and reshaping women's concerns. They are reconstituting their political agenda, remobilizing and in some cases demobilizing them, changing the conditions under which women organize, and forcing the development of new strategies. Restructuring makes visible the transiency and fragility of women's gains and the degree to which such gains are inextricably linked to the organization of state, capital, and workplace, and perhaps to a lesser degree to equality policies themselves.

All the articles collected here speak to the strategic implications of these changes. For example, Coulter and Wernersson note that, in the past, struggles for educational equity have made excellent use of the discourses and resources of the state; however, changing state forms may require a more oppositional politic in the realm of education. The fact that globalization and corporate rule are seriously undermining the role of national states in areas of reproduction, at the same time as they transform workplace organization and household responsibilities, suggests that women's organizing in the next millennium will need to shift direction away from both its focus and its reliance on the state. The following discussion briefly considers five arenas that will be of strategic significance: discursive struggle, revisioning the state, workplace control, coalitions and alliances, and a new internationalism.

Discursive Struggle

Counter-hegemonic interventions into discursive realities need to take up three related areas: first, the centrality of gender and race and other social inequalities to the restructuring process despite government, state, and corporate claims that they are insignificant; second, the implications of the corporate ideologies of competitiveness, privatization, decommodification, and radical individualism, especially for women and for families; and finally, the development of an alternative economic and social vision to challenge the primacy of marketplace discourse.[32] Any new vision must recognize the connection between the household and the workplace, and must challenge the privileging of paid work in the economic order. Armine Yalnizyan (1993: 90) calls for "reframing the notion of full employment, not in macroeconomic terms, but in terms of the individual's working life cycle. This would take account of the social dimension of full employment by including both paid and non-paid work. In this light, education and training, family formation and maintenance ... and volunteer activities in the community all contribute."

Brodie (1995) argues that in Canada "[C]ontesting the neoliberal orthodoxy [is] where a feminist politics of restructuring must begin" (80). In fact, she suggests that

> the Canadian women's movement has already begun to take the lead in interrogating restructuring discourse and the social relations it underwrites ... it has challenged the idea that market-driven development need not be held accountable for its impact on women ... As women's organizations contend, economic policies which make women less economically and socially secure, and contribute to women's vulnerability to social and sexual coercion and violence, are quite simply violations of their human rights ... This strategy provides a basis for coalitions both internally and internationally without assuming a unity of interests ... Equally important, the women's movement is attempting to write gender and systemic discrimination back into the neoliberal state's analysis of Canadian society. (80–3)

Re-visioning the State

The reorganization of states under the pressures of globalization has prompted renewed debate about the nature of the state in general and its contribution to equality agendas in particular. In the first instance, as Brodie stresses (1995: 51), "the ascendency of the market over politics does not mean that the state is disappearing. Rather, state power has been redeployed from social welfare concerns and economic management to the enforcement of a market model in all aspects of everyday life." Undoubtedly, women have unduly relied on states, much of women's organizing has focused on the state, and state-sanctioned and initiated equality policies have represented important successes. In her summary article on European women's movements, Threlfall (1996: 290–1) notes, "In all countries, the vast majority of feminists' claims ... involved directing demands at the state for law reform or state provision of facilities and benefits ... The public domain of institutions and the law has thus provided an immensely successful arena of feminist interventions, a development which had done much to significantly alter society's understanding of what constitutes a public or private sphere and a woman's role within it."

However, states have also co-opted women's organizing, reproduced patriarchal and heterosexist family forms, policed reproduction and sexuality, and disproportionately addressed the needs of some women over others. Labour-market regulation and government support for social programs and equality policies remain important, but the state also clearly requires re-visioning. New strategies are desperately needed to produce resisting states that are allies of the majority, rather than pawns of the transnational corporations. This outcome will only be possible if demands on the state are combined with strategies that decentre the state through a strengthened union movement and extra-institutional organizing in popular social movements.

Threlfall concludes that, "while state-directed strategies have chalked up a number of successes, feminism's influence in the sphere of the open labour market can be said to be patchy." In the search for new strategies, it is also worth remembering that women's organizing has had considerably less impact on the social and organizational relations of family and household life, even in Sweden, where government legislation has proactively intervened to encourage a shift in the sexual division of household labour (see Mahon). It has had even less success in transforming the organization of the workplace by, for example, shortening the working day or desegregating occupations and sectors.

Workplace Control

Unions are critical sites of resistance in the struggle against corporate rule. But to reinvigorate the struggle for workplace control, union movements in both Canada and Sweden need to be transformed. Unions must develop new visions of the organization of work that take account of household realities (such as the shorter working day).[33] At minimum, what is necessary is increased unionization in Canada and the democratization of the practices and policies of unions in both countries to ensure that the concerns of often-marginalized groups of workers are addressed (Briskin, 1998, 1997, and 1995). Since increasing competition among workers is at the heart of restructuring, equity and solidarity – unity in diversity – must be central to union responses.

The globalization of production, the mobility of capital, and competitive wage bargaining are clearly redefining the significance of *national* boundaries for unions. They must increasingly resist any form of isolationism and embrace coalitions with popular movements. They must also move across national boundaries to build alliances and cooperate with workers in other countries in order to limit the power of capital. Clearly, globalization has put international solidarity firmly on the agenda.

Coalitions and Alliances

Corporatization, workplace restructuring, changing state forms, and processes of decommodification have put the question of coalitions and alliances, both national and international, on the strategic agenda, more firmly than ever before. Alliances produce ideological solidarities and challenge the competitiveness and individualism at the core of the corporate agenda. They seek to invent and reinvent solidarities among women across class, race, and sexuality. What needs to happen is parallel to the paradigm shift that transformed the early second-wave call in North America for "abortion on demand" to the demand for "reproductive rights." This change reflected challenges by women of colour, who had deep concerns about forced sterilization programs. In the current period, it is critical to revisit arguments about social programs, pay equity, and employment equity and reconstitute them to support alliances among women. Cross-gender alliances in the labour movement must also be on the agenda.

Women organizing have different histories in Sweden and in Canada with regard to building coalitions – structural expressions of alliances. In Canada the building of alliances and coalitions across political current, sector, and institution to bring women together from the unions, parties, and community-based groups to cooperate nationally, provincially, and locally has been an important feminist strategy. The most successful formal expression of this process, but by no means the only one, is NAC, mentioned above.[34]

Many of the chapters in this book speak to coalition strategies in the Canadian context. Feldberg and Carlsson note that, at both grassroots and institutional levels, women in Canada have allied their campaigns for health with broader struggles for social justice. Cameron and Gonäs point out that NAC encouraged the establishment of coalitions of women specifically directed at opposing free trade and participated in ones uniting a broad spectrum of popular-sector organizations. Mahon concludes that by the 1980s coalition politics in Canada posed a challenge to traditional structures of representation.

The widespread practices of separate and autonomous organizing inside unions, political parties, and educational institutions and in the community have facilitated coalition strategies. These have also become increasingly important as a way of taking into account diversity and power issues among women based on race and sexuality; that is, coalitions represent an alternative to homogeneous organizations, which tend to silence marginal voices.

In Sweden organizing across sector, union, and party is made more difficult by the fact that there are few independent or autonomous women's rights organizations and less of a tradition of organizing "separately" in women's committees and caucuses inside institutions. Without a base of independent organizational structures, alliance building is necessarily more informal and local. It is also more apt to find a place within the political party structure.

Despite the strength of party loyalties in that country, women parliamentarians from across the political spectrum have cooperated in some critical instances to great success: passing abortion legislation in the 1960s, supporting the struggle for women's representation, and ensuring research funding for women's studies in the universities.[35] Not surprisingly, the structures of "political opportunity" situate coalitions in different arenas in the two countries – in Sweden inside the party system and in Canada in civil society.

A New Internationalism

Changes in the status of the nation state have also shifted the meanings of internationalism. As corporations operate transnationally and use nation states as vehicles for managing their interests, it is clear that social movements and labour organizations must also build communities of interest in the international arena. "Social movement scholars have become increasingly aware of the international nature of social movements, not only the diffusion of strategies and tactics but also the existence of common targets and international co-ordination among movements ... [S]ocial movements are not just prisoners of their national boundaries but are profoundly shaped by their international environments" (Jenkins, 1995: 32). This new internationalism requires cross-border alliances, especially inside and across regional trading blocks; the construction of social-movement organizations at the international level; and pressure on existing international organizations such as the United Nations to-play a greater role in monitoring the negative impacts of capital reorganization.[36]

Despite the self-evident need for a new internationalism, legitimate concerns about "international" politics have been raised. In this postmodern context of fragmentary and multiple identities and sensitivity to the dangers of reconstituting Western hegemony in international social-movement politics, there is a rejection of the global and a significant turn to the local. In keeping with Michel Foucault's call for dispersed struggles, Paul Patton suggests, "We should perhaps argue not for moving beyond the fragments toward the global politics of a new alliance but for multiplying the fragmentary effects of ... local campaigns" (quoted in Carroll, 1992: 14). This decentred politics refuses "to privilege any particular agent or structure" and suggests a metaphor of "localized guerrilla warfare."

In her work on lesbian identity and organizing, Shane Phelan (1993: 783) also calls for the elimination of "the grand narratives in favour of more local strategies." "A local politics also calls us to acknowledge our positions of privilege as well as of oppression. Grand theories work by subsuming all struggles under a single rubric ... Local politics and the theories that sustain them privilege no one axis of oppression but, instead, open space for a multiplicity of claims and struggles" (784).

Yet as Ratner (1992: 240) points out, the local is not protected from the global: "globalization trajectories also fragment societies from below, redefining and perhaps eradicating the spaces for popular politics and markedly influencing the availability of resources for collective action." Indeed, for those who study the structures and realities of transnational capital, the emphasis on the local seems inadequate in the face of an increasingly centralized corporate rule of disparate economies and peoples around the world. Yet the call for a return to the "old" political economy, and perhaps the privileging of class relations also, seems entirely insufficient to the struggle to address the diversities of race, gender, and sexual identity which have energized popular struggles in the last decades.

A more satisfactory approach is suggested by Inderpal Grewal and Caren Kaplan (1994), who argue for "transnational feminism." They specifically reject "global feminism." "'[G]lobal feminism' has stood for a kind of Western cultural imperialism ... [and] has elided the diversity of women's agency in favour of a universalised Western model of women's liberation that celebrates individuality and modernity. Anti-imperialist movements have legitimately decried this form of 'feminist' globalizing" (17).[37]

At the same time, Grewal and Kaplan recognize the imperative need to "address the concerns of women around the world in the historicized particularity of their relationship to multiple patriarchies as well as to international economic hegemonies ... We need to articulate the relationship of gender to scattered hegemonies such as global economic structures, patriarchal nationalisms, 'authentic' forms of tradition, local structures of domination, and legal-juridical oppression" (17). They use the term "transnational" "to problematize a purely locational politics of global-local or centre-periphery in favour of ... the lines cutting across them ... Transnational linkages influence every level of existence."[38]

Global feminism, then, asserts the commonality of women in an international arena. It is part of a Western master narrative and assumes alliances among women, rather than proactively taking up the differences between them in order to build links. In contrast, transnational feminism recognizes that the structures of global capitalism, corporate rule, and religious fundamentalism are affecting women everywhere, but in structurally asymmetrical ways. Alliances are possible, and necessary, because of these large structures. But they will only be successful if local differences are kept in focus and if the gaze on difference refuses to construct exotic subjects – that is, it is not a Western gaze.

Grewal and Kaplan use the example of fundamentalism to explore this approach. Women in the West often look pityingly on their counterparts in Iran, but they do not explore the reality of fundamentalism in the United States. So rather than simply condemning the Iranian fundamentalist death penalty against Salman Rushdie as an attack on free speech, Western feminists need to understand why Muslim fundamentalism appears in the media and other fundamentalisms (Christian, Jewish, Hindu) do not. They need to refuse to collaborate "with the construction of a 'progressive' and 'democratic' West against a despotic East" (23) and to call for a struggle against all fundamentalisms. Transnational feminist practices can "create affiliations between women from different communities who ... [work] against the links that support and connect very diverse patriarchal practices" (26).

The successful struggle to improve conditions in the plants in El Salvador that produce clothes for the Gap chain of stores is another example of such transnational work. A joint campaign was undertaken in the United States and Canada by unions and popular organizations and in El Salvador by workers who put their jobs and often their lives on the line. The goal was to compel the Gap to establish and enforce a code of conduct to improve working conditions and to extend the right to unionize to workers in the free-trade zones. The campaign used the power of Western consumers and the vulnerability of clothing retailers to public criticism. But it was also about protecting employment standards in the West, challenging deregulation, and preventing *maquiladora* working conditions from moving north. (In Ontario sweatshops women are now commonly forced to work for less than the minimum wage.) A common goal infused this coalition work – to "pressure retailers and major labels to take responsibility for the conditions under which their clothing is produced" in both industrialized and developing countries and a shared recognition of the impact, although asymmetrical, of the Gap's working conditions on workers in both the north and the south (Jeffcott and Yanz, 1997).

Transnational feminist solidarities are a new way of building alliances that go beyond simply recognizing difference, and certainly beyond the argument that alliances are not possible because of difference. It is this future that we must look towards: alliances on the basis of agency rather than victimization and an effective international resistance to transnational corporate rule. The chapters that follow makes visible women as agents and women's organizing as instrumental, and they give hope for the success of this most urgent project.

NOTES

1 West and Blumberg (1990: 13) develop a four-part typology to examine what issues draw women into social protest: (i) those directly linked to economic survival of their families and children – obtaining food, welfare, jobs, or housing; (ii) those related to nationalist and racial or ethnic struggles either in groups demanding liberation or equality or in countermovements demanding protection against erosion of the status quo, such as the Ku Klux Klan or the anti-busing movement; (iii) those addressing broad humanistic or nurturing problems such as peace, environmentalism, public education, prison reform, and mental health care; and (iv) those identified as "women's rights" issues where women have been activists on behalf of their own rights as women and for various groups of women (battered women, older women, child brides, etc.). Although gender and feminist consciousness may to varying degrees be part of all these kinds of struggles, this typology spotlights what is concealed about women's organizing if the focus is restricted only to what is explicitly identified as "feminist."

2 The notion of the political opportunity structure was originally elaborated by Peter Eisinger, who described it as "the openings, weak spots, barriers and resources of the political system itself" (quoted in Burstein et al., 1995: 288). Sidney Tarrow expanded on Eisinger's work and considered four dimensions: "the degree of openness or closure of formal political access, the degree of stability or instability of political alignments, the availability and strategic posture of potential alliance partners ... and political conflicts within and among elites" (quoted in Kriesi, 1995: 167). On this last point, Mahon in this volume notes that mobilization around childcare in Sweden was able to utilize already existing tensions among governing parties.

3 Using a similar argument, Jane Ursel sees the possibility of the convergence of state interests and women's interests. "The policy implications ... are to approach the state strategically, to select issues in which potential for convergence of interests does exist, and then to involve the state as much as possible in working toward those changes" (quoted in Eliasson and Lundy in this volume).

4 This comparison of the development of the two states comes from unpublished work done by Barbara Cameron. I am grateful to her for permission to use it here.

5 Reporting on the democratic audit of Sweden, Micheletti (1998: 4) concludes that "women can no longer be said to be political outsiders." Her assessment is based on the increase in women's political representation: "After the 1994 election the proportion of women in the cabinet was 50 percent, 48 percent in the county councils, 41 percent in municipal councils and 40 percent in parliament."

6 Diane Sainsbury comments on early second-wave organizing in Sweden: "contrary to several other countries where the new women's movement did not seek influence in male-dominated organizations, large numbers of Swedish women activists chose to work within the parties ... [S]pecific issues closely associated with the new women's movement and important for mobilization purposes – women's equality and abortion on demand – emerged relatively early in the 1960s and were incorporated into the policy agendas of the political parties. Such responses lent credibility to perceptions that working through party channels could pay off" (quoted in Maillé and Wängnerud in this volume).

7 Although the Fredrika Bremer Association is an "independent" group, it takes a traditional sex-role approach in the Swedish context. This means that the organization focuses on men and women having the same rights and responsibilities, and that it does not specifically take up women's rights or discrimination against women. The organization has always included men.

8 Note that when a source name is followed by "I," it indicates that the material came from an interview. The Swedish material is based in part on interviews done between 1992 and 1995. A total of thirty-seven open-ended interviews with trade unionists, community activists, feminist researchers, political party activists, and state officials averaging two to three hours in length were conducted. See the end of my article on unions in this volume for a list of those interviewed.

9 Joan Acker points out that in the 1950s in Sweden, "in the labour movement, independent feminist organization that might unite women across party and class lines was seen as a bourgeois movement that presented a danger to the unity of men and women in the working class.

With the increasing power of the labour movement, for many women, the way to get things done was through the labour unions and the Social Democratic party, not through independent organizing as women" (1992: 6). Given Maud Eduards's assessment of "state feminism," it is not surprising that she actively calls for women's separate organizing. "When women are separately organized and act explicitly on behalf of women, they win agency for themselves in politics" (1991: 705).

10 Many of those I interviewed stressed the informality of women's cooperation, its location at local, rather than central, sites, and the fact that it is often invisible publicly. Anita Dahlberg, a lawyer and researcher who runs the Centre for Women's Studies at Stockholm University, said (I, 1994): "The women's movement is under the surface. Some of the invisibility is an active strategy to resist co-optation by the state. Women find spaces within which to organize." It seems that women, often excluded from formal representation, are therefore less tied to these structures and their organizational norms. Informal local organizing is a subversive way to bypass structures.

11 This generalization is complicated by attitudinal differences to provincial and federal governments, especially in Quebec, where the struggle for the right to self-determination has often converged with feminist mobilizations. "Francophone feminists in Québec have considered the Québec state, since the beginning of the Quiet revolution in the 1960s, to be more progressive on women's issues than the federal state. Anglophone, allophone, and First Nations women in Québec, by contrast, have often been more favourably disposed to the federal state" (Vickers et al., 1993: 8).

12 In fact, strategic analysis of the state has focused heavily on the process of co-optation. See, for example, the special issue on the state put out by *Resources for Feminist Research* in 1988 and Walker (1990).

13 In addition to NAC, there are numerous other national organizations, for example, the Canadian Association of Sexual Assault Centres, the Congress of Black Women of Canada, the DisAbled Women's Network, the National Association of Women and the Law, the Native Women's Association of Canada, and the National Organization of Immigrant and Visible Minority Women of Canada.

14 Burstein and colleagues (1995: 277–8) summarize the aspects of *outsider status* that social-movement theorists find most relevant. "Gamson (1990) focuses on mobilization: challenging groups are outsiders largely because they seek to represent a constituency not previously mobilized to participate in politics. Tilly (1984) sees representation as crucial: the constituencies of social movements are outsiders because they lack formal representation in government decision making. McAdam (1982) focuses on tactics ... outsider status is defined by a willingness to use noninstitutionalized tactics ... Noninstitutionalized tactics customarily

have two defining characteristics: they involve activities that (1) are not part of the formal political process and (2) are intended to be disruptive (whether they are legal or illegal). Sit-ins, mass marches, and boycotts are examples. Not included are legally regulated components of the political process such as voting or lobbying; unregulated but non-disruptive tactics like letter-writing campaigns; and sometimes disruptive but institutionalized forms of participation such as continuous court challenges to proposed regulations."

15 Threlfall (1996: 289–90) argues that "engaging with the mainstream has not led to the feared one-sided dependence or absorption. On the contrary: women's groups have made creative use of opportunities provided by parties, institutions and governments, pushing for advantage and gaining access to different levels of power, and using them to defend or develop what was understood to be in women's interests ... The strategy of making use of existing institutions, whether understood as 'mainstreaming' or 'institutionalization' was distrusted in early stages of the movement and continues to be disparaged in some quarters. However ... few improvements occur without it."

16 This is a parallel argument to the one that I make about the hierarchy of oppressions (Briskin, 1990a: 103–4): "Rather than the abstract ranking of the relations of power inherent in class, race, gender, and sexual orientation, the focus is on the ways they intertwine, reinforce and contradict each other in historically specific contexts." Such an approach challenges "the primacy of class in socialist theory, and provides the basis on which to deconstruct the unified category of 'woman' sometimes found in feminist analysis." As we move away from abstractions, "we move toward a more conjunctural analysis of the relative weight of various relations of power and to a focus on the interrelationships between systems of power."

17 In interviews in 1993 both Margareta Winberg from the Social Democratic Party and Ulla Hoffman from the Left Party indicated that, as a result of this pressure from the outside, the political parties acted to address women's concerns about representation.

18 In his discussion of indicators of equality, Alan Siaroff (1992) notes that Sweden has the greatest equality of wages among the eighteen OECD countries for which there is data. The United States has the least equal pattern of wages, but the Canadian figures are not far behind. Family poverty is rarest in Norway (5.3 per cent), followed by Sweden (5.6 per cent), and most common in United States (17 per cent), followed by Canada at 12.5 per cent.

19 Sweden's attempt to balance out social injustices arising from regional differences has been regarded as a way of centralizing and homogenizing the nation. However, Swedish reality has always been and continues

to be more diverse than the discourse has suggested. For example, Forsberg's recent work (1998) highlights regional variants of gender relations.

20 A distinct and rather newly coined word (in the 1960s) is used to talk about equality between women and men: *jämställdhet* (as opposed to *jämlikhet*, which is used for other equalities). Women argued for a separate word because they had previously been grouped with people with disabilities, immigrants, and old people, but the new word does, intentionally, blur the differences between women and men (Annike Baude, I, 1994).

21 Many people whom I interviewed talked about the discomfort with difference that pervades Swedish society, the commonly held view that everybody wants or needs the same things, and the concomitant pressures to conform. See Ross and Landström in this volume on the implications of this ideology for lesbian visibility.

22 A 1979 poll indicated that 42 per cent of Canadian women called themselves "feminists"; by 1986 the proportion had grown to 47 per cent. A 1987 poll showed that 75 per cent of Canadians felt that the feminist movement has had a positive effect on Canadian society (Pierson et al., 1993: 27).

23 Many of those I interviewed indicated that in the current "third wave" of women's organizing in Sweden, women's attitudes to feminism and naming themselves feminists are shifting. Margareta Winberg, an important social democratic member of Parliament, reported that the 1993 Women's Congress of the Social Democratic Party discussed feminism for the first time and that she now calls herself a feminist (I, 1993). When the congress decided to call itself feminist, it made front-page news. In interviews in 1993, trade union women expressed a range of opinions about self-labelling as feminists: "I am a feminist, but I would never ever use that term. It puts up the flag in front of men" (Svensson); "The term 'feminism' is never used; feminism means I am against men. Feminism is seen as dangerous" (Magnusson); and "I wasn't a feminist when I started but I am now!" (Carlsson).

24 In contrast to the pattern in most Western countries, socialist feminism in Canada is more a current of the women's movement than of socialist or communist parliamentary parties or of the far left. In these latter cases, it might be more accurate to talk of "feminist socialism."

25 This picture provides a sharp contrast to the United States. Ruth Milkman (1985: 308) notes in her discussion of feminism and labour in that country since the 1960s that, "while in principle feminism offers collective solutions to gender inequality, in practice, there is a highly individualistic thrust to the women's movement ... [I]ts primary emphasis seems

to be on gaining more power for individual women within American society."

26 Recognizing the realities of gender-specific experience, discrimination, and strategies does not need to invoke biological essentialism. But activists often fear that such arguments can reproduce common stereotypes about women: that they are more nurturing, relational, and emotional *by nature*. A non-essentialist approach begins from the position that women's experiences are socially, not biologically, constituted.

27 A special opinion poll conducted in 1994 showed that the Swedish population had a particularly intolerant attitude towards Muslim immigrants, homosexuals, and atheist teachers (reported in Micheletti, 1998: 5).

28 For example, Burstein and colleagues (1995) conclude that "we still know little about the impact of social movements" (276). They quote McAdam, McCarthy, and Zald (1988): "demonstrating the independent effect of collective action on social change is difficult"; there are "evidentiary requirements ... generally beyond the means of most researchers" (291).

29 Burstein and colleagues (1995) note that Gamson's formulation leaves out "the political process occurring between the initial challenge and potential substantive political changes" (282). They find Schumaker's five stages of potential responsiveness helpful (1975): "access responsiveness, the willingness of the target to hear the concerns of the movement organization ...; agenda responsiveness, the target's willingness to place the movement's demands on the political agenda; policy responsiveness, the target's adoption of new policies (particularly legislation) congruent with the manifest demands of protest groups ...; output responsiveness, the target's effective implementation of its new policies; and impact responsiveness, the 'degree to which the actions of the political system succeed in alleviating the grievances of the protest group'" (282). Building on Kitschelt (1986), Burstein and colleagues add to Schumaker's model "structural impacts" which involve a transformation of political structures themselves and which "influence political outcomes for everyone, not only for themselves" (Burstein et al., 1995: 283).

Interestingly, Drude Dahlerup, in her introduction to *The New Women's Movement: Feminism and Political Power in Europe and the USA* (London: Sage, 1986), sees three such signs "of interaction and influence between the movement and the established political system" (16), although, in my view, her assessments seem overly positive. First, she argues that the "ideas of the movement [have] become absorbed by society or important sections of it," and she points to the fact that "the new women's movement has influenced the *programmes* of all the political parties in all the Western countries [although] the most positive response has come from the political parties on the left." She also calls attention to new "state machinery" established during the 1970s and 1980s "with the purpose of promoting equality between sexes" (17). (See Bergqvist and Findlay in this volume on such machinery in Sweden and Canada.) Second, Dahlerup notes that "the leaders of the movement are coopted into the mainstream of politics and society," which can be seen as "a symbol of success and a chance to influence." Finally, she identifies the fact that women, a former marginal group, have succeeded "in gaining access and influence in the political system and society at large" (18).

30 Ferre and Martin (1995) also identify both the vehemence of countermovements and the sheer number of feminist groups as measures of the effectiveness of feminist organizations.

31 Jana Sawicki's version of Foucault is much more accessible than his original writing, although the latter is certainly worth struggling with. For example, Foucault (1978) writes that we "must break free of the theoretical privilege of law and sovreignity if we wish to analyse power within the concrete and historical framework of its operation; we must construct an analytics of power that no longer takes law as a model and a code" (89). And further:

> Power's condition of possibility ... must not be sought in the primary existence of a central point ... it is the moving substrate of force relations which, by virtue of their inequality, constantly engender states of power, but the latter are always local and unstable. The omnipresence of power: not because it has the privilege of consolidating everything under its invincible unity, but because it is produced from one moment to the next ... Power is everywhere; not because it embraces everything, but because it comes from everywhere ... [P]ower is not an institution, and not a structure ... it is the name that one attributes to a complex strategical situation in a particular society ... Power is not something that is acquired, seized or shared ... power is exercised from innumerable points, in the interplay of nonegalitarian and mobile relations ... [R]elations of power are not in superstructural positions, with merely a role of prohibition or accompaniment; they have a directly productive role ... Power comes from below; that is, no binary and all-encompassing opposition between rulers and ruled. (92–4)

32 The need to develop an alternative economic vision to the corporate ideology of competitiveness is a central thrust in union discussions of economic restructuring in Canada (see Briskin, 1994).

33 A fascinating ongoing struggle in Sweden has been over the six-hour day, which was put on the agenda by the Social Democratic women's organization (now called Social Democratic Women in Sweden) in the 1970s.

It has produced serious tensions between women organizing and unions, who have remained ambivalent about it (see Mahon, 1996). In 1997 the demand was made again jointly by women from the Left, Centre, and Green parties (see Maillé and Wängnerud in this volume).

34 Other important coalitions and campaigns include the Justice for Women Campaign, the Equal Pay Coalition, the National Campaign Childcare Network, the March 8th Coalition in Toronto, the Ontario Coalition for Abortion Clinics, British Columbia's Women against the Budget, and recently the Common Front in Alberta, which brings together women's groups, women leaders, and organized women with gay activists, environmentalists, development agencies, grassroots community groups, and Workfare Hurts One and All. This last group links unions and community, women's, and First Nations organizations.

35 In Canada, Vickers (1997: 32) notes two instances of cross-party solidarity among women politicians: when women government members on a parliamentary committee united across party lines to support gun control, and when appointed women senators joined together to defeat the Conservative government's bill to recriminalize abortion.

36 The International Labour Organization, an agency of the UN, was established in 1919 and is the largest tripartite body in the world. It brings together governments, employers, and unions to negotiate improved working and living conditions and to promote basic human rights. In the summer of 1996, in an unprecedented and unsuccessful move, employers tried to block a proposed agreement on homework in order to have continued unregulated access to workers. The convention was a response to forced labour, child labour, and forced migration. This is the first time that the ILO has taken a position on setting labour standards in the informal sector (see Johnson, 1997).

37 Grewal and Kaplan build on the important argument made by Stuart Hall: "The global and local are two aspects of the same phenomenon. As the binary expression of a late-capital formation, the difference between global and local can mask the similarities or links ... In seeking to understand how late capital requires differentiation and the stylistic markers of 'otherness,' Hall identifies the oppositional nature of postmodernity; the return to the local as a response to the seeming homogenization and globalization of culture can only work for social change if it does not become rooted in 'exclusivist and defensive enclaves'" (Grewal and Kaplan, 1994: 11–12).

38 "Transnational feminist practices compare multiple, overlapping, and discrete oppressions rather than ... construct a theory of hegemonic oppression under a unified category of gender" (17–18). Feminists can begin to map these scattered hegemonies and link diverse local practices to formulate a transnational set of solidarities" (19).

REFERENCES

Acker, Joan. (1992). Two discourses of reform and women in the future welfare state. English manuscript; in Swedish in *Kvinnor och mans liv och arbete*, ed. Annika Baude (Stockholm: SNS Förlag).

Adamson, Nancy, Linda Briskin, and Margaret McPhail. (1988). *Feminist Organizing for Change: The Contemporary Women's Movement in Canada*. Toronto: Oxford.

Briskin, Linda. (1998). Gendering union democracy. *Canadian Woman Studies/Cahiers de la femme* 18 (1) (spring): 35–8.

– (1997). *Gendering Union Democracy: A Swedish-Canadian Comparison*. Working Paper Series no. 13, Centre for Research on Work and Society. Toronto: York University.

– (1995). Kvinnor och demokratiseringen av fackliga organisationer (Women and the democratization of the unions). In *Delad makt: kvinnor ock facklig demokrati*. Stockholm: Utbildningsförlaget Brevskolan. (translated into Swedish by Gunilla Persson).

– (1994). Equity and economic restructuring in the Canadian labour movement. *Economic and Industrial Democracy* 15 (1): 89–112.

– (1993). Union women and separate organizing. In Briskin and McDermott.

– (1990a). Identity politics and the hierarchy of oppression: A comment. *Feminist Review* 35 (summer): 102–8.

Briskin, Linda. (1990b). *Autonomy, Integration and Legitimacy: A Comparative Analysis of Socialist Feminist Practice in Canada, the United States and Western Europe*. Working Paper, Institute for Social Research, York University.

– (1989). Socialist feminism: From the standpoint of practice. *Studies in Political Economy* 30 (fall): 87–114.

– and Patricia McDermott (eds.). (1993). *Women Challenging Unions: Feminism, Democracy and Militancy*. Toronto: University of Toronto Press.

Brodie, Janine. (1995). *Politics on the Margins: Restructuring and the Canadian Women's Movement*. Halifax: Fernwood Publishing.

Burstein, Paul, Rachel Einwohner, and Jocelyn Hollander. (1995). The success of political movements: A bargaining perspective. In Jenkins and Klandermans (1995a).

Carroll, William (ed.). (1992a). *Organizing Dissent: Contemporary Social Movements in Theory and Practice*. Toronto: Garamond.

Carroll, William. (1992b). Introduction: Social movements and counter hegemony in a Canadian context. In Carroll (1992a).

Clement, Wallace, and John Myles. (1994). *Relations of Ruling: Class and Gender in Postindustrial Societies*. Montreal: McGill-Queen's University Press.

Dahlerup, Drude. (1986). Introduction. In Drude Dahlerup (ed.), *The New Women's Movement: Feminism and Political Power in Europe and the USA*. London: Sage.

Eduards, Maud. (1992). Against the rules of the game: On the importance of women's collective actions. In *Rethinking Change: Current Swedish Feminist Research*. Uppsala: Swedish Science Press.

– (1991). Toward a third way: Women's politics and welfare policies in Sweden. *Social Research* 58 (3): 667–705.

– (1988). Gender politics and public policies – in Sweden. Draft, Department of Political Science, University of Stockholm.

Egan, Carolyn, and Lynda Yanz. (1983). Building Links: Labour and the Women's Movement. In Linda Briskin and Lynda Yanz (eds.), *Union Sisters: Women in the Labour Movement*. Toronto: Women's Press.

Ferree, Myra, and Patricia Martin (1995). Doing the work of the movement. In Myra Ferree and Patricia Martin (eds.), *Feminist Organizations: Harvest of the New Women's Movement*. Philadelphia: Temple University Press.

Findlay, Sue. (1988). Feminist struggles with the Canadian state: 1966–1988. *Resources for Feminist Research* 17 (3): 5–9.

Forsberg, Gunnel. (1998). Regional variation in the gender contract: Gendered relations in labour markets, local politics and everyday life in Swedish regions." *Innovation* 11 (2): 191–209.

Foucault, Michel. (1978). *The History of Sexuality: An Introduction*. New York: Vintage.

Gelb, Joyce. (1989). Sweden: Feminism without feminists? In *Feminism and Politics*. Berkeley: University of California Press.

Grewal, Inderpal, and Caren Kaplan. (1994). Transnational feminist practices and questions of postmodernity. In Inderpal Grewal and Caren Kaplan (eds.), *Scattered Hegemonies*. Minneapolis: University of Minnesota Press.

Jeffcott, Jeff, and Lynda Yanz. (1997). Bridging the GAP: Exposing the labour behind the label. *Our Times* 16 (1): 24–8.

Jenkins, J. Craig. (1995). Social movements, political representation, and the state: An agenda and comparative framework. In Jenkins and Klandermans (1995a).

– and Bert Klandermans (eds.). (1995a). *The Politics of Social Protest*. Minneapolis: University of Minnesota Press.

– (1995b). "The politics of social protest." In Jenkins and Klandermans (1995a).

Jenson, Jane. (1987). Changing discourse, changing agendas: Political rights and reproductive policies in France. In Katzenstein and Mueller.

Johnson, Theresa. (1997). Home econmics: International labour standards for homework. *Our Times* 16 (1): 21–3.

Katzenstein, Mary. (1987). Comparing the feminist movements of United States and western Europe: An overview. In Katzenstein and Mueller.
– and Carol Mueller (eds.). (1987). *The Women's Movements of the United States and Western Europe: Consciousness, Political Opportunity and Public Policy.* Philadelphia: Temple University Press.
Kriesi, Hanspeter. (1995). The political opportunity structure of new social movements: Its impact on their mobilization. In Jenkins and Klandermans (1995a).
Lewis, Jane, and Gertrude Åstrom. (1992). Equality, difference, and state welfare: Labor market and family policies in Sweden. *Feminist Studies* 18 (1): 59–87.
Mahon, Rianne. (1996). Woman wage earners and the future of Swedish unions. *Economic and Industrial Democracy* 17 (4): 545–86.
Micheletti, Michele. (1998). The democratic audit of Sweden. *Viewpoint Sweden* (Swedish Information Service), no. 18 (February).
Milkman, Ruth. (1985). Feminism and labor since the 1960s. In Ruth Milkman (ed.), *Women, Work and Protest.* Boston: Routledge and Kegan Paul.
Phelan, Shane. (1993). (Be)Coming out: Lesbian identity and politics. *Signs* 18 (4): 765–90.
Pierson, Ruth, Marjorie Griffin Cohen, Paula Bourne, and Philinda Masters. (1993). *Canadian Women's Issues*, vol. 1, *Strong Voices.* Toronto: Lorimer.
Pocock, Barbara. (1996). Challenging male advantage in Australian unions. Unpublished PhD thesis, Department of Women's Studies, University of Adelaide.
Ratner, R.S. (1992). New movements, new theory, new possibilities? Reflections on counter hegemony today. In Carroll (1992a).
Ruggie, Mary. (1988). Gender, work, and Social Progress. In Jane Jenson et al. (eds.), *Feminization of the Labor Force.* New York: Oxford.
– (1987). Worker's movements and women's interests: The impact of labor-state relations in Britain and Sweden. In Katzenstein and Mueller.
Sawicki, Jana. (1986). Foucault and feminism: Toward a politics of difference. *Hypatia* 1 (2): 23–36.
Siaroff, Alan. (1992). The extent of the "gaps": Swedish-European versus Canadian-U.S. variations in economic and social policy. In *The Entry into New Economic Communities: Swedish and Candian Perspectives on the European Economic Community and North American Free Trade Accord.* Toronto: Swedish Canadian Academic Foundation, York University.
Scott, Joan. (1990). Deconstructing equality-versus-difference, or, The uses of poststructuralist theory for feminism. In Marianne Hirsch and Evelyn Fox Keller (eds.), *Conflicts in Feminism.* New York: Routledge.

Staggenborg, Suzanne. (1995). Can feminist organizations be effective? In Ferree and Martin.

Stark, Agneta. (1997). Combating the backlash: How Swedish women won the war. In Ann Oakley and Juliet Mitchell (eds.), *Who's Afraid of Feminism?* London: Hamish Hamilton.

Threlfall, Monica. (1996). Conclusion. In Monica Threlfall (ed.), *Mapping the Women's Movement: Feminist Politics and Social Transformation in the North*. London: Verso.

Vickers, Jill. (1997). Towards a feminist understanding of representation. In Jane Arscott and Linda Trimble (eds.), *In the Presence of Women: Representation in Canadian Governments*. Toronto: Harcourt Brace.

– (1991). Bending the iron law of oligarchy. In Jeri Wine and Janice Ristock (eds.), *Women and Social Change: Feminist Activism in Canada*. Toronto: James Lorimer and Company.

– Pauline Rankin, and Christine Appelle. (1993). *Politics as if Women Mattered: A Political Analysis of the National Action Committee on the Status of Women*. Toronto: University of Toronto Press.

Walker, Gillian. (1990). The conceptual politics of struggle: Wife battering, the women's movement and the state. *Studies in Political Economy* 33: 63–90.

West, Guida, and Rhoda Blumberg. (1990). Reconstructing social protest from a feminist perspective. In Guida West and Rhoda Blumberg (eds.), *Women and Social Protest*. New York: Oxford.

Yalnizyan, Armine. (1993). From the dew-line: The experience of Canadian garment workers. In Briskin and McDermott.

PART ONE

National Boundaries under Challenge

Women's Response to Economic and Political Integration in Canada and Sweden

BARBARA CAMERON AND LENA GONÄS

ABSTRACT

This chapter explores regional integration as a feminist issue, focusing on the political mobilization by Canadian women against the Canada–U.S. Free Trade Agreement (and later, the North American Free Trade Agreement) and by Swedish women around Sweden's entry into the European Union. The analysis is pursued through an examination of women's political organizing in the period leading up to the 1988 federal election in Canada and to the 1994 Swedish referendum on membership in the EU. A comparison of the arguments advanced by feminists in Canada and Sweden reveals a remarkable similarity in the issues identified as particularly affecting women. The concerns in both countries centred on the role of the state in the provision of social services and in the regulation of the labour market, particularly in relation to women's participation in the paid labour force. Despite these similarities, feminists in Sweden and Canada pursued quite different organizing strategies. In Sweden they participated primarily through organizations associated with established mixed-gender political and economic bodies. By contrast, Canadian feminist intervention came principally through autonomous women's groups. The chapter concludes with observations on the implications for future feminist organizing strategies of the new regional alliances.

Continental integration is gendered: its implications for women's equality must be central to public debate. This was the message of Canadian and Swedish women who organized in their respective countries around treaties directed at furthering the regional integration process in North America and Europe. Feminists in Canada began mobilizing against a bilateral Canada–U.S. Free Trade Agreement

(CUFTA) in 1985 and maintained a vigorous campaign against the project until its implementation in January 1989. When the federal government then began to pursue a wider North American Free Trade Agreement (NAFTA), involving Mexico as well as Canada and the United States, women again made their opposition clear.[1] Virtually all of the organized feminist movement, as well as the labour movement, in Canada opposed the free-trade strategy. In Sweden feminist and labour leaders campaigned on both the Yes and the No sides of the November 1994 referendum on that country's entrance into the European Union. Nonetheless, in Sweden, as in Canada, a significant gender gap appeared during the political campaign, with more women than men opposed to the EU project. The mobilization of Canadian women against the Canada–U.S. Free Trade Agreement and that of Swedish women both for and against their country's entry into the European Union provide a unique opportunity to compare women's organizing in Canada and Sweden.

GENDER REGIMES AND REGIONAL INTEGRATION

The starting point for our comparison is the concept of capitalist welfare-state regimes, as developed by Gøsta Esping-Andersen (1990) and modified by feminist scholars (O'Connor, 1993; Orloff, 1993; Sainsbury, 1994). According to Esping-Andersen, capitalist welfare states can be classified in three main clusters or regime types: the liberal, the corporatist, and the social democratic. These regimes differ in the extent to which social rights are recognized, the nature of stratification, and the state-market-family relationship. Feminists seeking to use the concept of welfare-state regimes have focused on the need to treat the family more fully in discussions of the the state-market-family triad. As Mary Daly (1994) points out, this emphasis is essential because "the family remains the most significant provider of welfare and care in all welfare states, even in those that are classified as social democratic" (107). Some feminists have sought to expand Esping-Andersen's identification of social rights with independence from the market in ways that recognize the importance to women of autonomy from male partners and the state. Feminists have also emphasized the need to expand the stratification dimension to include gender, as well as class, inequalities and have pointed to the need to recognize the importance of services as well as income-replacement programs in conceptualizing the relationship between welfare-state regimes and labour-market regimes.

Of particular relevance to our study are the attempts by feminist scholars to gender Esping-Andersen's explanation of the reasons for the differences in welfare-state regimes. He locates the source of difference in the interaction of three factors: "the nature of class mobilization (especially of the working class); class-political coalition structure; and the historical legacy of regime institutionalization" (Esping-Andersen, 1990: 29). Feminist critics argue that this conceptualization limits the significant political actors and organizations to those with a base in the labour market and focuses on mainstream political institutions. Social movements, such as the feminist movement, are excluded, as are the institutional responses of the state to these movements. Julia O'Connor (1993) argues that the conceptualization of politics in this model needs to be expanded in three ways: to recognize the influence of social movements other than those that are class based, to acknowledge the gender composition of mainstream political organizations, and to evaluate the historical institutional legacy "in terms of its conduciveness to facilitating or hindering the incorporation of women into the political process" (510). Differences in the conduciveness of institutions imply differences in the ways that women's interests are represented in various welfare-state regimes, with important consequences for women's organizing strategies.

While feminist research suggests that women will organize differently in various welfare-state regimes, it also points to a common basis for political mobilization of women across regimes. In all welfare-state regimes, gender remains a principle for the organization of work, with women having greater responsibility for the reproductive labour of society, both private and public, than men. As a consequence, they also have a different relationship to production than men do. The divergent locations of women and men in the division of labour lead to differences in the claims that they make on society. Ann Orloff (1993) has argued, "Men make claims as worker-citizens to compensate for failures in the labour market; women make claims as workers, but also as members of families, and they need programs especially to compensate for marriage failures and/or the need to raise children alone" (308). She suggests that men are politicized through their participation in and relationship to the labour market, whereas "women are politicized and mobilized by their ties to the state" (322). The different locations of men and women in the social division of labour also has implications for organization. Men's labour-market position provides the basis for organizations rooted in production. Women's weaker labour-market position and responsibilities for reproduction provide a weaker basis for economic organization. Hernes (1987) has suggested that women tend to have fewer organizational buffers than men between themselves and the state.

Beginning from Esping-Andersen's work, Annette Borchorst (1994) has explored the implications of the European integration process for women. She points out that the European Community (now the European Union) comprises examples of both corporatist and social democratic welfare-state regimes, with the corporatist predominating. This observation raises the question of which model will prevail in the process of harmonization associated with regional integration. Borchorst stresses the importance of recognizing the indirect, as well as the direct, effects of integration. In the case of the European Union, the direct effects arise from the equal-opportunity measures specifically aimed at improving women's status. The indirect effects, which relate to the impact of the integration process on the balance between the state, the family, and the market, could be more significant. She notes that the equality measures of the European Union have generally been progressive. However, the "highly monetarist character of the political and economic union" has implications for the state-family-market relationship. Borchorst notes that, "although the EC regulations have not aimed at strengthening the role of the family, they have certainly strengthened the market." Her own prediction is that the EU "will magnify differences between women, supporting those who can compete directly with men," and that it will reinforce a dualism in the labour market, which is structured along gender lines (Borchorst, 1994: 40).

The emergence of supranational regimes of regulation such as the European Union and the Canada–U.S. Free Trade Agreement raises interesting questions about the political mobilization of women. If it is true, as feminist scholars suggest, that women have seen their interests tied more directly to the national state than men have and that they are more reliant on state programs, one would expect to see differences in the political responses of men and women to the new treaties governing regional integration. This would particularly be the case if the new regional frameworks were seen to weaken or to improve existing national protections. One would also anticipate that this gender difference would be present irrespective of the type of welfare-state regime. At the same time, one would expect to find differences in the ways that women mobilize in various welfare-state regimes related to historically specific experiences of political mobilization, alliances, and institutional structures. New supranational regulatory regimes will also alter the "historical institutional legacy" of the national societies, a legacy that is the product of past alliances among a variety of social forces. This raises the question of what impact the new regimes will have on the existing national system of alliances. It also suggests the need to raise at the regional level the question that Julia O'Connor poses with respect to national welfare-state regimes: To what extent do the new supranational regimes facilitate or hinder the integration and political participation of women?

THE CASE STUDY

According to Esping-Andersen's typology, Canada and Sweden belong to divergent types of welfare-state regimes characterized by differences in the relationships among the state, the market, and the family. Sweden is the archetypical social democratic welfare regime, while Canada belongs to the liberal welfare regime cluster. In the 1960s Sweden officially embraced the dual-breadwinner model of the family and introduced taxation and family policies to support high levels of participation by women in the paid labour force. Reproductive labour is much more highly socialized in Sweden than in most other OECD countries, and a strong public sector provides employment for close to 60 per cent of the female labour force. The solidaristic wage strategy of the labour movement, pursued through a highly centralized system of collective bargaining, succeeded in narrowing considerably the gap between men's and women's wages. Strong universal benefits have resulted in low levels of poverty among single mothers, and there is little stratification among women based on their relationship with a man. The Swedish occupational and industrial structure, however, continues to be highly segregated along lines of gender, and women still have primary responsibility for domestic labour.

Canada also has high levels of female labour-force participation, and the two-wage-earner family has become the norm, with income from women keeping an increasing number of families above the poverty line. Except for health care and education, however, reproductive labour, including childcare and elder care, is treated in Canadian government policy as primarily a private responsibility to be provided either by families or by services purchased on the market. Public funding for social services other than health and education is targeted to the poorest sections of the population. At the time of the free-trade debate, Canada had a universal family allowance program and a universal old age benefit. The comparatively weak universal income-support programs were supplemented by employment-linked social insurance programs and targeted social assistance programs for the poor. There is a much higher degree of stratification in the Canadian than in the Swedish welfare-state regime, reflected in a wage gap of 30 per cent between full-time male and female workers, high levels of poverty among single mothers, and greater reliance by women over sixty-five than men on government income-support programs. As in Sweden, the occupational and industrial structure is highly segregated along lines of gender, and women continue to have primary responsibility for domestic labour. At the federal level and in some of the provinces, the women's movement has won equal-pay and affirmative-action legislation directed at countering wage inequality and occupational segregation.

The welfare-state regimes of Sweden and Canada diverge from those of their regional neighbours in ways that were important to the debates over the regional integration treaties. Sweden's Nordic neighbour Denmark, which has a social democratic welfare regime, is a member of the European Union and shares the Swedish commitment to high levels of social and gender equality. Finland is also a member of the EU, having joined at the same time as Sweden as the result of a much more positive referendum than in that country. However, the majority of the member countries of the EU are representative of the corporatist type of welfare-state regime. They are characterized by a strong reliance on employment-linked social insurance rather than universal programs and on the family for the provision of care for children and other dependants. There are high levels of stratification between men and women and between married women and single mothers. According to Esping-Andersen's typology, Canada and its partner in the Canada–U.S. Free Trade Agreement both belong to the liberal welfare regime cluster. Canadians, however, consider the American system to be much more market oriented than their own, an impression supported by a comparison of Canadian and American social programs conducted in the late 1980s by Canadian social scientist Keith Banting. He found that, while benefits for the elderly were roughly comparable, "the Canadian combination of universal health care, a much larger Unemployment Insurance program, richer child benefits and stronger social assistance provides more comprehensive protection for the non-elderly population" (Banting, 1997: 269). His analysis led him to conclude that there is "a firmer foundation for the welfare state in Canada than in the United States" (269).

Differences between the Canadian and Swedish welfare-state regimes are reflected in the divergent "institutional legacies" of the two societies. Joan Acker (1999) uses a framework of "two reform discourses" to understand the way that class and gender have been articulated ideologically and institutionally in Sweden and to explain the persistence of gender inequality despite state measures in support of the dual-breadwinner model. She describes the coexistence in Sweden of two reform discourses, whereby the female-dominated discourse of family and reproduction has been articulated with, but subordinated to, a male-dominated discourse of production and class. The discourse of class has been located primarily within the corporatist institutions of capital and labour, from which women have been largely excluded, while the discourse of family and reproduction has been located within women's organizations linked to political parties and unions, in certain branches of the state, and less frequently in small, autonomous feminist organizations. In comparison with other countries, the political parties and state legislative bodies in Sweden have been strongly conducive to women's political participation.

In contrast to the situation that Acker describes for Sweden, Canadian politics at the federal level have been organized around issues of region and nation, and political parties and legislatures have not been effective vehicles for the representation of those subordinate interests, including women and workers, that cut across geographic lines. Women's committees of political parties have existed in Canada since before the First World War, but their influence has rarely been significant. Canadian feminists have historically created non-partisan, autonomous, and often cross-class organizations of women to represent their political interests. In the period leading up to the free-trade fight, Canadian governments responded to the demands of the women's movement primarily within a liberal equal-opportunities framework, emphasizing the removal of discriminatory obstacles to women's participation in economic and social life, rather than the creation of the services to support this participation.

The main promoters of regional integration treaties in the two countries were organizations representing the largest corporations: the Business Council on National Issues (BCNI) in the Canadian case and the Swedish employers' federation (Sveriges Arbetsgivareforeningen, or SAF). In keeping with the interests of these organizations, the Treaty on European Union and the North American free-trade agreements have the common objective of achieving the free movement of goods, services, capital, and labour across national borders within a region. Both are directed at facilitating the operation of transnational corporations by harmonizing the regulatory frameworks governing their activities. They both, therefore, replace or alter important elements of the national system of regulation and have implications, either directly or indirectly, for the existing regimes of social welfare. There are, however, significant differences in the nature of the integration processes under the treaties in Europe and North America which are relevant to the general public debates in the two countries and possible future feminist political strategies.

The European Union is a political, monetary, and commercial, as well as an economic, union, whereas the Canada–U.S. Free Trade

Agreement is a commercial arrangement and does not cover trade relations with third countries. At the European level, there are regional policy-making institutions which have the authority to issue directives with respect to certain matters that are binding on member states. These institutions include a powerful Council made up of representatives of the governments of member states, a European Parliament elected on the basis of universal franchise in each of the member countries, and a European Court of Justice. In contrast, the regional institutions established by the CUFTA take the form of disputes-resolution mechanisms or procedures for future negotiations on liberalizing access to markets. There are no avenues for popular representation or consultation within CUFTA. An important feature of the Maastricht Treaty is the project of a European Monetary Union, which will subordinate national economic policies to the decisions of a powerful European Central Bank. In contrast, the harmonization of Canadian and American monetary policy did not require new regional institutions and has been achieved over the past two decades through the Bank of Canada's policy of following the leadership of the U.S. Federal Reserve in the establishment of interest rates.

The EU has a social dimension, which is reflected in the European Community Charter of the Fundamental Social Rights of Workers, signed in 1989, and the Protocol on Social Policy, or Agreement on Social Policy, agreed to in 1991 by all EU member countries except Britain. The Protocol on Social Policy covers matters related to the regulation of working conditions and the labour market, including health and safety, equal opportunities between men and women with regard to labour-market opportunities and treatment at work, and the social security and social protection of workers. Social services are the responsibility of national states. The treaty requires that "social partners" be consulted before social policy measures are introduced and identifies these parties as "in particular, representatives of producers, farmers, transport operators, workers, merchants, artisans, the professions and representatives of the general interests" (Treaty, 1992, articles 193 and 194; Addison and Siebert, 1994: 21). Women are not recognized as a distinct constituency. Social services were excluded from the services chapter of CUFTA, but the management of services such as health care was treated in the same way as commercial services and open to foreign investment. The failure of the Canadian negotiators to achieve a subsidies code led to concerns that public grants to non-profit services would have to be made available to United States–based providers of commercial services, and social transfers to individuals might be challenged as unfair subsidies. There are no explicit measures for the harmonization of working conditions within CUFTA and certainly no protective labour standards.

In Canada the debate on free trade was sharply divided between, on the one side, business organizations led by the BCNI, an organization representing the 150 largest corporations operating in the country, and, on the other side, popular-sector organizations, including unions, most farm organizations, women's groups, social-justice groups, and cultural organizations. Virtually all Canadian business organizations, including the Canadian Manufacturers' Association, the chambers of commerce, and representatives of small and medium-sized businesses such as the Canadian Federation of Independent Business, endorsed the free-trade project. Regionally based resource industries, particularly the oil and gas industry of Alberta, were strongly in favour. The Canadian Bankers' Association, representing the historically highly centralized and protected banking industry, offered lukewarm support. The political sponsor of the Canada–U.S. Free Trade Agreement was the Progressive Conservative government of Prime Minister Brian Mulroney, but the other major party traditionally enjoying business support, the Liberals, opposed it. The New Democratic Party, a moderate social democratic party with formal links to the labour movement, also opposed the project. Provincial Liberal and New Democratic governments did not support the federal government's free-trade initiative.

In Sweden opinion on membership in the European Union was also polarized, with the economic elites supporting membership and nonelite constituencies, including a majority of workers and women, opposing it. Throughout the Swedish debate, membership in the European Economic Area (EEA), which involved an agreement liberalizing trade in goods, services, capital, and labour between the Nordic countries and EU member countries without full integration into the political machinery of the EU, remained an alternative. The main promoters of full integration were the major business organizations: the powerful SAF and the Swedish manufacturers' organization (Industriförbundet). The EU option was strongly endorsed by two of the main bourgeois parties, the Liberals and the Moderates. Both the Christian Democrats, a bourgeois party, and the Centre Party, originally a farmer's group, were split. The Left Party and the Green Party were internally united in their opposition to the EU project. After November 1990 the bourgeois economic and political elites received the welcome support of the leadership of the Swedish Social Democratic Party (Sveriges Socialdemokratiska Arbetareparti, or SAP), which reversed the party's position and declared its support for membership in the European Union. It was a Social Democratic government that on 1 July 1991 submitted

Sweden's application for membership in the EU. The change in position by the SAP leadership resulted in a deep split within the party and within the unions, including those affiliated to the Swedish Trade Union Confederation (Landsorganisationen, or LO) and the Central Organization of Salaried Employees (Tjänstemännens Centralorganisation, or TCO). Negotiation of the terms of Sweden's entrance into the EU took place under a bourgeois government, in office from 1991 to 1994.

In both Canada and Sweden the opportunity to vote on the integration treaties came as a result of popular pressure. In Canada a Conservative prime minister was forced to call an election when the Senate, Canada's appointed upper house, dominated at the time by Liberals, refused to pass legislation implementing the Canada–U.S. Free Trade Agreement unless the government won an electioral mandate on the issue. The unprecedented decision of a modern Canadian Senate to oppose directly a major piece of legislation approved by the elected House of Commons was a response to the demand by the popular-sector opposition for an election on free trade. The election was held in November 1988, and the Conservatives won 43 per cent of the popular vote, which Canada's electoral system translated into a strong majority of the seats in the Commons. CUFTA came into effect on 1 January 1989. In Sweden the demand for a referendum on the question of membership in the European Union was launched as early as 1989, but it was not until April 1994, in the face of public opposition to the initiative, that the bourgeois parties then in government and the opposition Social Democratic Party agreed to hold a referendum two months after the September 1994 parliamentary elections. The referendum on Sweden's entry into the EU was held on 14 November 1994 and saw the Yes side win: 52.3 per cent voted for membership and 46.8 per cent were against, while 0.9 per cent turned in blank votes.

CANADIAN WOMEN AND THE FREE-TRADE FIGHT

Mobilizing Canadian Women: Institutions

Canadian women took part in the fight against the Canadian–U.S. Free Trade Agreement through a variety of organizations, the Canadian Labour Congress (CLC) and the federations of labour in Quebec and the provinces playing a particularly strong role. The CLC at that time was led by its first woman president, Shirley Carr, who was an effective spokesperson for the anti-free-trade forces. Another prominent woman and well-known feminist was Maude Barlow, once an adviser to former Liberal prime minister Pierre Elliott Trudeau and chairperson of the English-Canadian nationalist organization the Council of Canadians. However, leadership in defining and advancing issues of particular concern to Canadian women during the free-trade debate clearly belonged to the National Action Committee on the Status of Women (NAC), a Canada-wide umbrella organization of feminist organizations.

NAC had been formed in 1972 by thirty-two organizations located mainly in Ontario to lobby for the implementation of the recommendations of the Royal Commission on the Status of Women, whose report had been published two years earlier. By the time of the free-trade fight, NAC had grown to be a federation of over five hundred women's organizations in every region of the country, some small local groups with as few as ten members and others large national associations with tens of thousands of members. Among its affiliates are autonomous women's services such as rape crisis centres and community-based training organizations, advocacy organizations promoting the expansion of childcare services, business and professional women's organizations, church and farm women's organizations, women's committees of unions and political parties, and student organizations, as well as country-wide charitable organizations with origins in the first wave of feminism. Although member groups are located in every province and territory in the country, NAC's support has historically been weak among organizations of French-speaking Quebec feminists, who are represented through their own national organization. NAC has an annual general meeting (AGM) each year in Ottawa. On the Monday following the AGM a lobby is held during which several hundred feminists meet in the presence of the national media with the caucus members of each of the parties represented in Parliament. At the time of the free-trade fight, it also held a mid-year educational meeting in another city; its executive, with representatives from every region of the country, came together ten times a year. Between meetings, the NAC executive communicates with its members through publications, which at the time of the fight against free trade included an eight-page newspaper issued ten times a year.

NAC was among the first popular-sector organizations to speak out against free trade. The organization held a press conference on 4 September 1985, one day before the release of the report of the Royal Commission on the Economic Union and Development Prospects for Canada. Anticipating the pro-free-trade recommendation of the commission, NAC leaders declared the organization's opposition to a free-trade agreement with the United States (Dulude, 1985; Bashevkin, 1989: 367). Between September 1985 and the November 1988 federal election, NAC made opposition to the Canada–U.S. Free Trade

Agreement a major priority. In conducting its campaign, it used its own organizational structure and feminist networks to educate women about the potential effects of continental free trade on women's equality and found ways to intervene in the broader public debate. NAC's success in mobilizing feminists and in characterizing free trade as a women's issue forced free-trade supporters to make their own appeal to women and to defend their project against feminist critics.

NAC's federated structure and its annual general meeting (AGM) and mid-year educational meetings provided an effective network for building consensus among Canadian feminists, giving them the knowledge and skills to take part in debates in their local communities. In November 1985, little more than a month after the government's official announcement of its intention to seek a bilateral free-trade agreement with the United States, NAC made free trade a central focus of its mid-year meeting. The 1986 AGM officially established NAC policy on free trade by unanimously passing a motion condemning "government attempts to rely on the market to direct the economy; and opposed privatization, deregulation and free trade" (NAC, 1994: 11) Delegates from across Canada attending the 1987 NAC annual meeting passed a resolution to "endorse the executive's call for an immediate federal election" (NAC, 1994: 1), and the theme of the 1987 mid-year meeting, held in Edmonton, was "Using Power: Women and the Next Federal Election." It featured a debate on free trade between Marjorie Cohen, NAC vice-president, and the Conservative member of Parliament from the Edmonton West constituency (*Feminist Action*, February 1988). The AGM in May 1988 focused attention again on the demand for an election and the dangers of free trade to women. The meeting ensured that the issue would continue as a central priority for NAC by electing as president Lynn Kaye, a lawyer with ties to the labour movement who had been for many years an active member of NAC's employment and economy committee.

During the organization's annual lobby in 1986 and 1987, delegates to the AGM grilled members of the government on the effects of free trade on women. In 1988 the session of the annual lobby devoted to meeting the government featured a twenty-minute debate on free trade between representatives of the government and of NAC. Supporting the government's pro-free-trade position were Barbara McDougall, the minister responsible for free trade, and John McDermid, a Conservative member of Parliament. NAC was represented by Vice-President Marjorie Cohen, Madeleine Parent, the Quebec representative on the executive, and Lucia Spencer, from the National Organization of Immigrant and Visible Minority Women of Canada. During the lobby sessions with all political parties, NAC repeated the call for an election before the January 1989 implementation date for CUFTA (*Feminist Action*, September 1988). The effect of such lobby sessions was to communicate the organization's positions forcefully to the government and opposition parties, to educate women, and to gain media attention.

Throughout the free-trade fight, NAC used its tabloid newspaper, *Feminist Action*, and other publications to demystify an area of public policy previously inaccessible to most women and to provide the arguments that women needed to participate in debates at a local level. The organization's published positions were backed up with solid research by Marjorie Cohen, and the appearance in the spring of 1987 of her study *Free Trade and the Future of Women's Work* enhanced the credibility of NAC's case against free trade (Zwarun, 1987) The November 1987 issue of *Feminist Action* took the form of an election kit, outlining the key issues and providing tips to women on how to organize for an election campaign. Early in 1988 the organization published a pamphlet entitled *Free Trade: A Bad Deal for Women. Here's Why and What to Do* (NAC, 1988a), which listed activities that women could undertake to force an election, including contacting local members of Parliament and provincial legislatures, distributing the NAC pamphlet at work and in the community, joining local action against free trade, writing to local and national newspapers, setting up information meetings or debates on free trade, and sending for NAC's election kit (NAC, 1988a). For the 1988 election campaign NAC distributed shocking-pink buttons with the slogan "Women Vote" in black and produced a popular booklet, *What Every Woman Needs to Know about Free Trade.*

Throughout the three-year campaign against free trade, the organization's executive members used their frequent invitations to speak to women's organizations across the country to highlight the opposition of the women's movement. The local feminist media carried coverage of these speeches, as well as interviews with NAC leaders and analytical articles on free trade. (Waywanko, 1987; *Herizons*, 1987; Rudland, 1987). Shortly after her election as NAC president in May 1988, Lynn Kaye embarked on a two-week trek across western Canada and the north to organize women for the next federal election. Her speeches focused on free trade, childcare, and violence against women, but according to media coverage at the time, "Most of Kaye's scorn is reserved for the government's proposed free-trade agreement with the United States" (Wattle, 1988). NAC also encouraged the establishment of coalitions of women specifically directed at opposing free trade, such as the Toronto-based Women against Free Trade, composed of representatives of NAC, the Ontario Federation of Labour Women's Committee, the New Democratic Party, the Ontario Coalition for

Better Child Care, and other groups (Burstyn and Rebick, 1988). In the period leading up to the 1988 election, these coalitions were able to provide speakers for women's meetings and produce educational material of their own.

In addition to its campaigning through feminist networks, NAC found strategies to intervene in the broader public debate. It took advantage of public hearings by parliamentary committees at the federal and provincial levels to present well-researched briefs outlining the impact of free trade on women. As a way to increase the presence in the debate of the anti-free-trade forces and ensure the visibility of women's concerns, the organization helped to found and participated in coalitions uniting a broad spectrum of popular-sector associations. The first coalition against free trade came out of a meeting of representatives of women's, labour, aboriginal, farm, cultural, seniors', poverty, and religious groups convened by Laurell Ritchie, a NAC executive member, in November 1985. The meeting gave rise to the Ontario-based Coalition against Free Trade, which was co-chaired by Marjorie Cohen from NAC and John Foster from the United Church of Canada. In 1987 NAC, the Coalition against Free Trade, and many other popular-sector organizations came together under the name Pro-Canada Network, a nation-wide coalition that unified the popular-sector organizations fighting against the free-trade agreement. NAC encouraged its member organizations to build support in their communities for the public actions of the Pro-Canada Network and to become members of the local anti-free-trade coalitions.

At the time of the release of the draft free-trade agreement in October 1987, polls revealed that a gender gap had emerged on the issue, with 55 per cent of men, compared to 43 per cent of women, in favour. By December 1987 support among men stood at 47 per cent and among women at 34 per cent. (Bashevkin, 1989: 369) By January 1988 free trade was recognized as a women's issue not only by NAC and other feminist organizations but also by the government. With polls showing support for it declining and a significant gender gap, the government identified women as a key constituency in its fight for public opinion. Early in 1988 mothers across Canada opened their monthly family allowance cheque to discover a government brochure outlining the benefits of free trade to consumers. In March, Barbara McDougall, who was also the minister responsible for the status of women, began "blanketing the country with a glossy, full-colour brochure purporting to prove that free trade will benefit Canadian women" (Zwarun, 1988). Polls taken during the final month of the electoral campaign revealed that the gender gap persisted, and all parties targeted messages specifically to women in the closing weeks. John

Turner, leader of the Liberal Party, slammed the Conservative government for a "diabolical double whammy" on women by endangering their jobs with free trade and then picking their pockets with new taxes (*Winnipeg Free Press*, 7 November 1988). The Conservatives began running television ads directly aimed at women which claimed that the Government of Brian Mulroney had given them social justice by creating jobs.

Mobilizing Canadian Women: Arguments

Throughout the debate on free trade, the impact on employment generally was central to the arguments of both sides, and the implications for women's employment was initially the main focus of NAC's concerns. From the perspective of a traditional notion of trade as being in goods, the most readily recognized potential impact was on jobs in the manufacturing sector. Feminists argued that, while women comprised only 12 per cent of workers in manufacturing industries, they were concentrated in those industries that were most labour-intensive and that these were likely to be disproportionately affected by the elimination of tariffs (Dulude, 1985; Cohen, 1987a; Porter and Cameron, 1987). NAC's 1988 election brochure stressed the negative impact on women's employment in textiles, clothing, food processing, electrical and electronic products, and other consumer goods, and it maintained, "The women who will be particularly affected by job losses in manufacturing are immigrants, women of colour, older women, disabled women, and women with low levels of education" (NAC, 1988c).

A major contribution of NAC and of its vice-president, Marjorie Cohen, in particular was to broaden the free-trade debate and bring to public attention its potential impact on jobs in the service sector, which accounted for 83 per cent of women's employment, and on social services. As early as November 1985 Cohen had warned of the desire by the United States to extend trade to include services as well as goods, and she drew attention to the possible implications for women's clerical work in light of developments in communications technology (Cohen, 1985: 5–6.) This analysis was immediately reflected in NAC's public statements. In her speech to the Canadian Club on 11 November 1985, NAC president Chaviva Hosek maintained, "What the Americans want is free trade in services. It includes a lot of data processing, a lot of clerical work and a lot of areas where there are literally thousands of women" (Auman, 1985). The impact of free trade on women's service-sector employment was a continuing theme of NAC and its representatives throughout the free-trade debate (Hossie, 1985b; Cohen, 1987a; NAC, 1988b: 4).

In addition to highlighting a concern about employment in the service industries, NAC was also the first organization to emphasize the impact of free trade on Canada's system of social services. At the centre of its critique was a concern that free trade would take the Canadian system, currently a mixture of commercial, non-profit, and public services, increasingly in the direction of the primarily market-driven U.S. system. In a speech to a mid-year NAC meeting in Novembre 1985, Cohen linked the free-trade initiative to the emergence of a right-wing emphasis on market forces and argued that free trade could damage social protection measures, such as maternity benefits, which could be challenged as unfair trade subsidies (*Feminist Action*, January 1986). The link between free trade and social services was a theme of Cohen's speeches throughout 1987 (Waywanko, 1987: 20) and was emphasized in NAC's presentation to the 1988 parliamentary hearings on the implementation of the Canada–U.S. Free Trade Agreement (NAC, 1988b) and in the platform that it issued for the 1988 election campaign.

As the compaign progressed, NAC's focus increasingly became the threat to Canada's regime of social welfare posed by harmonization with the more market-oriented, more classically liberal welfare regime of the United States. The booklet *What Every Woman Needs to Know about Free Trade*, which was issued as part of the organization's 1988 election campaign, highlighted the potential impact of the free-trade agreement on health care and day care. The text on health care read in part: "Canada and the US have radically different ways of providing health care. In Canada it is publicly supported while in the US it is run by private enterprise. Under free trade, US businesses will be free to come in and manage (and/or own) our hospitals, nursing homes, homes for the disabled; our halfway houses, and community health clinic; our ambulance services, medical labs, x-ray labs, and even our blood banks." In a similar vein, the text on childcare began: "Under the investment chapter of the free trade deal, private US day care corporations could claim access to public funds for establishing centres here. They would be allowed to compete for such funding on an equal basis with our own non-profit day care centres. This could lead to a preponderance of 'for-profit' care delivery in Canada." The booklet drew links between the participation in these services of private American corporations and wages and working conditions, pointing to the practices in the few hospitals in Canada already run by U.S. management firms and the conditions in the existing commercial childcare centres.

NAC was also concerned that the free-trade agreement would strengthen the arguments of employers for lower standards for labour-market regulation in order to remain competitive. In response to the question of one interviewer about whether or not CUFTA could be used to prevent legislation directed at equality in employment, Marjorie Cohen stated: "I don't think it will be prohibited. I think it's going to happen in more indirect ways. I think workers are going to be blackmailed not to push for any improvement, whether it's wages or working conditions, and the threat will be, we'll have to shift production. Firms are already saying, look, we can't compete, Canadian labour legislation is too stringent, and if we meet all these regulations, pay equity requirements, we're going to price ourselves out of the market. The sad thing is, that in a sense, the threat's real" (Rowles, 1988: 16).

The November 1987 issue of *Feminist Action* featured an article by feminist political economist Isa Bakker, who maintained that "the increased competition of free trade will force firms to cut costs, thereby putting pressure on equal pay legislation." She also predicted, "American pressure on Canada to 'harmonize' its social programs with those of the US may affect the delivery of social services and lead to job losses. Efforts to bring Canadian tax programs in line with American ones may mean reduced revenues for government and may signal public sector spending cuts in response to deficits" (*Feminist Action*, November 1987: 2).

While the impact of free trade on women's employment, social services, and labour-market standards was the main focus of NAC's critique, other issues were addressed in its election material in response to claims made by free-trade supporters or the concerns of particular constituencies within the organization. To counter the Conservative government's appeal to women almost exclusively as consumers, NAC emphasized, "The consumer issues which are most worrisome to women have to do with the impact of free trade on product standards" (Pollak, 1988: 3; NAC, 1988b: 6). Its election material maintained that provisions in the free-trade agreement would replace Canadian product safety standards with lower American ones, and it challenged the claim of free-trade supporters that the agreement would bring lower prices by pointing out that the government intended to introduce a new sales tax to recoup the revenue lost by removing tariffs (NAC, 1988c).

NAC also raised the concerns of its membership about the impact of free trade on the environment and on peace. With regard to the environment, a major problem was the impact on Canadian environmental controls of the articles in the agreement regarding the harmonization of standards (NAC, 1988c). The other major environmental issue was the export of water. Along with other critics of the free-trade agreement, NAC maintained that the failure explicitly to exclude water from the agreement meant that the government could no longer exercise control over exports. Concerning peace, NAC argued, "Women are in the forefront of the peace movement and are concerned about the potential use of resources and labour for military purposes under free trade." The election booklet pointed out that the only industrial subsidies explicitly recognized by the agreement as permissible were those "sensitive to the defence of the country." Feminists feared that this aspect of the agreement would result in the militarization of Canada's regional economic development and job-creation programs (NAC, 1988c). The connection between free trade and a growing reliance on defence production was also a theme of an article in the summer 1988 issue of *Kinesis*, the newspaper of the Vancouver Council on the Status of Women (Grove, 1988).

The polarization that characterized the free-trade debate in Canada influenced the way in which the feminist leadership publicly defined the political role of the women's movement. This was a consequence of the growing awareness of free trade as an integral part of a broader, more market-oriented, and more American model of economic and social development. Feminist leaders, including NAC president Lynn Kaye, began to describe free trade as a Trojan horse being used to smuggle in right-wing policies similar to those of the Reagan administration in the United States (Wattle, 1988; Burstyn and Rebick, 1988: 141; Rowles, 1988). The women's movement was seen as part of a broadly based popular opposition to a right-wing agenda (Bursyn and Rebick, 1988: 141). This perspective was clearly articulated by Marjorie Cohen in a 1988 interview, in which she maintained, "The major interests behind the free trade decision were large US multinationals, the same people who have created Prime Minister Mulroney." She continued, "I think this is why free trade is such a divisive issue in Canada: it's government and big business against everybody else – women's groups, churches, trade unions, cultural groups, immigrant groups, farmers – because our interests are not the same, and they are pursuing an economic policy which is in the interests of the big and powerful" (Kjellberg, 1988: 20).

Women's Organizing in Canada: Conclusions

There were elements of the old and the new in the way that Canadian women mobilized around free trade. In keeping with their political traditions, they acted through non-partisan, gender-based organizations. That they chose this form, rather than political parties, is particularly notable given that the free-trade fight coalesced around a parliamentary election. In keeping with feminist traditions, the main focus of the struggle was the role of the state in the provision of services and the regulation of the labour market as it affected women's employment in manufacturing and equality legislation. During the campaign, NAC came increasingly to characterize free trade as a threat to Canada's regime of social welfare and to contrast the more universal and generous aspects of its social programs and stronger labour protections with the more market-oriented American system. A major new element in the free-trade struggle was a polarization of Canadian society with the "people," represented by a variety of popular-sector organizations that drew support from all regional and national groups in Canada, mobilized against a major initiative of Canadian business and the governing political party. In this encounter the largest and most influential feminist organization was clearly aligned with labour and other oppositional forces in a new way. Canadian feminists came to identify a "corporate agenda" as an anti-woman political project. The free-trade fight in Canada marked a final stage in the abandonment of the Keynesian social contract in the country and the embrace of neo-liberalism by the dominant political and economic elites. As such, it ushered in a new era of politics in which the demands for women's equality and for social equality generally and the organizations that promote them are increasingly defined as marginal to the main public agenda.

SWEDISH WOMEN AND THE EUROPEAN UNION

Mobilizing Swedish Women: Institutions

The debate in Sweden over entrance into the European Union in Sweden was characterized by clevages along a number of dimensions: non-elite/elite; female/male; young/old; public sector/private sector; and unemployed/employed. It is clear that membership in a particular socio-economic group determined how many people voted. Swedish society was also divided geographically between core and periphery. Here, the cleavage was two-dimensional: urban/rural and north/south. The largest spread in voting was between rural inhabitants in the northern part of Sweden, where 28 per cent voted yes, and urban voters in southern Sweden (the Stockholm area), where 66 per cent did so. In general, the northern parts of the country were strongholds for the No side; there over 60 per cent in all political parties other than the conservatives and the liberals voted no (Statistics Sweden, 1996).

The divisions within Swedish society over membership in the EU were reflected in splits within some of the political parties, giving rise to the need for new organizational forms to take part in the referendum campaign. For feminists of the professional and business classes, women's organizations linked to economic associations, in particular SAF and the farmers' organizations, played a particularly important role. The split in the Social Democratic Party and the unions led to the creation within these organizations of Yes and No groups. In order to avoid internal conflict, the leadership of the Social Democratic Women in Sweden did not take a position and carried articles on both sides of the issue in its monthly journal, *Morgonbris*. An autonomous feminist network, Stödstrumporna (Support Stockings), was also divided and did not take part in the debate, even though it had maintained a strong presence during the parliamentary election campaign two months before, threatening to start a women's party if the existing parties did not take up women's issues seriously.

From the beginning of the Swedish referendum campaign, the Yes side recognized the importance of women to the outcome of the vote and adopted a strategy of mobilizing them through women's organizations (Brantingsson, 1995). These were not, however, autonomous groups but were funded by and linked to other organizations on the Yes side. The main organization was Europea, a women's network affiliated to the Yes to Europe committee, which operated out of SAF's regional offices. Another pro-EU women's organization, the Network for Europe (Nätverk för Europa), was supported by the farmers' organization (LRF) and had its national office located in the LRF house in Stockholm. The women's organization of the Moderate Party supported the party's pro-Europe position but did no separate organizing during the campaign. The organizations of women on the Yes side were made up of women professionals, entrepreneurs, and farmers. Working-class women on the Yes, as well as the No, side participated in the campaign through mixed organizations formed within unions, the Social Democratic Party, and the Left Party.

The women's campaign on the Yes side benefited from the huge organizational and financial resources of the major Yes organizations. Operating out of the regional offices of SAF, women supporting the Yes position were able to create effective organizations at the regional and local levels. In addition, they also benefited from the professional, modern public-relations campaign conducted by the Yes side, which was unprecedented in Swedish political life. The main information bureau on the Yes side was Europa Fakta (Europe Fact), which SAF and Industriförbundet set up, staffed, and financed (Brantingsson, 1995). Feminists on the Yes side also made use of a report on the consequences of EU membership for social welfare and equal opportunities, which was one of six investigations into EU membership launched by the bourgeois government in 1993. This report, along with those of the other inquiries, was the basis of ostensibly neutral material circulated during the campaign by the government's Secretariat for Information on Europe. During the final weeks of the campaign, Europea organized a meeting for women Yes supporters under the name "Women's EU Parliament." The meeting was held in Älvsjömässan, the largest exhibition hall in Stockholm and an expensive one to rent. The main topics discussed were the EU, women, and welfare; food and the environment; jobs and the economy; and peace, democracy, and cooperation. The program featured prominent participants such as Antonia Axelson-Johnson, Anita Gradin, Deputy Prime Minister Mona Sahlin, Kristina Persson, and Annika Åhnberg, later minister of agriculture in the Social Democratic government.

In contrast to the Yes side's strategy of setting up women's organizations, feminists opposed to Sweden's entry into the European Union pursued a strategy of integration. For the most part, feminists on the No side worked within the mixed organizations that had historically represented their interests, where necessary as members of No committees, and participated with men in new organizations dedicated to the fight against EU membership. An exception to the strategy of integration on the No side was Kvinnofolkhögskolan, an autonomous feminist organization in Göteborg. It was not, however, a strong force in the Swedish referendum campaign. Women members of the Left, Centre, and Green parties participated in the general campaigns of these parties against EU membership and through the activities of No to Europe, an organization that the two parties helped found in the late 1980s. Feminist opponents within the much larger and more influential Social Democratic Party faced the challenge of a leadership primarily in support of the EU and a membership seriously divided on the issue. Initially, women and men "Eurosceptics" within the Social Democratic Party worked to challenge the leadership's support for the EU by calling for a debate on membership at the September 1993 party congress, but party leaders succeeded in having the debate postponed until after the completion of the EU negotiations. Feminists contributed to the material presented in the Social Democratic No report to the special party congress on the EU in April 1994 and participated in the congress debates. The Yes side carried the vote, but by a smaller margin than had been hoped by the leadership. Following the congress, Social Democratic feminists continued to participate in Social Democrats for the No and in No to Europe.

Lacking both the organizational and the financial resources of the Yes side, the opponents of Sweden's membership in the EU were forced to conduct a much more grassroots campaign based largely on the work of volunteers. The campaign centred on preparing, publishing, and distributing literature outlining the possible negative effects of membership in the EU and holding local meetings and seminars. The weekly paper *Kritiska EU fakta* (Critical EU facts), published by the No to EU organization, came to play an important role for the entire No movement and the umbrella No organization until the referendum. The No to EU also published a series of at least twenty booklets. Pamphlets were issued by other organizations, such as Alternatives to EU, an independent group founded in 1991 by publishers and journalists, and membership information leaflets were produced by the trade union EU critics and the Social Democratic No organization. Intellectuals associated with the No side contributed to these publications and also wrote articles for newspapers. Social democratic intellectuals who intervened in the public debate against EU membership included Rudolf Meidner, one of the founders of Swedish labour-market policy, and Walter Korpi, a professor of sociology. A leading feminist academic who wrote articles and spoke on the No side was Agneta Stark, an economist at the University of Stockholm and a founder of the Support Stockings, who was not identified with any party.

The No forces also made use of material produced by opponents of EU membership in other Nordic countries. The No to EU organization distributed material from the group Women in the Nordic Countries against EU. Four analyses prepared by journalist Else Skjönsberg for the Women's Front in Norway, which questioned EU membership from a woman's perspective, were circulated. The Norwegian movement No to EU (NEI til EF) had been well organized since the question of EU membership was first raised in the 1970s and proved to be a particularly valuable source of material. The Swedish No forces were also in contact with opponents of the EU in Denmark and Finland. The movement in Denmark, Junibevegelsen (or June movement), succeeded in stalling Danish membership in the European Monetary Union, thus forcing and winning a separate referendum on the EMU. The Danish resistance led to an exception related to the EMU in Denmark's agreement with the European Union. The opposition there focused on the indirect effects of the monetary union, and this line of argumentation was formulated by Danish feminist political scientists such as Drude Dahlerup, who was the chair of Junibevegelsen, and Annette Borchorst.

For most of the campaign, the strategy of feminists on the No side was to integrate their efforts with the general No campaign, contributing to publications and participating in and speaking at meetings. An example of how this integration strategy worked was a book published by the No side which included articles by members of the Left and Social Democratic parties. Contributors to the book included Lena

Gonäs, a researcher at the National Institute for Working Life and adjunct professor in economic geography, and Helena Johansson from the nurses' union (SHSTF), along with sociologist Walter Korpi and Sten Johansson, general director of Statistics Sweden, and Sture Ring, from the typographical union.

During the last month of the referendum campaign, women working under the No umbrella recognized the need to organize a women's network to respond to the massive publicity campaign directed at women by the Yes side. One of the tasks of the network was to produce a paper summarizing the main arguments against membership in the EU from a women's perspective. The publication, *Women against EU*, was financed by money from the various No groups, including the umbrella organization, Social Democrats against EU, and the trade union EU critics. An initial run of 100,000 copies of the paper was produced, followed by another of 40,000 copies. At a press conference, Margareta Winberg, at the time the minister of agriculture in the new Social Democratic government and a former chair of the Social Democratic Women in Sweden, introduced the feminist No network, the newspaper, and several of the contributors to the paper, including Agneta Stark, Gunilla Thorgren, and Lena Gonäs. Participants in the press conference criticized Europea, the women's network on the Yes side financed by the employers' federation, for organizing a meeting under the name Women's EU Parliament, at which only the pro-EU position would be represented. The women's No network distributed copies of *Women against EU* outside the exhibition hall south of Stockholm where the Women's EU Parliament was held. Their demonstration received more press coverage than the meeting inside the exhibition hall and included criticism of the one-sided representation in the women's parliament (*Dagens Nyheter*, 14 October 1994).

Another important element of the referendum campaign in Sweden was the participation as individuals of well-known women politicians, artists, and leaders of unions and other popular organizations as spokespersons for both sides. During the referendum campaign, Mona Sahlin, deputy prime minister in the newly elected Social Democratic government, often appeared together with Prime Minister Ingvar Carlsson to support membership in the EU. The head of the Yes to Europe umbrella committee was a woman, Agneta Dreber, a former member of the Stockholm City Council and general director of the Public Health Board, who had chaired the government investigation into the consequences of EU membership for social welfare and equal opportunities. The chair of the Social Democratic Yes organization was also a woman, Ines Uusmann, member of Parliament and later minister of transport in the Social Democratic government in 1994. Marit

Paulsen, an author and a columnist for the LRF newspaper *Land*, was an important spokesperson for the Yes position and participated in the final television debate, together with the chair of the Social Democrats and the leader of the Moderate Party. Similarly, for the No side Margareta Winberg, at the time minister of agriculture in the Social Democratic government and leader of the Social Democratic Women in Sweden, was identified as an individual with the women's network against the EU. Ulla-Britt Svensson, a member of the Social Democratic Party, was chair of the No to EU group, Among the other prominent women identified with the No side were Gundrun Schyman, chair of the Left Party; Eva Hellstrand, a milk farmer from Jämtland, vice-chair of the No to EU organization, and a participant in the final television debate; Birgitta Hambreus, member of Parliament for the Centre Party; and as previously mentionned, Agneta Stark.

Mobilizing Swedish Women: Arguments

The Swedish model of the welfare state was central to the debate on the EU. For the most part, the debate was between those on the No side, who argued that the economic policies which would flow from membership in the EU would undermine the Swedish model and with it women's equality, and those on the Yes side, who maintained that membership would ensure the ongoing economic growth required to support the model, that the equal-opportunity provisions of the Protocol on Social Policy would benefit women, or that social-welfare measures were national concerns unaffected by the treaty. The Yes side, however, was a coalition of forces and included Conservatives who did not fully support the Swedish model and, in particular, the family policy associated with it. A well-known feminist activist, Eva Moberg, pointed out the two sides of the Yes argument in a May 1994 article; she maintained that the Conservatives wanted to use membership as a tool to cut back the welfare state and curb the unions, while Social Democrats argued that membership was the only way to cut unemployment and curb capital (Moberg, 1994).

Disagreement over the impact of EU membership on the Swedish welfare state and on women's equality was reflected in the 1993 report of the government inquiry on social welfare and equal opportunities, one of six investigations into the consequences of joining the EU. In a reservation to the main report, Lena Gonäs and Margareta Persson, chair of the national confederation of organizations of people with disabilities, emphasized the implications of different welfare-state regimes for women and disabled people. They argued that women's position in the labour market was quite different in Sweden than in many EU countries and that Swedish women depended on the regulations and economic policies of the welfare state. People with disabilities in other European countries had to rely on care in the family, if they had one, instead of having the right to care by society, irrespective of family relations. In contrast, the majority argued that in the European Union social welfare and equal opportunities were national questions and that economic conditions were decisive for the development of social welfare. The chair of the investigation into social welfare and equal opportunities, Agneta Dreber, maintained that membership in the EU would create a more favourable climate for investment in Sweden than the European Economic Area agreement and would therefore lead to the increased economic growth needed to support social programs (SOU, 1993: 117, 231).

Many of the central arguments of the feminist Yes side were outlined in an article published in Sweden's second largest evening newspaper, *Aftonbladet*, in December 1993, at the time that the report of the investigation into social welfare and equal opportunities was released. Among the five authors of this article were two women who later became ministers in the Social Democratic government: Annika Åhnberg (later minister of agriculture) and Margot Wallström (*Aftonbladet*, 22 December 1993). The article maintained that if Sweden were to stay out of the EU, it "would have to offer more attractive conditions than in the surrounding world, meaning lower wages and lower taxes. That would lead to a decrease in welfare and lower living standards. A blue and yellow [the colours of the Swedish flag] social dumping instead of a progressive Sweden would be the result." The authors argued that the onus was on those opposing membership to show how Sweden could increase employment in industry and the public sector and how women's jobs could be protected without international legislation. They also emphasized that most, if not all, questions regarding the organization of welfare provisions and their scope, distribution, and financing would continue to be decided in Sweden. The authors argued that women in other European countries had benefited from the equal-wages directives, and they maintained that the Swedish equal-opportunities law was weaker than the EU rules.

Similar themes appeared in the arguments of all feminists on the Yes side, although the emphasis differed somewhat depending on the constituency being addressed. In general, feminists on that side argued strongly that the EU directives and policies on equal opportunities would benefit Swedish women, and this was a particularly important theme for liberal feminists. In their efforts to reach business women, female entrepreneurs, and self-employed women, the Network for Europe tended to emphasize that membership would create a favourable climate for investment. The investment argument, however, was also important to women members of LO unions. For trade union women on the Yes side, another important contention was that membership in the EU would allow for Sweden influence in the decision-making in the European Parliament and Commission, something not available through the EEA agreement (Carlsson, 1994). Some feminists on the Yes side acknowledged that women's employment and public services were threatened, but saw the problem as the result of Sweden's budget deficit, which they maintained would have to be tackled even more strongly if the country were outside the EU. They did not take up the argument of the No side that the real threat to social programs lay in the economic policies that Sweden would have to adopt to meet the criteria for membership in the European Monetary Union.

Feminists opposing membership in the EU contrasted the Swedish welfare model to those in the countries belonging to the EU (Nygren and Svensson, 1994). The Nordic norm of the dual-breadwinner family was contrasted to the male-breadwinner norm in the southern and middle European countries (Gonäs, 1992). It was pointed out that these countries relied heavily on insurance-based social-security systems and less on universal provisions such as allowances for children and housing. In Sweden the right to work and to a salary of one's own were important political objectives. Socialized childcare and elder care created the conditions for women's paid work, and the public sector was an important labour market for women. High rates of labour-market participation existed for Swedish women in all educational groups, those with a basic education having almost the same levels of participation as professional women (Stark, 1994). Feminists on the No side argued that these accomplishments had been achieved through policies of full employment which encouraged women's participation in the labour market, not through equal-opportunities legislation (*Socialdemokratisk Europainformation*, 1994). They challenged the claim that Swedish women would benefit significantly from the directives of the EU by pointing to the gap between the directives and reality. In an early article, Agneta Stark noted that during the 1980s the wage gap between women and men had increased in Denmark, Holland, and the United Kingdom and had not improved in West Germany (Stark, 1991).

At the centre of the opposition to Swedish membership, including feminist opposition, was the link between economic policy and social-welfare regimes. Gunilla Thorgren, chief editor of *Pockettidningen R*, a journal featuring debates on social and economic inequality issues, argued that a policy of full employment was essential in a society that promoted welfare and equality for both men and women. Yet the

Maastricht Treaty placed responsibility for the most important tool of economic policy, monetary policy, in the hands of the directors of the European Central Bank, who were outside the reach of democratic control. In her view, the treaty "gives constitutional protection to a policy which directly counteracts women's independence" (Thorgren, 1993; our translation). The specific criteria for joining the European Monetary Union were that the budget deficit of a country not exceed 3 per cent of GNP and that its total accumulated debt not exceed 60 per cent of GNP. Women from the Left, Centre, and Social Democratic parties argued strongly that meeting these criteria would lead to public-sector cutbacks and reduce women's employment opportunities (Nygren and Svensson, 1994; *Socialdemokratisk Europainformation*, 1994; Gonäs, 1992, 1993).

The concerns that women had about the public sector were summarized by Margareta Winberg, member of Parliament and chair of the Social Democratic Women in Sweden, in a campaign publication put out by the Social Democrats for the No. In answer to the question "Why do you think women react so strongly against cutbacks in the public sector?" she stated, "Because women are hit in double ways. The public sector is the most important labour market for women in Sweden. The sector also supplies a lot of important services (childcare, elder care, a solidaristic social insurance system) which are necessary for equality. If *dagis* [day-care centres] are closed and elder care deteriorates, we are back in the situation of the past with an old-fashioned view of women's issues" (Socialdemokratisk europainformation, nr 4, 1994: 5). In a similar vein, Helena Johansson, the deputy chair of the SHSTF and a member of the Left Party, stated during the campaign, "The cutbacks in the public sector will hit women in three ways. A large proportion of the jobs will disappear. Worsened child and elder care diminishes women's possibilities of taking the jobs that exist, and those women who still have a job in the sector have to work harder" (Johansson, 1994). This statement was published in a booklet written by members of the Left and Social Democratic parties.

A further argument advanced by feminists supporting the No option was that the economic costs of membership would increase the pressure to cut public spending. This position drew support from the dissenting opinion of Gonäs and Persson to the governmental investigation into the consequences of EU membership for social welfare and equal opportunities. They maintained that the costs of membership were being underestimated by the majority and that this underestimation was linked to failure to calculate properly the costs that would result from changes to welfare systems, equality, and women's employment (Gonäs and Persson, 1993: 117). Gonäs and Persson pointed out that membership fees in the EU would amount to 20 billion Swedish kronor a year, compared to the 700 million a year that membership in the EEA cost. Furthermore, adjustment in indirect taxes would lead to a loss of 20 to 30 billion a year. In their dissenting opinion, they estimated the total cost of EU membership at 50 billion kronor a year.

Women's Organizing in Sweden: Conclusion

The gender differences in voting in the Swedish referendum were clear and came as no suprise. A study of the referendum showed that 52 per cent of women voted no, compared to 40 per cent of men, and 46 per cent of women voted yes, compared to 59 per cent of men (Oskarasson, 1996). According to M. Oskarasson, the author of this study, there were three hypotheses that might be formulated to explain the scepticism of Swedish women about membership in the European Union: the "resource explanation": women have fewer political resources, skills, or interests; the "ideological explanation": women to a greater extent than men belong to economic groups (workers, public employees, low-income earners) that voted no; and the "consequence" explanation: women to a greater extent than men saw the consequences of EU membership as negative for the welfare state both as the prime labour market for women and as the creator of conditions for women's waged work. Oskarasson's research supports the third explanation; she concluded that the belief that membership in the EU would have negative consequences for social welfare and gender equality had strongly influenced the women who voted no, but not the men who did so (Oskarsson, 1996: 222). For both men and women, the strongest reason for voting no was the consequences for the Swedish economy and for national independence or autonomy of memberhip in the European Union.

As in Canada, there were old and new elements in the organization of Swedish women around their country's entry into the EU. The women who mobilized in support of the project did so in ways consistent with the "two discourses" tradition described by Joan Acker, even when they created new organizations such as Europea. They used separate women's organizations to raise issues of particular concern to women, but these groups were linked financially and administratively to major class-based organizations. In contrast, the anti-EU feminists pursued a strategy of integration that attempted to bring together discourses of class and social reproduction on more equal terms than suggested by the "two discourses" analysis. The feminist Eurosceptics participated in the debate through mixed-gender organizations and formed an ad hoc network of feminists to appeal to women as a separate constituency only in response to the separate women's organizing of the pro-EU forces. For feminists on both the Yes and the No sides in Sweden, the debate centred on the possible impact of the European Union on programs of the Swedish welfare state. The pro-EU feminists argued that new investment would sustain the programs, while the anti-EU feminists maintained that the harmonization implicit in the project would preclude the full employment policies on which the Swedish model was based. The division within Swedish society, particularly within the Social Democratic Party and the unions between leaders and members, was a new element in Swedish political life.

CONCLUSION

In both Canada and Sweden a gender gap existed in support for the regional integration treaties, with larger numbers of women than men opposed. Our study shows that the major reason for the greater opposition of women was the perceived threat of the Canada–U.S. Free Trade Agreement and the Treaty on European Union to the existing national regimes of social welfare. The question of the impact of these treaties on the existing relationship between the state, the market, and the family was at the centre of the debate for women in both countries. In Sweden the implications for the country's regime of social welfare were a central and explicit element of the debate on EU membership from the beginning. In Canada, in the course of the debate, the concerns of feminists crystallized around the threat of free trade to the Canadian system of social welfare from the more market-oriented U.S. regime. The fear of feminist opponents in both countries was that the treaties would undermine state programs, increasing reliance on the market or the family for the provision of necessary services and income support. Even for supporters of the EU project in Sweden, the main argument was that membership in the EU would create the investment climate needed to ensure the prosperity to sustain social-welfare programs. Our analysis is consistent with the argument of feminist theorists that women's specific relationship to the state is central to understanding differences in the political mobilization of women and men.

While the themes raised by feminists in the regional integration debates in Canada and Sweden were similar, the institutions that they used to mobilize women were very different. In both countries women used organizational forms that were consistent with the ways that class and gender had been institutionally articulated in their political systems in the past. In Canada feminists historically have used autonomous women's organizations to raise issues of particular concern to women. In the course of the free-trade campaign, the fight for women's equality came to be more and more identified as part of a popularly based opposition to a corporate agenda aimed at harmonizing the Canadian system of social programs and protections with the more market-oriented American system. The stronger identification of class and gender issues was expressed institutionally through the affiliation of autonomous organizations of women to broad popular coalitions uniting labour, farmers, environmentalists, students, peace activists, and church organizations. In Sweden political mobilization around women's equality has taken place primarily through political parties and women's organizations affiliated to them, rather than through autonomous women's organizations. The serious divisions in Swedish society over membership in the EU were reflected in splits within political parties and unions, making the creation of temporary organizations necessary for the referendum campaign. But women formed ad hoc organizations consistent with their own political traditions and the "institutional legacy" of Swedish society. Feminists worked through Yes and No committees created within working-class political and economic organizations, through women's organizations linked to class-based economic organizations, or through mixed-gender organizations.

Our study confirms the relevance for comparative research of Julia O'Connor's observation that studies of political mobilization must include social movements not directly based on the labour-market position of political actors, along with mainstream political and economic organizations. It also supports the importance of the conduciveness of institutions to women's participation as a factor in explaining the type of organization used to mobilize them. The political mobilization of Canadian women around the Canada–U.S. Free Trade Agreement could only be studied by examining the activity of a gender-based, cross-class organization, the National Action Committee on the Status of Women, which organizes women primarily in terms of their relationship to the state. In contrast, the greater conduciveness of Swedish institutions, particularly political parties, to women's participation meant that the mobilization of women around membership in the European Union took place through institutions associated with established mixed-gender political and economic organizations. Neither the regional institutions that are part of the European Union nor those found in the Canada–U.S. North American Free Trade Agreement are conducive to the political participation of women. The European framework, unlike CUFTA, does provide some avenues for democratic representation and popular consultation. Although the elected and appointed bodies of the EU are now male-dominated, the equal-opportunities program works to mainstream gender.

Inherent in both the Canada–U.S. (and later, the North American) Free Trade Agreement and the Treaty on European Union is a legal dichotomy between, on the one hand, formal national responsibility for matters related to social reproduction and, on the other hand, the strategies related to production, which are assigned to regional institutions or to private corporate actors. One consequence of the dichotomy is the disruption of the institutions and alliances associated with the previous welfare-state regimes, as reflected in a disenchantment among large sections of the non-elite population with existing political institutions and a growing sense of powerlessness. This dichotomy of responsibility is particularly problematic for women: the social services that are a condition of their social equality are the responsibility of a national state whose capacity to provide them depends on economic policies increasingly determined at a regional level. Another consequence of the dichotomy is likely to be a growing social polarization between those who have the skills and resources to compete in a regional labour market and those who rely on the state to provide the regulations, services, and benefits that decommodify labour. For feminists these consequences necessitate a search for new political strategies, new alliances, and, perhaps new institutional arrangements. The search is likely to be a long and difficult one. But whatever strategies are adopted, they will be informed by the unique political traditions of feminists in Canada and Sweden, which now include the organizations and arguments used to mobilize women in the fights around CUFTA/NAFTA and the Treaty on European Union.

NOTE

1 NAFTA extended the provisions of the Canada–U.S. Free Trade Agreement to Mexico and included a greater liberalization of trade in services that was particularly important to women. However, the popular mobilization in Canada occurred primarily around the earlier agreement, and this study is confined to examining women's organizing leading up to the 1988 Canadian "free-trade election" on CUFTA.

REFERENCES

Acker, Joan. (1999, forthcoming). *Developing a Feminist Sociology.* Cambridge: Polity Press.

Addison, John T., and Siebert, W. Stanley. (1994). Recent developments in social policy in the new European Union. *Industrial and Labour Relations Review* 48 (1): 5–27.

Aftonbladet Debatt. (1993). EU är bra för jämställdheten. 22 December.
Åkerman, N. (1994). EU avskaffar vår välfärdsstat. *Dagens Nyheter*, 16 October.
Atkin, Wendy. (1988). Women and free trade. *Jurisfemme*, 8, no.4 (spring).
Auman, Ann. (1985). Women seen suffering most from free trade. *Toronto Star*, 12 November, D1.
Bakker, Isa. (1987). Free trade: What's at risk. *Feminist Action*, July.
– (1988). Women and free trade. What's at risk? *Canadian Dimension*, January, 4–5.
Banting, Keith. (1997). The social policy divide: The welfare state in Canada and the United States. In Keith Banting, George Hoberg, and Richard Simeon (eds.), *Degrees of Freedom: Canada and the United States in a Changing World*. Montreal and Kingston: McGill-Queen's University Press.
Baril, Joan. (1987). Casting a big net: NAC's new president tackles free trade, privatisation and Mulroneyism. *Herizons*, January/February, 28–30.
Bashevskin, Sylvia. (1989). Free trade and Canadian feminism: The case of the National Action Committee on the Status of Women. *Canadian Public Policy* 15 (4): 363–75.
– (1991). NAC's opposition to free trade: The costs and benefits. In her *True Patriot Love: The Politics of Canadian Nationalism*. Toronto: Oxford Univerity Press.
Borchorst, Anette. (1994). Welfare state regimes, women's interests and the EC. In Diane Sainsbury (ed.), *Gendering Welfare States*. Sage Modern Politics Series, vol. 35. London; Thousand Oaks; New Delhi: Sage Publications.
Brantingsson, Ch. (1995). *De många samtalen om EU*. Stockholm: Ekerlids förlag.
Buchignani, Walter. (1988). Election 88. The woman's angle: "Women's issues" are people issues. *The Montreal Gazette*, 13 November, A-6.
Burstyn, Varda, and Judy Rebick. (1988). How "Women Against Free Trade" came to write its manifesto. *Resources for Feminist Research*, September, 139–42.
Buussemaker, Jet, and Kees van Kersbergen. (1994). Gender and welfare states: Some theoretical reflections. In Diane Sainsbury (ed.), *Gendering Welfare States*. Sage Modern Politics Series, vol. 35. London; Thousand Oaks; New Delhi: Sage Publications.
Cameron, Barbara. (1995). NAFTA, GATT and women's rights: A Canadian case study. In *From Basic Needs to Basic Rights*. Washington, DC: Institute for Women, Law and Development.
Canada. (1985). Royal Commission on the Economic Union and Development Prospects for Canada. *Report*. Ottawa: Supply and Services Canada.

Canada. (1990). Women's Bureau. Labour Canada. (1990). *Women in the Labour Force, 1990–1991 Edition.* Ottawa: Supply and Services Canada.

Canadian Press. (1987). Labour congress opens anti-free trade fight. *Vancouver Sun*, 8 June, C8.

Carlsson, B. (1994). *EU kvinnofälla eller möjlighet.* Stockholm: Svenska Kommunalarbetareförbundet.

Cohen, Marjorie. (1985). The Macdonald Report and its implications for women. Toronto: National Action Committee on the Status of Women. Photocopy.

– (1987a). *Free Trade and the Future of Women's Work.* Toronto: Garamond Press and the Canadian Centre for Policy Alternatives.

– (1987b). *Free Trade in Services: An Issue of Concern to Women.* Ottawa: Canadian Advisory Council on the Status of Women.

– (1995). Feminism's effect on economic policy. In Ruth Roach Pierson and Marjorie Griffin Cohen (eds.), *Canadian Women's Issues: Twenty-Five Years of Women's Activism in English Canada.* Vol. 2, *Bold Visions.* Toronto: James Lorimer & Company.

Dagens Nyheter (1994). 14 October.

Daly, Mary. (1994). Comparing welfare states: Towards a gender friendly approach. In Diane Sainsbury (ed.), *Gendering Welfare States.* Sage Modern Politics Series, vol. 35. London; Thousand Oaks; New Delhi: Sage Publications.

Deverell, John. (1986). Carr vows jobs showdown with Ottawa. *Toronto Star*, 2 May, A13.

Doern, G. Bruce, and Brian W. Tomlin. (1991). *The Free Trade Story: Faith and Fear.* Toronto: Stoddart.

Dulude, Louise. (1985). [Untitled article]: *Feminist Action*, October.

Eduards, Maud L. (1991a). The Swedish gender model: Productivity, pragmatism and paternalism. *Western European Politics* 14 (3): 166–81.

– (1991b). Toward a third way: Women's politics and welfare policies in Sweden. *Social Research* 58 (3): 677–705.

Esping-Andersen, Gøsta. (1990). *The Three Worlds of Welfare Capitalism.* Cambridge: Polity Press.

Feminist Action. Various issues, 1985–88.

Gonäs, Lena. (1992). Kvinnors arbetsmarknad i det framtida Europa. In *Kvinnors och mäns liv och arbete.* Stockholm: SNS.

– (1993). Visionerna om Europa. In *Det nya riket: 24 kritiska röster om Europaunionen.* Stockholm: Tidens förlag.

– and M. Persson. (1993). Reservation, In SOU, *Den sociala välfärden och kvinnors arbete.* Stockholm: Allmänna förlaget.

Grove, Marion. (1988). Free trade: Putting more lead on the table. *Kinesis*, July/August, 7.

Herizons. (1987). January/February.
Hernes, Helga Maria. (1987). Women and the welfare state: The transition from private to public dependence. In Ann Stackhouse Sassoon (ed.), *Women and the State*. New York: Routledge; Oslo: Norwegian University Press.
Hossie, Linda. (1985a). Free trade would hurt, women told. *Globe and Mail*, 3 June, M7.
– (1985b). Trade pact would hurt women, meeting told. *Globe and Mail*, 26 November, A18.
Jenson, Jane, and Rianne Mahon. (1993). Representing solidarity: Class, gender and the crisis in social-democratic Sweden. *New Left Review* 20.
Johansson, H. (1994). Hur går det med den generella välfärden och kvinnors arbete om Sverige går med i EU? In H. Johansson et al., *Facket, EU och massarbetslösheten*. Stockholm: Fackliga EU-kritiker.
Kinesis. Various issues.
Kjellberg, Judith. (1988). Free women – trade the multinationals: An interiew with Marjorie Cohen. *Women and Environments*, 20.
Kommunal. (1994). *EU – kvinnofälla eller möjlighet?* Stockholm: Svenska Kommunalarbetareförbundet.
Kvinnor mot EU. (1994). Stockholm: Folkrörelsen mot EU, Socialdemokrater mot EU, Fackliga EU-kritker och andra EU-kritiska organisationer.
Lewis, Jane, and Gertrude Astrom. (1992). Equality, difference, and state welfare: Labor market and family policies in Sweden. *Feminist Studies* 18 (1) 59–87.
Macmillan, Katie. (1987). Free trade and Canadian women: An opportunity for a better future. Ottawa: Canadian Advisory Council on the Status of Women.
Marsden, Lorna. (1992). *Timing and Presence: Getting Women's Issues on the Trade Agenda*. Working Paper Series, GSD-3. Toronto: International Federation of Institutes for Advanced Study. Gender, Science and Development Program.
Moberg, E. (1994). Strutspolitik. *Dagens Nyheter*, 26 May.
Molgat, Anne. (1987). An action that will not be allowed to subside. Toronto: National Action Committee on the Status of Women. Photocopy.
National Action Committee on the Status of Women (NAC). (1988a). *Free Trade: A Bad Deal for Women. Here's Why and What to Do* ... Toronto.
– (1988b). Presentation to the parliamentary committee hearings on Bill C-130. Photocopy.
– (1988c). *What Every Woman Needs to Know about Free Trade*. Toronto.
– (1993). NAC brief to the sub-committee on international trade. 10 February. Toronto.
– (c. 1994). *Index of Abridged Resolutions 1972 to 1993*. Toronto.

Nygren, E., and E.-B. Svensson. (1994). *Hotet mot välfärden*. Stockholm: Nej till EU:s skriftserie.

O'Connor, Julia. (1993). Gender, class and citizenship in the comparative analysis of welfare state regimes: Theoretical and methodological issues. *British Journal of Sociology* 44 (3): 501–18.

Ontario (1987). Cabinet Subcommittee on Free Trade. Proceedings of hearings. 10 October 1987.

Orloff, Ann Shola. (1993). Gender and the social rights of citizenship: The comparative analysis of gender relations and welfare states. *American Sociological Review* 58: 303–28.

Oskarsson, M. (1996). Kvinnorna och . . . In M. Gilljam and S. Holmberg (eds.), *Ett knappt ja till EU*. Stockholm: Norstedts juridik.

Peritz, Ingrid. (1988). Turner gets benefit of the gender gap. *Montreal Gazette*, 13 November, A1 and A6.

Pockettidningen R. (1989). På väg mot EG. Nr 2–3. Stockholm.

– (1990). Den svenska modeleln och internationaliseringen. Nr 3–4. Stockholm.

– (1991). Europa, samtal, tankar, ideer. Nr 5. Stockholm.

– (1992). Fåvälde eller folkvälde-om EG och den hotade demokratin. Nr 1–2. Stockholm.

Pollak, Nancy. (1988). Free trade: Government propaganda aims at mothers. *Kinesis*, June, 3.

Porter, Ann, and Barbara Cameron. (1987). *Impact of Free Trade on Women in Manufacturing*. Ottawa: Canadian Advisory Council on the Status of Women.

Rowles, Mary. (1988). In Conversation with Marjorie Cohen: Free trade is a Trojan horse. *Our Times*, March/April, 15–16.

Rudland, Lorri. (1987). Free Canada, trade Mulroney. *Kinesis*, May.

Sainsbury, Diane. (1994). *Gendering Welfare States*. Sage Modern Politics Series, vol. 35. London; Thousand Oaks; New Delhi: Sage Publications.

Sears, Val. (1988). Election will be bandwagon for special-interet groups. *Montreal Gazette*, 11 June, B6.

Skjönsberg, E. (1993). *Kvinnoliv i EU*. Oslo: Kvinnor i Norden mot EU.

Socialdemokratisk Europainformation. (1994). nr 4.

SOU. (1993). *Den sociala välfärden och kvinnors arbete*. Stockholm: Allmänna förlaget.

Stark, A. (1991). Sluta Nyckla om EU. *Dagens Nyheter*, 28 August.

– (1994). Mannen är norm i EU. *Kvinnovetenskaplig tidskrift* 15 (2): 3–11.

Statistics Sweden. (1996). *Folkomröstningen om medlemskap i EU*. Stockholm.

Sweden. (1990/91). Om åtgärder för att stabilisera ekonomin och begräns, tillväxten av de offentliga utgifterna. (Government bill 1990/91: 50).

Thorgren, G. (1993). Norden har chansen. In Lotta Gröning (ed.), *Det nya riket. 24 kritiska röster om Europaunionen*. Stockholm: Tidens förlag.
Toronto Star. (1988a). Deal makes cabinet all-powerful, women say. 27 July, A26.
– (1988b). Women hurt worst by pact, MPs told. 27 July.
Wattle, Chris. (1988). Federal election heads feminist's busy agenda. *Calgary Herald*, 1 September, C3.
Waywanko, Andrea. (1987). Who pays for free trade? *The Newsmagazine*, January/February, 20–2.
Winnipeg Free Press. (1988). Women told jobs on line. 7 November, 20.
Women's Economic Agenda. (1988). *Three Deals, One Game: B.C. Women Look at Free Trade, Meech Lake and Privatization*. Vancouver.
Zwarun, Suzanne. (1988). Free trade: What's in it for Canadian women? *Calgary Hearld*, 23 March, A8.

Women's Organizing and Immigration: Comparing the Canadian and Swedish Experiences

WUOKKO KNOCKE AND ROXANA NG

ABSTRACT

Historically, as now, both Canada and Sweden have been immigration countries; that is, people have been allowed to enter as immigrants or as refugees or asylum seekers and can eventually acquire citizenship status. But despite this overall similarity, the policies regulating immigration in the two countries are quite different. As well, the lives of immigrant and minority populations are subjected to different integration rules. This divergence also extends to the composition of immigrant and minority populations.

One notable feature in immigrant recruitment, which speaks to the pervasiveness of a male-chauvinist power structure and sexism in both countries, is the lack of consideration of women's contribution. The official discourses and practices have largely focused on men. Policies have been developed from their vantage point and experiences. This characteristic has led to the marginalization of immigrant women in the host society.

This chapter examines and compares three areas where women are marginalized: in the policy process, in the integration and settlement process, and by extension in the labour market. We confine our discussion largely to the period after the Second World War (from the mid-1940s onward). We then examine how women attempt to overcome their marginalization and make visible their concerns to the larger society through various forms of organizing. We end with a reflection on our attempt to compare the experiences of immigrant women.

Until the emergence and subsequent burgeoning of feminist scholarship, women were invisible as subjects. Such has been the case for women in general, but more so for those in migration. In addition to racial prejudice, ethnicism, cultural stereotyping, and overt discrimination, an important way that immigrant women are disadvantaged is through the formal systems of rights. This chapter begins by exploring one such crucial formal system: the policies pertaining to immigration and settlement. The second part of the chapter concentrates on immigrant and minority women's organizing and the ways in which official policy measures have shaped the form and content of their organizing. More specifically the aim is to analyse and compare the impact of official policies on immigrant and minority women's organizing efforts in Sweden and Canada. We argue that gender-neutral or male-biased (sexist) state policies pertaining to immigrants have rendered women marginal, eclipsed their experiences, and made their social, cultural, and economic contribution to society invisible. These are also the dynamics that underpin immigrant women's organizing in both countries.

IMMIGRATION

Policy Formation and Orientation

In both Canada and Sweden immigration matters fall first and foremost under the jurisdiction of the national (Sweden) or federal (Canada) government.[1] A major contrast between the two countries with regard to the policy formulation process has to do with the role played by the respective governments in mediating the interests of labour and capital. In Sweden there are three influential actors in the policy formation process: the state, represented by the social democratic government; capital, represented by the employers and their association (SAF); and the trade union movement, represented by the Trade Union Confederation (LO).

As a key player in the Nordic region, Sweden has been deeply involved since the mid-1930s in the negotiations for a common Nordic labour market for the free movement of workers. Negotiations were interrupted by the war, but resumed soon afterwards. Citizens from the Nordic countries have been allowed to take up employment in Sweden without work permits since 1943. A common Nordic labour-market agreement was signed in 1954, giving citizens the right to settle and work in any of the Nordic countries without a residence or work permit. The agreement remains in force today.

After the war, when Sweden experienced a severe labour shortage, the concerns and interests of Swedish capital and the social democratic government converged, and immigration was seen as the most efficient labour recruitment strategy. The labour unions and women's organizations were against "the importation of foreign labour," as it was called then. Instead they wanted to activate domestic labour reserves, principally the large number of married women, but also the elderly and partially handicapped (Kyle, 1979). Although the unions were opposed to worker immigration, they did not try to stop it. They had to accept that it would have been both too slow and too costly to start training women and other domestic reserves to provide them with necessary industrial skills (SOU, 1967). It was only in the mid-1960s, when Sweden witnessed a sudden and dramatic increase of spontaneous immigration from Yugoslavia, Greece, and Turkey (Wadensjö, 1973), that the National Labour Market Board (AMS)[2] and the LO, two of the most influential actors, urged the government to regulate immigration (Knocke, forthcoming). In 1967 the immigration of non-Nordic workers was controlled in that a work contract, a work permit, and housing had to be arranged before arrival in Sweden (Widgren, 1980: 14; SOU, 1967).

In 1972 the LO decided, with reference to the labour-market situation, to put a stop to worker immigration from outside the Nordic countries (Hammar, 1988). This move was an indication of the powerful and influential role that the trade union movement had over post-war worker immigration. The stop came before the first oil crisis and coincided with the introduction of separate taxation for couples, making it economically more attractive for women to take on paid employment. Industrial jobs were decreasing, and women's labour was needed for the expanding public-welfare sector. Thus in the post-war period, immigration went through a dramatic change, from labour recruitment and spontaneous labour immigration to family reunification. Since 1972 humanitarian considerations have also taken precedence, and political refugees and persons who needed shelter on grounds of religious or other kinds of persecution have been welcome.

As a colony of first France and then Britain in the "new" world, Canada has always used immigration to meet its economic, labour-market, and demographic needs. Although selection criteria are purported to be based on economic and sociocultural, as well as humanitarian, grounds, in actual fact, economic consideration has dominated policy orientation.[3] On the whole, the government has acted in the interests of capital by using immigration to fill gaps in the labour market (e.g., by bringing in special groups of workers such as the Irish and the Chinese to build the railway in the 1880s) and boost the economy. More recently, in order to attract foreign capital, the level of business-class immigration[4] was increased, with a corresponding decline in independent and family-class immigrants. As well, there has been a steady increase in the use of guest workers through the Non-Immigrant Employment Authorization Program to meet labour needs in selected sectors (see Sharma, 1995).

Because of Canada's historical use of immigrants and guest workers to increase competition among workers, the labour movement in Canada traditionally resisted immigration (see Campbell, 1980), and from time to time it was successful in preventing certain groups from entering the country as immigrants. An example is the role played by Canadian workers in lobbying for the institution of a head tax for Chinese immigrants, thereby restricting the entry of workers from China at the end of the nineteenth and the beginning of the twentieth centuries (Wickberg, 1982). At present, public pressure and public sentiment, comprising a wide range of interests from anti-immigrant groups to human-rights groups and ethnocultural communities, in addition to economic interests, are at play in influencing government decisions around immigration (Simmons and Keohane, 1992).

There are major policy differences between Canada and Sweden with regard to immigration. For Canada, immigration policy is salient to understanding the marginality of immigrant women after arrival. In Sweden the policy serves as an initial guideline governing who comes into the country. But once someone has entered and received a residence permit, a separate and explicit policy – the policy for immigrant integration – provides the framework for settlement. This major difference shapes how immigrant women subsequently negotiate their way through the larger society after arrival.

Immigrant Classification

Since the end of worker immigration in 1972, newcomers to Sweden have been confined to two major categories: refugees or asylum seekers (with subcategories, approximately 35 per cent a year) and family-reunification cases (around 60 per cent a year). The exception was between 1993 and 1995, when the proportions were reversed as a result of the influx of refugees from the former Yugoslavia. Foreign citizens who enter the country to marry or live in partnership with a Swedish citizen or a permanently settled immigrant receive a resident permit for six months at a time. The marriage or partnership status is reviewed every six months. Only when the relationship has lasted for at least two years is the applicant granted permanent residence. A notable feature of the latter category is that same-sex couples are recognized as a family unit in Sweden, which is not yet the case in Canada.

The concept of a guest worker system never took root in Sweden. The fundamental right of families to unite was never questioned, and family reunion was accepted without any special political decision. Family reunion includes the spouse and children up to the age of eighteen and only in exceptional cases parents past the age of sixty. Very important from a gender perspective is the fact that women, even those who join a husband, are given the status of independent legal subjects with the right to their own residence and work permits. This policy is in striking contrast to those in many other labour-importing countries, including Canada, where women's legal position is dependent on the male breadwinner and where they are given only derived rights of settlement (Knocke, 1994a). It is therefore all the more surprising that the official discourse takes so little notice of them. We come back to this issue later in the chapter.

In Canada immigrants are considered according to four major classes: independent immigrants (including nominated relatives), business-class immigrants, family-class immigrants (who are sponsored by either the independent immigrants or family members who are already residing in Canada), and refugees (who are further subdivided into two classes) (Segal, 1994). The economic orientation of the policy is reflected in the utilization of a points system, developed in 1967, to determine eligibility. Immigrants are selected on the basis of the points that they earn in nine areas such as education, language, and occupation. The points assigned to different areas are constantly revised to reflect the demands of the Canadian economy.

Our discussion here focuses on the relationship between independent and family-class immigrants, because it pertains most directly to immigrant women's experiences in Canada. The Immigration Act establishes a multi-tiered structure of rights and privileges among immigrants based on the points system. An independent applicant is granted landed-immigrant status on the basis of the accumulated points that she or he has earned for education, work experience, occupation, and economic resources under the system. A family-class immigrant is someone who cannot qualify to enter Canada under the points system; such an individual is granted this status through the sponsorship of an immediate family member who is either an independent landed immigrant or a Canadian citizen. The family-class category usually includes the spouse, children under eighteen, or parents over sixty-five, of the independent immigrant.

Usually, in an immigrant family only one member is granted independent status. In most cases, it is the husband who is so designated, because he is perceived to be the head of the household, and the wife is categorized as a family-class immigrant along with the children. Statistics released by Employment and Immigration Canada up to 1988 shows that the majority of family-class immigrants were female

(59 per cent) (Immigration Canada, 1989). Although these figures do not specify the age breakdown of the male and female immigrants, it is likely that most male immigrants in the family-class category are the children or retired parents of the independent immigrant.

This classification system ignores the fact that the wife may have comparable education and work experience with the husband, and may have made essential contributions to the family income before immigration. For example, among industrial workers in Hong Kong and other Southeast Asian urban centres, which are one of the sources of immigrants to Canada, the family of two income earners is the norm (Salaff, 1981). Moreover, once they have immigrated, the financial security of many immigrant families often depends on the labour-force participation of the wife initially and later that of both spouses. This outcome has to do with the structure of the Canadian labour market, where there are more demands for cheap labour in the marginal sectors of the economy. Coupled with the increasing necessity for Canadian families to survive on at least two incomes, it means that, in fact, most immigrant wives have to join the paid labour force as wage earners. Yet the assignment of family members according to the categories of "independent" and "family class" negates this reality. The official view of the immigrant family, according to Canadian policy, is that of one "independent" member on whom others depend for their sponsorship, livelihood, and welfare. It can be seen that the process systematically structures sexual inequality within the family by rendering one spouse (usually the wife) legally dependent on the other (Ng, 1993).

The system does not distinguish between white and non-white women as such. However, immigration officers have a great deal of discretionary power, and they exercise this power according to their assumption of certain gender and racial stereotypes. These stereotypes, together with the accreditation process, which gives more weight to education and training obtained in the Western, English-speaking world, may mean that non-white women from the third world are more disadvantaged in the immigration selection and assessment process. Thus racist practices are implicit in the provisions of the policy.

Furthermore, it is important to note that the sponsorship system places many immigrant women in a totally dependent and subordinate position vis-à-vis the sponsor, who is legally responsible for their financial welfare for a period of five to ten years. A woman's entry into Canada is conditional upon the financial support of her sponsor. If for some reason the sponsor should be deported, it is likely that she will be forced to leave also. Thus prior to an immigrant woman's entry into the country, her legal status as a dependent is already established.

It can be seen that this dependence is built into the institutionalized (sexist) practices of the policy. Its apparently neutral language renders invisible this difference, thus eclipsing the situation of women in the immigration application process (see Ng, 1993).

IMMIGRANT INTEGRATION AND SETTLEMENT

Official Ideology

The ideology of the two countries with regard to immigrant settlement has been remarkably similar. Up to the late 1960s both Canada and Sweden held the official position that immigrants should be assimilated. As demographic, social, and political realities changed in the 1970s, the two countries tended to emphasize integration. Although this shift had different origin, both countries officially recognized the concepts of equality and freedom of cultural choice.

In Canada the move from assimilation to integration arose out of several interrelated processes: the Quiet Revolution in Quebec, which culminated in the FLQ crisis of October 1970; increasing militancy among Canada's aboriginal peoples and ethnocultural minorities; and the search for a unique Canadian identity separate from the "melting pot" model of the United States. In October 1971 an official cultural policy – multiculturalism within a bilingual framework – was instituted by the Liberal government to give all Canadians, regardless of their ethnic and racial origin, freedom of choice in the cultural sphere (see Ng, 1995). This policy was enshrined as law by the Progressive Conservative government in 1988.

In Sweden, except for the initial period when migrants were thought to be guest workers, the implicit ideology until the late 1960s was that immigrants should become assimilated. The growing awareness that assimilation was not as unproblematic as had been assumed led to a shift in ideology to an emphasis on integration and social adjustment, and a recognition of social, cultural, and ethnic differences and the special difficulties faced by immigrants (SOU, 1967). The principle of equality with Swedish citizens in the treatment of immigrants was confirmed by Parliament in 1968, 1975, and 1986. The goals of the immigrant settlement and integration policy were expressed in the concepts of equality, freedom of cultural choice, and partnership in cooperation, in terms of establishing a multicultural society, a concept that until today has never been defined.

An important point of difference between Sweden and Canada is that since 1975 Sweden has had an official immigrant policy, unanimously adopted by Parliament, which provides guidelines for the integration of immigrants into society. No such policy exists in Canada. In spite of the ideological similarity and the supposed rights of equality in treatment, we will show that the implementation process continues to render immigrants, especially women, marginal to both Canadian and Swedish societies.

Service Provision

In Sweden, state authorities in their respective policy areas, principally the AMS with its subsidiary organizations, the National Board of Education, the National Health Care Authorities, and the National Board of Health and Welfare were given the task of managing questions related to the immigrant population. At the local level, social assistance, information, and counselling in personal matters, housing subsidies, public childcare, and other social issues were catered for by municipal Social Welfare Committees.

One of the earliest concerns was language training, which, through an initiative of the National Board of Education, started to be offered free of charge in 1965 for both working and non-working immigrants.[5] Soon, information on Swedish society was made an integral part of language courses. The AMS, together with employers and unions, developed introductory programs at the workplace and gave orientation on practice and norms in the labour market. Written information was made available in several foreign languages. This kind of close collaboration among state, capital, and labour regarding the welfare of immigrants is not found in Canada.

The end of the 1960s saw the establishment of an institutional structure dedicated to immigrants in Sweden. At the central level the Aliens Commission was replaced by the National Immigration Board (SIV) in 1968. It was responsible for granting residence and work permits, deciding on citizenship issues, and similar matters. At the ideological level SIV took care of information to immigrants and minorities, and public awareness of the situation of immigrants directed to the Swedish public. Special information offices for immigrants (*invandrabyraer*) were started under the administration of local authorities. Today information offices, refugee reception centres, and other services to immigrants, with interpreters and translators, are found at the municipal level across the country which provides counselling to immigrants and information to the Swedish public on the ethnic and cultural backgrounds, motives for coming to Sweden, living conditions, and special needs of ethnic and minority groups. They also act as points of liaison between immigrant organizations and various societal bodies (SIV, 1985).

In spite of these lofty goals, however, there are difficulties in translating the vague policy guidelines into working instruments, especially for local civil servants, who since the early 1980s have been responsible for the welfare and integration of immigrants. Evaluations and criticisms indicate that the policy guidelines have provided either contradictory messages or little discernable impact (Alund and Schierup, 1991). At any rate, the marginalized situation for Swedish immigrant populations and refugees in the mid-1990s bears clear evidence that neither integration nor equality has been achieved. Extremely high proportions of these populations have lost their jobs through technological restructuring and as a result of the economic crisis. Women in particular have been made redundant through work-related injuries caused by their monotonous jobs. On the whole, the "host" society has dictated the norms and rules to be followed and assigned the models of how cooperation should be enacted, defining Swedish values, norms, and culture as superior. Those who do not comply are seen as intruders, deviants, and "others" (Czarniawska-Joerges, 1994). Ethnicism and racism have confined immigrants in general and immigrant women in particular to the margins of work life and society in a gender-segregated Sweden (Knocke, 1991; 1994b).

In Canada a landed immigrant can apply to become a Canadian citizen by passing a citizenship examination after residing in the country continuously for three years. Thereafter she or he is granted the right to vote as other Canadians and, apart from family-class immigrants, is entitled to the same social benefits (e.g., social assistance). Services provided to immigrants are less extensive in Canada. There is also a difference in entitlement according to the classes of immigrants mentioned earlier in the chapter. First, with the exception of the initial period after immigration, the welfare of immigrants, once they are in the country, comes under the jurisdiction of provincial and municipal governments in whose territory they reside. Secondly, services to immigrants are provided indirectly, by means of special grants to institutions and non-governmental organizations at the local level.

Upon landing, the independent applicant, assumed to be the household head, is eligible to enrol in English-language or skills-upgrading programs paid for by the federal government. Usually, it purchases places for new immigrants in language or job-training classes run by local community colleges or boards of education. While the immigrant is enrolled in these classes, he or she is given a living allowance. Other members of the household, who are considered "family class" immigrants, do not enjoy this privilege. Thus if an immigrant woman wishes to take an English-language or job-training program, she has to pay for it herself. As a result of agitation by women's and other equality-seeking groups in the 1980s, some money is now allocated to community groups and the continuing education division of local boards of education to run language classes for immigrant women who are homemakers. However, many immigrant women complain that these classes, while serving to break down their isolation, do not provide English at a level that would enable them to participate in the labour market (see Ng, 1993).

Furthermore, during the five-to-ten-year sponsorship period, family-class immigrants are not eligible for social assistance provided by the provincial or municipal government. If they apply for it, they can be deported. This stipulation adversely affects many women who are family-class immigrants because in abusive situations they feel unable to leave the household of the sponsor, thus deepening the dependency of women created by the immigration process. Although, in reality, few cases of the deportation of family-class immigrants have been documented, fear of it serves as an effective deterrent for women to leave unpleasant or violent relationships.

Given the minimal provision of services to newcomers, historically their welfare was taken care of within the ethnocultural communities to which they belonged. This was especially the case for groups that were seen as undesirable, such as the Chinese community until very recently. The lack of official services to immigrants prompted the formation of voluntary and benevolent associations within ethnic and racial communities. While these associations in principle provided services to both men and women, they were male-centred as a result of the historical development of many ethnic communities. In many cases, especially before the two world wars, men were the first to immigrate because it was their labour that was sought. When women joined their husbands later on, their needs were frequently subsumed under those of the men. Furthermore, these associations were frequently formed along clan, locality, or political lines, thus reinforcing intra-group rivalry and the containment of immigrants within their perceived cultural communities. This pattern persists today, as, for example, the Somalian community in Toronto.

Although ethnocultural organizations provide some measure of security for male and female immigrants in an alien and sometimes hostile environment, many of them were and remain male-dominated. They may in fact perpetuate traditional (sexist) values that keep women in their place. However, especially for minorities who experience racism in Canadian society, women (as well as men) are reluctant to move outside these community boundaries precisely because of the unfavourable conditions of the host society. This pattern again reinforces women's (and children's) dependency on both the spouse and the community, especially in abusive situations.

State-funded, community-based organizations also do their share to respond to the needs of immigrants. They may be specific to ethnocultural communities or cut across them. Thus, while in Sweden immigrant services are coordinated by the SIV (since 1 July 1998 the responsibility of the National Integration Office), in Canada they are less coordinated and are carried out largely by non-government organizations both within and outside ethno-specific communities.

THE MARGINALIZATION OF IMMIGRANT WOMEN IN THE LABOUR FORCE

It is not the purpose of this chapter to analyse the labour-force participation of immigrant women in detail. However, we want to outline their location in the labour market to show their relative marginality in both societies. In spite of the structural differences between Canadian and Swedish labour markets and the different approaches to immigration rights and integration, immigrant women's locations in the workforce in the two countries are remarkably similar: they are found in the lower rungs of the occupational hierarchy.

In Sweden high labour-force participation (in 1981, 73 per cent for foreign-born and 65.3 per cent for Swedish-born women between the ages of sixteen and seventy-four) has long been considered the most successful sign of their integration. Structural change and recession in recent years has brought the figure of foreign-born women down to 51.4 per cent (vis-à-vis 75.5 per cent for Swedish-born women) in 1994, indicating immigrant women's vulnerability and insecure position and the failure of integration.

As a result of the powerful role of the trade union movement in Sweden in matters of immigration, an overwhelming majority of all immigrants, both women and men, become organized upon taking a job (Knocke, 1982 and 1986). Union density in most blue-collar unions has generally been around 90 per cent, a pattern that holds true for female and male immigrants. The exceptions are the building maintenance and hotel and catering workers' unions, where jobs are often temporary, part-time, or carried on during irregular working hours. In these unions the degree of organization has been around 50 to 60 per cent irrespective of national origin or gender. Because immigrants, especially women, from certain nationalities have been overrepresented in these jobs, they have also had lower union membership. As Knocke's earlier studies (1982 and 1986) show, the unions had no difficulties in recruiting the immigrant workforce, and their primary task was to defend their interests at work. There was never any major problem where wages were concerned, given that the workers were unionized. Swedish unions have, by and large, not taken up the issue of affirmative action for women, even less for immigrant women. The problem has been that even qualified immigrant workers often ended up in unskilled jobs. The women have been trapped in female job ghettos without any help from the unions to better employment, on-the-job training, career development, or jobs that corresponded to their qualification levels (Knocke, 1986; 1993; 1994b).

Since many immigrant women ended up at the bottom of the work-life hierarchy – as chars, in female-typed industrial jobs, or as health-care auxiliaries – a persistent problem has been their invisibility and silence in the official discourse. Only male immigrants were considered in policy texts, parliamentary debates, and government investigations (see e.g., Prot., 1947 and 1966). It has been difficult for them from their lowly positions in the labour market to make their voices heard or to build a public platform from which to speak and represent themselves. Thus neither formal equality with male immigrants nor equal rights and duties with the native population have helped immigrant women to gain a place in the public arena of Swedish society. We argue that this invisibility is one of the most fundamental reasons for their structural subordination and persistent powerlessness in society and work life.

There are two striking contrasts between Canada and Sweden in overall employment and unionization patterns, however. First, according to the OECD employment outlook in 1996, among the industrialized nations, Sweden had the lowest incidence of low-paid full-time workers (5.2 per cent), whereas Canada had the highest incidence (23.7 per cent), second only to the United States (25 per cent). The incidence of low-paid employment for Canadian women was even worse (34.3 per cent; Sweden's figure was 8.4 per cent – CLC, 1997: 4). These statistics mean that, in general, women workers are much worse off in Canada than in Sweden. Secondly, the unionization rate is much lower in Canada than in Sweden. A recent report on women's work by the Canadian Labour Congress (CLC), the largest umbrella organization of Canadian trade unions, indicates that the overall unionization rate for full-time workers is 34.7 per cent, with that for women being 31.6 per cent (CLC, 1997: 22). Immigrant women had a slightly higher labour-force participation rate than Canadian women generally. However, many of them are in sectors, such as the garment, textile, and food-processing industries, that have low union density. The CLC report found that the unionization rate of visible-minority women is slightly lower than for other Canadian women (26.7 versus 28.6 per cent – CLC, 1997: 51).[6]

In this overall context, immigrant women in Canada are found among the upper and lower echelons of the occupational hierarchy, either in highly skilled professional and administrative positions or in job ghettos. Many of those holding managerial, administrative, and professional positions are from Britain or the United States and are not normally seen as immigrants. The majority of the non-English-speaking and non-white women are confined to jobs that are low paid and make use of traditional female skills developed from housekeeping and child rearing. In other words, in addition to immigrant status, the occupational hierarchy is stratified by ethnicity and race. Like immigrant women in Sweden, the latter group of women too are in the female job ghettos – in domestic work, the service sector, and light manufacturing (Boyd, 1986; Ng, 1993).

Until recently, most labour unions have not really made a concerted effort to organize women workers in general and immigrant women workers in particular (see White, 1980). In the current climate of globalization, many sectors that have made used of immigrant workers, such as the garment and textile industries, have undergone tremendous restructuring, with the resultant displacement of these workers from the labour force. In the garment sector, for instance, restructuring has resulted in women doing piecework at home. These women are seen to be self-employed; they are not allowed to unionize and are not covered by labour-standards legislation. Thus immigrant women are among the most exploited workers and enjoy fewer privileges and rights than do other members of society, but their working conditions remain largely invisible because of their isolation and low union density rate. Their labour-market conditions, as well as their status, created through immigration policy, have shaped the organizing of women in both societies.

WOMEN'S ORGANIZING

Throughout Swedish and Canadian history, immigrant women have organized themselves, their families, and their communities to alleviate the strains of immigration. Our discussion here is confined to the post-war period, especially since the 1970s, and the focus is on the organizing efforts by and directed at immigrant women themselves (rather than at their families and immigrant communities more generally). The efforts that we found occur at the national and local levels in Sweden and at the national, provincial, and local levels in Canada. Although we discuss these activities separately for this presentation, in reality they may overlap for a particular group.

Organizing around Social Support

Historically, immigrants in both countries have organized along ethnically homogeneous lines because the first impulse for forming associations was, and still is, to alleviate the isolation that they felt and often continue to feel in the host society. In Sweden the driving force for pre-war associations and for organizations created in the 1950s and 1960s was to enable the different groups to meet socially in their own cultural setting, enjoy the company of people from their home countries, celebrate their national or religious holidays, and create niches where they could speak their own language (SIV and Arb.markn. dep., 1991).

With official acceptance of the freedom of cultural choice in Sweden, immigrant organizing, especially in the early years of many groups, was supposed to be around "immigrant culture," defined narrowly and superficially by mainstream society as singing, dancing, and music. Culture was equated with folklore (Knocke, 1991; Ålund and Schierup, 1991). This view was due in part to the fact that funding was easily available for such activities, but it was also an expression of the immigrants' own wish to gather around activities that confirmed their common origin. Immigrants of the labour-migration generation felt the need to come together socially with compatriots.

In the case of Finnish women, for example, the primacy of the social motive for creating associations in the early days is confirmed by the coordinator for women's issues at the national association level. She said emphatically: "First and foremost it was being together socially that was important, to meet other Finnish women who were in the same situation – having their relatives back home and their children here and all that ... Social togetherness was important."

In addition to intra-group associations, earlier efforts by immigrant women in Canada to deal with an inhospitable environment took the form of support groups. Many women met informally in each other's homes, when their husbands and children were out for the day, in order to break down the isolation they suffered as a result of the immigration process. As early as 1958, a group of West Indian domestic workers in Toronto met at the YWCA on Thursday evenings, which was known in the city as the "maid's day out." They formed the Caribbean Club, the first known support group for domestic workers and immigrant women from the Caribbean in the province of Ontario. The group lasted for twenty-two years (Das Gupta, 1986).

It is difficult to find records of such groups in both societies because they were voluntary and informal. Group memberships changed according to women's family responsibilities and other circumstances. Although these kinds of informal networks were not given a lot of credence in the larger society, they were, and continue to be, an important vehicle through which women could deal with the trauma of immigration. They served to validate women's experiences, frequently ignored and denigrated in a patriarchal and sexist society. These kinds of support groups are still being formed today, both spontaneously among immigrant women in neighbourhoods and through community organizations.

Separate and Autonomous Organizing

An interesting contrast between Canada and Sweden concerns the mode of organization developed by immigrant women. Historically, they seem to have organized more autonomously in Canada; that is, they have formed organizations of their own independent of their ethnic and racial communities and the mainstream women's movement. This is an indication that the country's immigration policy has produced common conditions among female immigrants despite their cultural diversity. Their organizing efforts, although not directly aimed at challenging the policy, nevertheless reflects their marginalization in Canadian society as a result of this initial experience. In Sweden the tendency has been to organize separately; that is, women immigrants formed women's committees within national ethnic organizations. However, autonomous organizing has begun to occur there also, as will be seen later in the chapter.

In Canada the second-wave feminist movement, which began in the 1960s and 1970s, has had a great indirect influence on the configuration of intergroup organizing among immigrant women. Although the women who joined the second-wave movement were largely white and middle class and they were not attentive to the special needs of immigrant women, their struggle created a social climate for women from diverse backgrounds to speak up about their oppression as housewives, as immigrants, and as workers. In this social and political climate, immigrant women too began to speak about their experiences of marginality and the unequal treatment that they received under the law, in the workplace, in the educational system, and in the family. As these efforts evolved, women organized around services aimed at improving their livelihood and around collective action, including advocacy and lobbying for social and legal changes. Thus, even though immigrant women's unequal position in Canada is shaped initially through immigration policy, they are organizing around a multiplicity of issues pertaining to their experiences, from family violence to the lack of specialized services for their needs.

Since International Women's Year (1975), many immigrant women's groups that consisted of members across ethnic and racial lines were formed in major Canadian cities. Some examples are the Multicultural Women's Group in Vancouver (Ng, 1991) and the Immigrant Women's Centre in Toronto (Ng and Ramirez, 1981). The latter was one of the first groups to specialize in service provision to immigrant women in Canada. A group that combines friendship network, service provision, and advocacy is Women Working with Immigrant Women (WWIW) in Fredericton (Ng, 1991). Indeed, outside major cities, where the immigrant population is small, local groups working with immigrant women serve a number of functions to meet these women's multiple needs. Apart from groups organized by immigrant women themselves, community organizations, both in the mainstream and within ethnic communities, have begun to recognize immigrant women's unique experience and are providing services and programs directed to their needs.

One group that deserves special mention is INTERCEDE. It began with a number of domestic workers and activists getting together in Toronto in the late 1970s to see how to bring about legislative changes to immigration policy and the labour code in order to improve the employment conditions of domestic workers. It is now a nationally recognized organization playing a central role in monitoring conditions and pressuring for changes in aspects of immigration policy that affect domestic workers. As well, it provides information to workers about their basic rights and serves as a reference point for domestic workers in the Toronto area. While keeping the interest of those workers as its focus, INTERCEDE also works with other women's and community groups on human-rights and social-justice issues. The work of this organization illustrates how, beginning from the unique position and experiences of one group, immigrant women are able to make linkages with other groups of citizens to work on more general social and political issues (Ng, 1991).

By the 1980s the immigrant women's movement had created its own voice through the formation of provincial and national organizations. In all the provinces, networks were formed to give women a voice independent of service-oriented community and local groups. The relationship between local, provincial, and national organizing is not a simple one. Whereas some provinces have networks that act as a support for local groups, in other provinces local group formation has taken place and has thrived without provincial coordination. As the National Organization of Immigrant and Visible Minority Women of Canada (see next section) consolidated itself, there was and is increasing tension among the national, provincial, and local groups with regard to communication, leadership, and allocation of resources, notably human and financial resources. Many women who were active locally are being recruited to provincial and national organizing simultaneously, leaving the local groups short of woman power to carry out the daily work of the organization. In provinces where there is a strong provincial network, the three tiers of an organization experience tension about the appropriate mechanisms of communication (Ng, 1991).

Immigrant women, together with women of colour, are also challenging traditional assumptions of the women's movement with strong middle-class and racial biases. They draw attention to the fact that demands of the feminist movement are defined according to white middle-class women's perspectives and priorities. Quoting Angela Davis, Noga Gayle (1991), a black feminist scholar and activist, pointed out that the emphasis on women working outside the home, one of the major efforts of the feminist movement in the 1960s and 1970s, stemmed largely from the concerns of middle-class women who had the privilege to be full-time homemakers. Immigrant and black women have always worked outside the home. Similarly, feminist theorization of women's oppression, based mainly on the experiences and perspectives of white women, is being challenged by immigrant women, women of colour, and "third world" women. They point out the Eurocentric nature of these theories and draw attention to the diversity of women on the basis of race, class, religion, and other attributes.

These debates, while ridden with tension and leading to divisions within the feminist movement, have also contributed to new theorization and creative alliances. Many mainstream women's organizations, such as the National Action Committee on the Status of Women (NAC) and the Canadian Research Institute for the Advancement of Women (CRIAW), were forced to examine their own practices and to develop more inclusive approaches to organizing.[7] The Women's Legal Education and Action Fund, for example, has taken up cases concerning immigrant women in their court challenges to the Canadian constitution. These examples indicate the dialectical relationships between and among diverse groups of women, and show how their struggles with each other and with the larger society inform and transform their practices.

In Sweden since the early 1980s, immigrant women have begun to organize separately in committees and sections within the older national associations established by labour immigrants and in more recent organizations created by refugees. These efforts have been made in a period when gender equality and equality of opportunity, codified in the Equal Opportunity Act of 1980, gained momentum in Swedish society. Even though immigrant and minority women are not covered as a category by the act, there seems to have been a congruency in timing between immigrant women's organizing and the increasing attention to women's position at work and in society at large.

This was also the moment when immigrant women who had been active behind the scene in their associations stepped into the foreground. An excellent example is that of the Finnish women, who now call themselves "Sweden-Finns."[8] Many years before any action was taken in women's organizing at the national level, Finnish women took the initiative to form local associations. One of Knocke's informants at the national association level gave the following account: "When I have spoken with women in our local associations, many of them say, 'It was us, the women, who took the initiative to form an association.' Simultaneously, they often also created a women's section. But it has been a bit different across the country. It is also that some associations have had women's committees, which later have been discontinued. We have been pushing from the national association that all local associations should have a women's committee, that all districts should have a women's committee as well. But it is difficult to tell when exactly the first women's section was founded. It simply varies from one place to another."

At the national level, the initiative to create a separate women's section came in 1981, when the executive board agreed to set up a working group for women's issues. At that time, no woman had yet been elected as a regular board member. After the ground was prepared through discussions in the working group and at special women's seminars, and after a women's activities program had been set up, the women's section came into being at the national level in 1984.

By May 1993 as many as twenty-three different national associations had separate women's committees or sections. New committees have been created since, such as the one established by the more recently arrived Albanian women, who soon after their arrival started organizing and mobilizing their women. In at least two of the "older" organizations, the Portuguese and the Polish national associations, women run most of the activities. In the Polish association they make up the majority of members of the executive board. A recent important victory for the Sweden-Finnish women was when the National Congress voted for gender equity in the executive board and other decision-making bodies in accordance with the objectives of the women's policy program of 1991. The executive board of the Chilean National Association is composed of equal numbers of women and men, but does not feel the need of a separate women's committee (Jasim, 1994). Several other national associations have appointed special representatives for women's issues, among these, two of the older associations, the National Association of Immigrants and the Central Federation of Immigrants.

A major problem for these women's committees at the national association level has been the lack of separate state funding.[9] These committees and sections are supposed to present their budget requirements to the national group in order to receive a share of the organization support granted to the national associations. Pressure from women's committees and sections for independent funding has not been successful. In this way, the notion that democracy is gender neutral works to the disadvantage of women. As M. Regina Tavares Da Silva (1993), a member of the Council of Europe, pointed out in the context of human rights and gender, "democracy ... has disregarded the question of gender and has even denied or concealed it in the name of universality" (4).

Although presenting a claim for a portion of the association's budget has worked well for some women's committees, this is not a satisfactory solution because of the male-dominated nature of these associations (Jasim, 1994). As one woman put it, "the women are in the hands of the executive board."[10] Even where women are successful in having their activities included in the budget, the proportion of funds that they receive is too limited. This is especially the case in the many national associations where women are the most active members. An example is the Women's Organization of the Portuguese National Association. The women receive only 20 per cent of the funding for organization support for their activities, although they initiate more and more varied activities than their male compatriots. Funds channelled through the common budget are simply not enough, but the women are determined to succeed.

Women who work within their national associations have to wage a double struggle. For example, in building up their activities, the Sweden-Finnish women had first to make the Swedish authorities recognize and support their plans. Then they had to convince the men in their own organization to give them their backing. In spite of higher representation on the executive board, it is still difficult for women to become part of the decision-making bodies. However, in the words of one of Knocke's informants, "the men are also a bit scared to see so many able and knowledgeable women, who are difficult to be kept down."

Although most immigrant women have tended to organize separately within their own national associations, as we mentioned at the beginning of this section, some have also chosen to organize across the divide of nationalities and ethnicities. Currently, at least three women's organizations have status and funding as national associations. All three have a membership composition that crosses national or ethnic boundaries. The oldest women's organization, the National Federation of International Associations for Immigrant Women (RIFFI), which started as a local association in Stockholm in 1968, dates from 1974. It was the creation of a Greek woman, Mira Kakossaios, feared by local and central authorities for her determination and strength. For her, bureaucratic rules and regulations were obstacles to be fought and overcome. The organization is still flourishing today, with a truly international membership, a small staff, a number of dedicated volunteers, excellent localities, and a decent amount of state funding.

More recent is the National Association of Latin-American Women (ALAM), which started as a local organization in a suburb of Stockholm more than ten years ago. After establishing several more local groups throughout Sweden, it gained its present status and has moved to new localities in central Stockholm.[11] The third organization, the International Women's Association, is located in a traditional textile and garment industry town and is run by women who came there as labour immigrants. Long settlement in Sweden and many years of experience in organizational work has made them highly competent in managing the association successfully in accordance with the Swedish model (see the next section).

In a similar fashion to their Canadian counterparts, immigrant women in Sweden have started to organize around tasks that have been part of public-sector responsibility, such as socially oriented activities with the young or the second generation, with elderly and retired persons, with the unemployed, and with drug abusers and victims of domestic violence. They have stepped in and mobilized around issues and needs that were simply disregarded by the larger society or where public support fell short.

Although traditional women's activities such as needlework, weaving, and the like still have their appeal for the older Sweden-Finnish women of the first generation, over the last ten years there has been a shift of focus from traditional activities to social issues with relevance for women's welfare. A number of projects have centred around women's work life, issues relating to health and physiological and psychological well-being, and other questions of importance in women's situation. Gender equality and equality of opportunity have been high on the agenda and have become a major challenge to be tackled both within their own community and in relation to mainstream society.

Frustrated by the lack of proper attention from Swedish society, women who have been made redundant and forced into early retirement because of health problems have also organized. There are now networks for unemployed Sweden-Finnish women. One district in western Sweden is developing models for working with unemployed women that can be used in other parts of the country. Many of the discussions in these groups are aimed at encouraging the women, who often have not had a chance to improve their Swedish, to enrol in studies or attend courses in Finnish-speaking folk high schools.[12] Another initiative is the building up of "friendship services" with courses around the country to prepare these groups to support and help their own members. These are examples of the autonomous organizing that immigrant women in Sweden have undertaken.

State Intervention

A common theme that runs through our examination of immigrant women's organizing in Canada and Sweden is the extent to which the state intervenes, directly or indirectly, in women's efforts. Since both countries are democratic welfare states – a social democratic one in the case of Sweden and a liberal one in Canada – women look to the government for support of their activities. This dynamic produces interesting tensions for them. In both countries, state control is not so much exercised by coercion, as one researcher would have it for Sweden (Schierup, 1991), as through administrative rules and regulations.

The Swedish welfare state has been supportive of immigrants' organizing through relatively generous funding. Compared to immigrants in other countries, including Canada, they have achieved what many others have to struggle for. Nevertheless, gender-neutral formal institutional structures and administrative rules have made it more difficult for women to organize. For example, in order to qualify as a national association, a group must have a minimum of a thousand members and geographical representation in at least three local associations. Some national or ethnic groups may simply be too small or too scattered geographically. Implicitly, these requirements also contain an important gender aspect, in that gender-neutral administrative rules do not take account of the different life situations for women and men. For women, meeting the administrative requirements means coping with the manifold responsibilities of their private lives and their jobs, and at the same time with organizational activity. As with other groups, potential members are likely to be spread throughout the country.

Contacts must be established and initiatives taken over large distances. More than anything, women with organizational experience need time and money to assist less-experienced members of their group to organize.

A concrete illustration of this difficulty is the Kurdistani Women's Association. It started as an independent women's organization, but did not manage to survive economically. The women were simply not in the position to meet the requirement of having groups in several local communities, nor were they able to recruit a sufficient number of members to be considered for organization support. Project support covered their activities, but was not enough to maintain an administrative base or to pay for localities. Eventually, the women had to join with the men of the Kurdistani National Association, which gave them access to administrative services and localities. They still call themselves the Kurdistani Women's Association and are now in the process of recruiting more women in other local communities. In sum, funding restrictions have made it difficult for immigrant women to organize autonomously, even though the National Immigration Board in principle is in favour of women's organizing efforts.

Similarly, state funding has a way of both enabling and restricting the activities of immigrant women's groups in Canada. In examining the work of a community-based organization set up to act as an advocate for immigrant women in the labour market, Ng (1996) found that, because of the funding requirements, which focused on job placement rather than the experiences of immigrant women, the organizational objective changed from one of working on behalf of immigrant women to that of providing services to both employers and immigrant workers. Another documented example is the experience of WWIW in Fredericton, New Brunswick. The group discovered that obtaining funding to administer two programs called ISAP and HOST[13] meant increased administrative work for the group and led to a concomitant change in the relations of group members (Ng, Kwan, and Miedema, 1991).

However, the way in which immigrant women's groups work with the state has been different in the two countries. As already mentioned, the receptivity of the Swedish welfare state to immigrants has meant that the relationship between it and immigrant women has been more collaborative and consultative. They have managed to establish a partnership with the state, as the experience of the Coordinating Body for Immigrant Organizations (SIOS) shows. SIOS is an umbrella group of ten national associations, mostly those of traditional worker immigrants, and it acts to promote immigrants' interests in relation to Swedish society with the authorities, in order to provide information on politically relevant issues. SIOS is not equivalent to a national association, and funds are therefore issued under a special government ordinance. In 1991 women representing the national SIOS organizations were invited to be present at its congress. They decided to suggest a Women's SIOS, a proposal that was accepted by the congress. The decision was based on the view that important questions relating to gender equality would never be addressed without a coordinating body for women. The Women's SIOS depends on project support for its activities. As coordinating bodies for ten immigrant organizations, both SIOS in general and the Women's SIOS have gained increasing importance as partners in consultation with state authorities. This example shows the willingness of the state to work with immigrant groups, its openness to consult and cooperate with them on issues of common concern, and immigrant women's capacity to work on common issues across ethnic and nationality borders. However, it does not guarantee that women's voices and concerns are heard in the larger society. Ironically, the paternalism of the state ensures that immigrant women's concerns are confined to the structured ethnic-relations apparatus of the state.

In Canada the relationship between immigrant women's groups and the state has been more contentious and at times confrontational, as the following example shows. In 1982 the federal government, through the Department of the Secretary of State, organized a national conference on immigrant women, bringing together academics, bureaucrats, and "experts" to discuss the problems of such women in Canada. Women from the community were not invited. Immigrant women, especially those in the Toronto area, where the conference was held, mounted an intense protest. Eventually, representatives were invited from each province, and immigrant women from the community in Toronto were allowed to attend the conference. They used this forum to drive home the iniquitous treatment that they received. A follow-up committee was established to plan another conference for immigrant women in two years' time. (In actual fact, this conference did not take place until 1986; see Ng, 1991). Members of the follow-up committee began to make contacts across the country. This process infused new energy into local organizing efforts. Not only did local activities expand, but provincial and national linkages were forged. For example, WWIW in Fredericton was formed as a result of a visit by members of the committee to meet with immigrant women in New Brunswick (Ng, 1991). At the second national immigrant women's conference, held in Winnipeg in November 1986, the National Organization of Immigrant and Visible Minority Women of Canada was formed. This body serves as a national coordinating and lobbying association for immigrant women. Its membership is made up of provincial and territorial immigrant women's groups.

In order to understand the political context of immigrant women's organizing in Canada, therefore, it is important to see that the state has played, and continues to play, a major role in mediating these attempts at the local, provincial, and national levels. One notable feature of the immigrant women's movement, which is similar to the feminist movement generally, is its dependence on state funding as groups at various levels struggle to establish themselves. In local groups, there is a tendency to move from lobbying and advocacy to the provision of services funded through various state programs (see Ng, 1996; Ng, Kwan, and Miedema 1991). At the provincial and national levels, initiatives launched by immigrant women are closely monitored by state officials, notably by the Women's Program, which has provided the bulk of funding for organizations at these two levels. The need to develop an autonomous movement and the concomitant dependence on state funding constitute one of the many contradictions that are hotly debated within the immigrant women's movement.

In particular, the federal government has played a central role in encouraging and facilitating the establishment of a national body by organizing the national conferences of 1981 and 1986 and through funding. It is clear that, as immigrant women become a visible pressure group, the state is attempting to incorporate them into the electoral process: immigrant women can now be counted upon as a constituency within the formal political apparatus. While a national body enables immigrant and visible-minority women to have a united voice in lobbying government, it also provides a vehicle through which politicians and government departments can consult with this particular constituency without having to respond to the myriad grassroots groups directly. By channelling much of the Women's Program funding to the national group, the federal government has also created competition among all immigrant women's groups. As their movement develops, new contradictions, tensions, and alliances are and will continue to be generated, both within the movement itself and in relation to the larger society.

SUMMARY AND REFLECTIONS

We have found it difficult to make direct comparisons between Sweden and Canada because, in spite of certain similarities, policy development and women's organizing have occurred under different historical circumstances and have taken divergent trajectories. We offer the following reflections instead of a definitive conclusion.

It is clear that state policies in the two countries regarding immigration, immigrant settlement, and immigrant women's organizing are in flux at the moment, particularly with globalization, which is affecting both countries. An obvious example in the Canadian case is the institution and augmentation of business-class immigration, with a corresponding decrease in the quota for family-class immigrants, thus affecting who will enter the country and where they will be located in the Canadian economy and labour market. We are surprised that, in spite of the strong presence of labour in the formation of state policies and class discourse in the Swedish society, organizing among immigrant women there has been based on identity in a way similar to the Canadian situation. From our examination, it seems that the experience of marginality is an important and galvanizing force regardless of state policies and the overall strength of labour in these two advanced industrialized nations.

The forging of the European Union in the Swedish context and the effects of neo-liberal economic strategies in Canada (an example being the signing of the North American Free Trade Agreement, discussed elsewhere in this volume) have led to a period of drastic restructuring and rapid transformation in the labour market and in the welfare state. What we found in both countries was the progressive marginalization of immigrant women as a result of these changes. We have already stated that their organizing has been in large part shaped by state policies and by their labour-market conditions. Although it is still too early to determine how their organizing will change in response to globalization, it is reasonable to assume that women will continue to organize around the current changes in spite of decreased government support in both countries. Indeed, one major conclusion that we can point to is the tenacity of immigrant women in their attempt to overcome societal barriers and define a space for themselves in the host society.

In reflecting on the forms that their agency has taken in the two countries, we found one striking difference in immigrant women's organizing. While those in Canada have taken to lobbying and advocacy, at times militantly, their counterparts in Sweden have pursued a quieter course. Paradoxically, the benevolent and paternalistic Swedish state, which has encouraged and funded immigrant women's organizations and their projects, has also channelled their activities in accordance with its own administrative framework. Thus militancy has had no ground on which to develop. Interestingly, militancy has been directed more towards the male counterparts of their organizations.

What is certain in terms of the picture we presented here is that new contradictions and alliances are occurring. They will continue to do so, opening up new possibilities and imposing new limits on immigrant women's organizing. But only time will tell how these dynamics will play out.

NOTES

This chapter is the result of a three-year project comparing social policies and women's organizing in Canada and Sweden directed by Linda Briskin (Canada) and Mona Eliasson (Sweden). We are grateful to members of the project, especially the editors, for comments on earlier drafts of the manuscript.

1 While constitutionally, immigration matters are administered jointly by the federal and provincial governments (for example, in determining immigration levels in the provinces), in fact, apart from Quebec and Alberta, immigration is controlled federally.

2 The National Labour Market Board (AMS) is the central state authority responsible for labour-exchange offices and for the implementation of labour-market policy measures. Until the beginning of the 1980s, it was also responsible for the reception of workers and refugees; subsequently, this area was transferred to the National Immigration Board (SIV).

3 Although Canada is a member of the United Nations, and in accordance with the International Convention of Refugees, the Canadian Immigration Act allows immigrants to enter the country under the refugee classification, in fact – and in contrast to the Swedish situation – refugees constitute a small percentage of the immigration program.

4 The business-class program was instituted in 1978 to encourage the immigration of entrepreneurs (Man, 1994). Since 1980s, in order to attract foreign investment, the definition of the latter category was expanded to include investors. These immigrants bypass the points system if they have enough money to invest in Canadian businesses and industries. The amount of capital required for applicants to be eligible for this classification changes from year to year; it has been increasing.

5 In 1973 a law came into force giving immigrants the legal right to 240 hours of language training during paid work. Since the early 1980s the number of hours has been extended to approximately 600, and is available to all workers as well as to non-workers.

6 The CLC report does not use immigrant women as a category. "Visible minority" refers to immigrant groups from countries other than those in the Americas and Europe. Thus these are not comparable statistics, strictly speaking. Nevertheless, they indicate the comparative working conditions of Canadian and minority workers, many of whom are immigrants.

7 An indication of the integration of concerns of women of colour into the mainstream feminist agenda is the fact that they and immigrant women are now in leadership positions within major women's organizations. The past president of NAC, Sunera Tobani, was an immigrant and a woman of colour; its current president, Joan Grant-Cummins, is originally from the Caribbean. One of the authors of this article (Roxana Ng) was president of CRIAW in 1995–96.

8 "Sweden-Finns" and "Sweden-Finnish" are terms used by the large minority of people from Finland who have settled in Sweden and who aspire to the position of a national minority in the country. They should not be confused with the Swedish-speaking population of Finland, which since historical times has been a minority group there with full national, linguistic, and other rights.

9 There are two principal types of state funding for which national and local associations, as well as other groups who want to initiate activities, can apply to the National Immigration Board: organization support and project support. Organization support, the most important and continuous form of funding, is exclusively reserved for national associations. To qualify, an association must have at least three affiliated local groups and a membership of at least a thousand persons. Project support is the major source of funding for specific activities initiated by local assocations or other groups below the national level. It is normally given on a one-year basis.

10 This quotation is from an interview conducted by Knocke.

11 Unfortunately, this group had to discontinue its activities because of the financial misconduct of one of its board members.

12 The so-called folk high schools are educational institutions for adults who want to improve their educational level or learn skills of various kinds (both practical and theoretical) without the pressure of having to earn diplomas or credentials. It is education for the sake of education.

13 ISAP and HOST were programs instituted by Employment and Immigration Canada (or CEIC, as it was called at the time), in "partnership" with voluntary organizations, to provide reception services to new immigrants. They had different and strict funding criteria. Services such as information and orientation, referral to community resources, counselling, and translation provided by voluntary groups were funded by ISAP. HOST made use of volunteers, who acted as "hosts" to refugees at their point of entry into the country. HOST funding covered the salary of a volunteer coordinator and subsidies to refugees for transportation, clothing, food, and shelter for a short period. For a critique of these programs and how they affected the internal relations of voluntary groups, see Ng, Kwan, and Miedema (1991).

REFERENCES

Ålund, Aleskandra, and Carl-Ulrik Schierup. (1991). *Paradoxes of Multiculturalism: Essays on Swedish Society.* Aldershot: Avebury.

Boyd, Monica. (1986). Immigrant women in Canada. In R.J. Simon and C.B. Brettell (eds.), *International Migration: The Female Experience.* Ottawa: Rowman & Allanheld.

Campbell, Marie L. (1980). Sexism in British Columbia trade unions, 1900–1920. In Cathy Kess and Beth Latham (eds.), *In Her Own Right: Selected Essays in Women's History in B.C.* Victoria: Camosun College.

Canadian Labour Congress (CLC). (1997). *Women's Work – A Report.* Ottawa.

Czarniawska-Joerges, Barbara. (1994). Editorial: Modern organizations and Pandora's box. *Scandinavian Journal of Management*, 10 (2): 95–8 (special issue on "The Construction of Gender in Organizations").

Das Gupta, Tania. (1986). *Learning from Our History: Community Development by Immigrant Women in Ontario, 1958–1986.* A Tool for Action. Toronto: Cross-Cultural Communication Centre.

Gayle, Noga. (1991). Black women's reality and feminism: An exploration of race and gender. In Dawn Currie and Valerie Raoul (eds.), *Anatomy of Gender: Women's Struggle for the Body.* Ottawa: Carleton University Press.

Hammar, Tomas. (1988). Mellan rasism och reglering. Invandrarpolitikens ideologi och historia. *Arbetarhistoria*, 12 (46): 11–14.

Immigration Canada. (1989). *Immigration to Canada: A Statistical Overview.* Ottawa.

INTERCEDE. (n.d.). *Toronto Organization for Domestic Workers; Rights, Orientation Kit for Newly-Arrived Foreign Domestic Workers.* Toronto: Author.

Jasim, Mohamed. (1994). Trångt for jämstalldheten. *Nya Sverige*, 6: 40–1.

Knocke, Wuokko. (1982). *Invandrare möter facket.* Stockholm: Arbetslivscentrum.

– (1986). *Invandrade kvinnor i lönearbete och fack.* Forskningsrapport nr. 53. Stockholm: Arbetslivscentrum.

– (1991). Women immigrants – What is the 'Problem'? *Economic and Industrial Democracy*, 12 (4): 469–86.

– (1993). De invandrade kvinnornas arbetsmarknad. In *Kvinnors arbetsmarknad. 1990-talet – återtågets årtionde?* Stockholm: Arbetsmarknadsdepartementet.

– (1994a). *Tendenser och utveckling på kvinnornas arbetsmarknad inom den europeiska gemenskapen.* Working Paper Series, no. 17. Stockholm: Arbetslivscentrum.

– (1994b). Gender, ethnicity and technological change. *Economic and Industrial Democracy* 15 (1): 11–34.

– (forthcoming). The case of Sweden: Insiders outside the mainstream. In R. Penninx and J. Roosblad (eds.), *Trade Unions, Immigration and Immigrants in Western Europe, 1960–1993*. Amsterdam: International Institute of Social History and Institute for Migration and Ethnic Studies.

Kyle, Gunhild. (1979). *Gästarbeterska i manssamhallet.* Stockholm: Liberforlag.

Loney, Martin. (1977). A political economy of citizen participation. In L. Pantich (ed.), *The Canadian State: Political Economy and Political Power.* Toronto: University of Toronto Press.

Man, Guida. (1994). The effect of immigration policy on the experiences of Chinese immigrant women in Canadian history and in contemporary Canadian society. Unpublished manuscript, Department of Sociology, Ontario Institue for Studies in Education.

Ng, Roxana. (1991). Finding our voices: Reflections on immigrant women's organizing. In Jeri Wine and Janice Ristock (eds.), *Women and Social Change: Feminist Activism in Canada.* Toronto: James Lorimer & Co.

– (1993). Racism, sexism, and nation building in Canada. In C. McCarthy and W. Crichlow (eds.), *Race, Identity and Representation in Education.* New York: Routledge.

– (1995). Multiculturalism as ideology: A textual analysis. In M. Campbell and A. Manicom (eds.), *Knowledge, Experience, and Ruling Relations: Studies in the Social Organization of Knowledge.* Toronto: University of Toronto Press.

– (1996). *The Politics of Community Services: Immigrant Women, Class and State.* 2nd ed. Halifax: Fernwood Books.

– Elizabeth Kwan, and Baukje Miedema. (1991). State funding and immigrant services: The experience of an immigrant women's group in the Maritimes. *Canadian Review of Social Policy* 27: 49–67.

– and Judith Ramirez. (1981). *Immigrant Housewives in Canada.* Toronto: Immigrant Women's Centre.

Protokoll. (1947). Parliamentary discussion on measures to transfer foreign labour, etc. Prot. I:24:2. 23 March.

– (1966). Parliamentary discussion on the long-term social and cultural problems connected with continuous immigration to Sweden. Prot. I:2:5. 9 December.

Salaff, Janet. (1981). *Working Daughters of Hong Kong: Filial Piety or Power in the Family.* Cambridge: Cambridge University Press.

Schierup, Carl-Ulrik. (1991). Ett etniskt Babels torn: Invandrarorganisationerna och den uteblivna dialogen. *Sociologisk Forskning* 3: 3–22.

Segal, Gary L. (1994). *Immigrating to Canada*. North Vancouver and Bellingham: Self-Counsel Press. (First published in 1975).

Sharma, Nandita R. (1995). The true north strong and unfree: Capitalist restructuring and non-immigrant employment in Canada, 1973–1993. Unpublished MA thesis, Department of Sociology and Anthropology, Simon Fraser University.

Simmons, Alan B., and Kieran Keohane. (1992). Canadian immigration policy: State strategies and the quest for legitimacy. *Canadian Review of Sociology and Anthropology* 29 (4): 421–52.

SIV. (1985). *Invandrarbyråer: Information*. Norrköping: Statens invandrarverk.

– (1991). *Myndigheternas ansvar för invandrarna*. Norrköping: Statens invandrarverk.

– (1994). *På tal om invandrare*. Norrköping: Statens invandrarverk.

– and Arbetsmarknadsdepartementet. (1991). *Invandrarföreningar*. Norrköping: Statens invandrarverk.

SOU. (1967). *Invandringen*. Stockholm: Arbetsmarknadsdepartementet.

Tavares Da Silva, Maria Regina. (1993). Human rights and gender. Paper prepared for the interregional meeting organized by the Council of Europe in advance of the World Conference on Human Rights. Strasbourg: Council of Europe.

Wadensjö, Eskil. (1973). *Immigration och samhällsekonomi*. Lund: Studentlitteratur.

White, Julie. (1980). *Women and Unions*. Ottawa: Canadian Advisory Council on the Status of Women.

Wickberg, Edgar (ed.). (1982). *From China to Canada: A History of the Chinese Communities in Canada*. Toronto: McClelland and Stewart Ltd.

Widgren, Jonas. (1980). *Svensk invandrarpolitik*. Lund: Liber Laromedel.

PART TWO

Organizing Contexts

Representing Women's Interests in the Policy Process: Women's Organizing and State Initiatives in Sweden and Canada, 1960s–1990s[1]

CHRISTINA BERGQVIST AND SUE FINDLAY

ABSTRACT

Women in both Sweden and Canada have been seriously under-represented in all aspects of the policy process, and their interests have scarcely been reflected in government policies. In the last three decades, governments in both countries have taken measures to increase women's participation in public life. In this chapter we explore these measures, and compare and contrast the ways that women in these countries have organized themselves in order to influence the development and implementation of change.

We conclude that women's organizing as "insiders" and "outsiders" was and still is central to the success of government policies to increase the participation of women in public life. While some might argue that the greater effectiveness of Swedish policies reflects that country's "passion for equality" and its tradition of more democratic forms of representation, women in both Sweden and Canada have learned that commitments to equality are not free of gender bias. The success of government initiatives also depends on the extent to which women can organize themselves to counter the resistance that men mount to policies that challenge their traditional domination of the public sphere.

The 1960s in both Canada and Sweden were a period marked by debates about the status of women and by organizing by women to pressure governments for policies that would increase their representation in public life. In Canada women had won the right to vote earlier in the century, but political rights had not removed the barriers that limited their participation in public life. Nor had they worked to integrate women's interests into the governments' policy processes. By the 1960s women in Canada were severely under-represented in political parties, in the governing bodies at all levels of the political system, and in the institutions that administered government policies. And their right to social and economic equality had been largely ignored in the design of the welfare policies that had addressed the quality of working life for men in Canada since the 1930s.

In Sweden the barriers to women's equality were different. They were relatively well represented in Parliament, and the interests of working women had to some extent been reflected in Sweden's welfare-state policies since the 1930s. However, as a group, women were still poorer than men, and they were not as well represented in public life as men were, particularly on the powerful commissions and public boards that constituted Sweden's corporatist system of policy-making. Regardless of the benefits that they had won, they too saw the need to take up the issue of women's equality. Parity between women and men in public life was still an issue.

We begin this chapter by looking at the different ways that women in Sweden and Canada organized themselves to take up the debate about women's equality. In Sweden they worked from their position as "insiders" within political parties and Parliament to organize a public debate that set the tone for a government policy of gender equality (*jämställdhet*). This policy argued that women should have an equal partnership with men in public and private spheres. In Canada the debate about women's equality was slow to move beyond groups of women. These women had little impact on the men who dominated political organizations. As "outsiders," they found it necessary to pressure the federal government to appoint a royal commission to investigate the status of women in Canada and advise it on strategies to promote women's interests. When the Royal Commission on the Status of Women was appointed in 1967, women organized themselves at both the national and the local level to identify their interests and to present them at the commission's hearings, which took place across the country.

In the next section of the article, we examine the initiatives that our respective governments have introduced to implement commitments to represent women's interests in the policy process over the last three decades, beginning with Sweden's Commission for Gender Equality between Men and Women and the development of Canada's policy machinery in the 1970s. We then explore the initiatives that both governments introduced in the mid-1980s to increase the representation of women in state institutions and the effect that these have had in giving women a voice in making government policy. We conclude the chapter with an overview of what we have learned about the way that women's organizing has influenced the introduction of government initiatives to integrate women's interests into the policy processes of our governments and to give women themselves a voice in these processes. We argue that these initiatives must be attributed as much to the success of women's organizing as to any commitments that our respective governments have made to women's equality or the "passion for equality" that is embedded in our political culture.

WOMEN'S ORGANIZING

Women in both Canada and Sweden have played an active role in defining the barriers to women's equality and the policies that governments could use to promote it. However, the way in which they have organized themselves to do so has differed quite radically. These differences reflect the very divergent ways in which women in Canada and Sweden have participated in the political process in the twentieth century, as well as the very dissimilar commitments to equality that are embedded in our political cultures and shape our systems of representation. In Sweden the "passion for equality" set the stage for a public debate about ways to promote women's equality. In Canada equality was a contentious issue, prompting women and government leaders to rely on a royal commission to mediate the conflicting perspectives that the Canadian public had about it.

Women's Organizing in Sweden: Working from the Inside

In the 1960s Sweden was characterized by its "passion for equality" (Graubard, 1986). According to Swedish political scientist Maud L. Eduards (1991), equity and equality are "probably the most basic values in Swedish – and Nordic – political culture" (169). This passion for equality set the stage, then, for a public debate about women's equality. Women were well represented in this debate. They had a relatively strong voice in Parliament and in political parties. Compared to women in other non-Nordic countries, Swedish women had played a significant role as members of Parliament since the introduction of universal suffrage in 1919. By 1965 their representation in Parliament had risen to almost 11 per cent. Twenty-one per cent of Social Democratic members were women, although only one, Ulla Lindström, had been appointed to the cabinet (Bergqvist, 1994). Women's relatively high representation in Parliament reflects Sweden's use of a proportional list system to organize the electoral process. This system is generally considered to be more inclusive than the "first past the post" system that characterizes Canada's electoral process (see Maillé and Wängnerud in this volume). It also reflects the strong presence that women have had in political parties. Four out of five parliamentary parties had affiliated women's sections in the 1960s. These groups used their power in political parties to put women candidates on the parties' lists. The Social Democratic Party in particular had put women candidates into winnable positions on the party list for some time. During the long period when it was in power in Sweden (1932–76), many of its women candidates won seats in Parliament. The social and economic policies that the Social Democratic government introduced in this period provided working women in particular with significant benefits.

In spite of these policies, however, there was increasing evidence in the 1960s that vast inequalities still existed between women and men, and that women did not participate in public life on an equal basis with men. In that decade women and men in Sweden's political parties made women's equality the focus for public debates. They were supported by women from community-based organizations and unions, as well as by professional and highly educated women.

In the public debates in Sweden, two main lines of argument emerged about how to promote women's equality. These views cut across party affiliations. One position was quite conservative. It supported the existing male-breadwinner model, arguing that women should wait until their children were older before they tried to combine their primary role as mothers with a professional one. This model outlined social reforms to support housewives and women who "had" to work, and benefits for the main (male) breadwinner (Bergqvist, 1994; Sainsbury, 1993, 1994).

The second line challenged the traditional male-breadwinner model and sex roles that made women responsible for family life, and it argued for a model of gender equality. A starting point for the radicalizing of the debate was an essay written in 1962 by Eva Moberg, a young liberal. In her article, "Kvinnans villkorliga frigivning" (Women's conditional liberation), Moberg argued that women's liberation should not be restricted because of motherhood. Rejecting a society based on different roles for women and men, she talked about the "human role" and the freedom of the individual regardless of sex (Moberg, 1962; *Kvinnans jämlikhet*, 1964). She argued for the reconstruction of the old sex roles in order to make it possible for everyone to combine paid work and responsibilities for the family regardless of sex or the age of the children. Moberg's model was based on the idea of an equal partnership between women and men that would support the capacity of both to live fully human lives and participate actively in the workforce. Unless men were prepared to change the division of labour within the home, women would never be able fully to exercise their rights to participate in the workforce on the same basis as men. Among the proposals made to promote this new partnership were a revised individual tax system that broke with the breadwinner model, more and better public day-care facilities, sex-neutral education, and a more liberal abortion act.

To promote this model of gender equality, its advocates organized a network of young social democratic, liberal, and leftist women and men (journalists, researchers, and politicians) to take the debate into the mass media, political parties, unions, and universities (Moberg, 1962; Baude, 1992). The members of Group 222, as they were called, supported their case for the dual-income model with new research which indicated that women's participation in the labour market was actually higher than statistics suggested if part-time work was included. According to their research, the number of women entering the labour market was growing each year. They also argued that more women would do so if they could get childcare. Women wanted paid work, and they were needed in the growing public-service sector as well as in the textile and food industries. To support its arguments, Group 222 also used the 1953 opinion poll that the SSKF (Social Democratic Women in Sweden) had carried out among its members, which showed that women working outside the home were more satisfied with their situation than those working at home (Karlsson, 1996).[2] From the mid-sixties on, important groups such as SSKF, the Social Democratic Youth organization, the LO (Swedish Trade Union Confederation), and social democrats and liberals in general aligned themselves with the advocates of the dual-income model, supporting their claims for the promotion of public day care, parental leave, and a more liberal abortion act.

In 1969 the Social Democratic Party made gender equality a goal and "defined equality between the sexes as an integral part of the party's aspirations to achieve equality" (Sainsbury, 1993: 280). In that same year, the party released "Towards Equality," a report prepared by a committee headed by Alva Myrdal. This report put gender equality at the top of the government's political agenda.

Women's Organizing in Canada: Working from the Outside

In Canada the under-representation of women reflected the limited commitment to equality and representation that marked the governing process. In its review of the participation of women in public life, the Royal Commission on the Status of Women concluded, "It appears to have been much easier for Canadian women to engage in politics indirectly than to run for elected office" (Canada, 1970: 350). Women in Canada did play a role in public life, but it was one that was largely restricted to the relatively elite group of women who were the leaders of women's national voluntary organizations. As a consequence, women organized themselves as "outsiders."

There was little evidence of any widespread public support for reforms to promote women's equality in Canadian society in the 1960s. Canada's welfare state had been shaped by policies that supported the roles that women had traditionally played and maintained the sexual division of labour that seemed to work in the interests of capital (Scott, 1996; Ursel, 1992). "The deep roots of liberalism in Canada, the federal political structure, and the circumscribed role of class-based, gender-based, and other progressive movements have all contributed to the emergence of a liberal welfare regime" (Scott, 1996: 10). By the 1960s, the Canadian government offered few of the benefits that accounted for the high participation rate of women in Sweden's workforce. The issue of women's equality had not found a place in the struggles for equality that were led by the new social movements in Canada at the time. Women's interests were simply not part of the policy processes of political institutions, nor were they on the agendas of the new social movements that were challenging the failure of Canadian governments to represent the interests of the marginal groups in society at this time.

In the 1960s the leaders of established women's organizations who had taken up women's equality argued that a royal commission was needed to document women's issues and persuade the government to take action. Although socialist women and the "new feminists" were organizing women at the community level to challenge the very fundamental way that capitalism and patriarchy reproduced women's inequality in Canadian society, the strategies of the more "liberal" women captured the support of the majority of Canadian women and the ear of government. In 1966 leaders from the Canadian Federation of University Women, the Business and Professional Women's Clubs, the National Council of Women, the Young Women's Christian Association, and even the more recently established and more radical Voice of Women came together as the Committee for the Equality of Women and launched a militant and very well publicized appeal to members of the federal cabinet for a royal commission. The audacity of these women, particularly as it was reported in the press, resonated with the anger that more and more Canadian women were feeling as they struggled to enter public life. Pressure from the Committee for the Equality of Women for a royal commission was reinforced by the growing demands from the United Nations and the International

Labour Organization to address the issue of women's rights (particularly the under-representation of women in the federal public service), as well as demands from the few women inside the government, such as Secretary of State Judy LaMarsh. The government had often used royal commissions and similar public bodies to define government responsibilities for the contentious social issues that marked the 1960s.

On 16 February 1967 the prime minister of Canada appointed the Royal Commission on the Status of Women. It was headed by a well-known female broadcaster, Florence Bird, and its members included human-rights advocates. Only one of them, Elsie Gregory McGill, called herself a feminist. The commission was asked to "inquire into and report upon the status of women in Canada, and to recommend what steps might be taken by the Federal Government to ensure for women equal opportunities with men in all aspects of Canadian society" (Canada, 1970).

Between 1967 and 1970 the seven commissioners criss-crossed Canada listening to the stories that women told them about the problems they faced in their communities. In the report that they tabled in 1970, the commissioners used these stories in their documentation of the status of women and offered the government 165 recommendations to improve the status of women in Canada. The thousands of women who had participated in the commission's work embraced the report and supported the development of a network of more-permanent women's organizations at the community level to lobby provincial and federal governments for the implementation of the recommendations.

At the time, the Royal Commission on the Status of Women gave women in Canada a badly needed and very timely opportunity to speak publicly about the issues that shaped their lives. However, there were many factors that limited its usefulness as a strategy to represent women's issues or to influence government (Ashforth, 1991; Findlay, 1995). The Canadian government's limited commitment to equality was reflected in the commission's equal-opportunity framework, a factor that inhibited the development of recommendations for active policies such as affirmative action (Arscott, 1994). The conservative political perspectives of the government-appointed commissioners limited their responsiveness to the radical and socialist feminists who were organizing in this period. In this context the "new feminists" had little impact on the analysis that the commissioners conducted about the status of women (Begin, 1992.) These factors and their marginal position in the policy process as members of a quasi-governmental body led the commissioners to argue for a "pragmatic" perspective on the development of recommendations and to tailor the diversity of women's interests which they had heard about to models that they hoped would make sense to the men inside who dominated the policy process.

In particular, the commission's recommendations about women in public life were very limited (Begin, 1993). By urging the government to increase its funding to established women's groups so that they could represented status-of-women issues in their communities (Canada, 1970: 49), the commissioners essentially legitimated the "outsider" role that women had historically played, rather than challenging the exclusive nature of the existing system of representation, And finally, the procedures of the commission – relatively formal hearings that emphasized the authority of the commissioners, written presentations, the machinery required for simultaneous translation, and reliance on expert witnesses – privileged the voices of the more-conservative women from the elite classes in Canada in the deliberations of the commission. The majority of presentations came from established women's groups. Women from these groups were more comfortable with these procedures than working-class, poor, immigrant, and ethnic women. They were more familiar with commissions of inquiry than most of the other women, and as members of these national organizations, they had acquired the skills required to partipate in forums such as the commission. Few came from unions, churches, political parties, or native and minority groups (Findlay, 1995: 64–6).

In summary, by the mid-1960s women in both Sweden and Canada had organized themselves to put women's equality on the political agenda. In Sweden they, and some of their male colleagues, had worked as insiders, building networks and alliances with those who shared their passion for equality in order to shape a public debate about how to promote women's equality. The gender-equality model that emerged from these debates reflected Sweden's long history of social and economic reforms to promote equality, as well as the success that women and men in the Social Democratic Party had in organizing a radical coalition to offset the more traditional perspectives about women's role in public life that still existed in Sweden in the 1960s. The gender-equality model went well beyond the policies for working women that the government had supported since the 1930s to focus on the development of more equal partnerships between women and men at work and in the family. Government responsiveness to it reflected Sweden's "women-friendly state" (Hernes, 1987), as well as the pressure that women could exert on the policy process as members of Parliament and of political parties.

In Canada women who took up the issue of women's equality were "outsiders" in the male-dominated political system of representation, sidelined as lobbyists and forced to rely on the mechanism of a royal commission to influence the "insiders." Although the appointment of the Royal Commission on the Status of Women did provide the impetus for public hearings that engaged thousands of women in debates about their status, the radical nature of their demands was subdued. Debates were dominated by a ruling class of women, and the commission's recommendations were shaped to fit a relatively conservative equal-opportunity model that the commission hoped would "make sense" to the mandarins who dominated the state bureaucracy. But the commission was a relatively powerless agency on the fringe of the federal policy-making process. Responses to its report were slow, and when they emerged, they reflected a defence of the very narrow form of representation that had shaped Canada's political system to represent and protect the particular interests of a ruling class of men.

STATE INITIATIVES TO PROMOTE WOMEN'S EQUALITY

Governments in both Canada and Sweden have been heralded by feminists throughout the Western world for the initiatives that they introduced to promote women's equality. In Canada in the 1970s the federal government was noted for the machinery it inaugurated to add women's interests to the policy process; in the same period the Swedish government was praised for its far-reaching commitment to a policy of gender equality. By the 1980s, however, the focus in both countries had shifted to the issue of representation. In this period Sweden and Canada were pressured by women for stronger commitments to increase the representation of women in state institutions and the policy process more generally.

Representing Women's Interests in the Policy Process: Sweden's Commission for Gender Equality between Men and Women

In 1972 the Swedish government appointed the Commission for Gender Equality between Men and Women (Delegationen för Jämställdhet mellan Män och Kvinnor) to define and implement its commitments to the gender-equality model. This commission was decidedly more powerful than Canada's Royal Commission on the Status of Women. Unlike in Canada, commissions in Sweden are a permanent and central feature of the country's corporatist system of making policy. In these commissions, representatives of the key interest groups in Swedish society work with elected members of Parliament and state administrators to develop government policies. The Commission for

Gender Equality was first attached to the Office of the Prime Minister and subsequently moved to the Ministry of Labour Market Affairs.

The appointment of the commission reflected Sweden's decision to integrate gender equality into the development of its social and labour-market policies. The commission was charged with the task of developing policies that would promote an equal partnership between women and men. To do so required the transformation and modernization of older welfare programs that had supported the traditional male-breadwinner model and/or the introduction of gender-neutral social reforms to strengthen women's positions and possibilities on the labour market and men's responsibilities in the family. Examples of such reforms were the extension of childcare services and parental leave and the separation of taxes for spouses. Special treatment or positive action for women was only considered as an exception (SOU, 1975; Eduards, 1991).

It is important to note that the emphasis on gender neutrality in this period reflected a radical shift from a more traditional view of gender relations (SOU, 1975). It was a period of "sex roles in transition" (*roller i omvandling*), which was the name of a report from the Commission for Gender Equality. However, public documents that emerged from the commission reflected a consensus within Swedish society that improvements in gender equality would benefit everyone and hence were simply a question of new reforms and attitudes.[3] Voices from the more radical feminist groups that raised questions about women's sexuality, pornography, and violence against women, such as Group 8, were largely absent. There was little evidence of the conflict of interests between women and men that these women had identified. Relations between the sexes were portrayed as basically harmonious, and the nuclear, heterosexual model that framed these relations in the family was unquestioned. A 1975 governmental report expressed it this way: "The goal now is that it should be possible to combine children and paid work in a harmonious way and that it would be positive for men, women and children – for the whole society. However, this goal demands huge changes both in the home and in work life" (SOU, 1975).

The election of a more conservative coalition government in 1976 brought with it a reduced commitment to the corporatist system of policy-making and to the more democratic form of representation that it had supported. The Commission for Gender Equality between Men and Women was replaced with a Committee of Gender Equality, which was attached to the Ministry of Labour Market Affairs. Its membership was more restricted, made up of representatives from all the parties in Parliament. Anti-discriminatory measures began to replace the social and economic reforms that women needed to participate equally with men.

In 1980 the government introduced the Equal Opportunity Act, a special gender-equality law against sexual discrimination. This initiative reflected the appeal to legal solutions that characterized reforms in Canada and other countries dominated by liberal and conservative governments. Social Democrats, as well as the strong organized interests in the labour market, saw the new legislation as an attempt by the more conservative government to replace with gender issues the class issues that had dominated established corporatist decision-making circles. An equal-opportunity ombudsman (JämO), supported by the Equal Opportunity Commission (Jämställdhetsnämnden), was appointed to force employers to take active measures to comply with the Equal Opportunity Act.[4]

In 1982 the Equality Affairs Division was established to coordinate issues of gender equality within government. The division was small (five to six employees), and its status depended on that of the various ministries to which it has been attached, as well as of its director. From the start, it focused specifically on women and labour-market issues. The work of the division was supported by the Council on Equality Issues, an advisory body that is made up of representatives from women's organizations, political parties, and other organized interests,[5] as well as from the Working Group on Men's Roles (Arbetsgupp om Mansrollen). The issues for the latter group included those related to their roles as fathers, lovers, or divorced parents. Gender-equality units were more permanently established inside the ministries of the state administration.

In 1994 Prime Minister Ingvar Carlsson made gender equality one of the priorities of the new Social Democratic government, moving the Equality Affairs Division back to the Office of the Prime Minister under Deputy Prime Minister Mona Sahlin. However, the subsequent removal of Sahlin from public office and the retirement of Carlsson have both weakened the government's commitment to implement this priority.

Representing Women's Interests in the Policy Process: Policy Machinery in Canada

In the 1970s the men who dominated the federal government in Canada were faced with an unfamiliar challenge. They had neither the expertise inside the policy process nor the relations with women outside it who did to mount an effective response to the recommendations of the Royal Commission on the Status of Women or to the growing number of questions about the status of women that came from an increasingly enlightened and vigilant constituency of women (Findlay, 1987). New machinery and new appointments were a necessary first step.

A coordinator was appointed to the Privy Council Office in 1971 to oversee the Cabinet's response to the royal commission, and a senior minister was delegated to represent women's interests in Cabinet. The priority for government leaders was rather specific, reflecting messages that both the United Nations and the royal commission had sent to them about the serious under-representation of women in Parliament and in the federal public service. What they wanted were strategies that would respond to this situation. In 1971 the Public Service Commission established the Office of Equal Opportunity for Women. Complementary advisers on women's equal-opportunity employment were appointed to the Treasury Board Secretariat. Departments also acquired their own equal-opportunity coordinators. Between 1972 and 1975 policy advisers were appointed in departments that clearly had some responsibilities for policies related to women's equality, including those of Justice, Health and Welfare, Employment and Immigration, and the Secretary of State. The Department of Labour had established its Women's Bureau in 1954.[6] The government created the Canadian Advisory Council on the Status of Women in 1973 to advise the minister responsible for the status of women on a permanent basis and to inform the Canadian public about the key issues affecting women's status.

This machinery was intended to implement two major cabinet directives. In 1971 the Cabinet had issued a directive to deputy ministers to increase the participation of women in middle and upper echelons of the public service. Responsibility for the implementation of this directive was delegated first to the Public Service Commission and later to the Treasury Board. In 1975, Cabinet directed deputy ministers to develop mechanisms to integrate women's interests into all government activities. The Office of the Coordinator on the Status of Women was given the responsibility of monitoring and coordinating the implementation of this directive, and many departments established intradepartmental "integration" committees. In 1976 the Office of the Coordinator on the Status of Women was given departmental status. Subsequently much of its activity has focused on the preparation of Canada's official report to the United Nations on government commitments to promote women's equality since International Women's Year.

These initiatives constituted a model that still exists – in a more limited way – within the federal bureaucracy today. During the 1970s and 1980s this model was extended in various forms to most provincial and territorial governments through the creation of a number of official and unofficial interprovincial committees on status-of-women issues.

The effectiveness of the model has been limited by a number of factors, however. In the first place, the women who were appointed to implement the model had little or no power over the men who dominated the policy process. Status of Women Canada and departmental advisers on the status of women have from the beginning been faced with persistent resistance from the "gatekeepers" of the federal bureaucracy. These individuals have found numerous ways to resist the implementation of these directives from Cabinet. Status-of-women personnel have had neither the staff nor the authority needed to challenge senior managers and their defence of the sexual division of labour that has shaped the Canada's federal bureaucracy, or the unequal structure of representation that has privileged the interests of a ruling class of men in the policy process (Mahon, 1977). The Canadian Advisory Council on the Status of Women was equally powerless. Council members rarely saw the minister responsible for the status of women – they were sidelined in the policy process as "outsiders."

The effectiveness of the model was also limited by the government's failure to build into it any requirement for ongoing consultations between the advisers inside and feminists and/or the women at the community level about women's interests and the policies that could reflect them. The advisers who were hired were professional public servants – expected to "reflect" women's interests rather than engage with them to determine what they wanted. Feminists were actively discouraged from applying for most of the advisory positions created in the federal government (Morgan, 1987; Findlay, 1995). Government leaders had no interest in the kind of model that Australia had introduced, a model that put "femocrats" (i.e., community-based feminists) into state administrations to implement policies to promote women's equality. Nor were they interested in following the Swedish model and incorporating feminist "outsiders" into a more democratic form of representation.

A certain amount of collaboration between the advisers on the inside and representatives from the network of feminist organizations such as the National Action Committee on the Status of Women (NAC) did occur in the 1970s. NAC had been established in 1972 to pressure the federal government to implement the recommendation of the commission. But the advisers themselves were relatively powerless and clearly accountable to government priorities rather than to the interests of women. Internal meetings with "insiders" (departmental advisers) were increasingly substituted for consultations with the "outsiders" – or indeed, for a strategy that would have brought the "outsiders" inside to represent women's interests in the development and implementation of policies to promote women's equality. In any case, feminists outside tended to concentrate on elected officials, with whom they could use their lobbying skills and their political connections to pressure for reforms. In 1976 NAC was successful in persuading members of the federal caucuses to meet with its members on an annual basis. In the same year it persuaded federal officials to include legislation requiring equal pay for work of equal value in the new Canadian Human Rights Act. The Canadian Advisory Council on the Status of Women offered no alternative. Saddled with government appointees, these bodies had few members with the roots in the feminist community that they needed to represent women's issues effectively.

By the end of the 1970s the government had failed to implement the more substantive recommendations that the royal commission had made to increase the representation of women in the public service, to decriminalize abortion, to put a national day-care program into effect, and to amend the Indian Act to give Native women equal status with Native men. Government reforms seemed to be at a standstill (CACSW, 1979).

In the 1980s the effectiveness of the model was even more limited as the new Progressive Conservative government moved to reassert its commitment to the dominance of the increasingly well organized and powerful business class. Between 1984 and 1993 the government consistently cut back on the meagre commitments that the Liberal governments of the 1960s and 1970s had made to a more representative form of policy-making (Phillips, 1991).[7] In response to protests from feminists, it argued that women's interests could be more legitimately represented by the women who had been elected to Parliament and/or appointed to Cabinet rather than by representatives of community-based feminist groups such as NAC that had no real system of accountability to the women of Canada. It also questioned the right of these organizations to criticize government policy. Those who protested against such policy were negatively characterized as part of an "extra-Parliamentary opposition." By the mid-1980s the federal Conservative government refused to participate in NAC's annual lobby. Consultations with members of feminist groups continued, but they were more clearly organized and controlled by government officials and focused on government priorities rather than on women's demands.

Funding for feminist projects was also under attack. In 1986, responding to pressure from REAL Women (an anti-feminist group that lobbied government for a return to traditional values), the government also initiated a parliamentary review of the Women's Program, the main source of government funding to feminist groups since the early

1970s. It threatened to substantially reduce grants to NAC, feminist publications, and women's centres (the infrastructure of the movement) and to tighten critieria for funding. The Women's Program was instructed to exclude lesbian projects and those related to abortion reform. In other departments, grants were replaced by contractual "partnerships" between government departments and individual feminist groups to deliver their commitments on issues such as violence against women at the community level.[8]

In the 1990s the retreat from initiatives to promote women's equality has continued, in spite of the return to power of the Liberal Party in 1993. The portfolio for the status of women has been delegated to women with junior status in the Cabinet. In March 1995 the Canadian Advisory Council on the Status of Women was closed. On 1 April the same year the research program of the council and the funding program for feminist groups (the Women's Program) became part of the responsibilities of Status of Women Canada. The minister responsible for the status of women stressed the positive side of this "consolidation." She suggested, "The consolidation will create a single-window operation, enhancing communication and access to government: from local grassroots groups, through the regional staff of the Women's Program, to government policy-makers, and right back to the Cabinet table – and back" (Finestone, 1995: 2).

It is hard to see how such an amalgamation can increase women's access to the policy process. Neither the minister nor Status of Women Canada (or comparable groups at the provincial level, such as the Ontario Women's Directorate) has the authority to make its perspectives heard in the policy process. Nor can they draw on the support of organized feminists as they did in the 1970s. As a former coordinator of Status of Women Canada reflected, "There is not the same easy back and forth between the women's movement and the women who staff the different parts of the federal machinery that existed 10 years ago" (O'Neil, 1993: 22).[9] If there is still a place within state bureaucracies where women can have voice in the struggle for women's equality, it seems to be within the line departments and ministries that have been given the task of implementing government commitments. Advisory councils and the policy-coordinating units for status-of-women issues such as Status of Women Canada may still have some symbolic value for feminists inside and outside the state, but the success of government reforms today may well depend on the everyday work of the women who are responsible for putting government commitments into practice in the respective departments and ministries and the links that can be forged between them and women at the community level.

DEMOCRATIZING REPRESENTATION: POLICIES TO GIVE WOMEN A VOICE IN THE POLICY PROCESS

By the 1980s women in both Canada and Sweden were pressuring their governments to give them a voice in the policy process of state institutions. Seeing the limits of the initiatives that their respective governments had introduced since the 1970s, they argued that women must have a voice in the policy process. Governments in both Canada and Sweden responded by appointing commissions to investigate policies to meet the demands for more and better representation.

Sweden's Commission of Inquiry on Women's Representation

Anita Gradin, a cabinet minister in the Social Democratic government elected in Sweden in 1985, proposed the appointment of a commission of inquiry to investigate women's representation on public bodies and to recommend measures to improve it. Support for feminist values was apparent in the proposal for the commission and the appointments to it. Implicit in its establishment was the government's concern over the under-representation of women on commissions and boards of public bodies (SOU, 1987: 193–9). The investigation of women's representation marked a shift in the public discourse on gender equality towards a more open discussion about relations of power between women and men.

In their first report, *Is the Future Society Also Going to Be Designed Solely by Men?* (Ds A, 1986:4), the commissioners linked the question of women's under-representation to issues of power and democracy, arguing that equality between the sexes was far from achieved and that women as a group had far less influence than men. They talked about a male-dominated society where men's experiences and values were still the norm. They also claimed that women were systematically discriminated against. The language of the report was grounded in a woman's perspective rather than the gender-neutral viewpoint that had shaped public documents on equality in the 1970s and early 1980s (Bergqvist, 1994: 232; Eduards, 1991: 695).

In their final report, *Every Other Seat for a Woman* (*Varannan damernas*), the commissioners outlined the gender patterns in commissions of inquiry and lay boards of state administration in 1986. These institutions are of great significance for the political decision-making process in Sweden. Commissions prepare the documents for political decisions, and boards of state administration implement these decisions. These bodies are not apolitical or neutral. Their "organization and decisions are about politics, i.e. have significance for the distribution of values in society, of who gets what, when and how" (Rothstein, 1991: 8). In both commissions and lay boards, corporatist arrangements are common: representatives from organized interests are participants in their deliberations.

The commission's strategy to increase the representation of women on commissions and public boards included goals to be achieved in two stages over a three-year period. They proposed that the three-year project be divided into different stages. In the first, women's representation would have to increase to at least 30 per cent by 1992. The next stage called for women's representation to increase to 40 per cent by 1995, and the third to 50 per cent by 1998. The 1990 government proposition on gender equality established the same goals (Proposition, 1990/91).

The government supported the commission's recommendations, including its proposal that the Equality Affairs Division make a yearly report to Parliament on the distribution of women and men on public bodies. Such a report had been suggested by several of the groups involved as a way to make women's under-representation more visible.[10]

Women's representation has increased greatly since the Commission of Inquiry on Women's Representation tabled its final report in 1987. Reviews of the project to date show that the boards of public administration have reached the first goal of 30 per cent at the central level. In 1992 women accounted for 36 per cent of the members of these boards. By 1997 their participation had risen to 43 per cent.

Much of this progress reflects the role that members of the commission played in cooperation with female politicians in order to change institutionalized norms, thus illustrating the impact that "femocrats" can have in implementing changes that favour women's interests when they have allies at the top of the hierarchy (Levy and Edwards, 1990: 151). However, it also reflects a number of other factors that strengthened the commission's power during its investigation and encouraged those who administered the commissions and public boards to take steps to increase the representation of women in the corporatist system even before the commission made its final report. For example, using information that the commission gathered about how organizations nominated representatives to commissions of inquiry and boards of state administration, the government applied pressure on departments to take a more active role in implementing the recommendation to nominate both a woman and a man that had been introduced in 1982. This show of government support for the findings of the commission in turn strengthened the influence of the commissioners in their negotiations with the responsible groups. In their final report they wrote:

"In our interviews with those in power we got the same answer again and again to the question of how to improve women's representation: make us stand in the dunces' corner. Almost all of them testified to the opinion-making effect of our investigation. The risk of being pointed out as the villain of the piece contributes to raising consciousness and to applying existing rules" (SOU, 1987: 164–5).

The government also took steps to improve coordination between the ministries, giving the Equality Affairs Division a key role in this process. As well, the project mobilized a wide range of women's organizations and networks and involved unions, political parties, and workplaces in its implementation at the local and central levels. And lastly, media coverage of the commission's work made the way that nominations to corporatist boards worked more visible to the public.

What we learned from this process is that femocrats can collaborate with sympathetic politicians to produce a policy that works in women's interest. Women politicians from all parties, as well as the women representatives from the organized interests, were in complete agreement with the goal of making visible the gender dimension in corporatist arrangements that the Commission of Inquiry on Women's Representation had established. In the 1970s a similar strategy adopted by women in political parties and elected bodies had contributed to significant increases in the participation of women in political office. In the 1980s and 1990s many of these women were involved in alliances to find strategies in order to integrate women into all parts of the political decision-making process. This approach also shows that a unit such as the Equality Affairs Division can play an important role if the political context is favourable and the minister in charge is committed to women's equality.

But we also learned that men in decision-making positions in Sweden still resist the introduction of policies that they believe will shift the balance of power which has historically defined relationships between women and men and limited women's access to public life. Men feared that commitments to increase the proportion of women in the policy process would mean that the recruitment of men would almost stop and that many men would have had to leave their places earlier than they expected. Although the body of the commission's report showed no signs that the feminist values of the commissioners were co-opted by powerful interests in Swedish society, the strength of men's resistance is reflected in their actual recommendations. In spite of the fact that the commission's studies had shown that the legislated quota systems adopted by other Nordic countries were most effective in increasing representation, the commissioners chose a system that relied on recommended quotas and the cooperation of those who managed Sweden's commissions and public bodies to meet them.

In the 1990s, concern about the issue of representation increased. The election of a right-wing coalition to Parliament resulted in an actual drop in the representation of women from 38 to 33 per cent, indicating the very limited commitment that some of the more conservative parties in the coalition had to the election of women to Parliament. It also led women in Sweden to question their participation in these political parties as the most effective form of influencing the policy process. In 1991 several key women decided that they might have more success as "outsiders." Forming a network that crossed party lines, the Support Stockings, as they called themselves, mounted a strong attack on the undemocratic nature of Swedish party politics and appealed to the country's "passion for equality." They called on political parties to nominate more women for the next election. "The whole salary and half the power" was their slogan, conveying their demands for wage equality with men as well as equality in representative institutions. These "outsiders" threatened to form a women's party if the existing parties did not take women's interests seriously. Women (and men) from all parties supported their claims (Eduards, 1992: 86), although women politicians from the non-socialist parties were more negative than their social democratic counterparts about the idea of a women's party.

In 1993 the government responded to their campaign by shifting responsibility for gender equality from Birgit Friggebo, minister of immigration and gender equality, to Bengt Westerberg, leader of the Liberal Party, deputy prime minister, and minister of social affairs and a strong proponent of gender equality and a universal welfare state. Most of the parties promised to nominate as many women as men on the party lists. Using the Support Stockings' threat to form a women's party, women inside the party system were able to put gender equality on the political agenda. In the 1994 elections women won 41 per cent of the seats in Parliament, and the new Social Democratic government appointed equal numbers of women and men to its cabinet.

Canada's Royal Commission on Equality in Employment

By the early 1980s, feminists in Canada were endorsing a demand for employment equity which they hoped would overcome the resistance that had met government initiatives to bring women into decision-making positions in state institutions as well as in the private sector. The 1971 directive to increase the participation of women in upper-echelon positions had suggested a willingness on the part of the governing party to do just this, but the very vague nature of the directive and the sexism of the men who dominated senior management positions in federal government departments had seriously limited results. Attempts to bolster the equal employment opportunity program in the late 1970s and early 1980s failed, prompting the government to introduce an affirmative-action program for women, Native people, and those with disabilities in the public service in 1983.

In 1983 the Liberal government took a further step with the appointment of the Royal Commission on Equality in Employment to investigate "the opportunities for employment of women, Native people, disabled persons and visible minorities in certain crown corporations and corporations wholly owned by the Government of Canada" (Canada, 1984: ii). This was not the first investigation that the federal government had initiated to define its responsibilities as the major employer of women in Canada. In the late 1960s, pressured by those at home (e.g., the 1962 Commission on Government Organization) and abroad (e.g., the United Nations' Status of Women Commission and the International Labour Organization) to align its employment practices with its apparent commitment to democratic and representative institutions, the federal government ordered the Public Service Commission to investigate the persistent under-representation of women in the public service (Archibald, 1970). The report from this investigation, "Sex and the Public Service," provided the basis for the commission's report to the Royal Commission on the Status of Women as well as for the government's 1971 directive.

The appointment of the Royal Commission on Equality in Employment reflected a different set of factors, however. Governments at all levels in Canada were facing serious pressures from a strong business lobby, which wanted more flexible hiring policies to support competition in the global economy and was fundamentally opposed to more representative and democratic forms of policy-making, and from the new equality-seeking groups, who articulated demands for more-equal employment opportunities. The conflicts inherent in liberal democracy between the principle of equality (as upheld by the equality-seeking groups) and commitments to a free market (as supported by organized business interests) were increasing.

The task of the commission was to establish a new consensus about ways to promote equal employment opportunities – one that would appeal to employers as well as members of the equality-seeking groups. Neither the passive equal-opportunities programs that the federal government had initiated in the 1970s nor the affirmative-action policies introduced in the early 1980s were considered suitable. Equal-opportunity programs were too weak for the equality-seeking groups; affirmative-action policies were too threatening to employers.

The commissioner (Judge Rosalie Abella) won the support of legal feminists with a report that recommended legislated employment equity. "All federally regulated employers should be required by legislation to implement employment equity" (Canada, 1984: 255). But her proposals for legislated employment equity was tempered by recommendations that gave employers the right to implement the legislation in a way that fit with their human-resources needs and their strategic operations. As the commissioner argued, the opening of employment opportunities for the designated groups would require a "special blend of what is necessary, what is fair and what is workable" (Canada, 1984: 254).

In 1986 the federal government introduced its Employment Equity Act, legislation that was largely based on the commission's recommendations. It stipulated that all federally regulated employers and crown corporation with a hundred or more employees must design a program to implement employment equity and submit annual reports on their progress to the Canadian Human Rights Commission. Failure to comply could result in a fine of $50,000, and evidence of discrimination in a complaint under the Canadian Human Rights Act. At the same time, the government introduced the Federal Contractors Program to extend the commitment to employees of companies who had contracts of $200,000 or more with the government. In 1985 it introduced its Employment Equity Policy for designated groups in the public service, an expanded version of its affirmative-action program that would also cover visible minorities.

By 1992, however, there was a strong consensus emerging that the act was essential unenforceable. In that year the Canadian Human Rights Commission appeared before the special parliamentary committee that reported on the operation of the act to argue that the act was too vague and that the commission lacked the mandate to monitor its implementation effectively. According to one critic, "The changes achieved by the Act have been small and there is a problem relating to the identification of what is a change – a change in job title does not necessarily denote a an increase in pay and/or promotion aspects ... Gender segregation has declined but at a slow rate and then only at the upper end of the occupation distribution" (O'Connor, 1998: 95, 96). While representation in the managerial-administrative and professional groups had increased, women were still located at the bottom of these categories: "numerical integration may mask significant intra-occupational segregation" (O'Connor, 1998: 97). A similar pattern could be seen in the implementation of employment equity in the city of Toronto (Findlay, 1993). Hopes were higher for the implementation of the employment-equity legislation introduced by Ontario's New Democratic government in 1993. But the legislation was abolished by the Conservative government in October 1995.

The federal Parliament passed a new Employment Equity Act (Bill C64) in October 1995. This legislation extends coverage to all employees in the federal public service. But more important, it strengthens the powers of the Canadian Human Rights Commission. Under it the commission is empowered to conduct audits of all public and private employers covered by the legislation in order to verify compliance and to ensure final enforcement when needed in both the private and the public sectors. Unfortunately, the new authority accorded to the commission has not been matched by an increase in the resources required to exercise it fully. Implementation in the private sector continues to be a problem.

CONCLUDING REMARKS

Over the last three decades, governments in both Sweden and Canada have introduced initiatives to promote women's equality. These have included commissions of inquiry, machinery to represent women's interests in the policy process in state administrations, and policies to give women themselves a voice in the policy process. Today women in Sweden have a stronger and more powerful voice in policy-making. They are better represented in Parliament and in the Cabinet of the governing party, and have won appointments to the powerful boards and commissions that develop official policy. They have not yet achieved full equality with men, however. In Canada the evidence is not so positive. The representation of women in the policy process has increased to some extent, but for the most part these changes reflect the placement of women in temporary and entry-level positions rather than in positions that would give them power.

Explanations for Sweden's relative success vary. Some argue that its "passion for equality" and the construction of the welfare state have been of more importance than the "gender equality machinery." Helga Hernes sees the success of Swedish commitments to increase the representation of women in public life as a reflection of the willingness of Nordic social democracies to support a "women-friendly" state that "would enable women to have a natural relationship to their children, their work, and public life" (Hernes, 1987: 15). Presumably she would argue that Canada's more limited responses to feminist demands for women's equality reflect the much narrower commitment to democratic (i.e., gender) representation that is embedded in Canada's political processes and state institutions.

However, this is not the whole story. Regardless of the fact that Sweden has demonstrated a greater commitment to women's equality than Canada, resistance to the introduction of initiatives that threatened the traditional balance of power between women and men in public life continues. The selection of two of the three leading members of the Support Stockings who had criticized Sweden's system of representation was soundly condemned. Given this resistance, women's organizing has played and continues to play a necessary and central role in pressuring governments to introduce policies to promote women's equality in both Sweden and Canada since the 1960s.

The ways that women in Sweden and Canada have organized themselves have differed, however. In Sweden in the 1970s and 1980s, they worked as "insiders" in a system that was, as Hernes argued, "women-friendly." With the commitment to equality that had characterized Swedish politics for decades and the power that they could exert on the political process as members of the ruling Social Democratic Party and of Parliament, women in Sweden were successful in putting the issue of women's equality on the political agenda. By the 1990s, however, they were organizing themselves as "outsiders." A more conservative perspective dominated Sweden's political process, and the representation of women in Parliament actually decreased. Arguing that they must now rely on each other to put forward women's claims, rather than on the conservative men who dominated the political system, Swedish women organized the Support Stockings and forced political parties to find ways to increase the representation of women in Parliament in the next election.

In Canada, women have always worked as "outsiders" in the political process. In the 1960s the leaders of women's national voluntary organizations converged to pressure the federal government to appoint the Royal Commission on the Status of Women. In the following decade, women organized themselves as feminists to lobby federal and provincial governments to implement the commission's recommendations. Since then, the number of feminist organizations has expanded, as have their demands. These organizations are still active in the ongoing struggle for government policies to promote women's equality. Today, however, their voices have little impact on the conservative governments, which have insulated themselves against the "special-interest groups," including organized feminists.

As in Sweden, it is time for feminists in Canada to reassess the strategies that they have relied on since the 1960s. The development of alternative strategies has, however, been stymied by conflicts between white women and women of colour within feminist organizations. Since the mid-1980s women of colour have consistently challenged the white women who historically dominated feminist organizations to give up their privileges and develop a more inclusive and democratic form of politics (Working Group on Sexual Violence, 1985; Findlay, 1995). Struggles about identity and representation still tend to mark feminist organizations in the 1990s, dividing women from each other and diverting feminists from the much needed dialogue about political strategies.

What we have learned from our exploration of Swedish and Canadian initiatives to promote women's equality, then, is the strength of the resistance to the integration of women's interests that is embedded in our structures of representation and the practices of the men who still dominate them. Regardless of the fact that Sweden – with its passion for equality and its tradition of social democratic governments – has supported a greater degree of commitment to equality than have Canadian governments, neither system has accorded women equal power in public life. Women's organizing has played a necessary and central role in the campaign for women's equality in both Canada and Sweden. The relative and continuing success of the Swedish campaigns, however, ultimately reflects the degree to which women in that country have broken with political tradition and countered the gradual weakening of political commitments to equality that has accompanied the era of global competition by organizing a more general appeal to the passion for equality that the Swedish people continue to embrace.

NOTES

1 In this chapter we both draw quite extensively on our respective theses: Findlay (1995) and Bergqvist (1994).

2 Even though the SSKF did not share the view of those who argued for new sex roles, it defended women's freedom of choice. It spoke for the interests of both the homemakers and the working mothers (Karlsson, 1990: 86ff).

3 "Sex Roles in Transition" was the title of a report to the United Nations women conference in Mexico City in 1975, and "Roller i omvandling" the title of the final report by the Commission for Gender Equality (SOU, 1976).

4 The Equal Opportunity Act has been criticized for being ineffective. In mid-1994 it was strengthened, and an equality expert was nominated for each of the twenty-four counties in Sweden.

5 In 1995 twenty-seven of the thirty-one members were women. Among the organizations represented were all six parties in Parliament as well as the Christian Democrats, women's separate party organizations in the labour market, and various women's groups.

6 Earlier pressures from women's organizations had forced the government to establish the Women's Bureau in the Department of Labour in 1954 to address the "special problems facing women workers."

7 In the televised leaders' debate in 1988, Brian Mulroney argued that he did not need to consult with the Canadian Day Care Coalition because he had a woman in his cabinet, Barbara McDougall.

8 In 1991 the national office of Canada's YWCA signed a contract with the minister for Health Canada for a $1.2 million project, Community Action on Violence against Women. This project called for the development of partnerships with most sectors in the community, including business, social work, and various identity groups. The requirement for partnerships almost paralysed the project and diverted most of its resources from community action to meetings of these sector representatives (Findlay, 1995).

9 Maureen O'Neil was coordinator of the status of women at Status of Women Canada in 1978–85.

10 An evaluation of projects has been undertaken by Eduards and Åström (1993).

REFERENCES

Archibald, Kathleen. (1970). *Sex and the Public Service*. Ottawa: Queen's Printer for Canada.

Arscott, Jane. (1994). *Women's Representation in the Mirror of Public Policy*. Paper presented at the meeting of the Colloquium on Women and Political Representation of Women in Canada, Ottawa, September 1994.

Ashforth, Anthony. (1990). Reckoning schemes of legitimation: On commissions of inquiry as power/knowledge forms. *Journal of Historical Sociology*, 3 (1): 1–29.

Bäck, Mats, and Möller, Tommy. (1994). *Partier och organisationer*. Stockholm: Allmänna förlaget.

Baude, Annika (ed.). (1992). *Visionen om jämställdhet*. Stockholm: SNS Förlag.

Begin, Monique. (1992). The Royal Commission on the Status of Women: Twenty years later. In Constance Backhouse and David H. Flaherty (eds.), *Challenging Times: The Women's Movement in Canada and the United States*. Montreal and Kingston: McGill-Queen's University Press.

Bergqvist, Christina. (1990). Myten om den universella välfärdsstaten. In *Statsvetenskaplig Tidskrift*, 3: 223–33.

– (1991). Corporatism and gender equality: A comparative study of two Swedish labour market organisations. In *European Journal of Political Research* 20: 107–25.
– (1994). *Mäns makt och kvinnors intressen*. Stockholm: Almqvist and Wiksell International.
– (1995). The declining corporatist state and the political gender dimension. In Lauri Karvonen and Per Selle (eds.), *Women in Nordic Politics: Closing the Gap*. Aldershot: Dartmouth.
Birgersson, Bengt Owe, and Jörgen Westerståhl. (1992). *Den svenska folkstyrelsen*. Stockholm: Allmänna förlaget.
Canada (1970). Royal Commission on the Status of Women. *Report*. Ottawa: Information Canada.
– (1983). Status of Women Canada. *Toward Equality for Women*. Ottawa: Minister of Supply and Services.
– (1984). Royal Commission on Equality in Employment. *Equality in Employment*. Ottawa: Minister of Supply and Services.
– (1987). House of Commons. Standing Committee on Secretary of State. *Fairness in Funding: A report on the Women's Program*. 33rd Parliament, 2d Session, 1986–87.
Canadian Advisory Council on the Status of Women. (1979). *Women in the Public Service: Barriers to Equal Opportunity*. Ottawa.
Dahlerup, Drude (ed.). (1986). *The New Women's Movement: Feminism and Political Power in Europe and the USA*. London: Sage.
– (1988). From a small to a large minority: Women in Scandinavian politics. *Scandinavian Political Studies* 4: 275–98.
Ds A. (1986). Ska även morgondagens samhälle formas enbart av män?: Report from the Commission on Women's Representation. Stockholm: Ministry of Labour.
Eduards, Maud L. (1991). Toward a third way: Women's politics and welfare policies in Sweden. *Social Research* 58 (3): 677–705.
– (1992). Against the rules of the game: On the importance of women's collective actions. In M. Eduards et al. (eds.), *Rethinking Change: Current Swedish Feminist Research*. Stockholm: HSFR.
– and Gertrud Åström. (1993). *Många kände sig manade, men få blev kallade – en granskning av arbetet för ökad kvinnorepresentation*. Stockholm: Socialdepartementet.
Findlay, Sue. (1987). Facing the state: The politics of the women's movement reconsidered. In Meg Luxton and Heather Jon Maroney (eds.), *Feminism and Political Economy*. Toronto: Methuen.
– (1993). Democratizing the local state: Issues for feminist practice and the representation of women. In Gregory Albo, David Langille, and Leo

Panitch (eds.), *A Different Kind of State: Popular Power and Democratic Administration.* Toronto: Oxford University Press.

– (1995). Democracy and the politics of representation: Feminist struggles with the Canadian state, 1960–1990. PhD. diss., University of Toronto.

Finestone, Sheila. (1995). In *Perspectives*, 8 (1): 2.

Graubard, Stephen R. (ed.). (1986). *Norden: The Passion for Equality.* Oslo: Norwegian University Press.

Haavio-Mannila, Elina, et al. (1983). *Det uferdige demokratiet: Kvinner i nordisk politikk.* Oslo: Nordisk Ministerråd.

Hernes, Helga M. (1987). *Welfare State and Woman Power: Essays in State Feminism.* Oslo: Norwegian University Press.

Karlsson, Gunnel. (1990). *Manssamhället till behag?* Stockholm: Tiden.

– (1996). *Från broderskap till systerkap: Det socialdemokratiska kvinnoförbundets kamp för inflytande och makt i SAP.* Lund: Arkiv.

Kvinnans jämlikhet. (1964). Stockholm: Tiden.

Levi, Margaret, and Meredith Edwards. (1990). The dilemmas of femocratic reform. In M. Katzenstein and H. Skjeie (eds.), *Going Public: National Histories of Women's Enfranchisement and Women's Participation within State Institutions.* Oslo: Institute for Social Research.

Lovenduski, Joni, and Pippa Norris (eds.). (1993). *Gender and Party Politics.* London: Sage.

Mahon, Rianne. (1977). Canadian public policy: The unequal structure of representation. In Leo Panitch (ed.), *The Canadian State.* Toronto: University of Toronto Press.

Moberg, Eva. (1962). Kvinnans villkorliga frigivning. In *Kvinnor och människor.* Stockholm: Bonniers.

Morgan, Nicole. (1987). *The Equality Game.* Ottawa: Canadian Advisory Council on the Status of Women.

Norris, Pippa. (1985). Women's legislative participation in western Europe. *West European Politics* 4: 90–101.

– (1993). Conclusions: Comparing legislative recruitment. In J. Lovenduski and P. Norris (ed.), *Gender and Party Politics.* London: Sage.

O'Connor, Julie S. (1998). Employment equity strategies and their representation in the political process in Canada, 1970–1994. In M. Tremblay and Caroline Andrew (eds.), *Women and Political Representation in Canada.* Ottawa: University of Ottawa Press.

O'Neil, Maureen. (1993). Ensuring gender equality. Paper presented on behalf of the North-South Institute.

Orloff, Ann Shola. (1993). Gender and the social rights of citizenship: The comparative analysis of gender relations and welfare states. *American Sociological Review* 58.

Oskarson, Maria, and Lena Wängnerud. (1995). *Kvinnor som väljare och valda*. Lund: Studentlitteratur.
Ostrom, Elinor. (1986). A method of institutional analysis. In F.X. Kaufmann, G. Majone, and E. Ostrom, *Guidance, Control, and Evaluation in the Public Sector*. Berlin/New York: de Gruyter.
Petersson, Olof. (1989). *Maktens nätverk*. Stockholm: Carlsson Bokförlag.
Phillips, Anne. (1991). *Engendering Democracy*. Cambridge: Polity Press.
Phillips, Susan. (1991). How Ottawa blends: Shifting government relationships with interest groups. In Frances Abele (ed.), *How Ottawa Spends: The Politics of Fragmentation*. Ottawa: Carleton University Press.
Proposition. (1990/91). Om en ny jämställdhetslag, m.m. (1990/91: 113).
Raaum, Nina Cecilie. (1995). The political representation of women: A bird's eye view. In L. Karvonen and P. Selle (eds.), *Women in Nordic Politics*. Aldershot: Dartmouth.
Rothstein, Bo. (1991). *Politik som organisation: Förvaltningspolitikens grundproblem*. Stockholm: SNS.
Sainsbury, Diane. (1993). The politics of increased women's representation: The Swedish case. In J. Lovenduski and P. Norris (eds.), *Gender and Party Politics*. London: Sage.
– (ed.). (1994). *Gendering Welfare States*. London: Sage Publications.
Scott, Katherine. (1996). The dilemma of liberal citizenship: Women and social assistance reform in the 1990s. *Studies in Political Economy* 50: 7–36.
Skjeie, Hege. (1992). *Den politiske betydningen av kjønn: En studie av norsk topp-politikk*. Oslo: Institutt for samfunnsforskning.
SOU. (1975). *Målet är jämställdhet*. 1975: 58. Stockholm.
– (1987). *Varannan damernas*. 1987: 19. Stockholm.
– (1990). *Demokrati och makt i Sverige*. 1990: 40. Stockholm.
Statistics Sweden. Allmänna valen (The general elections).
Ursel, Jane. (1992). *Private Lives, Public Policy: One Hundred Years of State Intervention*. Toronto: Women's Press.
Women and Men in the European Union: A Statistical Portrait. (1995.) Luxembourg: Office for Official Publications of the European Communities.
Working Group on Sexual Violence. (1985). *Feminist Manifesto*. Vancouver: Women's Research Centre.

Unions and Women's Organizing in Canada and Sweden[1]

LINDA BRISKIN

ABSTRACT

This chapter explores women's organizing in Swedish and Canadian unions. Part one examines the dramatic differences in union density. It then considers the interplay between collective bargaining and legislation in the attainment of wage equality, highlighting centralized bargaining, bargaining strength, adversarial-versus-corporatist bargaining, and class-versus-gender discourses. Part two looks at four areas of organizational and strategic interventions: representation, ways of working, separate organizing, and alliances and coalitions. First, the distinction between sex-proportional representation and representation of organized interests provides a basis for comparison. Secondly, despite tremendous differences, evidence suggests that "women's ways of working" in both countries are more focused on local organizing, on process, and on participation. Thirdly, separate organizing has been a key strategy of Canadian union women. Their Swedish counterparts have been reluctant to organize separately, an ambivalence reinforced by resistance from the unions. Finally, in Canada there has been an emphasis on the building of alliances and coalitions to bring women together from unions, parties, and community-based groups. In Swedish unions, women's mobilizing across blue- and white-collar lines and unions has some precedents. However, it is considerably less institutionalized than in Canada and comes up against opposition. The current crisis in Swedish unions is reconfiguring the practices around women's organizing.

In the 1990s the union movements in Canada and Sweden are facing serious and similar challenges. High unemployment, changes in welfare-state regimes, and employer-initiated changes in collective bargaining and work organization are reshaping labour markets, unions, and union women's organizing. These challenges are linked to and compounded by processes of globalization through the European Union (EU) and the North American Free Trade Agreement (NAFTA), which are weakening national states.

To survive the crisis of economic and political restructuring, unions in both countries are trying to increase rank-and-file participation in and commitment to unions. As part of this process of democratization, the unions are attempting to expand the involvement of their women members. In fact, a developing discourse increasingly sees women's contribution to the unions as critical to their survival (see Mahon, 1996: 546; Briskin, 1994; Jenson and Mahon, 1993; Briskin and McDermott, 1993).

In Canada this focus on women has been both a cause and an effect of a strong movement among union women which has enjoyed considerable success in transforming the structures, practices, ideologies, and policies of the unions. These successes, however, have not translated into major collective bargaining gains. The Swedish unions, on the other hand, have been known for their commitment to social democracy and have had the political and economic strength to pursue full employment; a universal and comprehensive welfare state, which has eased tensions between waged and unwaged work; and wage solidarity, which, for blue-collar women, has significantly reduced the wage gap. What has been less visible has been women's organizing in the unions. In the current context, Swedish women are actively resisting attacks on the public sector that affect women disproportionately. Pia Laskar (I, 1993)[2] characterized this period as a "third wave" of women's organizing, evidenced by changes in women's consciousness and the emergence of new organizing strategies (Nickell, I, 1994; Acker, 1992; Eduards, 1991 and 1992).[3]

This chapter explores women's organizing in the unions, focusing on strategies that women have used to change union structures and practices, organize themselves as a constituency, and/or affect union or social policy. Part one opens with a consideration of union density and representation, and then examines the interplay between collective bargaining and legislation in the attainment of equality goals, using the example of organizing around wage inequities. This discussion affirms the degree to which context shapes organizing strategies. Part two explores four areas of organizational and strategic interventions: representation, ways of working, separate organizing, and alliances and coalitions.

Before I turn to the unions, the project of comparison merits some comment. Inevitably, especially in a work of this short length, it is necessary to compare at a level of generality that flattens out complexity and makes invisible not only the subtle texture of union realities but also the multiplicity of competing views and practices in each country. At the same time general comparisons can reveal patterns – in this case, about women's organizing – which might not be visible in the detail.

Unlike many in this volume, this chapter has not been co-authored with a Swedish researcher. As a result, and despite extensive research undertaken in Sweden between 1992 and 1995, there is an inevitable privileging of my Canadian perspective and point of view.[4] For example, separate organizing has been a critical strategy of union women in the Canadian, but not in the Swedish, context. The way it is positioned in the text implies that it is an "absence" in Sweden and needs to be explained. However, if the chapter were written from a Swedish perspective, a discussion of separate organizing would have been fairly marginal, and its absence would not necessarily require any explanation.[5]

To complicate matters, my identity as a white professional living in a urban area in central Canada is not unproblematic; further, given tremendous regional diversities, the entity "Canada" exists only at a high level of abstraction. Finally, both Canada and Sweden are in tremendous flux. It is difficult in text to capture the sense of fluidity and change and to underscore effectively that the snapshot which this chapter provides holds history unrealistically stable.

PART ONE

Union Density and Representation

Union density patterns and access to union representation differ dramatically in Canada and Sweden. The union density of Swedish workers is the highest in the world – about 85 per cent, compared to 34 per cent in Canada. The latest available Canadian figures show that, in 1992, 38.2 per cent of men and 31.2 per cent of women were unionized.[6] Women made up 41 per cent of union membership. In Sweden in 1994, 87.1 per cent of women were unionized, compared to 84.2 per cent of men (Mahon, 1995: 10). The high density in Sweden is in part a result of a different kind of union structure. Almost all workers, regardless of their workplace or its size, have the right to be represented by a union. This right does not depend on an adversarial struggle to certify workplaces as it does in Canada. Further, since it is through union membership that many social-security, insurance, and unemployment benefits are most easily accessed (the Ghent *systemet*), the vast majority of Swedish workers choose to belong to a union.[7] Despite the accessibility of union membership, however, Swedish unions have been experiencing a decline in membership, especially among younger male workers. In an interesting parallel with Canada, where women accounted for 79 per cent of the total growth in union membership between 1983 and 1992 (Statistics Canada, 1995), the organization of blue-collar women has been critical to the maintenance of density levels in the period 1975–94 (Kjelberg; reported in Mahon, 1996: 576–7).

Although Canadian workers have the formal right to be in a union, organizing one is a difficult, lengthy, and often unsuccessful undertaking. Employers have various legal means to interfere with union organizing. Furthermore, the entrenchment of right-wing governments with intensely anti-labour agendas has increased the ability of employers to prevent unionization (Panitch and Swartz, 1988). Should an organizing drive be successful, employers often resist the successful negotiation of a first contract, without which union certification is not possible.

Organizing the unorganized, then, is a major problem for Canadian unions, and organizing women who work in difficult-to-organize sectors and locations (small workplaces, part-time work, and the retail and financial sectors) poses a special challenge, one not always taken up seriously by Canadian unions.[8] In the new context of economic restructuring and direct attacks on unions, they have become more active in trying to organize women to strengthen their membership base. Concomitantly, women workers have been more concerned to gain the protection of union status; they have initiated and led some very militant strikes for first contracts. No doubt, the difficulty in accessing union status in Canada, and the relative ease in Sweden, has had a differential impact on worker commitment and attitudes towards unions.

Collective Bargaining, Legislation, and Wage Inequality

Not surprisingly, variations in union density and access to representation reflect different degrees of union strength and a different relation among the state, employers, and unions. In Canadian unions the restricted scope of collective bargaining, its decentralized structures, and its adversarial nature reflect and reproduce the weakness of the union movement; they also help to explain union demands for state intervention in the labour market. The accord between unions and employers generally restricts the areas about which unions negotiate to wages, benefits, and job-related issues such as seniority. The adversarial nature of collective bargaining, combined with fragmented structures that restrict the impact on the labour market of significant gains in one workplace (Whitehorse, 1992: 80), limit the possibilities for widespread negotiation of meaningful equality measures. Pressed by the demands of an organized movement of union women, unions in Canada have been active advocates for legislation about equality – pay equity, employment equity, and protection against sexual and racial harassment.

Pradeep Kumar (1993: 221) found that most collective bargaining gains for women in Canada have been made in areas where legislative standards have been mandated. Such gains in Canada, then, may well depend upon a multi-pronged strategy that emphasizes the links between legislation and bargaining, and simultaneously builds alliances with those fighting for similar issues in the women's movement outside the unions and in other progressive movements. The critical location of legislation in the Canadian union context may help to explain the strategic significance of and commitment to strategies of coalitions and alliances, a point that I expand upon below.

Sweden provides an interesting contrast. There the strength of the unions, a long tradition of centralized bargaining structures through labour centrals, corporatist rather than adversarial bargaining, and a considerably wider scope for negotiations (to include such issues as workplace democracy) have meant, in general, a focus on collective bargaining rather than on legislation. Indeed, the union centrals, especially LO (Landsorganisationen i Sverige; with about 3 million members and twenty-four unions), have argued for self-regulation and have often tried to prevent direct state intervention in the labour market. Stemming from the 1938 Saltsjöbaden agreement, Swedish corporatism has emphasized that "labour market parties would themselves settle their differences through negotiation and that the state would not intervene through legislation" (Acker, 1992: 8). The unions have strongly resisted the development of equality (*jämställdhet*) legislation, arguing that women's concerns could be addressed most effectively through bargaining. This approach has indisputably led to some significant successes.

To the extent, then, that the Swedish unions have taken up workplace-equality issues such as wages, hiring, and promotion, it has been largely through negotiations.[9] Extensive social policy, especially on family issues, has also provided a boundary demarcating the issues that unions address. Those benefits provided by the welfare state have not entered into the process of collective bargaining. In Canada, given the weaker government commitment to the welfare state and the difficulties and limits of adversarial and fragmented bargaining, unions have been forced to seek legislative intervention more aggressively in order to pursue similar gains.

Among Swedish scholars and activists, explanations for the unions' resistance to equality legislation vary. Although the unions have emphasized the power struggle with the state and employers, part of their reluctance reflects the positioning of equality legislation in Sweden and the recognition of the need for collective solutions. Lena Sveneaus, equality ombudsman for the government, pointed out that, in addition to the lack of political will in Sweden, there is no human-rights legislation (the rules in the Constitution are very general and are not working tools for lawyers) and no tradition of individuals bringing discrimination cases to the courts. The equality legislation is confined to the labour courts (discrimination against women is seen as a labour-market, rather than a general social problem), and the provisions are not well developed. After 1986 most cases brought to the labour courts were lost. All these factors help to explain the historic reluctance of unions and individuals to use the legislation, and the choice to seek collective solutions through workplace negotiations (I, 1994).

Swedish feminists have often identified the power struggle between women and men as significant in understanding union reluctance. For example, Kristina Persson, previously with TCO (Tjänstemännens Centralorganisation; about 1 million members and twenty unions, only in the white-collar sector) and currently governor of Jämtland, argued: "The rejection of the legislation by the trade unions has been an effective means of keeping women out and maintaining status quo" (I, 1994). This line of argumentation is supported by the fact that LO broke the Saltsjöbaden agreement around industrial democracy. Active debates and initiatives about workplace democracy culminated in the Co-Determination Law (MBL) of 1977, which legislated active involvement by workers in changes to workplace organization. The fact that the same willingness was not extended to the equality legislation reflects the way that "class" took priority over "gender" (Mahon, 1996: 556).[10]

Although generalizations are difficult to make, the balance between collective bargaining and legislation in each country is clearly different. To the extent that unions have collective bargaining strength (through size and centralization of bargaining), they will be less interested in legislative initiatives. So in Sweden, LO, by far the largest and strongest of the union centrals, has been considerably more resistant to legislative initiatives than TCO. The unravelling of corporatist structures and centralized bargaining over the last decades as a result of pressures from employer organizations is weakening the bargaining strength of the unions; concomitantly, there has been more emphasis on legislative intervention. In fact, Sture Nordh, past president of Sveriges Kommunaltjänstemannaförbund (SKTF/TCO) and currently under-secretary of labour in the Social Democratic government, pointed out that, given the new degree of employer resistance, it is no longer possible to use collective bargaining without legislation to deal with equality. His union is "no longer negative to legislation" especially as it tries to negotiate pay equity (Nordh, I, 1993). Kristina Persson made a similar point: "Resistance of unions to legislation is weaker now because the movement is weaker (I, 1994)."

These complex differences in the two countries are visible in union strategies around gendered wage inequality. These struggles also highlight the relative positioning of gender and class debates not only in the two countries but also in different union sectors inside each country.

In Canada, on average, women workers make approximately 65 per cent of what men earn, although the gap is narrower for unionized women (White, 1993: 65). To the extent that the wage gap between women and men has been addressed seriously in Canada, it has been driven primarily by a gender, rather than a class, analysis and by a legislative, rather than a bargaining, strategy. Some individual Canadian unions, more often in the industrial sector, have attempted to flatten the wage hierarchy (similar to solidaristic wage bargaining in Sweden), but this effort has had a limited impact because of occupational and bargaining segregation (Warskett, 1996: 615). Most unions have supported the introduction of and used provincial pay-equity legislation as a vehicle to improve women's wages.[11]

In coalition with community-based feminist organizations, union women lobbied successfully for such legislation, which is now established in most provinces. The Ontario Pay Equity Act, which came into force in January 1988, broke new ground in its application to both private- and public-sector workers, in its rejection of an individual complaints-based procedure in favour of mandated standards and procedures, and in its provision of a mechanism – through the Pay Equity Commission – for resolving disputes which does not rely on the bargaining strength of the parties (Fudge and McDermott, 1991: 8).

Ironically, at a time in Canada when feminist unionists are arguing for more centralized bargaining (broader-based and sectoral bargaining) as a means of addressing the weakness of the collective bargaining system and the wage gap (Fudge, 1993),[12] centralized bargaining and bargaining cartels are breaking down in Sweden, and there is a growing interest in legislative intervention.

In Sweden, LO and TCO provide very different contexts for organizing around wage inequality and underscore the significance of centralization and bargaining strength. Based on a strong class discourse and from a position of bargaining strength, LO has been instrumental in narrowing the wage gap between the highest and the lowest paid (most of whom were women) through solidaristic wage bargaining. So in 1992 the average wage for a blue-collar woman was 81 per cent of the male wage. Yet, as Eivor Englund (I, 1993), among many others, pointed out, "A class-driven policy of wage solidarity in LO did help women, but its motivation was to make men's wages more secure, i.e. to reduce the competition of the bottom" (see also Ruggie, 1987; Whitehorse, 1992).

In recent years, Svenska Kommunalarbetareförbundet (municipal workers' union), the largest LO union, which organizes primarily blue-collar public-sector women, has initiated, under the leadership of Lillemor Arvidsson, the first woman to lead an LO union, some radical gender-specific strategies on the wage front, in particular the *kvinnopotter.* Instead of reliance on solidaristic strategies, *kvinnopotter* called for supplements to women's wages (Higgins, 1996: 189).[13]

TCO and its member unions have had a stronger platform on equality issues, but with its decentralized structure and greater range of occupational groups, it has had no official policy to narrow the gap and been much less successful in affecting the wage rates of its predominantly female membership.[14]

As a result of employer strategies, the wage gap is widening (Mahon, 1996: 564; Acker, 1991: 249), inspiring more organizing by women for pay equity and more demands for legislative intervention. Currently, women across the union centrals and across the "collar" (blue and white) divide are organizing around job evaluation and pay equity, neither of which is new to Sweden, but widespread interventions in the past have not focused on gender.[15] Surveys suggest extensive support for women's wage demands.[16]

Anita Nyberg (I, 1994) observed that a focus on "pay equity" in Sweden will encourage equalizing wages inside class rankings and inside professions, but will not be effective in narrowing the wage gap across classes. This interpretation implies that pay equity will undermine, rather than complement, solidaristic wage strategies.[17] In Canada the issue of raced and classed wage differences has been raised, although rarely with significant success. In the absence of other solidaristic wage strategies, negotiated pay equity mandated by legislation has led to hefty increases for women workers in some Canadian jurisdictions.[18]

PART TWO

Dominant discourses about class/gender and equality/difference in each country provide a frame within which to understand organizational and strategic interventions by union women around representation, ways of working, separate organizing, and alliances and coalitions. In Sweden an emphasis on common interests between women and men is often expressed in gender-neutral policies which focus, not on women's issues, women's rights, or discrimination against women, but on the family and the labour market. In the unions this focus on family and labour-market issues has not encouraged gender consciousness or facilitated organizing a constituency of women.

In Canada, gender-neutral approaches have usually worked against the specificities of women's concerns, hidden the practices that privilege men, and made it difficult to talk about power imbalances and conflicts of interest. Common interests are increasingly rejected as a basis for strategy or public policy, such rejection providing support for affirmative action and autonomous organizing by women. In sharp contrast to their counterparts in Sweden, Canadian women unionists have organized from a gender-conscious perspective. They have successfully pressured the unions to take up childcare, abortion, sexual harassment, pay equity, affirmative action, and employment equity as both women's and union issues. Around each of these issues, union men and union hierarchies questioned the legitimacy of unions addressing such questions. With each victory (expressed in policy statements, expansion in the collective bargaining agenda, changes to political focus), the boundaries of what constitutes a legitimate union issue have shifted, the understanding of what is seen to be relevant to the workplace has altered, and the support for a more social and political analysis of the role of unions has increased. A dramatic case in point is the growing union involvement, with active support from top leadership, in the broad issues around violence against women. These campaigns go well beyond a focus on employer harassment or even co-worker harassment, and many have successfully integrated issues around racial harassment and violence.[19]

The transformation in the union agenda to address women's concerns has set the stage for two other shifts. First, gendering issues has meant a subtle move from an identification of a women's platform to a recognition of the gender implications in all issues. This new awareness is evident in recent discussions on free trade, economic restructuring, seniority, health and safety, and telework. Second, issues are frequently scrutinized for their impact on diverse groups of women. For example, discussions of sexual harassment acknowledge the specific forms of harassment experienced by women of colour. Considerations of family benefits increasingly reject traditional definitions of the family that exclude gay and lesbian couples. In Canada the paradigm of diversity which recognizes difference – based not only on gender but increasingly on race, sexuality, ability, region, or language – and the acknowledgment of privilege, discrimination, and power dynamics have gradually been integrated into union discourse.

These shifts in the understanding of what constitutes a union issue and the increase in gender visibility and specificity have had impacts on the collective bargaining agenda. In the most recent and only national assessment of the gains made by women through collective bargaining in Canada, Pradeep Kumar (1993: 207) concludes that there is now "widespread consensus within the Canadian labour movement that unions need to escalate their efforts towards labour market equality, safe and harassment-free work environments, and policies and practices to make it easier for women to balance more effectively their work and family life."

Representation

In most unions in the Western world, women are under-represented in positions of union leadership: less so in local or club positions and more so in the central halls of power.[20] Unions in both Canada and Sweden have been concerned with this under-representation and have sought ways to encourage women's participation in leadership positions.

In an attempt to address the under-representation of women in top elected positions, many key Canadian unions and centrals have adopted affirmative-action policies which allocate seats (either designated or added) on leadership bodies to women. In 1983 the Ontario Federation of Labour (OFL) broke new ground by amending its constitution to create five "affirmative action" positions on its executive board. The leadership role played by the movement of union women, especially the Women's Committee of the OFL, was crucial to winning the affirmative-action policy. They organized a grassroots campaign among the membership, and simultaneously promoted an analysis linking employment equity in the workplace with affirmative action in the unions. In 1984 the Canadian Labour Congress (CLC), the main labour central, also adopted a constitutional change calling for a minimum of six female vice-presidents out of thirty-two.[21] Subsequently many large labour federations and unions across the country did the same.

Undoubtedly, these policies have increased the numbers of women in top leadership positions in unions. A recent study reports that "of the ninety-five executive seats held by women in these organizations, fully thirty-nine of them (41 per cent) are affirmative action positions. Without them, the representation of women on these labour central executives would fall from 28 to 18 per cent" (White, 1993: 105). The increased concern with representation of women in top leadership positions has had spin-off effects in other areas: employment equity for union staff, affirmative-action seats for visible minorities and gays and lesbians, equity representation in education courses, and improvements in gender distribution in local leadership.

In Sweden, gender representation strategies have focused on the need for parity. A government report, *Varannan damarnas* (*Every Other Seat for a Woman*, 1987), sparked a society-wide discussion of representational inequality and led to major initiatives in many institutional contexts, including the unions.[22] For example, in LO it resulted in the publication in 1987 of *Women in the Union: An Activity Program to Get More Women Involved in Union Work*, an ambitious report with a fifteen-year action plan. Despite these interventions, in recent years, the number of women in union posts in LO has been decreasing (LO, 1994). In response, the board has approved a new action plan to achieve parity representation by 1998 (quoted in Mahon, 1996: 562). In TCO unions every decade since 1945 has seen a deterioration in gender equality in top leadership positions (Bergqvist, 1991: 113; Irlinger, 1990).

A distinction between sex-proportional representation and the representation of organized interests in which women "are elected or appointed not as individuals and not simply as members of a gender category but specifically to speak for the members of a disadvantaged social group: women" (Cockburn, 1996: 20) offers a useful reference point for considering the situation in Canada and Sweden. Representational strategies in unions in both countries have been driven by concerns about proportionality. Sometimes this has meant targeting on a few high-profile leadership positions (for example, designated affirmative-action positions), and sometimes a more general argument that women (and other marginalized groups) should be represented in proportion to their numbers.

However, a focus on proportionality, rather than on politics, means that when women are elected to positions of leadership, there is no guarantee – nor should there be – that they will represent women's interests. As might be expected, however, evidence suggests that the line between sex-proportional representation and representation of women as an organized interest group is necessarily blurry. In Canada, women who fill affirmative-action positions established to redress proportional inequalities can face considerable resistance, their credibility challenged and their ability to fill their mandate hampered by their association with affirmative action. Research shows that they may encounter systematic exclusion from information networks and from formal and informal decision-making processes; ghettoization in narrowly defined areas of "women's issues," and feminist and lesbian baiting (Briskin, 1990b; Cuneo, 1993).[23]

It is also the case that women elected to top positions give visibility to women in leadership, challenge stereotypes, and provide role models. Since some of these women are committed to addressing the specific concerns of women as workers and unionists, the profile of these issues has also increased. Penni Richmond of the CLC Women's Bureau reports that the presence of "outsiders" on the CLC executive has "changed the issues raised, changed who gets to hear what we talk about, and changed rank-and-file perception of who has power; in fact, it has put the discussion of power itself on the agenda" (I, 1994).

In Sweden, debates about sex-proportional representation are informed by widespread corporatist practices which integrate organized class interests into decision-making (for example, the involvement of unions in a government commission). In a common-sense way, such practices are understood to build equality, consensus, and cooperation; they are, at their core, also about representation.[24] However, women have not been perceived as an organized interest group to be included, and simultaneously, sex-proportional representation has been viewed negatively – as undemocratic (Bergqvist, 1991: 123).

Although strong evidence indicates that women, women's interests, and women's organizations have not been adequately represented in corporatist decision-making, there are differing assessments by scholars of the degree to which corporatism has supported women's interests. Mary Ruggie (1987), who has examined solidaristic wage bargaining, suggests that corporatism has worked for women despite (or perhaps because of) its lack of specific attention to them. By and large, however, feminist scholars have seen corporatism as reproducing male domination and marginalizing women and women's interests (Bergqvist, 1991).[25] "Measures have rarely been taken specifically in favour of women or by women. Their conditions have, as it were, rather been a byproduct of the comprehensive welfare project" (Eduards, 1991: 699). Hernes argues that "the collaboration between economic organizations which is inherent to the system not only excludes individual women: it also keeps out and subordinates important areas which concern women," such as reproductive work (quoted in Eduards, 1991: 700).

In the unions, women need both proportional representation and also representation as an organized interest. In Sweden, where there is a tradition of corporatist decision-making, struggles to ensure the recognition of women as an organized interest will be critical. In Canada, where no such tradition exists,[26] in addition to fighting for representation, women have been forced to look for other vehicles, such as women's committees, both formal and informal, to represent their interests.

Ways of Working

Dramatic changes in the political climate, the labour process, and the realities of bargaining have forced unions in both countries to re-examine the way they organize their membership and undertake their work, to reconsider the meaning and role of the club or local, and to encourage more membership involvement. This section of the chapter considers some of the dynamics around centralization and decentralization which affect the way that women organize in unions, and it also looks at women's "ways of working" which offer new and timely directions to, and untapped resources for, union transformation. Despite the tremendous differences in union realities, structures, and ideologies in each country, it is around these ways of working that a surprising number of parallels emerge. Evidence suggests that women's ways of working in both countries are more focused on local organizing, on process, and on participation.

Not only has collective bargaining been centralized in Sweden, but so have union structures and practices. Organizational centralization has created limited space for ongoing rank-and-file membership involvement and initiative, and has contributed to producing and reproducing the unions as "service" organizations for their members. "The very centralization of union activity that was so vital to the consolidation of the working class as a national political collectivity ... resulted in a stagnation of the workshop clubs that had constituted the building block of Swedish unionism" (Mahon, 1991: 303).[27]

In fact, several of those I interviewed said that unions were not part of a political movement but more like insurance companies, a comment connected only in part to the fact that Swedish unions administer social-security benefit programs.[28] Sture Nordh (SKTF) pointed out that, "having achieved the laws in the 1970s, unions became more like accountants than a force for social change. We didn't need organizing activities and rallies. We could deal with it the Swedish way: if we wanted something, we could deal directly with government" (I, 1993).

As a result of these centralized structures, most major initiatives for women have come from union leaders or equality officers, often without active support or organized pressure from women members.[29] Kristina Persson, previously the TCO equality officer, said, "Initiative came from TCO, not from outside pressure or from below. It is important for the equality officer to take the initiative and formulate directions" (I, 1993).[30]

Although many of the union equality officers whom I interviewed in 1993 and 1994 felt quite isolated, few saw organizing an active constituency of women members as part of their mandate.[31] None thought it accurate to talk about a "movement of union women" (although conditions are changing rapidly). And certainly, those scholars who have written about the unions in the past would concur. Qvist, Acker, and Lorwin (1984: 281) point out that "there has been no autonomous or semiautonomous women's movement within the trade unions"; and Mary Ruggie, who agrees, suggests the following explanation: "Part of the answer rests on the dominant mode of interest aggregation in Sweden which is relatively passive, making few claims on rank-and-file initiatives, and gives much authority to representatives at the top of organizational hierarchy which remains male dominated" (1988: 180).

The process of decentralization, however, is changing the relationship among elected leaders, staff, and membership and how leadership and accountability are understood. There is also a shift towards more emphasis on the local level and greater efforts to encourage more membership involvement. Nordh of SKTF/TCO said, "Now we need to mobilize the membership like we've never done before" (I, 93). LO has taken a major initiative through the organization of the "Justice Project."[32]

The discussion about structural change in the unions is often gendered. In almost all the interviews with unionists, centralized, hierarchical, and bureaucratic structures were identified as barriers to women's participation. Irene Sundelin from Svenska Industritjänstemannaförbundet (SIF/TCO) said: "Women don't like the way that the union is working: the formal meetings which just rubber stamp. The union is looking for ways of leading the organization differently to encourage involvement and to give members more power to influence" (I, 1994). Annica Magnusson of Svenska Hälso och Sjukuårdens Tjänstemannaförbundet (SHSTF), the nurses' union, envisioned "a flatter structure" for the hospitals, and she pointed out that "men's hierarchial thinking" had heretofore dominated the workplace (I, 1993). Sture Nordh said that SKTF is "now more open, flexible, less hierarchical"; he attributed these changes to women's influence (I, 1993).

Organizational decentralization may increase membership participation, especially the involvement of women, thereby strengthening the unions and their ability to resist the encroachments of economic restructuring. In particular, it will provide a foundation for revaluing the local work and informal leadership of women – a concern in both countries (see Cuneo, 1993). Traditionally, women have been better represented in local leadership positions and have often wanted to work at the local level.[33] Many of the Swedes made the point that "women have different life priorities than men" (Svensson, I, 1993), and that women prefer to work at the local level. "When asked, women say they like to work at the local level where they are more directly involved with membership service; they also like their jobs and want to stay in them" (Englund, I, 1993). Jeanette Olsson, on staff with LO, explained:

> For the majority of women [who work as union representatives] it is important to maintain contact with club members and to try to mobilise them and to share their knowledge. They retain a lay role. Many men more easily take on the role of specialists and spend more time thinking about how to tackle their management counterparts than thinking about the members ... It is not obvious that what men consider to be "competence" and "ability" in union work is the same as the way women define these things. We need to change the union rule of the game to both masculine and feminine ways of being. (quoted in Briskin, 1996: 15)

These comments reflect many of the criticisms that Swedish women unionists have made of union organization: that it validates central and top leadership work over local work; that it encourages leaders and staff to become "experts" removed from the daily work experiences of the membership, thus producing hierarchical and undemocratic structures, which in turn reproduce male domination; and that these patterns make invisible – indeed, devalue – women's ways of working and organizing, and exacerbate their low status in the unions.[34] The move towards decentralizing union work addresses some of these concerns: for example, shifting from full-time union representatives as experts who spend their time negotiating with management to part-time reps (some working on teams) who engage in a dialogue with members, the goal of which is to empower rather than speak for them.

These changes in the way that Swedish unions do their work clearly present opportunities for women; however, in the Australian context, where bargaining has also traditionally been centralized and has recently been decentralizing, with accompanying changes in union structures, Barbara Pocock (1996: 59) concludes that "a dis-aggregated union movement ... lacking the capacity for movement-wide dialogue and decision is a much more difficult prospect for women to affect. This is because the development and dissemination of policy is much more difficult in a diverse, disorganized, and divided set of organisations than where a single channel of discussion exists." It may well be that decentralization will improve the representation of women but not necessarily make it easier for their interests to be represented.[35]

Canadian unions are much more decentralized than Swedish ones, both structurally and in terms of bargaining. In fact, some unions, such as the Canadian Union of Public Employees and the Canadian Auto Workers (CAW), pride themselves on the strength of their local structures. This decentralization has meant a stronger rank-and-file presence in unions, but it has not ensured participatory organizational strategies. A debate continues about whether the unions should have a business perspective with a narrow definition of the union role and responsibility (on wages and benefits) that is organizationally reflected in "service" structures or a social unionist one that sees the union as a broader social movement concerned with a wide range of social and economic issues, reflected in a more activist structure.[36]

In contrast with Sweden, most initiatives for women came originally from rank-and-file women organizing on the margins of unions with very little credibility (Briskin and Yanz, 1983). These women put pressure on the unions to take up women's issues and address their organizational criticisms. Over the last decade, unions have responded to these demands, in part by allocating staff and union resources to organizing women. Women's departments and/or staff responsible for these issues exist now in many unions, but they continue to rely on the pressure of the constituency of union women to support their work. Indeed, one of the major tasks of Canadian equal-opportunity officers is to support and encourage the self-organization of rank-and-file women so that they can speak for themselves. Organizing the constituency of women unionists – building a movement – has been a central strategy of activists in Canadian unions.

As a result of women's organizing in unions, and in response to male-dominated and hierarchical union practices, a new politic of leadership and alternative ways of working can be identified which emphasize process, accountability, and constituency building; participation rather than representation; greater democracy in decision-making and more openness of union structures; and the sharing of work collectively and consensus decision-making (Little, 1989; Briskin, 1990b).[37] Informed by the organizing strategies of the grassroots women's movement, this politic supports the decentralization of power traditionally associated with leadership positions and provides "members opportunities to develop their own power and the self reliance required to effect democratic changes in the union" (Edelson, 1987: 6; also see Needleman, 1988: 10). The new approach is reflected in the different work styles of male and female representatives. In the dominant male model, the staff members act as authority figures, experts, and "white knights" who charge in to rescue weak locals. In contrast, women staff members tend to promote a participatory approach whose aim is to develop the confidence and skills of members (Stinson and Richmond, 1993; see also Heery and Kelly, 1989).

Separate Organizing

Separate organizing by women, or self-organization, takes a variety of forms within the union movement: an informal women's network or caucus; a formal, sometimes elected, regional or national women's committee; women-only educational conferences and targeted educational programs that address women's issues; a women's local or auxiliary of a mixed union; or a women-only union such as the Federation of Women Teachers Associations of Ontario. Separate organizing is often supported by union resources and facilitated by equal-opportunity coordinators, women's bureaux and departments, and so on. Separate organizing has a long and complex history in trade union movements around the world; for example, German and Austrian unions have had women's divisions since the 1890s, replicated at each level of confederation and national union life (Cook, Lorwin, and Daniels, 1992: 50).[38]

In the last few decades, union women in Sweden and Canada have developed different strategies and attitudes towards separate organizing, influenced by the country-specific ideologies around equality, diversity, and power and the practices around representation. In Canada, separate organizing has been a central and effective strategy of union women. In the last twenty years – but not without struggle – such organizing has been legitimized and institutionalized.[39] In Sweden, union women have been reluctant to organize separately, especially through formal structures, inside or outside the unions, an ambivalence reinforced by structural and ideological resistance from the unions. Unlike in Canada, where women's committees are now institutionalized at all levels of the labour movement, there are almost no women's committees as such in the Swedish unions.[40]

The interviews that I conducted with union ombudsmen (equality officers) in Sweden underscored the reluctance to organize as women and around "women's" issues, as well as a general uneasiness with equality issues. Where committees exist, they are called "equality committees," and most operate only at a central level. One exception is SIF/TCO, which has elected equality groups in sixteen of its twenty-five regions. But even SIF, which has a very extensive equality program, has "not been allowed to have *women*'s committees" (Sundelin, I). Irene Sundelin, the equality officer, supports this approach. "Typically Swedish," she said, and she underscored that equality committees "do not close men out" (I, 1993).

Most unions have equality officers, but the Civil Engineers (Civilingenjörsförbundet, or CF), the largest union in SACO (Sveriges Akademikers Centralorganisation; with about 300,000 members and twenty unions), does not, nor does it have its own equality policy. Ing-Mari Svensson, currently a negotiator for CF and previously an equality officer for a LO union, says: "We can do so much about equality without talking about it. You don't have to say a word about equality, but if you give working-class women more influence and power at work, then it will change the way women see themselves. Maybe I can do more work for equality where I am not appointed as 'equality ombudsman.' Then I don't face a wall of resistance" (I, 1993).

Kerstin Stjernberg, whose responsibilities at Lärarförbundet (the teachers' union) include equality issues, did not think it "good to have equality issues on their own. In Sweden, equality is not such a high priority question and if this is your only question, then you would not be taken seriously. The assumption will be that if you open your mouth, they know what you will say and they will lock their ears" (I, 1993).

Yet this is also a period of change. Sture Nordh of SKTF/TCO made the point that there are more separate activities for women around training, education, networks, and conferences.[41] Further, "there is a change in debate in this country, a process moving from a debate about equality to a situation where we talk about women's matters. This is an important next step. We are not advanced in seeing gender discrimination; rather, we have talked about equal opportunity. We need to accept women's experiences in challenging male structures" (Nordh, I, 1993).

At a meeting of the International Federation of Chemical, Energy and General Workers Unions in 1992, Swedish women delegates concluded: "We thought for a long time that the differences in treatment between men and women would solve themselves when the differences between the classes were evened out. Now we know that this is not the case and in order to create a just society both a class and a gender perspective must be borne in mind" (quoted in Pocock, 1996: 167).

Furthermore, recent attacks by conservative forces on the welfare state and the established practices of unions are shifting patterns of women's organizing in Sweden (Eduards, 1992). The development of Tjejligan (the Girls' Gang) in LO is one concrete example. Tjejligan started in 1991 as part of the SAP (Social Democratic Party) election campaign. Its structure was influenced by visits to Canada and the United States, and the first LO women's conference, held in 1988 on health issues. By 1993, fifteen groups in Stockholm were working on different questions. They choose their own focus: for example, childcare, representation, violence against women, sexual harassment, unemployment, or women and power. "Tjejligan, with its 11,000 members across the country, has become the exemplar of the new, unconventional way of organizing ... Tjejligan focuses on the local level, where women are more likely initially to become engaged. It has demonstrated a capacity creatively to combine social and political action. Unafraid to resort to unconventional tactics like street theatre, it functioned as one of the most visible bases of grassroots union mobilization against the unpopular policies of the Bildt government" (Mahon, 1996: 560–1). Tjejligan's way of working is consistent with the broader trends to decentralization and democratization. In an interview in 1993, Boel Carlsson, LO's equality officer, talked enthusiastically about Tjejligan: "Its organization is very different. They are free to make their own decisions. The union can't give them orders. It is a new kind of democracy" (quoted in Briskin, 1996: 16).

Paradoxically, coincident with the reluctance to organize openly as women, the lack of formal structures such as women's committees, and policy commitment to gender neutrality, evidence from interviews suggests that Swedish women unionists actively use informal ways of networking. In fact, Tjejligan may be paradigmatic of this approach in its informal and local strategies. Cook, Lorwin, and Daniels (1992: 126) also found such evidence. "Although the Swedish unions decided in the early 1970s to abandon in the name of equality their women's divisions and special classes for women, we nevertheless found women meeting together in nearly all the unions and shops we visited. Some meetings were initiated by women shop leaders, others by women members, and both were tolerated but not strongly supported by skeptical local male leaders."

In Canada, separate organizing has been a central and successful strategy of union feminists. By highlighting the specificity of women's concerns as workers and unionists, women's committees and caucuses have mobilized them in large numbers – in formal and informal settings (some elected, some appointed) and at all levels of union structures. More than fifteen years of such committees has not led to a decline in this organizing. Peggy Nash, a vice-president of the CLC and a women's organizer for the CAW, a male-dominated union mostly organizing industrial workplaces where "women have to get along with the guys to do anything," commented: "It used to be the kiss of death to be involved in the women's committees in terms of other involvement in the union. Most women activists don't feel this way now. There is a growing sense that 'sisterhood' in the union is a good thing, that organizing separately is a good thing, and that fighting to include women of colour and lesbians strengthens the women's movement inside the union" (I, 1994).

In fact, the trajectory has been to seek more arenas in which women can organize separately. Growing acceptance and legitimation of women's organizing can be documented, as can the increasing institutionalization and formalization of structures to facilitate it: constitutional clauses to incorporate women's committees, policy statements to address their concerns, allocation of staff and financial resources, educational courses designed specifically for women activists and leaders, regularly scheduled women's conferences to develop new initiatives and policy, and other such activities.

Union women's struggles have demonstrated not only the need for separate organizing but also its efficacy in the Canadian context.[42] In an interesting study of public-sector unions in Quebec using statistical path analysis, Barbara Nichols-Heppner (1984: 294) concludes that establishing women's committees is a more effective strategy than seeking greater electoral representation, and that such committees "evoke more organizational responsiveness from unions" and are "the strongest determinant of the negotiation of collective agreement provisions favourable to women unionists."

Despite these successes, women's relationship to separate organizing in Canada has been marked by an ambivalence, reminiscent of Swedish attitudes, which reflects the struggle to be integrated as equals into the structures of unions and the simultaneous recognition that women are discriminated against as women and may need special measures to make such integration possible.

Alliances and Coalitions

An important feminist strategy in Canada has been the building of alliances and coalitions across political current, sector, and institution to bring women together from the unions, parties, and community-based groups to cooperate nationally, provincially, and locally (Colley, 1983; Egan and Yanz, 1983; Antonyshyn, Lee, and Merrill, 1988; Kome, 1995; Ash, 1996). The most successful formal expression of this approach, but by no means the only one, is the National Action Committee on the Status of Women/Comité Canadien d'Action sur le Statut de la Femme (NAC), a binational (includes Quebec), bilingual umbrella organization of over six hundred member groups which celebrated its twenty-fifth anniversary in 1997. This cooperation has meant that trade union women work with community-based feminist groups, both to build coalitions around key issues such as childcare and pay equity and to pressure the union movement to respond to the feminist challenge. Trade union women, in turn, have had an important impact on the politics and practices of the Canadian women's movement, weakening the tendency towards individualistic solutions and introducing (and reintroducing) a class perspective (Briskin, 1990a).

Such organizing has helped to legitimize coalition-building with groups outside the union movement, thus actively challenging traditions of union isolationism, and has provided a model for coalition-building that Canadian unions are now adopting. Monique Simard (1988: 37–8), a union and feminist activist in Quebec, concludes: "Women have been so successful that other popular movements have been adopting the kind of flexible coalition work that has made the women's movement in Québec so resilient."

Three recent innovative initiatives are worthy of note. NAC and the CLC teamed up to promote a Toy Awareness Campaign around Christmas in 1995 to increase public awareness about the working conditions of Asian women who produce toys. The campaign was part of an international effort to pressure the toy companies to improve working conditions (Imada, 1996). In June 1995, after a year of intense planning, three branches of the ten-day Quebec Women's March against Poverty converged on the National Assembly in Quebec City to join 15,000 supporters. This march was initiated by the Fédération des Femmes du Québec and organized by more than forty groups, including unions, anti-poverty groups, immigrant groups, and women's organizations. It was quite a success: in response to its nine demands, the Quebec government agreed to raise the minimum wage, introduce a proactive pay-equity law, deduct child support payments automatically, set aside 5 per cent of social housing for poor women and five places for every fifteen in non-traditional trades, reduce the length of sponsorship for immigrant women, allocate money to the "social economy" to generate jobs, extend basic employment standards to those on workfare, and freeze student fees (Nadeau, 1995). NAC and the CLC sponsored a national women's march against poverty, "For bread and roses, for jobs and justice," modelled on this initiative in May and June 1996. Caravans travelled from both the west and east coasts to Ottawa to demonstrate against the right-wing corporate and government agenda. Barb Byers, president of the Saskatchewan Federation of Labour, saw the march as an opportunity for "the labour movement and the women's movement ... to form new and stronger coalitions" (quoted in *Kinesis*, May 1996).

The fact that separate organizing is widespread inside unions, political parties, educational institutions, and the community has facilitated a coalition strategy and inter- and extra-union cooperation. Union women's committees create many opportunities for women unionists to work across the borders of union, sector, and province.

In Swedish unions, women mobilizing across blue- and white-collar lines and across unions certainly has a few precedents – for example, around wage equity – although it is considerably less institutionalized than in Canada. In Sweden such organizing comes up against both structural and ideological resistance. The structure of the labour movement with three union centrals (TCO, SACO, and LO) often in competition with each other for members, does not facilitate cooperation. There are few formal contexts in which the three centrals work together, a fact that has limited joint initiatives among women unionists. Further, the traditional strength of the labour movement in Sweden (exemplified by the long association between LO and SAP) mitigated its need to rely on co-operation with other groups.

Ideological resistance is expressed in strong class and party loyalties that discourage women from working together. For example, loyalties to union centrals deter LO and TCO women from cooperating; loyalties to the Social Democratic Party limit alliances with women outside the party structures, although they may encourage alliances with LO women. Almost all the women I interviewed talked about loyalty to parties and unions keeping women from working together. Margareta Winberg (I, 1993), from the Women's Federation of the Social Democratic Party and a member of the Riksdag (Parliament), said, "In the recent past, we were not allowed to cooperate with other women's political organizations, but now we allowed to do it." As in other contexts, informal local organizing is a subversive way to bypass structures. Karin Karlsson (I, 1994) of SKTF/TCO pointed out that, "although there are few formal contexts to work together, women unionists have looked for ways to work together. We saw we had joint interests. We wanted to work together, and we were willing to break the rules to do it." She described some of the early attempts at the end of the 1980s by women across union and union centrals to organize around pay equity: "Women unionists worked together across unions, but this wasn't allowed; it was not the acceptable way. Now it is more legitimate. In last five years, the unions have become more flexible about choosing partners."

A number of factors are changing attitudes and practices towards cross-sectoral alliances: moves to decentralize unions and changes in collective bargaining are shifting attention from the centre to the workplace and creating the conditions for cross-collar and cross-union organizing, especially around "solidaristic work" (Mahon, 1991 and 1996) and the reorganization of work (Higgins, 1996). Attacks on the welfare state, which disproportionately affect women's work, are also inspiring new forms of organizing and new alliances such as the August 1994 campaign Kvinnors Rätt till Arbete (Women's Right to

Work), which brought women together from TCO, LO, and SACO. Many saw this campaign as a turning point (Hultin, I, 1994).[43]

Strategies of cooperation and coalition building among union women in Canada are shaped by the reality that only 30 per cent of Canadian working women are unionized. In order to reach out to the majority of working women, alliances and coalitions across the union–non-union divide are necessary. In Sweden virtually all working women are unionized, but not inside the same union central. It may be that increased cooperation across the TCO-LO-SACO borders, such as the Kvinnors Rätt till Arbete campaign in 1994, will be the critical factor.

CONCLUSION

Despite the inevitable and significant differences in context, ideology, union practices in Sweden and Canada, this chapter highlights some common themes: wage discrimination and under-representation, and struggles to make women's issues visible and to legitimize women's ways of working. At the same time, strategic differences around attitudes and practices to separate organizing and to alliances and coalitions are instructive. They help to deepen our understanding of the nature of the union movements and the political culture in each country.

In Canada the unions have now become a central vehicle for organizing around women's issues and a key player in the women's movement. This change has not occurred without resistance; indeed, union women have struggled for more than twenty years to make it a reality. The process is helping to revitalize the unions, which, in turn, will perhaps be part of a strategy for revitalizing the practice of politics.

In Sweden, unions have not been seen as a major vehicle for women's organizing (Eduards: I, 1993 and 1994). The common-sense view, supported by research, is that the political parties are more responsive to women's needs, perhaps in part because they are more visible and accountable institutions (Karin Karlsson, I, 1994). In Canada the opposite is true: unions are considerably more responsive to women's concerns and more innovative in their organizing strategies.

Ironically, it may be that the less-powerful, more marginal nature of Canadian unions has provided space for oppositional ideology and practice, and thereby for women's organizing. Swedish unions have been centrally located in the map of institutional and political power, traditionally involved in corporatist initiatives, and as a result, less amenable to certain kinds of internal challenge. The current crisis in Swedish unions, however, is reconfiguring the possibilities. Given the degree of unionization of women, Swedish unions may be the decisive arena for women's organizing.

NOTES

1 Research on Sweden was funded by various programs of the Social Sciences and Humanities Research Council of Canada, the Scandinavian-Canadian Academic Exchange, the Faculty of Arts at York University, and the Marvin Gelber Award for International Academic Exchange. I appreciate their support. I am also indebted to the many Swedish activists, unionists, and scholars who agreed to be interviewed in 1992–93, and in many cases reinterviewed in 1994. Finally, I would like to thank Rianne Mahon for translating and thus making accessible to me two documents from LO and the paper by Ann-Sofie Hermansson, and Mona Eliasson for her helpful comments.

2 Note that when a source name is followed by "I," it indicates that the material came from an interview. The Swedish material is based in part on interviews done between 1992 and 1994. See pages 178–9 for a list of those interviewed. A total of thirty-seven open-ended interviews with trade unionists, community activists, feminist researchers, political party activists, and state officials, averaging two to three hours in length, were conducted by the author in Sweden. The lists of respondents were drawn up on the basis of a number of strategies. In the case of the unions, for example, letters were written to the union head offices asking them to identify an appropriate person. In the case of community activists, several well-placed activists made recommendations, key organizations were contacted for suggestions, and so on. Letters were sent by the researcher to identified respondents (including a list of the open-ended questions), and follow-up telephone calls were made to set up meetings. As a result of the first set of interviews conducted in 1992 and 1993, a draft paper entitled "Mapping Swedish women's organizing: A Canadian perspective" was sent to all respondents. In 1994 second interviews were held with eleven of the first group of respondents, in which the paper provided a vehicle for discussion; for the new interviews conducted in 1994, eleven of the respondents also read the paper. Interviews based on the paper helped to identify and negotiate disjunctures (discrepancies, contradictions, inconsistencies) in interpretation about the Swedish context, not for the purposes of achieving a consensus but to highlight the assumptions that inform these differences and to problematize the disjunctures as a site for understanding my own assumptions about Canadian feminism.

3 In North America the "third wave" has referred to the shift away from a focus on differences between women and men and towards diversity among women, and to organizing among women of colour, immigrant women, native women, and poor women – that is, marginalized women.

4 It was largely in response to these difficulties that I undertook to organize, with Mona Eliasson of Uppsala University, the project that has generated these comparative articles. It was motivated in part, by a desire to find ways to do comparative research that were well grounded in the realities of each country. In fact, the more research I did in Sweden, the more I became aware of the complexity and pitfalls of writing about a country not one's own and of doing comparative research. Unfortunately, because of unforeseen circumstances, this chapter was written without a collaborator.

5 This problematic privileging resonates with critiques of the way that Western women have written about third-world women (see Mohanty, 1991).

6 In contrast to the situation in some European countries, these figures seem low; however, in the North American context, Canadian unions have maintained density rates far more successfully than in the United States, where in 1990 unions represented only 21.4 per cent of men and 14.5 per cent of women, although the gender breakdown of union membership is about the same (Cobble, 1993).

7 It is possible, however, just to join the union-administered programs.

8 Sweden has the highest rate in Europe of women working part-time; unlike in Canada, however, these workers are mostly unionized. In Sweden, then, employers cannot use a move to part-time work as a strategy to increase the exploitation of labour.

9 "The unions, especially the LO, had been the initiating agents, or at least actively supported, legislative and administrative efforts related to income tax reform, day care, parental leave and labour market measures to reduce sex segregation. But on issues of labour relations, such as wages, hiring, and promotion, the unions opposed legislation and insisted that such matters were best settled by collective bargaining" (Qvist, Acker, and Lorwin, 1984: 271).

Under the terms of the 1991 Equality Act, employers with more than ten employees must draw up a plan aimed at promoting equality which ensures that "working conditions shall be appropriate for both men and women"; facilitates "the combination of gainful employment and parenthood"; ensures that "no employee is subject to sexual harassment"; and promotes occupational integration (see Sweden, 1991). These requirements mean that unions who employ more than ten people must also draw up such a plan. It would be interesting to study these plans and to research their impacts on the equality agendas of unions in relationship to their own membership.

10 Researcher Eivor Englund (I, 1993) reports that a study which she did in 1980 on fifty workplaces indicated that neither employers nor unions

had used the MBL to get more information about equality issues. The increase in workplace democracy was not seen as a mechanism to address women's concerns or equality issues.

11 Pay-equity legislation addresses equal pay for work of equal value. Equal pay for equal work has been part of provincial employment-standards statutes for many decades.

12 Many of those I interviewed in Sweden fear the impact on women of the breakdown in centralized bargaining (Sundelin, I, 1993; Svensson, I, 1993; Stjernberg, I, 1993). Research confirms these fears (see Whitehorse, 1992, and Hammond and Harbridge, 1995).

13 The municipal workers' union has been seen "as expressing more militant and all encompassing demands than traditionally aggressive male-dominated metal trade unions. The municipal workers demand radical wage redistribution between different categories of employees and sexual equality as well as shorter hours, maintained services and workplace democracy. Male-dominated unions recurrently press what can be seen as narrower demands focused on the real wage package" (Woodward and Leiulfsrud, 1990: 411).

14 Although TCO has never itself bargained for its member unions, it has organized bargaining cartels to bring unions together; these structures are also now breaking down.

15 A number of major municipalities in Sweden have hosted projects on work evaluation, seeking a fairer and more rational basis for comparative wage rates. These projects have been funded through the local government initiative known as KOM (Kvinnor och Män Tillsammans, or Men and Women Together; reported in Higgins, 1996: 190).

16 A 1993 survey indicated that over 90 per cent of LO, TCO, and SACO members felt that pay equity and job evaluation should be among the unions' top priorities (quoted in Mahon, 1995: 31).

17 "Job evaluation was opposed by many trade unionists because, as a management controlled tool, it could be used as an argument for wage differentiation, thus undermining worker solidarity" (Acker, 1991: 252).

18 In July 1998 the Canadian Human Rights Tribunal ruled that the governement owes about $4 billion in back pay and interest to 200,000 employees, mostly women. This decision represents a landmark in a fourteen-year fight by the Public Service Alliance of Canada (reported in the *Montreal Gazette*, 30 July 1998).

19 Three recent innovative union documents on violence against women are *Taking Action: A Union Guide to Ending Violence Against Women* (1992), a joint publication of the British Columbia Federation of Labour and the Women's Research Centre; "We Can Do It: End the Violence Against Women," a policy statement from the 19th Constitutional Convention of the Canadian Labour Congress, June 1992; and "Racial and

Sexual Harassment, and Violence against Women: Policy and Prevention," from the United Steelworkers of America (undated).

20 In LO in 1983, women constituted 42 per cent of members and 7 per cent of the executive committee; by 1993 they represented 45 per cent of members and 13 per cent of the EC. In TCO in 1983, women accounted for 60 per cent of members and 21 per cent of the EC; there was virtually no change by 1993. Reported in Sweden, 1994: 29; see also Bergqvist (1991) and Irlinger (1990). For Canadian figures, see White (1993).

21 As of February 1997, women filled fifteen of the forty-four positions on the CLC council. This body includes the key executive committee (of which two must be women), the presidents of the twelve provincial federations of labour, and eighteen vice-presidents at large (of which four must be women).

22 Rianne Mahon argues that this report "helped to spark the rebirth of the Swedish women's movement." And within LO "it marked the beginning of a concerted campaign to bring women and gender relations into the organization" (Mahon, 1996: 558). In Sweden, government reports such as this one and later inquiries into wage inequity have had a major social impact. The same cannot be said about government commissions in Canada. For further discussion, see Bergqvist and Findlay in this volume.

23 In Sweden there is certainly an awareness of this danger. For example, Irene Sundelin, equality officer at SIF/TCO, said that SIF has not decided if it will move in the direction of quotas, "but it may be necessary." She was ambivalent about this strategy. She is not afraid that "quotas will mean that we will not get good women but rather that if women are appointed the thought will be that she is not so good and that she got the job because she is a woman. And she will be forced to represent her sex. This is true now and it is harder on women. A lot of men don't live up to standards but they don't stand in for all men" (quoted in Briskin, 1996: 13).

24 Diane Sainsbury (1988: 341) considers two meanings of corporatism: first, "as the integration of organized interest in the governmental decision-making process," and second, "as a particular set of relations between labour and capital characterized by harmonization of interests ... and a growing role of government – or what other analysts have referred to as 'tripartism.'"

25 It in an interesting but understandable paradox that in Sweden, while women are seriously under-represented in the decision-making processes of unions and in corporatist arrangements, after the 1994 election the proportion of women politicians was the highest in the Western world.

26 There are no equivalent corporatist structures in Canada. Attempts at various forms of tripartism (among governments, employers, and unions)

have been unsuccessful and strongly resisted by Canadian unions. In contrast to corporatist structures of bargaining, Canadian unions operate under a strongly adversarial regime.

27 On this issue Kerstin Sandell, a union activist in SAC, wrote in a letter of May 1994, "It is very difficult to get workers to act in even small questions at a workplace. The action should be done by ombudsmen ... The centralized organization is taking away from the agency of the workers/unionists. That is part of why militancy and direct action is unheard of in Sweden. And that is devastating for the women's movement who has, as a founding element, localized direct action. So the lack of women's agency is linked to the lack of agency on the local level for everyone."

A major and quite successful initiative by Kommunal, the municipal workers' union, around work reorganization in the caring sector emphasized democratic, bottom-up, and from-within strategies that drew on the "silent knowledge" of the mostly women workers. Ironically, it came up against a hierarchical union structure that marginalized women members (reported in Higgins, 1996: 181–2, 187).

28 Karin Karlsson (SKTF) also connected this pattern to the ease of joining unions and the high rate of unionization (I, 1993).

29 Anita Dahlberg from the Centre for Women's Studies at the University of Stockholm (I, 1994) pointed out that the original women's studies *fora* (associations) at the universities were initiated by the state and driven by state money provided in 1978 and 1979. She saw this as an example of state feminism; the state wanted research on the situation of women in the universities as part of its equal-opportunity program. "The Fora were not a movement from below. Money drove the organizing. Women were brought together by money from the state." This scenario presents such an interesting contrast to the development of women's studies in Canadian universities. Like union women, feminist academics organized from the margins, pressuring universities to allow them to teach courses on women. To this day, despite their size and success, these programs remain on the margins and are very underfunded.

30 Rianne Mahon (1996) reports on some of the important initiatives taken by women union officials: for example, the production of the important document *Class and Gender* for the 1991 LO congress.

The exceptions to this generalization are also instructive. Although she agreed that most initiatives "come from above," Karin Karlsson (SKTF/TCO) described one taken on pay equality in the mid-1980s with Lena Sveneaus, then on the LO staff and now the equality ombudsman for the state. Working with other unionists, the two women developed a booklet and planned seminars around country. The project ended when it lost its funding. One of its express purposes was to "create pressure from below" (Karlsson, I, 1994): "We did not work on this in our formal capacity. We did it on a voluntary basis to spread the message. We didn't want to take away from the traditional role of unions but wanted to create pressure from women members, to create pay equity consciousness."

31 Svenska Industritjänstemannaförbundet (SIF/TCO) is unusual in its commitment to organizing its women membership. The first equality officer was appointed in 1969, the same year as equality groups began. Her mandate, seen to be atypical, was to start up such groups, which in the early years raised the issue of women's wage inequality. The groups called for across-the-board increases. Sundelin (I, 1994) pointed out that making this unpopular argument was "like swearing in the church." She stated, "The groups still operate but if I look back over the last five years, they haven't been pressure groups. Everyone thought equality was fixed. As a result of the research done on women's wages, they are now again operating as pressure groups: both on women's wages, unemployment, and on how to work with Jämo" (Sundelin, I, 1994). Sundelin concluded that she "finds her work easier when groups make demands."

32 The Justice Project used the remand method: "One of most intensive forms of grass-roots consultation and education is the 'remand' method of LO and TCO ... Remand involves reaching thousands of members in small study groups, and sometimes, later, in regional conferences with informative materials and specific questions related to a single major issue on which the organization is developing its position. Thus, in the LO remand on the pending national occupational health and safety bill in 1973, over 85,000 members expressed their views and brought about a major change in the draft law enacted the following year" (Cook, Lorwin, and Daniels, 1992: 125).

33 The tendency to undervalue local work and see it as only or primarily a stepping stone to higher positions (see, for example, Elkiss, 1994; Melcher et al., 1992) reinforces the individualism of personal success stories and the hierarchy associated with male-dominated and bureaucratic unions, and simultaneously makes less visible the commitment of local women activists to union transformation. The focus of affirmative action on top leadership positions and, in staff positions, on expertise has not only made the leadership contributions of elected women at the local level less apparent but has also made invisible the informal leadership that women often provide.

34 These findings are consistent with recent research by Johanna Esseveld (1997). She concludes that "gender relations look different within the unions depending on where in the hierarchy somebody is located. There are clear differences in women's accounts of how trade unions limit and open up in different ways for their actions on different levels. Most women we have interviewed at the central (national) level claim that

meeting styles and work conditions at this level discriminate against them, while most women at lower and middle levels find that there are possibilities to redefine both union work traditions and contents of union tasks at these levels. It is also in the accounts of these women that we find visions of future working modes which are more network-like and less bureaucratic." Thanks to Mona Eliasson for providing this translation.

35 "The decentralization of collective bargaining can be seen as one element in a broader design which has been described as a kind of enterprise corporatism ... The employers' new strategy aims to provide the institutional foundations for an identity alternative to that of 'wage-earner.' The latter, constituted at the level of the nation as a whole through solidaristic bargaining and the welfare state, is to be replaced by a new unity of white- and blue-collar workers at the level of the individual firm and its subunits. The new identity of *medarbetare*, in turn, complements that of the atomized consumer individual" (Jenson and Mahon, 1993: 94–5).

36 This is also clearly a debate about democracy: the wider the reach of union concerns and the more participatory and decentralized the organizational structure, the more inclusive and democratic the practices of the union will be. Practices of union democracy have also been encouraged by the movement to Canadianize unions (gain autonomy from American parent unions) and by the movement of union women; simultaneously these have created more space for union women's organizing (see Briskin, 1998).

37 For example, self-conscious strategies to address the issue of accountability inform the election to affirmative-action seats in some jurisdictions. In response to what was seen as a top-down and male-dominated mechanism for selecting women to fill designated affirmative action positions in the CLC, women in the Alberta Federation of Labour won the right for the women's caucus to elect the women who would stand for these positions (Cuneo, 1993). In the Quebec Federation of Labour, "an all-women caucus elects the women's affirmative action positions, which are then confirmed by a vote of all Convention delegates. The purpose of this election process is that the women elected to these positions should reflect the needs and concerns of the women members" (White, 1993: 105).

38 It is useful to distinguish between separatism as a *goal* – an end in itself – and separate organizing as a *strategy* – a means to an end. Separatism often includes an explicit refusal to work with men; it frequently focuses on building alternative communities as a solution, rather than on the transformation of dominant social structures. By contrast, separate organizing is a strategy of empowerment for women in their struggle to alter

political and economic configurations. Union women have mostly argued for separate organizing rather than separatism; however, separate organizing by union women has often been discredited on the assumption that it is separatist. The conflation of the two means that separate organizing by women is often seen as a divisive strategy in the union movement, rather than as a means to strengthen the voice not only of women but of the union movement as a whole. The point is that taking account of gender differences in power and experience does not create divisions among union members; rather, it acknowledges differences that already exist. In so doing, the unions build *equality in practice* and establish the foundation for a transformed and inclusive union movement (see Briskin, 1993).

39 In Canada, women's separate organizing has also provided a precedent for organizing by women and men of colour, lesbians and gay men, and Native peoples, who are now organizing "separately" inside the union movement, often through human-rights committees, "pink-triangle" committees, aboriginal circles, and the like.

40 The historical development of the approach by Swedish unions to women's committees remains to be told in detail. Sigrid Ekendahl filled the position of ombudsman in LO from 1946 to 1964; her role was to organize, inform, and activate women in all LO unions. She organized women's committees around the country; by 1964 there were 175 such committees but it is unclear what exactly happened to them. More is known about the Women's Council, set up with employers in 1947, which eventually included both LO and TCO unions. The council carried out a key investigation into childcare and was instrumental in bringing about the Swedish childcare program. For complex reasons connected to its focus on women, to new governmental initiatives on equality introduced by Prime Minister Olof Palme (the government was increasingly seen as more appropriate venue to handle such issues), and to a change in union attitude towards cooperation with employers, the LO unions withdrew from this council in 1967, and SAF and the TCO unions decided to end it in the early 1970s (see Englund, 1988, and Englund, I, 1993).

41 Cook, Lorwin, and Daniels (1992: 127) report the following example: "In the metalworkers club at the ball-bearing plant in Gothenburg, women numbered seven hundred, or one-fifth of the total membership. We were told that earlier only one woman was enrolled in the union's study circles, despite attempts of the local education officer to recruit others. When, however, he offered two courses for women only, each enrolled some fifty members."

42 In *Women and Decision-Making in Trade Unions*, an extensive study done for the European Trade Union Confederation, Mary Braithwaite

and Catherine Byrne (1995: 2–3) draw the following conclusions: "Those confederations with markedly low levels of female representation within the confederation structures have no such [women's or equality] committee suggesting that women's or equality committees are a necessary part of achieving better female representation ... Those confederations with no women's or equality department have low levels of representation of women in key decision making areas ... [T]here appears to be a strong correlation between the existence of a regular women's congress or conference and higher levels of female representation in decision making positions and structures."

43 Karin Karlsson's description of the process of organizing this campaign illuminates some of the political culture around union women's organizing in Sweden. "On Sept 21, 1993, a meeting of about one hundred people was held. There was a widespread invitation to unions to get people there. A core of local groups were formed. We organized them geographically and told them, "It is up to you to do whatever it is that you want to do." They looked very surprised and then they said, 'Is that right? Can we really do that?' because they have never been allowed to do what they wanted to, not when the initiative came from the central level. There has usually been rather strict regulations or advice about what you should do. Throwing the ball to them, they had all kind of wild ideas at the beginning" (I, 1994).

INTERVIEWS, 1992–94

(an asterisk indicates interviews in two different years)

Trade Unionists

Boel Carlsson, Landsorganisationen i Sverige (LO)
Karin Karlsson, Sveriges Kommunaltjänstemannaförbund (SKTF/TCO)*
Annica Magnusson, Svenska Hälso och Sjukuårdens Tjänstemannaförbundet (SHSTF/TCO)
Sture Nordh, Sveriges Kommunaltjänstemannaförbund (SKTF/TCO)
Kristina Persson, Tjänstemännens Centralorganisation (TCO) and Social Democratic Party (SAP)*
Kerstin Stjernberg, Lärarförbundet (TCO)
Irene Sundelin, Svenska Industritjänstemannaförbundet (SIF/TCO)*
Ing-Mari Svensson, Civilingenjörsförbundet (SACO)

Community Activists

Eva Bohlin and Joan Haavie
Amanda Golert

Lilian Hultin
Catharina Landstrom
Pia Laskar
Karin Lindeqvist and Anna Karin Granberg*
Eva Nickell
Helena Norberg
Inga Lisa Sangregorio*
Eva Stigsdottir
Nina Yderberg

Feminist Researchers

Annike Baude, Arbetslivsinstitutet*
Elizabeth Cedersund, Linkoping University*
Anita Dahlberg, University of Stockholm
Maud Eduards, University of Stockholm*
Mona Eliasson, Uppsala University
Eivor Englund*
Lena Gonas, Arbetslivsinstitutet
Ann Britt Hellmark, Arbetslivsinstitutet
Gunnel Karlsson, University of Göteborg*
Arja Lehto
Anita Nyberg, Linkoping University
Kerstin Sandell
Elisabeth Sundin, Linkoping University

Party Activists and State Officials

Ulla Hoffman, chair of the Women's Committee of the Left Party
Lena Svenceaus, ombudsman, Jämo
Margareta Winberg, National Federation of Social Democratic Women and member of the Riksdag (Parliament)

REFERENCES

Acker, Joan. (1992). Two discourses of reform and women in the future welfare state. English manuscript; in Swedish in *Kvinnor och mäns liv och arbete,* ed. Annika Baude. Stockholm: SNS Förlag.

– (1991). Pay equity in Sweden and other nordic countries. In Fudge and McDermott.

Antonyshyn, Patricia, B. Lee, and Alex Merrill. (1988). Marching for women's lives: The campaign for free-standing abortion clinics in Ontario. In Frank Cunningham, Sue Findlay, Marlene Kadar, Alan Lennon, and

Ed Silva (eds.), *Social Movements, Social Change: The Politics and Practice of Organizing*. Toronto: Between the Lines.

Ash, Shannon. (1996). More cuts, few benefits. *Kinesis*, December-January.

Bergqvist, Christina. (1991). Corporatism and gender equality: A comparative study of two Swedish labour market organisations. *European Journal of Political Research* 20: 107–25.

Braithwaite, Mary, and Catherine Byrne. (1995). *Women in Decision-Making in Trade Unions*. Brussels: European Trade Union Confederation.

Briskin, Linda. (1998). Gendering union democracy. *Canadian Woman Studies/Les Cahiers de la femme* 18 (1) (spring): 35–8.

– (1996). *Gendering Union Democracy: A Swedish-Canadian Comparison*. Working Paper Series, no. 13, Centre for Research on Work and Society, York University. Includes the English version of "Kvinnor och demokratiseringen av fackliga organisationer" (Women and the democratization of the unions), originally published in 1995 in *Delad makt: kvinnor ock facklig demokrati* (Stockholm: Utbildningsförlaget Brevskolan). Translated into Swedish by Gunilla Persson.

– (1994). Equity and economic restructuring in the Canadian labour movement. *Economic and Industrial Democracy* 15 (1): 89–112.

– (1993). Union women and separate organizing. In Briskin and McDermott.

– (1990a). *Autonomy, Integration and Legitimacy: A Comparative Analysis of Socialist Feminist Practice in Canada, the United States and Western Europe*. Working Paper, Institute for Social Research, York University.

– (1990b). Women, unions and leadership. *Canadian Dimension* 24: 38–41.

– and Patricia McDermott (eds.). (1993). *Women Challenging Unions: Feminism, Democracy and Militancy*. Toronto: University of Toronto Press.

– and Lynda Yanz (eds.). (1983). *Union Sisters: Women in the Labour Movement*. Toronto: Women's Press.

Cobble, Dorothy. (1993). Remaking unions for the new majority. In Dorothy Cobble (ed.), *Women and Unions: Forging a Partnership*. Ithaca: ILR Press.

Cockburn, Cynthia. (1996). Strategies for gender democracy: Strengthening the representation of trade union women in the European social dialogue. *European Journal of Women's Studies* 3: 7–26.

Colley, Susan. (1983). Free universal daycare: The OFL takes a stand. In Briskin and Yanz.

Cook, Alice, Val Lorwin, and Arlene Daniels. (1992). *The Most Difficult Revolution: Women and Trade Unions*. Ithaca: Cornell University Press.

Cuneo, Carl. (1993). Trade union leadership: Sexism and affirmative action. In Briskin and McDermott.

Edelson, Miriam. (1987). *Challenging Unions: Feminist Process and Democracy in the Labour Movement*. Ottawa: Canadian Research Institute for the Advancement of Women.

Eduards, Maud. (1992). Against the rules of the game: On the importance of women's collective actions. In *Rethinking Change: Current Swedish Feminist Research*. Uppsala: Swedish Science Press.

– (1991). Toward a third way: Women's politics and welfare policies in Sweden. *Social Research* 58 (3): 667–705.

Egan, Carolyn, and Lynda Yanz. (1983). Building links: Labour and the women's movement. In Briskin and Yanz.

Elkiss, Helen. (1994). Training women for union office: Breaking the glass ceiling. *Labour Studies Journal* 19 (2) (summer): 25–42.

Elman, R. Amy, and Maud Eduards. (1991). Unprotected by the Swedish welfare state: A survey of battered women and the assistance they received. *Women's Studies International Forum* 14 (5): 413–21.

Englund, Eivor. (1988). Arbetsmarknadens Kvinnonamnd. (On the women's committee in LO; part of a symposium celebrating the fiftieth anniversary of Saltsjöbads.) Stockholm: Arbetslivscentrum.

Esseveld, Johanna. (1997). Om kvinnliga förtroendevalda, makt och könsrelationer i fackföreningar. In Anita Nyberg and Elisabeth Sundin (eds.), *Ledare, makt, kön*. Statens Offentliga Utredningar #13. Stockholm: Arbetmarknadsdepartmentet.

Fudge, Judy. (1993). The gendered dimension of labour law: Why women need inclusive unionism and broader based bargaining. In Briskin and McDermott.

– and Patricia McDermott. (1991). Introduction: Putting feminism to work. In Fudge and McDermott (eds.), *Just Wages: A Feminist Assessment of Pay Equity*. Toronto: University of Toronto Press.

Hammond, Suzanne, and Raymond Harbridge. (1995). Women and enterprise bargaining: The New Zealand experience of labour market deregulation. *Journal of Industrial Relations* 37 (3): 359–76.

Heery, Edmund, and John Kelly. (1989). "A cracking job for a woman" – A profile of women trade union officers. *Industrial Relations Journal* 20 (3): 192–202.

Higgins, Winton. (1996). The Swedish municipal workers' union – A Study In The New Political Unionism. *Economic and Industrial Democracy* 17: 167–97.

Imada, Andrea. (1996). Trouble in toyland. *Kinesis*, December-January.

Irlinger, Irma. (1990). TCO *och kvinnorna: Tidsperioden 1944–74*. Uppsala: Uppsala University.

Jenson, Jane, and Rianne Mahon. (1993). Representing solidarity: Class, gender and the crisis of social-democratic Sweden. *New Left Review* 201: 76–100.

Kome, Penney. (1995). Common front de-Kleins cutbacks. *Herizons*. spring.

Kumar, Pradeep. (1993). Collective bargaining and women's workplace concerns. In Briskin and McDermott.

Little, Margaret. (1989). Women and unions: Movement make over. *Our Times*, December, 12–14.
LO. (1994). *Förslag till landssekretariatet angäende ökad kvinnorepresentation i LO*.
Mahon, Rianne. (1996). Woman wage earners and the future of Swedish unions. *Economic and Industrial Democracy* 17 (4): 545–86.
– (1995). Swedish unions in new times: Women workers as the basis for renewal. Paper prepared for the annual meeting of the American Political Science Association.
– (1991). From solidaristic wages to solidaristic work: A post-Fordist historic compromise for Sweden. *Economic and Industrial Democracy* 12 (3): 295–325.
Melcher, Dale, Jennifer Eichstedt, Shelley Eriksen, and Dan Clawson. (1992). Women's participation in local union leadership: The Massachusetts experience. *Industrial and Labor Relations Review* 45 (2): 267–80.
Mohanty, Chandra. (1991). Under Western eyes: Feminist scholarship and colonial discourses. In Chandra Mohanty, Ann Russo, and Lourdes Torres (eds.), *Third World Women and the Politics of Feminism*, Bloomington: Indiana University Press.
Nadeau, Denise. (1995). For bread and roses. *Kinesis*, July-August.
Needleman, Ruth. (1988). Women workers: A force for rebuilding unionism. *Labor Research Review* 11 (spring): 1–13.
Nichols-Heppner, Barbara. (1984). Women in public sector unions in Quebec: Organizing for equality. Unpublished PhD thesis, McGill University.
Panitch, Leo, and Donald Swartz. (1988). *The Assault on Trade Union Freedoms*. Toronto: Garamond.
Pocock, Barbara. (1996). Challenging male advantage in Australian unions. PhD thesis, University of Adelaide.
Qvist, Gunnar, Joan Acker, and Val Lorwin. (1984). Sweden. In Alice Cook, Val Lorwin and Arlene Daniels (eds.), *Women and Trade Unionism in Eleven Industrialized Countries*. Philadelphia: Temple University Press.
Ruggie, Mary. (1988). Gender, work, and social progress. In Jane Jenson et al. (eds.), *Feminization of the Labor Force*. New York: Oxford.
– (1987). Worker's movements and women's interests: The impact of labor-state relations in Britain and Sweden. In Mary Katzenstein and Carol Mueller (eds.), *Women's Movements in United States and Western Europe*. Philadelphia: Temple University Press.
Sainsbury, Diane. (1988). The Scandinavian model and women's interests: The issues of universalism and corporatism. *Scandinavian Political Studies*, special issue on Feminism and Politics, 11 (4): 337–46.
Simard, Monique. (1988). Quebec: Fighting the right in coalitions. *Canadian Dimension* 22 (March/April): 37–40.

Statistics Canada. (1995). *Women in Canada: A Statistical Report.* 3rd ed. Catalogue no. 89-503E. Ottawa.
Stinson, Jane, and Penni Richmond. (1993). Women working for unions: Female staff and the politics of transformation. In Briskin and McDermott.
Sweden. (1994). Ministry of Health and Social Affairs. *Shared Power/Responsiblity: The National Report by the Government of Sweden for the Fourth World Conference on Women in Beijing 1995.* Stockholm.
– (1991). Jämställdhetsombudsmannen. *Act Concerning Equality between Men and Women.* Stockholm. Translation of Swedish Code of Statutes (SFS) 1991: 433.
Warskett, Rosemary. (1996). The politics of difference and inclusiveness within the Canadian labour movement. *Economic and Industrial Democracy* 17 (4): 587–625.
White, Julie. (1993). *Sisters and Solidarity: Women and Unions in Canada.* Toronto: Thompson Educational Publishing.
Whitehouse, Gillian. (1992). Legislation and labour market gender inequality: An analysis of OECD countries. *Work, Employment and Society* 6 (1): 65–86.
Woodward, Alison, and Håkon Leiulfsrud. (1990). Masculine/feminine organization: Class versus gender in Swedish unions. In Stewart Clegg (ed.), *Organization Theory and Class Analysis.* Berlin: Walter de Gruyter.

Looking for New Opportunities in Politics: Women's Organizations and the Political Parties in Canada and Sweden

CHANTAL MAILLÉ AND LENA WÄNGNERUD

ABSTRACT

This chapter compares the ways in which women in Canada and Sweden have organized in order to influence the political scene. It starts with a brief discussion on the concept of representation and its possible meanings from a feminist perspective. This first section also deals with the issue of representing women's interests: how far can the presence of women in political institutions take us in terms of presenting a feminist plan and initiating a change for women in society? The article then looks at what can be considered an indicator of a given group's degree of representation within political structures – namely, the percentages of women elected in political positions in both countries – and formulates different explanations for the variations, looking more specifically at the impact of variables such as the type of electoral system and the measures adopted by political parties in each country to encourage female participation. Finally, the article examines women's own organizations and their impact in the field of politics. Our conclusion brings us to consider the need to reform parliamentary democracy and political institutions in order to make them more compatible with a feminist vision of power.

Why do women organize in the field of politics? The question is deliberately naive. It is a historical matter of fact that women, at least since the turn of the century, have gotten together around political issues. An obvious answer is that they want to have a say in the socio-economic and political events that shape their lives. However, the answer is more ambiguous if one considers the severe critique that feminists have made of political institutions.

Since the latest surge of feminism in the late 1960s and early 1970s, there has been an ongoing debate about the validity of representative democracy. The fundamental question is whether or not participation in established representational structures is beneficial to women. Feminists and other social activists argue that parliaments tend to over-represent the dominant groups and block the presence of disadvantaged ones such as women, poor people, and ethnic or racial minorities (Phillips, 1995).

Despite this ongoing questioning, political parties continue to be a part of women's lives; they are the vehicle of political power, and they contribute to the improvement or worsening of women's social and economic conditions. But women are not totally dependent on parties to gain access to the political agenda; various types of women's organizations have, for example, been able to function as alternative channels for affecting government policies. This chapter compares the ways in which women in Canada and Sweden have organized in order to influence the political scene. It contrasts the organizational *forms* that women have chosen and the *goals* that they have formulated, and evaluates their success in influencing politics.

The first impression is that we deal with two countries that differ immensely: Sweden has the highest proportion of women elected – 42.7 per cent in 1998 – in the world, while Canada had 20.5 per cent of elected women in the 1997 federal election. However, by going beyond questions of sheer numbers, we are able to bridge that gap and show pros and cons for women in both systems.

We begin with a brief discussion of the concept of representation. We then look at the number of women in political positions in both countries and provide explanations for the variations. Finally, our article examines women's own organizations and their impact. In the course of our review of the subject, we hope to provide some answers to the question of whether a feminist political plan can work within the confines of existing institutions, or whether women must look for other ways of putting forward a feminist point of view.

REPRESENTATION: THEORETICAL PERSPECTIVE

For many feminist writers the strength of the feminist perspective in the field of politics lies in the politicization of activities considered by classical political science to be outside the political sphere. Kirstie McLure (1992) states: "The critical power of feminism ... lies in its politicization of activities traditionally excluded from 'the political,' and more specifically in its erasure of distinctions between public and private life, between political and domestic economy. Its 'new definition of politics' is thus represented as analogous to nineteenth-century politicization of the realm of production and exchange" (346). For McLure, what distinguishes feminist political theory from other concepts is the notion that activities in one's personal life are considered to be part of one's political functions.

However, the very idea of representation implies a delegation of power, resulting in a concentration of power seemingly irreconcilable with feminism. The problem does not stem entirely from electoral systems. Representation itself implies an inequality between the one who is representing and the one who is represented, limiting each group to a specific role.

Virginia Sapiro (1990) proposes that women's political involvement assumes many forms and cannot be reduced to their participation in structures that have until recently completely excluded them. It can also be said that levels of power which are less structured and where the stakes are lower present fewer obstacles for women, and are thus a better choice in their quest for integration. This observation supports Thelma McCormack's view (1975) that the forms of political involvement developed by women in Western society arose out of activities centred on the community – activities where prestige is not very important.

Jane Arscott and Linda Trimble (1996) propose a distinction between two aspects of representation: "representation by women (which obviously can only be done by women) and representation for women (which can be undertaken by either men or women). Only by combining the quantitative and qualitative aspects of representation are we likely to achieve a comprehensive understanding of representation and its significance for their public life" (8).

A similar distinction has been made by Joni Lovenduski and Pippa Norris (1993). However, their comparative research on Western democracies has shown that, even though analytically separated, the two aspects of women's representation – the quantitative and the qualitative – in practice tend to go hand in hand. They conclude that historically, women's issues have been brought to the political agenda mainly by women: "Prominent party women, supported by women's organizations and networks raised issues of sex equality in the parties. Often they began with demands for policies to secure sex equality in employment, but the implications of equality for childcare, reproductive rights and family policies were also issues" (4).

This result concurs with the argument that women legislators, the problems of representation considered, can nonetheless make a difference (Carroll, 1985; Purdy, 1991; Thomas, 1994). According to Jane Arscott (1993), "The difference that sex difference in legislators can make includes the expansion of the range of issues considered to be political, the bringing of a gender-specific perspective to bear on already established issues, including the entire gamut of taxation, defense and economic issues of general interest to the public and a symbolic presence that helps in the continuing task of eliminating sex-based discrimination" (16).

REPRESENTING WOMEN'S INTERESTS

What we are heading towards is a question positioned at the core of the feminist debate: How far can the presence of women in political institutions take us in terms of presenting a feminist plan, thus initiating a change for ordinary women in society?

The notion of a "critical mass" is very important here. This is the idea that women have a meaningful presence in decision-making processes when their representation is above a given percentage (Vickers, 1996). Studies (Gingras et al., 1989) show that women who are active in politics are critical of the culture underlying political life and the parliamentary system, where loyalty to the party line takes precedence over other types of solidarity. The milieu makes it difficult for female politicians to defend women's interests with any forcefulness. However, studies from countries where women constitute more than a third of the members in political institutions indicate a context more responsive to women's demands (Skjeie, 1992; Wängnerud, 1998). A "critical mass" strategy might therefore be a justifiable solution in the short term.

A series of interviews with female politicians in Quebec (Maillé, 1990a) has shown that, although these women are few in number, they tend to think of themselves as representatives of women in general when they take the floor. They say that this identification has been forged out of experiences in their personal and family lives as well as their advocacy work. In Sweden as well, female politicians are aware of being representatives of women's issues and concerns in their parliamentary work (Oskarson and Wängnerud 1995: 128–30).[1]

It is obvious that the political representation of women involves much more than the mere presence of women in political office. But what exactly does it entail? Looking at the participation of women in politics from a feminist point of view, we propose that political representation involves both the presence of women in formal political structures and their involvement in autonomous women's organizations – in pressure groups, community groups, and volunteer work.

WOMEN IN POLITICAL POSITIONS

In this section, we start by looking at something often considered to be one of the most important indicators of a given group's degree of representation within formal political structures: the percentage of its members elected to positions of power. We have already pointed out the fundamental problems inherent in these institutions. We therefore do not suggest that the percentage of elected women is a *sufficient* indicator of the degree of women's political representation. However, it seems possible that by studying available data more closely, we can understand the relationship between women and the political institutions of the society in which they live.

Over the second half of the twentieth century, there has been a net increase in the number of women at all levels of government in Canada and Sweden; however, the increase has been significantly more rapid in Sweden. This development has, in both countries, taken place without a formalized system of quotas that would reserve a certain number of seats for women. In Canada the 1997 federal election result confirmed the trend of a rising number of women elected (table 1). In that campaign 62 women won 20.5 per cent of the seats, an increase of 9 over the 1993 election. However, nearly half the women who ran for office in 1993 and 1997 represented small parties or ran as independents, with practically no chance of being elected because of the type of electoral system. (Canada is characterized by a single-member plurality system, meaning that one representative is elected from each constituency. The government is formed by the party that has obtained the highest number of elected candidates, and the leader of this party becomes prime minister.)

The emerging trend of increased representation holds some promise in the struggle to change the status of women in Canadian politics. However, progress remains very slow and random, in part because the political parties have not instituted any mandatory regulations to increase women's participation. If women members of the federal Parliament are elected at the same rate as they were between 1993 and 1997, and if the number of seats remains constant at 301, it will take more than seven elections before an equal number of women and men are elected to the House of Commons. It is important to note that this scenario is based on continuity of growth. In reality, some ground is likely to be lost unless specific measures are taken to increase the number of women elected.

Despite the fact that two of the three important political parties at the federal level in Canada have had women leaders, this degree of political involvement still remains largely out of reach to women as a

Table 1
Canada: Percentage of women candidates in federal elections and percentage of women elected, 1921–1997

Election Year	*% of women candidates*	*% of women elected*
1921–67	2.4	0.8
1968	3.5	0.4
1972	6.4	1.8
1974	9.4	3.4
1979	13.8	3.6
1980	14.4	5.7
1984	14.5	9.6
1988	19.2	13.2
1993	22.0	17.9
1997	24.4	20.5

Note: Data for 1921–84 from Canadian Advisory Council on the Status of Women and for 1988, 1993, and 1997 from Elections Canada.

group. In the 1993 federal election, Progressive Conservative leader Kim Campbell lost her seat and led her party to one of the most stunning defeats in Canadian political history, while New Democratic Party leader Audrey McLaughlin won her own riding and ended up with a caucus of only nine (the NDP had held 43 seats at dissolution). Canada had reached a milestone in 1993 by electing its first woman to the top of the political pyramid, but Kim Campbell survived only five months as prime minister.

In Sweden the 1970s are generally seen as the breakthrough for women in politics. In 1973 the number of women elected to the national parliament, the Riksdag, surpassed those elected in the Canadian federal election of 1993. In the Social Democratic cabinet of the mid-1990s, half the appointed ministers were female (11 of 22), although only one of the seven major Swedish parties was headed by women leaders (the Left Party).[2] Similarly, in the current (1998) Social Democratic cabinet, half the appointed ministers are female, although among the major parties in Sweden, only the Left Party is at present led by a woman.

According to political scientist Wilma Rule (1993), the Canadian electoral system is not "woman-friendly." A proportional system based on party lists, such as the one in Sweden, is considered to be more advantageous. The basic difference between the two countries is that in Sweden more than one candidate is elected from each constituency. A list details the candidates who stand for each party, and the seats are distributed proportionally to each party that receives more than 4 per cent of the votes. A big party usually gets more than one candidate elected from each constituency. This process means that women do not have to be in a top position to get elected. Even numbers three and four might have a chance.[3]

British political scientist Pippa Norris has discussed why a party-list system facilitates women's entry into politics; one reason is that the parties have the ability consciously to compose and balance their lists. It is easier to respond to demands for female candidates when there are more seats to deal with. Norris also points to the fact that greater proportionality generally increases the number of seats which change hands in each election. This pattern improves political newcomers' access to Parliament (Lovenduski and Norris, 1993: 314–15).

However, in addition to proportionality and the use of lists, other features of the Swedish electoral system encourage women's representation. One is the use of large multi-member constituencies. The country has twenty-eight constituencies, roughly corresponding to the provinces. On average, about 12 MPs represent each constituency. The second factor is that the Parliament is comparatively large in relation to the size of the electorate. The Riksdag is composed of 349 MPs, who represent an electorate of approximately six and a half million voters (Sainsbury 1993: 266).

On the whole, we agree with Norris when she says that a party-list system is a necessary, but not sufficient condition for high levels of female representation (Lovenduski and Norris, 1993: 314). To elaborate this argument further, we will, in the case of Sweden, look more closely at differences between the parties in levels of women's representation. Since 1970 there have not been any major changes in the Swedish electoral system, which means that this factor cannot – at least not solely – be used to explain the rapid increase of women in the Riksdag over the past twenty to twenty-five years.

The presence of women in the top levels of politics is characteristic of all the Nordic countries.[4] The growth of the welfare state and an egalitarian political culture, along with the similarities in electoral systems, are important to that development. The expansion of the welfare state has meant an integration of women into the labour market as well as an assimilation of traditional female areas of responsibility – including family policy and care of the elderly – into politics.

By contrast, Canada has a low percentage of female MPs, a much more liberal state, and as we stated earlier, a woman-unfriendly electoral system. The notion of equality is present in the Canadian political culture, but little attention has been paid to numerical representation of the different politically significant groups that have forged Canadian society. Also, in Canada the state has provided much less support for parental responsibilities (i.e., day-care facilities), leaving the burden of

Table 2
Sweden: Percentage of women elected to the riksdag in national elections, 1971–1998

Election year	*Parliament average*	*Percentage of women by party*							
		Left	*Soc.*	*Cent.*	*Lib.*	*Mod.*	CD	*Green*	ND
1971	14	18	17	13	9	10	—	—	—
1973	21	21	23	24	15	16	—	—	—
1976	23	21	23	24	15	16	—	—	—
1979	28	25	28	33	26	25	—	—	—
1982	28	20	30	32	14	24	—	—	—
1985	32	16	35	32	39	22	—	—	—
1988	38	38	41	38	43	27	—	45	—
1991	34	31	41	39	33	26	31	—	12
1994	41	46	48	37	35	28	33	56	—
1998	43	42	50	56	35	31	40	50	—

Note: Complete names for the parties are as follows: the Left Party, the Social Democratic Party, the Centre Party, the Liberal Party, the Moderate Party, the Christian Democratic Party, the Green Party, and the New Democracy Party. Statistics from official parliamentary records. Number of seats in Parliament: 349 (350 in 1971 and 1973).

juggling work and family responsibilities to individuals, specifically to women.

Norwegian political scientist Helga Hernes characterizes not just the electoral system but society in general as "woman-friendly" in Nordic countries (Hernes, 1987; see also Graubard, 1986). However, common structural features such as the ones discussed above still do not explain the variations shown in table 2 in the number of women in the Riksdag. The Swedish experience reveals the importance of discussing party ideology within this context.

There are three parties with an almost equal share of women and men in their 1998 parliamentary representation: the Centre Party, the Social Democratic Party, and the Green Party. A second grouping in the contemporary Riksdag consists of the Left Party, the Christian Democratic Party, and the Liberal Party, which all have about 40 per cent female representation. A third element comprises the Moderate Party, which has about 30 per cent women. The Moderate Party is actually the most remarkable within the Swedish context. The 1980s were a period of electoral success for the party; however, this has not been reflected in any significant growing female parliamentary representation. The Moderate Party is the most right-wing in Sweden.

While we would not suggest a complete correspondence between party ideology and the number of women elected, left-wing and middle-positioned parties tend to have more female representatives than do parties to the right. Over the past decade the ideological base seems to have become more and more important in explaining the number of women elected to the Riksdag. Before 1970 there were few systematic variations between the parties, and the development since then cannot be sufficiently explained by factors such as party size, electoral success, or political establishment. The Green Party, for example, is a small newcomer to Swedish politics, while the Social Democratic Party is a big party that has dominated the political scene since the 1930s (Oskarson and Wängnerud, 1995: 100–2; Wängnerud, 1998: 29ff).

Pippa Norris sums up the importance of looking at party ideology when it concerns getting women into political positions. "Just as parties of the right tend to favour a minimal role for government in the free market economy, so they lean towards non-intervention or regulation of the candidate recruitment process" (Lovenduski and Norris, 1993: 320).

In Canada the situation is quite different: "The combination of Canada's single-member plurality electoral system and the extremely decentralized candidate-selection process makes it very difficult for parties to adopt any kind of workable affirmative-action program for women or other underrepresented groups" (Young, 1996: 86). But in addition to the type of electoral system and candidacy designation, Canadian political parties are characterized by a more pragmatic approach to issues and programs. "Political parties, especially Canada's brokerage parties, are pragmatic institutions whose logic is defined by the objective of capturing political power" (Gotell and Brodie, 1991: 60). "Lacking clearly delineated policy programs, brokerage parties seek to build coalitions among various groups within the electorate. This characteristic of Canadian parties created space for the expression of variants of feminism within the party caucuses. Because Canadian parties generally seek to act as brokers among competing interests (usually regionally based) and have avoided taking distinctive ideological stances, women within parties can advocate certain feminist policy stances as a means of attracting female voters" (Young, 1996: 100). In the following section we focus in more detail on the extent to which parties in Canada and Sweden intervene to regulate women's representation.

WOMEN IN POLITICAL PARTIES

Some parties have adopted far-reaching strategies, such as quotas, to encourage female participation, while others have not. Why? Pippa Norris has, as mentioned, pointed to the role of party ideology. Her observation is based on broadly conducted comparative studies of Western democracies, which show that social democratic and green parties are generally more likely than others to adopt strategies to regulate representational imbalances (Lovenduski and Norris, 1993: 320).

However, it is also important to keep the specific milieu of each country in mind. It might be that, once certain actions are taken by one party to increase women's representation, other parties within that specific political system will follow suit. Arguably, the most radical measure taken within a country-specific context will become a sort of "standard" to which all others will be contrasted.[5] Here we look at strategies implemented by the parties in Canada and Sweden to get more women involved in electoral politics. We also discuss the role played by caucuses and women's federations inside the established party structure.

In recent years the major Canadian federal parties have demonstrated a new interest in the issue of women's representation during public leadership conventions. But so far no party has adopted any quotas for women's representation or other measures such as reserving certain ridings for female candidates. However, the Liberal Party for the 1997 election adopted a goal of 25 per cent of female candidates and "airlifted" them into some ridings, bypassing the usual nomination process. The party also distributed a document for female candidates that generated a lot of both positive and negative comments, since it included tips on how to dress and make up properly for the electoral campaign. Before women's caucuses in political parties were established at the federal and provincial levels in Canada, the parties had no specific objectives with regard to encouraging female candidates. But in the 1970s the long-established women's caucuses, energized by the women's liberation movement, became places where women finally took power. "Despite continuing tensions within party organizations, older auxiliary-type attitudes and women's groups are gradually being replaced either by more explicitly pro-feminist ones, or by integrated structures that do not include women's units of any type. Unlike traditional associations, which frequently functioned as support structures for mainstream parties, newer party women's groups tend to emphasize increased female representation in party activities" (Bashevkin, 1993: 132).

Today each of the three major federal parties in Canada has created a special fund to support female candidates. The initiative shows a new degree of consciousness surrounding the under-representation of women in decision-making positions within the political parties. The fact remains, however, that the sums allocated to women are minimal.

In Canada, as well as in Sweden, women are well represented among the membership and lower ranks of the political parties. But the higher the rank, the fewer the women. This fact is attributable to several factors: socialization, failure to conform to the socio-economic model favoured by political parties, weak networks within the parties, the demands of child rearing, and exclusion of informal power networks from the structure. Sylvia Bashevkin (1993) has noted the under-representation of women in Canadian parties. "Party activity in Canada has been characterized by an absence of females in upper-echelon elite positions, particularly in organizations that hold, or are likely to take over, the reins of government. Empirical evidence for 'the higher the fewer' and 'the more competitive the fewer' was found in data on local constituency executives, convention delegates, campaign managers, party-office holders, candidates for public office, legislators and cabinet appointees" (145).

What, then, can be done to promote women in Canadian politics? The electoral system seems to represent just one more obstacle to increasing the number of elected women. Adopting a system of proportional representation could mean a more representative democracy with greater room for parties reflecting special-interest groups. Political parties in Canada could make more concerted attempts to encourage female candidates and representatives to join their ranks. They could make a special effort to recruit more women candidates in ridings that are winnable. Arscott (1993) has noted: "When women candidates win nominations in federal electoral contests they have tended to be selected all too often in situations in which their party has little possibility of gaining power or the party candidate in the riding has little prospect of winning."

The parties could also lend potential candidates practical and realistic support. Women interested in running as candidates could network among themselves to avoid feeling isolated and to get the moral support and solidarity that they may not receive from others in their party. And since many women interested in running for office cannot do so for lack of money, controlled public funding of all election campaigns would ensure a greater measure of equity and might well result in significantly more female candidates.

In its final report, the 1991 Royal Commission on Electoral Reform and Party Financing in Canada (Lortie Commission) did not endorse proportional representation. It did, however, recommend many other measures that might facilitate women's access to elected positions. The report's most important proposals, which would afford women greater access to elective legislative office, included "(1) mandatory leaves of absence granted by employers to employees seeking nomination and candidacy; (2) spending limits in nomination contests; (3) tax receipts to nomination campaign contributors; (4) tax deductibility for child care if the primary caregiver sought nomination on election; and (5) formal party search committees and other processes that demonstrably promote the identifications and nomination of broadly representative candidates" (Bashevkin, 1993: 101–2).

One recommendation of the Lortie Commission was more specifically targeted at increasing opportunities for women to be nominated for electoral campaign through party bonuses; the report stated:

> We recommend that should the overall percentage of women in the House of Commons be below 20 per cent following either of the next two elections, then: (1) at the two elections following the next election, the reimbursement of each registered political party with at least 20 per cent female MPs be increased by an amount equivalent to the percentage of its women MPs to a maximum of 150 per cent; (2) this measure be automatically eliminated once the overall percentage in the House of Commons has attained 40 per cent; and (3) following the third election, if this measure is still in place, the Canada Election Commission review it and recommend to Parliament whether it should be retained or adjusted. (Canada, 1991: 280)

We would not suggest that there are no obstacles to women in the Swedish political system; "the higher the fewer" and "the more competitive the fewer" are plausible descriptions, even if the gender representation in positions of power is more balanced than in Canada. One important distinction between the two countries is the electoral campaign. In Sweden, campaigns are organized around parties, not individual candidates, and to a large extent are based on governmental party subsidies. This policy means, for example, that the individual candidate does not have to seek her own funding. Another difference is that in Sweden the nomination process is formalized. The party is much more of a focus there than the candidate.[6] The strategies to increase women's representation have therefore mainly centred on balancing the composition of different levels within the party structure. In the 1970s doing so basically meant adopting measures to increase women's presence in *internal* party boards, committees, and other bodies. This can be seen as a first stage of developing women's representation.

The gender-equality discussion in Swedish politics emerged mainly within the Social Democratic Party. During the 1960s a high-level committee was appointed (with the prime minister as honorary chair) which for the first time ever adopted a special women's program. In 1969 an all-party document, *Towards Equality*, placed equality and the means to achieve it at the top of the political agenda in Sweden. Political scientist Diane Sainsbury has described the vitalizing effect that the new women's movement had on the debate on women's representation during this period. She also points to the "domino-effect" of the measures taken within the Social Democratic Party. Once the party had subscribed to the goal of equality, *all* party women could use it as leverage in their claims for representation (Sainsbury, 1993: 280).

During the 1990s a new wave of feminist critique has emerged within the political debate in Sweden. The results of the 1991 general election fuelled this development as the average number of women in the Riksdag decreased from 38 to 34 per cent (table 2). Although the development reflected an upswing for the Swedish right wing, it highlighted weaknesses in all the parties concerning their strategies to increase women's representation. The Swedish parties have been hesitant to use a formalized quota system to regulate their electoral party lists. Any measures stronger than recommendations or encouragement have been seen as interfering too much with local party nomination processes. In Norway, by comparison, quotas have been more readily accepted (Skjeie, 1992; 1993).

However, the drop in women's parliamentary representation in 1991 led to the formation of a feminist network, made up of both feminist activists and women involved in political parties, called the Support Stockings.[7] Their work is behind the fact that a new standard was set within the Swedish political context. In September 1993 the Social Democratic Party congress passed six bills requiring – not just recommending – that all lists used in the election be regulated, with every second seat reserved for a woman.[8]

In the discussion of how to increase women's representation in Canadian politics, the importance of support and solidarity from other women has been central. In Sweden, women's federations were established during the 1920s and 1930s in all major parties. They have to a great extent functioned as significant channels for women to get into positions of power. They have also been important in work on equality. It would be wrong to describe them as merely auxiliaries in the party system. The women's federations within the Social Democratic and the Centre parties in particular have generated ambitious women's programs of their own. The federations have also offered educational programs directed towards women. Diane Sainsbury (1993) concluded: "[H]istorically, the women's party organizations [in Sweden] both fought unrelentingly for increased political representation, and they have offered a power base for women. In a cross-national perspective, these organizations appear to have more political clout than their counterparts in other countries" (276).

The influence of these federations has to be seen in the light of their size. During the 1970s the women's federations in the Social Democratic, Centre, and Moderate parties had 50,000 to 70,000 members each. Today these organizations are shrinking. This development seems like a paradox considering the rising number of women in the Riksdag. But the overall political involvement of Swedish women is not decreasing. On the contrary: in terms of their own reported political interest, voting, participation in demonstrations, and protest activities, it is rising (Oskarson and Wängnerud, 1995: 38–55).

The decline in membership is not confined just to women's federations. Many parties in European democracies that were founded at the turn of the century are losing ground among ordinary citizens. Interviews conducted with the presidents of the Swedish women's federations confirm that women today look for new models of cooperation to meet the demands of more "updated" ways of conducting politics (Wängnerud, 1994).

WOMEN IN AUTONOMOUS WOMEN'S GROUPS

We have stated that to look only at the presence of females in formal institutions is not enough in order to understand the degree of women's political representation. In this section we therefore look at organizing in autonomous women's groups in Canada and Sweden. A brief review of the different forms of representation demonstrates that the representation of women in Canada is related more to the existence of a strong women's movement than it is to the presence of women in political office. The women's movement acts as a transmitter, making sure women's concerns are being heard by traditional representative institutions. Over the years, women have made significant advances in the area of rights.

The 1970s in Canada saw the first initiatives in women's groups specifically oriented towards increasing the representation of women in politics and educating women in all forms of political participation. Part of the solution to dealing with the state seemed obvious – get more women involved in formal politics. Women's groups across the country were established to encourage women to run for office (Cohen, 1993: 23). These initiatives coincided with a general trend towards more-specialized activities organized by women's groups. While political parties took steps to promote women's participation, women's groups began to present more focused activities in workshops, seminars, and conferences. They also published helpful guides and prepared other resource materials for would-be candidates and appointees. Although the women's groups did not launch a planned cooperative effort, some of them simultaneously reached the conclusion that political power was the nerve centre for social change. They realized the need to claim power in their own right and to find ways to overcome the obstacles responsible for the political under-representation of women.

The National Action Committee on the Status of Women (NAC) has carried out a variety of activities designed to promote women's political representation. During the 1984 federal election, it organized a debate between the party leaders on women's issues. "The spectacle of three men, who at best had been heavily briefed by the women in their party in order to debate each other on how women would be best treated by their own party, was an historic first that feminists thoroughly enjoyed" (Cohen, 1993: 23).

During the 1988 and 1993 federal elections, NAC conducted an advertising campaign, distributed buttons, and encouraged all women in Canada to use their vote. NAC members received an election kit containing a list of questions to ask the political candidates which focused on four subjects: free trade, violence against women, abortion, and childcare centres. A questionnaire was sent to three major federal parties, and the responses received were made public through the media. In the 1997 election, NAC organized another debate on women's issues with representatives from the five most important political parties. Only one national leader, though, accepted the invitation: Alexa McDonough from the New Democratic Party, the only female leader of a federal party. Other parties sent female representatives. The event did not get all the media coverage that it deserved, as if to suggest that women's issues were not central to this electoral campaign.

Other groups have been directly involved in promoting women in politics. In 1984 a group of women set up the Committee for '94, whose objective was gender parity in the House of Commons by 1994. Based in Ontario, it organized a variety of activities to promote the visibility of women in politics. In 1986, the group co-organized the Ryerson Conference in Toronto on "Women in Politics"; two years later it held a press conference to denounce the lack of women's representation in Parliament. In 1990 the Committee for '94 released its brief on public funding to the Royal Commission on Electoral Reform and Party Financing. The brief called for a system of public financing for candidates in elections in order to level the playing field for women, ethnic and racial minorities, and poor people. Finally, the group created an internship program enabling women to familiarize themselves with government structures and lobbied for the appointment of women to senior government positions. It disbanded in the mid-1990s, having foundered with the arrival on the political map of far-right women politicians (Hurst, 1997).

An organization called "The 52% Solution" was created in Newfoundland in 1986. Its purpose was to foster equality and peace by offering a feminist analysis of political problems and their possible solutions. The group was structured informally and was modelled after the Icelandic Women's Alliance.

In Quebec a number of women's groups have encouraged women's political participation, including the Association Féminine d'Education et d'Action Sociale (AFEAS, or Women's Association for Education and Social Action), the Fédération des Femmes du Québec (FFQ, or Quebec Women's Federation), and the Femmes Regroupées pour l'Accès au Pouvoir Politique et Economique (FRAPPE, or Women Organized for Access to Political and Economic Power). AFEAS sponsored an event called "Women and Political Power" in 1985. During the two-day workshop, participants and experts formerly active in various areas of politics discussed the problems associated with political participation. AFEAS also launched a step-by-step guide to running for municipal, provincial, or federal office. Local political clubs were created to provide the necessary support and information to women interested in doing so.

The FFQ, the largest umbrella organization of women's groups in Quebec, has also undertaken specific measures to increase women's political representation. In 1987 it held a symposium called "Women and Political Power: Do They Mix?" at which were debated the strategies that feminists should adopt vis-à-vis political power. Participants discussed issues surrounding their relationship to the political system, such as whether to support all female candidates or only those who agreed to defend FFQ policies and who tried to establish links between women's groups and female politicians. Several suggestions were made, including creating support groups for candidates and developing ties between the FFQ and female incumbents. However, no specific organizations were created as a result of this symposium. In June 1995 the federation successfully organized a rally, the "Bread and Roses" march, in which hundreds of women walked for more than ten days, their goal to present the provincial government with a list of nine demands aimed at fighting women's poverty. The success of the event, as well as the wide media coverage it received, have reaffirmed the leadership position of the FFQ within the women's movement in Quebec (Maillé, 1996).

In 1985, FRAPPE (whose acronym means "to hit or strike" in French) was created to help women penetrate the bastions of political and economic power by supporting female candidates, providing training, and organizing discussions with political personalities. FRAPPE emphasized the importance of networking as a key to spheres of influence and maintained a non-partisan stance. Its political support was limited to the period prior to nominating conventions, and it did not continue its involvement once the candidates were chosen. FRAPPE's goal was to ensure that the greatest possible number of nominations were won by women, regardless of their political allegiance. In 1997 the group reduced its activities, but it still organizes networking activities such as cocktail parties with high-profile and political women.

Several groups across the country have taken the name "Winning Women" and have set up informal networks in Alberta, British Columbia, Manitoba, Nova Scotia, and Saskatchewan. They had a common goal: to increase political participation and representation of appointed or elected women at all levels of government. The groups have operated autonomously, and none has had a full-time office. The British Columbia section of Winning Women put an end to its activities when members realized that much of the work needed to elect more women was now being accomplished by the women's caucuses of political parties. In Nova Scotia the Winning Women local section disbanded after the 1991 conference "Skills for Women in Politics." The grassroots initiative for this network can be attributed to women working in different organizations: junior leagues; local Councils of Women; university departments of political science, continuing studies, and women's studies; and various women's groups.

Canadian women's groups have already begun a process of education and organization around the issue of political representation. The net effect of these efforts has been to increase public awareness of the under-representation of women and to place pressure on the parties to remedy the situation. Groups such as the Committee for '94 have also fostered the creation of informal networks of women involved in partisan politics, which have in turn facilitated the diffusion of ideas and information regarding techniques for electing women (Young, 1996: 88). Such initiatives must be pursued in the years to come. These efforts could be given a formal framework: for example, they could be integrated into the college or university curriculum of adult or community education programs. At present most of these activities rely on volunteer work and would benefit from institutional support. As well, they would reach more teenagers and young women if they were offered through teaching institutions. Following the model of the Center for Political Leadership in the United States, universities could offer certificates and introductory training sessions in political work. Women's groups are fighting battles that will be decided mainly on the political front. For many, recognition of this fact has stimulated efforts to promote the involvement of women in politics. However, in Canada this approach may present a significant problem for elected female representatives: they must reconcile party loyalty with their solidarity towards women's groups. It might be wise to develop new ties between female politicians and women's groups in order to give the politicians access to a network of support and information, while offering the groups an effective channel for making their voices heard by governments. This avenue requires further consideration.

A lot of the work that has been done by autonomous women's groups in Canada has in Sweden been carried out by women inside the parties. However, of the autonomous groups, the Fredrika Bremer Association is worth mentioning. Founded in 1884, it is the oldest women's organization in Sweden, and its impact upon politics has been significant. The association has acted as an external pressure group, putting forward proposals and stating party positions in an innovative and active way over a long period (Clayhills, 1991: 137–8; Sainsbury, 1993: 279). However, the association can also be seen as working partly from the inside. Women from the Liberal Party in particular have combined a party career with active membership in the association (Sainsbury 1993: 279).

North American feminist scholars are sometimes astonished when they notice the "lack" of women's autonomous organizing in the field of politics in Sweden (e.g., Gelb, 1989). To some extent this reaction can be explained by a misunderstanding of the role that the women's federations have played in the Swedish political system. The description of the strategies used by women in Sweden to influence politics is often highlighted as a dual one of working simultaneously outside and inside the parties. Diane Sainsbury writes about the strategies of the new women's movement during the 1960s and 1970s:

> Thus, contrary to several other countries where the new women's movement initially did not seek influence in male-dominated organizations, large numbers of Swedish women activists chose to work within the parties. There are several reasons for this development. Among the most important was that specific issues closely associated with the new women's movement and important for mobilization purposes – women's equality and abortion on demand – emerged relatively early in the 1960s and were incorporated into the policy agendas of the political parties. Such responses lent credibility to perceptions that working through party channels could pay off. (Sainsbury, 1993: 276; see also Dahlerup and Gulli, 1985)

There are, of course, various types of women's groups in Sweden. However, with few exceptions, such as the Fredrika Bremer Association, there are really no autonomous women's organizations that work to increase women's political representation in a focused way on a long-term basis. There have been some attempts to form women's parties (the first took place during the late 1920s). In 1985 a party was created with the aim of applying "a women's perspective to society at large." However, in the parliamentary election of 1991 it received only 500 votes. The party has been described as invisible by political scientist Maud Eduards (1992: 89).

The feminist network Support Stockings, mentioned earlier, is a very loose formation. Nonetheless, it has managed to make gender issues visible in the Swedish media during the 1990s. Partly this success is due to the fact that the leaders of the network are well established within the media structure in Sweden (see Eduards, 1992). The Support Stockings threatened to form a women's party that would take part in the 1994 electoral race. However, this threat was never realized, and because one of the network's main goals – greatly increased representation of women in politics – has been fulfilled, it currently has a lower profile.

Canada was also the site of a feminist party. Founded in 1979, the Feminist Party of Canada wanted to bring feminist perspectives to policy-making arenas, and it was organized with the intention of fielding candidates. But by 1982 this organization had almost disappeared, following internal disputes over membership issues and goals (Burt and Lorenzin, 1996: 205). In 1990 women from the three major federal parties formed the Association of Women Parliamentarians. The association was open to all female MPs and was created in response to the negative aspects of parliamentary life experienced by women, including the chauvinism of their male colleagues. It served as a forum for discussing common experiences (Young, 1996).

There is a debate in feminist literature on the political situation of women in the Nordic countries. In terms of numbers, they are fairly well represented. Some feminists researchers argue that this has also meant substantial changes in policy outcomes (see Karvonen and Selle, 1995). Studies of legislative behaviour also show clear linkages between women in the Riksdag and women citizen-voters in terms of policy priorities and positions on policy issues (Oskarson and Wängnerud, 1996; 1995). Diane Sainsbury notes that feminist demands such as women's equality and abortion rights were easily incorporated into the agendas of established parties some twenty to thirty years ago. Today we can see how women from different parties in Sweden are working together to strengthen a long-standing feminist demand for the six-hour working day.[9]

One conclusion that can be drawn from the Swedish experience is that women in the established political structure do represent other women and women's specific issues and concerns (Wängnerud, 1998). However, there is also a pressure on women to go along with party loyalties. Maud Eduards argues that there has been no real space for women to act "as women" in Swedish politics. She analyses the attempts to organize specific women's parties as follows: "It can be said that the threat of a women's party is a response to an instrumental, measure-oriented, partially woman-friendly politics which nevertheless lacks a sex/gender-political analysis, and which is thus arbitrary" (Eduards, 1992: 97).

Clearly, the way that women have organized in Sweden has been successful when it concerns getting women into political structures; the 40:60 gender balance in the present parliament is unique from an international perspective. Women inside the structures have been pushing for change; they have been able to transmit ideas from the women's movement. However, it is not clear to what extent this effort has changed the societal position of ordinary women.[10]

Today there is a wide-ranging restructuring of welfare policies in Sweden. The situation is different from the 1970s, when the welfare state and women's political representation were both expanding very quickly. Women in Sweden today are worried about cutbacks in welfare spending; the social-service sector has facilitated their entry into public life and what will happen now no one really knows. The gains that women have made seem to be based on a shaky foundation. The Canadian situation is very similar in many aspects – the gains made by women in Canada over this century are not to be taken for granted either.

Eduards has pointed to the need for women's collective action to secure their interests in society. What might emerge from the contemporary changes in Sweden is perhaps more cross-political action among women. We think that some useful experience can be drawn here from the way that women have worked together in local or regional organizations and in strong national umbrella organizations to put pressure on the political system in Canada.

CONCLUSION

In this article, we have looked at the ways in which Canadian and Swedish women have organized in order to influence the political agenda. Our analysis has rested on the assumption that the numerous presence of females within formal institutions is not enough to provide an understanding of the reality of women's political representation.

The differing electoral systems have had major impacts on the percentage of women elected in each country. In addition to having an electoral system that favours women, Sweden is a more "woman-friendly" society, with its comparatively strong public-welfare sector. In Canada the rise of neo-liberalism has had a major impact on society in general, with the dismantling of the welfare state and its woman-friendly social programs. This development helped to produce a political climate that discourages women's interest in politics. However, although Sweden has a much higher number of elected women at the national level, the position of women in political parties in the two countries is quite similar: they are well represented among the membership and lower ranks of the parties; but the higher the rank, the fewer women there are.

One of the important differences between the two countries lies in the regulations that in Sweden secure seats for female candidates. Canadian political parties have adopted only mild incentives to encourage female candidates, such as special funding, but these are more symbolic than real incentives, given the cost of running campaigns at the national level. Nonetheless, all major federal parties (Liberal, Conservative, and NDP) have women's caucuses that can be labelled "profeminist," and these caucuses have long-established traditions. One of the newly formed parties, the Reform Party, is much more "feminist-unfriendly." Lisa Young observes: "The Reform Party's ideological stance is hostile toward feminism, and party leaders have been unwilling to engage in any way with 'special interests,' like organized feminism" (Young, 1996: 101).

Sweden has similar women's caucuses in national parties, but their major impact seems to be to attract female candidates and not to influence the parties' agenda as in Canada. However, there is evidence that elected women in that country have been important in the development of an expanded political agenda that includes gender equality as well as issues traditionally seen as women's areas of responsibility.

Among the differences that we can identify, the structure of autonomous women's groups and their political influence seems to be the most striking. In Canada, women's organizations are strong and plentiful. These groups are important vehicles of women's political representation, and they function as transmitters of women's concerns to governments. This institutionalized form of lobbying can compensate for the weakness in terms of numbers and power of women who are members of parliament. However, over the course of the thirty-fourth Canadian parliament (1988–93), female members demonstrated that gender does affect legislature behaviour. In their effort to bring more women into the political process and to pursue feminist policy issues, the women worked within the constraints of the party system and on occasion tested its limits (Young, 1996).

In Sweden, women are much more organized around political parties than autonomous groups, and therefore in some ways they reinforce the monopoly that the parties have over the country's political agenda.

However, despite these important differences, Canada and Sweden share a similar concern for electing more women, and in both countries attempts are made by women's groups and the women's caucuses of political parties to develop strategies from a feminist point of view.

It seems likely that in both countries the numbers of women elected nationally will remain at the same levels for years. This is particularly a problem in Canada, where the percentage of elected women is unacceptable, and there are no specific or radical measures adopted to change the situation. Prioritizing the election of women might become a more central issue in the context of the neo-liberal politics that will prevail for the coming years.

Another concern that is shared in both countries is the importance of getting younger women involved in women's organizing and politics. It is impossible to improve the quality of women's political representation if those who are the most concerned, women, do not maintain a sustained interest in the representation of their interests.

Lastly, our chapter brings us to consider the need to reform parliamentary democracy and political institutions in order to make them more compatible with a feminist conception of power. As we discussed earlier, from a feminist standpoint, existing forms of Western democracy by no means reflect the full spectrum of women's political activism. Much of the work that women do in civil society – their fights to give meaning to their status as citizens – is an important dimension of women's political activism that needs to be incorporated into the understanding of their relationships to politics. New political institutions could emerge from this serious rethinking of governance and citizenship.

NOTES

1 Yet the underlying assumption of the idea that women politicians represent all women is that there is something common to all women and that, by virtue of their gender, they all belong to one analytical category. This kind of statement has been rejected by many contemporary feminists, who instead use the framework of identity politics – race, class, or sexual orientation and sometimes age and ability – to draw lines in terms of women's interest. This approach tends to bury the universal woman brought to life by Simone de Beauvoir, which was at the core of the second wave of feminism.

2 There have, for shorter periods, been women leaders also for the Centre and the Liberal parties in Sweden.

3 However, as will be argued later on, this is not the only factor that can explain the number of women in political positions in Sweden. There are

many countries that work with a proportional system which do not elect higer percentages of women than Canada does (see Inter-Parliamentary Union, 1933).

4 In 1995 the proportion of women in Parliament was 40.4 per cent in Sweden, 39.4 per cent in Norway, 33.5 per cent in Denmark, and 25.4 per cent in Iceland. Iceland is the Nordic country where the development in women's representation has been slowest.

5 Although all parties will not adopt the same strategies, they will be compared to each other in debates and in the media. The argument that a sort of "standard" of women's representation is set is demonstrated, for example, at the cabinet level in Sweden. Regardless of which parties have formed the government, there has not been since 1970 any government with fewer female members than the preceding one (Sainsbury, 1993: 273).

6 This pattern might change in the future since a "personal vote" is now part of the Swedish electoral system. The personal vote is, however, quite restricted. A voter can (voluntarily) choose to mark one candidate on the list that the party has put up before the election. To alter the list a candidate needs marks from 8 per cent of the voters in his or her constituency. The personal vote was used for the first time on a large scale in the election of 1998.

7 The aim of the network was to put pressure on the parties so that they would present truly gender-balanced tickets in the election of 1994 (Eduards, 1992).

8 Material from the Social Democratic Party congress (*Partistyrelsen utlåtande över motioner om demokrati, Socialdemokraternas ordinarie kongress den 15–21 september 1993*, 31–2).

9 In a recent article (7 January 1997) in *Dagens Nyheter*, the most influential daily newspaper in Sweden, leading female politicians from the Left, Centre, and Green parties put forward the demand that the working day be shortened.

10 To some extent, this lack of knowledge can be explained by an absence of research. However, we also emphasize that the question of women's societal position is wide-ranging and hard to give a clear-cut answer to.

REFERENCES

Arscott, Jane. (1993). Between the rock and a hard place: Why so few women have been elected to the legislatures of Newfoundland and Nova Scotia. Paper presented at the 1993 annual meeting of the Canadian Political Science Association, Carleton University.

– and Linda Trimble. (1996). *In the Presence of Women: Representation and Canadian Governments*. Toronto: Harcourt Brace.

Bashevkin, Sylvia. (1993). *Toeing the Lines: Women and Party Politics in English Canada.* Toronto: Oxford University Press.

Burt, Sandra, and Elisabeth Lorenzin. (1996). Taking the women's movement to Queen's Park: Women's interests and the New Democratic government of Ontario. In Jane Arscott and Linda Trimble (eds.), *In the Presence of Women: Representation in Canadian Governments.* Toronto: Harcourt Brace.

Canada. (1991). Royal Commission on Electoral Reform and Party Financing. *Reforming Electoral Democracy.* Vol. 2. Ottawa: Canada Communication Group Publishing.

Carroll, Susan J. (1985). *Women as Candidates in American Politics.* Bloomington, Ind.: Indiana University Press.

Clayhills, Harriet. (1991). *Kvinnohistorisk uppslagsbok.* Stockholm: Rabén & Sjögren.

Cohen, Marjorie. (1993). The Canadian women's movement. In Ruth Roach Pierson et al. (eds.), *Canadian Women's Issues,* vol. 1, Strong Voices. Toronto: James Lorimer.

Dahlerup, Drude, and Brita Gulli. (1985). Women's organizations in the Nordic countries: Lack of force or counterforce? In Elina Haavio-Mannila et al. (eds.), *Unfinished Democracy: Women in Nordic Politics.* Oxford: Pergamon Press.

Eduards, Maud L. (1992). Against the rules of the game: On the importance of women's collective actions. In Eduards et al., *Rethinking Change: Current Swedish Feminist Research.* Stockholm: HSFR.

Gelb, Joyce. (1989). *Feminism and Politics: A Comparative Perspective.* Berkeley: University of California Press.

Gilljam, Mikael, and Sören Holmberg. (1995). *Väljarnas val.* Stockholm: Norstedts Juridik.

Gingras, Anne-Marie, et al. (1989). *Sexes et militantisme.* Montréal: CIDIHCA.

Gotell, Lise, and Janine Brodie. (1991). Women and parties: More than an issue of numbers. In Hugh Thorburn (ed.), *Political Parties in Canada.* 6th ed. Scarborough: Prentice-Hall.

Graubard, Stephen R. (1986). *Norden – the Passion for Equality.* Oslo: Norwegian University Press.

Hernes, Helga M. (1987). *Welfare State and Woman Power: Essays in State Feminism.* Oslo: Norwegian University Press.

Hurst, Lynda (1997). Women: Why the house is not a home. *Toronto Star,* 19 April, C1.

Inter-Parliamentary Union. (1993). *Les femmes au Parlement au 30 juin 1993.* Geneva: Inter-Parliamentary Union.

Karvonen, Lauri, and Per Selle (eds.). (1995). *Women in Nordic Politics: Closing the Gap.* Aldershot: Dartmouth.

Lovenduski, Joni, and Pippa Norris (eds.). (1993). *Gender and Party Politics*. London: Sage Publications.

McCormack, Thelma. (1975). Towards a non-sexist perspective on social and political change. In M. Milman and R. Moss Kanter (eds.), *Another Voice: Feminist Perspectives on Social Life and Social Science*. New York: Doubleday.

McLure, Kirstie. (1992). The issue of foundations: Scientized politics, politicized science, and feminist critical practice. In Judith Butler and Joan W. Scott (eds.), *Feminists Theorize the Political*. New York: Routledge.

Maillé, Chantal. (1996). Challenges to representation: Theory and the women's movement in Quebec. In Jane Arscott and Linda Trimble (eds.), *In the Presence of Women: Representation in Canadian Governments*. Toronto: Harcourt Brace.

– (1990a). *Les Québécoises et la conquête du pouvoir politique*. Montréal: St-Martin.

– (1990b). *Primed for Power: Women in Canadian Politics*. Ottawa: Canadian Advisory Council on the Status of Women.

Oskarson, Maria, and Lena Wängnerud. (1995). *Kvinnor som väljare och valda: Om betydelsen av kön i svensk politik*. Lund: Studentlitteratur.

– (1996). Vem representerar kvinnorna? In Bo Särlvik and Bo Rothstein (eds.), *Vetenskapen om politik: Festskrift till professor emeritus Jörgen Westerståhl*. Göteborg: Statsvetenskapliga institutionen.

Phillips, Anne. (1995). *The Politics of Presence*. Oxford: Clarendon Press.

Purdy, Elizabeth R. (1991). *The Representation of Women and Women's Issues: Differences in Voting Patterns of Male and Female Members of the House of Representatives*. Ann Arbor: University of Michigan Press.

Rule, Wilma. (1993). "Woman-friendly to woman-unfriendly electoral systems. Paper presented at the Fifth International Interdisciplinary Congress on Women, San José, Costa Rica.

Sainsbury, Diane. (1993). The politics of increased women's representation: The Swedish case. In Joni Lovenduski and Pippa Norris (eds.), *Gender and Party Politics*. London: Sage Publications.

Sapiro, Virginia. (1990). Political connections: Gender and the meanings of politics." In *Les Avenues de la science politique*. Montréal: Editions de l'ACFAS.

Skjeie, Hege. (1992). *Den politisk betydningen av kjønn: En studie av norsk topp-politikk*. Oslo: Institute for Social Research.

– (1993). Ending the male political hegemony: The Norwegian experience. In Joni Lovenduski and Pippa Norris (eds.), *Gender and Party Politics*. London: Sage Publications.

Thomas, Sue. (1994). *How Women Legislate*. Oxford and New York: Oxford University Press.

Vickers, Jill. (1996). Toward a feminist understanding of representation. In Jane Arscott and Linda Trimble (eds.), *In the Presence of Women: Representation in Canadian Governments*. Toronto: Harcourt Brace.

Wängnerud, Lena. (1998). *Politikens andra sida: Om kvinnorepresentation i Sveriges riksdag*. Göteborg: Statsvetenskapliga institutionen.

– (1994). Interviews conducted for this chapter with representatives of women's political federations in Sweden (unpublished material).

Young, Lisa. (1996). Fulfilling the mandate of difference: Women in the Canadian House of Commons. In Jane Arscott and Linda Trimble (eds.), *In the Presence of Women: Representation in Canadian Governments*. Toronto: Harcourt Brace.

PART THREE

Domestic Policy

Education, Gender Equality, and Women's Organizing in Canada and Sweden

REBECCA PRIEGERT COULTER AND INGA WERNERSSON

ABSTRACT

Women's organizing in education has a long history and involves efforts by women as teachers, mothers, students, and "femocrats" to work individually and collectively through women's organizations, political parties, unions, and other social movements. In both Canada and Sweden, to speak of women's organizing in education is to focus primarily on their strategic use of the state. In Sweden, because of the nature of the state and because there is a national education system, women's efforts have been directed towards making change through the state administration. In Canada, where each of the ten provinces is responsible for its own education system, female teachers have launched the majority of gender-equality initiatives in the schools and have utilized their teachers' federations to this end.

This chapter explores these different contexts for women's organizing efforts around gender and education over the last twenty-five years in Canada and Sweden, while summarizing the many similarities that can be found in theory and practice in the two nations. Using the example of girls and women in science and technology, the article illustrates how women's organizing strategies have been particularly effective when they utilize and expand upon an existing discourse of equality and when they are seen to meet or match other types of policy objectives. Finally, the chapter concludes that shifts in analysis and strategy will be required to take account of new economic and social realities.

Women's organizing in education covers at least two centuries of more or less constant activity by women as teachers, mothers, students, and "femocrats"[1] working individually or collectively through women's organizations, political parties, unions, or social movements. They have been agents of change in a multitude of contexts in education in both Canada and Sweden, whether to promote their own or their students' interests or wider social reforms. Women have been adept at seizing opportunities and gaining access to funding in order to develop a panoply of approaches in the struggle for equality.[2] While it is often difficult, especially in the Swedish context, to isolate and identify specific forms of organizational activity or to generalize about how women organize in education, there is no doubt that in both Canada and Sweden, women have worked on many fronts and with a great deal of flexibility in order to achieve their goals.

One thing is clear: to speak of women's organizing in education is to focus on their strategic use of the state. In both Canada and Sweden, education is publicly funded and state controlled, although it is organized and administered in somewhat different ways.[3] Despite these differences, the form and content of education is a key component of public policy in both countries, and women seeking to effect change in educational policies as they relate to gender must, of necessity, work almost exclusively with, and often within, established institutional frameworks. This reality has had both advantages and disadvantages for women's organizing in education, and it helps to explain why women in Canada and Sweden, while often having similar goals, have organized in somewhat different ways to achieve them.

PUTTING GENDER EQUALITY ON THE AGENDA

When the "sex-role question" was put on the agenda in both Canada and Sweden in the 1960s, education was the obvious tool to change attitudes and reshape conceptions of sex-appropriate work. This was not surprising since achieving equality has been seen as an important purpose of education in each nation for a considerable period of time. For historic reasons, this tendency has been somewhat stronger in Sweden. As part of the "old world," it has an earlier history of explicitly class-based forms of state organization. That one's social position might be more important than individual merit in obtaining social rewards thus has been made more obvious. The educational system was, in this context, identified early as a tool to promote equality. In Canada, class issues in schooling have been less emphasized historically than debates about religion and language. Those debates, however, have also focused on the provision of equal opportunities. The point here is that education in Canada and Sweden has been acknowledged as a tool to achieve equality, so it is understandable that those seeking gender equality would turn to the schools for solutions.

In terms of schooling, equality in both countries has been understood to mean open access and a reward system based on individual merit. Put another way, the emphasis has been on equality of opportunity, although it is not clear that *jämlikhet* is exactly parallel to the Canadian understanding of equal opportunity. The Canadian and Swedish governments point to the fact that the vast majority of young people now complete secondary school as evidence of the success of their respective equality programs. Further evidence is provided in statistics which show that in Canada 58 per cent of males and 63 per cent of females proceed to some form of post-secondary education (Human Resources Development Canada, 1994). In Sweden, 31 per cent of females and 26 per cent of males go on to post-secondary education within three years of completing secondary school *(Bakgrundsmaterial för vuxenutbildning*, 1995: 1). Over a lifetime, 53 per cent of females and males combined seek post-secondary education (Statistics Sweden, personal communication). Over all, the trend in educational attainment statistics suggests that gender equality, understood as equality of access, has essentially been achieved in Canada and Sweden.

As early as 1970, however, this narrow definition of equality had already been challenged by women who seized on the existing discourse about education and equality and refocused it specifically on gender. Initially, attention was directed towards sex roles. In Sweden both men and women were viewed as victims of obsolete sex-role patterns. Through changes in education (and socialization) boys would learn to cook, care for babies, show their feelings, and cry when hurt. Girls would learn to play football, climb trees, and choose jobs that would bring them good salaries, social prestige, and power. By the late 1970s in Sweden, the view of the gender structure as equally evil to males and females rapidly changed. An understanding of the gender system as a power imbalance between males and females developed and increasingly put girls in focus.

In Canada the sex-role issue was from the start primarily constructed as a women's question, and measures taken within the educational system were mostly directed towards girls and women. The Royal Commission on the Status of Women, established in 1967 as a result of the forceful lobbying of Canadian women, identified education as one of nine areas "particularly germane to the status of women" (Canada, 1970: ix). Relying on sex-role socialization theory drawn from the social science research of the day, the commission and many women's groups argued that sex-role stereotyping, the lack of strong female role models for girls, and inadequate career counselling were key factors contributing to women's inequality in Canada. For the best part of the next two decades, this type of analysis shaped educational policy-making around gender issues, and it resulted in remarkably similar initiatives across the country.

Early research in Canada and Sweden exposed sex-differentiated patterns of subject and program choice, the sexual division of labour in education, sex-role stereotyping in textbooks, and the absence of information about women's lives and contributions in the curriculum. An example of an early study from Sweden is Ingrid Fredriksson's analysis of textbooks in history and social studies, which found that girls and women were poorly represented in every possible respect (Fredriksson, 1969). The book, *Kvinnors liv och arbete*, published in 1962, included articles on sex-role socialization by several Norwegian sociologists (Harriet Holter, Sverre Brun-Guldbrandsen, and Per-Olov Tiller) and was an important influence even though it did not deal with education directly. Educational researchers such as Härnqvist (1960) and Svensson (1971) included sex as a variable in their different analyses of the impact of social background on educational opportunity, an approach that, in a sense, made gender relations an aspect of equality. Somewhat later, studies of classroom interaction patterns demonstrated the dominant position of boys despite the explicit policy of equal treatment (Wernersson, 1977).

In Canada during the 1970s, several studies on stereotyping in textbooks were published (Cullen, 1972; Batcher et al., 1975; Women in Teaching, 1975; Ad Hoc Committee Respecting the Status of Women in the North York System, 1975). The studies were consistent in identifying the pervasiveness of sex-role stereotyping and bias in textbooks and curriculum materials. The study by Batcher and colleagues concluded from its review of all the reading series approved for use in grades four to six in Ontario schools that none could be termed "positive-image" or "non-sexist" (1975: i). The North York study found ample evidence of sexism in the readers used in grades one to three, as well as "shocking evidence of various other kinds of rigid stereotyping and of racism" (Ad Hoc Committee Respecting the Status of Women in the North York System, 1975: 16).

ORGANIZING AROUND GENDER AND SCHOOLING IN SWEDEN

Official response to the identification of gender inequalities within the school system occurred more quickly and more thoroughly in Sweden than in Canada. This was probably because public policy in Sweden had long been favourable towards equality between the sexes and women had a history of successfully working within established political bodies, such as the parties, Parliament, and government committees. In addition, within these organizations, some key decision-makers were women who had developed a pronounced gender perspective on issues. Baude (1992) describes how an informal group (Group 222, which can be called an elite network) was formed in the mid-1960s to discuss sex-role issues and strategies to achieve gender equality. The political stands of the members varied from liberal to Marxist; they were active in political parties or unions, worked in governmental agencies or organizations, or were employed as journalists or authors. The aim of the group was to share knowledge and ideas on gender issues, to plan strategies, and to influence decision-makers. The initiative was taken by a woman, Annika Baude, but the group included both men and women in accordance with the understanding of the sex-role question as equally important to both women and men. Group 222 had connections to the educational sphere through Ingrid Fredriksson and Margareta Westin. Olof Palme, who was the minister of education from 1967 to 1969, when he became prime minister, also was a member, as was his wife, Lisbeth Palme, a child psychologist. In retrospect, this informal organizing is judged to have had great importance.

In Sweden the most effective way of working for women's equality in education was through the state administration, supported by a sympathetic Social Democratic government. A significant result of women's organizing inside the established bodies occurred in 1969 when the second regular national curriculum (*läroplan*, or "Lgr 69"), a document describing the goals and content of compulsory education in Sweden, came into force. The first regular *läroplan* had been implemented in 1962 and had contained some very cautious notions of gender equality. For example, it said that boys or girls who showed an interest in atypical occupational or educational choices should not be discouraged. The 1969 version went much further. The sections on gender equality in "Lgr 69," written by Ingrid Fredriksson at the Ministry of Education, were probably much more radical at the time the document appeared than either public opinion or the views of the ordinary teacher. It discussed how and towards what ends equality between men and women should be enforced in and through the compulsory school system. Education was described as a powerful emancipatory instrument for social change, and equality between men and women was identified as one of the most important changes.

In addition, because the central issue in the sex-role debate was the division of labour and the possibility of women being active in the labour market on the same terms as men, the most important single goal of "Lgr 69" was to prepare boys and girls for the same occupational roles. To make this possible it also was judged necessary to promote equal sharing of family responsibilities between men and women. "Lgr 69" outlined educational approaches that were thought to be effective. Curriculum content was seen as central. The concerns were, first, that boys and girls be given the same knowledge in general and in all subject areas and, second, that all students be provided with knowledge about the issue of equality, including, for example, a critical analysis of the historical roots of traditional roles for and stereotypical attitudes about men and women. A third type of knowledge deemed important to gender equality was reflected in a new compulsory course geared towards preparing boys and girls to share childcare and work in the home.

Equal treatment in school was seen as another important tool to promote equality. It was argued that the school should be a model for the rest of society by showing the possibility of equal treatment for boys and girls. That girls and boys with new attitudes and substantive knowledge about the mechanisms of the sex-role system would influence both their parents and other adults in society was expected. For example, in the obligatory introduction to working life (grades eight to nine), all students were to try at least one "atypical" job, partly to demonstrate to employers the ability of both sexes to do all kinds of work. The major emphasis was on the sameness of boys and girls and on social change through the systematic socialization of the young. On the whole, there was a great belief that rationality and enlightenment would transform society.

To implement "Lgr 69" the National Board of Education started the "Sex Role Project" in the early 1970s. This endeavour was led by Margareta Westin, a member of Group 222, who was working with educational and occupational counselling at the National Board of Education. Westin describes herself as ideologically fairly traditional at the start of the project. She writes, "In my duties as a central bureaucrat and travelling secondary school consultant, I was to cover 'girls' educational choice.' Initially my interest in this part of the job was lukewarm. In my own life I had not hesitated to 'act like a man,' i.e., to go out and work. That 'women's two roles' were open to me, however, depended on the possibility at the time of keeping (underpaid) help in the home, living in collective housing with organized day care and after school activities (and having a husband who loved children)" (Westin, 1992: 107; translated here). She also describes how, in a book on occupational choice, she gave fairly traditional advice to girls about the need to prepare for paid employment in case they could not find men to support them.

Later, however, the discussions in Group 222 gave Westin "new eyes" and "new ears" and a much more radical outlook. The Sex Role

Project which she led produced two large reports that explored almost every possible angle (biological, moral, psychological, sociological, etc.) on sex roles and sex differences and included the results of school-based research. The reports were condensed in a smaller and more popular book (*Ett friare val*, 1975) and an action plan for the promotion of gender equality in the school in 1978 (*Ett friare val*, 1978). Some of the new ideas in the action plan were a "geared introduction to working life" (at least one non-traditional choice had to be made), career planning programs, and programs for the in-service training of teachers.

The ideas of "Lgr 69" and the Sex Role Project played an important part in shaping how teachers and parents perceived the situation of boys and girls and the mission of the school with respect to gender equality. However, the ideas were not implemented fully, largely because very little was done in teacher education.[4] In-service training also became somewhat diluted since it mixed "gender equality" and "international understanding" and confused the issues. However, the pattern of women's organizing at the centre and inside the existing political bodies persisted despite uneven implementation.

In the later national curricula ("Lgr 80" and "Lpu 94"), a general commitment to gender equality is expressed in much the same way as it was in 1969. However, the analysis of the nature of the problem changed. By 1994 the idea of a basic similarity between boys/men and girls/women had given way in official policy to the concept that basic differences should be taken into account in teaching. An action report on gender equality (*Vi är alla olika*, 1994) initiated by the former Conservative minister of education leans heavily on assumptions of stable female and male characteristics rooted in biology. Thus, while left-wing and right-wing politicians agree that gender equality is desirable, they differ when it comes to the substantive content of that agenda.

Given that the state and its agencies have a pronounced policy actively to promote gender equality, the most obvious strategy for women who want to act to change education or educational practices is to turn to the National Agency of Education (formerly the National Board of Education) or to the Ministry of Education to find financial, ideological, and moral support. In general, people in those organizations working with gender issues are expected to be not only women but also feminists in some sense of the word.[5] A personal commitment to and enthusiastic action about gender equality – not cool objectivity – is anticipated from civil servants in such positions. This expectation also illustrates that individuals inside the system have played important leadership roles. Although laws, regulations, and national policies promoting gender equality were developed early in Sweden, it is still the case that there is no automatic awareness of equality issues at all levels in the education system. Appropriate responses have to be brought about by extraordinary efforts and the personal involvement of civil servants at all levels. What this means is that the "women friendliness" of Swedish educational policy ensures that initiatives developed by individuals (often femocrats) are not rejected; but if there is no femocrat around to press for change, nothing will happen. Perhaps gender equality can best be described as having passive acceptance in the education system. This response could also be understood as a kind of repressive tolerance – women will get what they are entitled to, but only if they fight for it.

Finally, a variant of the strategy of separate organizing can be considered. One of the very few examples of a school with a pronounced feminist base can be found in adult education. Kvinnofolkhögskolan (Women's Folk High School), situated in Göteborg, was founded in 1985. It is connected to the century-old Nordic tradition of folk high schools where "ordinary people" can get an education outside the formal system and in a school free from grading and examinations. Many of the folk high schools are connected to various popular movements, political parties, unions, or other organizations and are intended to be places for the free development of the individual. Kvinnofolkhögskolan has its roots in the women's movement of the 1970s. From the start a goal was to guarantee diversity among the students by encouraging immigrant women to take the courses. The school has several different types of programs – full courses with content similar to those secondary schools or on selected themes and short courses on specific topics. Some are designed especially for immigrant women. The school has a day-care centre for the students' children, and to keep costs down, the students take turns cooking lunch. Connected to this school there is also an organization, Feminist Pedagogues, which can be described as a network for feminist teachers, researchers, and others interested in teaching. However, even though the school essentially operates as an independent women-only organization, it is publicly funded and must be viewed as a good example of women's strategic use of the state.

ORGANIZING FOR GENDER EQUALITY IN CANADA

In Canada, women's organizing takes on a somewhat different shape. This can be partly explained by the fact, that unlike in Sweden, where one national system of education exists, education in Canada is controlled by ten different provincial governments, which are, for the most part, not particularly sympathetic to women's concerns. However, at different historical moments in some provinces, individual ministers of education or femocrats in women's directorates, women's secretariats, or ministries of education have been supportive and influential, and the federal and provincial governments have in place fairly weak, non-directive policy statements on education and equality. By far the most important women's organizing around gender issues in schools has occurred through the teachers' federations or unions, in particular their status-of-women committees (Julien, 1987), where women with a consciously feminist analysis provide leadership and direction.

Women's organizing in schools revolves primarily around two axes. One has to do with the education of students, especially female students, although increasingly there is a growing concern about changing boys too. The other axis of concern has been with women teachers and workplace issues, most particularly the under-representation of women in administrative positions such as principalships, and with the lack of women occupying executive and staff positions within teachers' federations. In the organizing around these issues, the specific contexts of education in each province and the particular backgrounds and experiences of activist teachers play a large role in shaping the possibilities for change. Many female teachers have learned organizing skills not just within teachers' federations but through involvement with women's groups, whether caucuses of political parties, status-of-women groups, day-care cooperatives, or any one of the many other forms of organizing that women have engaged in over the last few decades. In addition, the political context in each of the provinces means that some teachers' federations are more open to women organizing for change than others. The contrasting cases of British Columbia and Alberta illustrate this fact.

The British Columbia Teachers' Federation (BCTF) established a permanent Status of Women Committee in 1977 after a small group of female members took the initiative in 1969 and began to lobby for action against sex discrimination in the schools. From the start, the BCTF status-of-women program consciously emphasized two things. One was the need to build a grassroots movement within the federation. Hence there was an emphasis on finding and educating local representatives who would build the program in each school district. Considerable attention was given to building and maintaining local programs and developing communication networks within the province.

A second objective was "to stress that the program is one designed to help solve sex discrimination in the educational system, not a vehicle for women to rise in the hierarchical structure" (Shuto, 1974). That is, the BCTF program eschewed a major focus on women and leadership and opted instead for an emphasis on curriculum, classroom interactions, and teacher attitudes. With the possible exception of the Centrale de l'Enseignement du Québec, the BCTF has been the most progressive teachers' union in Canada and has emphasized the social responsibility of teachers. This attitude was reflected in and strengthened by the status-of-women program, which emphasized the links between sexism, racism, and classism and named "the system under which we live ... a system that values competition, aggression and domination over co-operation and sharing and caring about other people" (Shuto, 1975: 5) and as being responsible for, among other things, the oppression of women.

Implementing the status-of-women program was not always easy. Reflecting back on the early work of the program, Shuto (1984) notes that "the first objective was to raise the consciousness of teachers and to establish a high-profile program that would engender credibility and support. The membership as a whole was not behind the program" (12). During its first year, 1973–74, a Status of Women Task Force began a series of intensive meetings with forty-one local teachers' associations and with all educational stakeholders, including community and women's groups. Status-of-women contact people were named in seventy-two locals. A major conference for teachers and the public was organized, and registration had to be capped at 500. As Shuto (1984) puts it, "The times were with us. Preparations for '1975, International Year of Women,' were underway. Women's programs and groups were blossoming everywhere. Media attention was high" (12). The Status of Women Task Force found that, as teachers' consciousness of the issues was raised, they began to support the program. The task force was able to utilize the resources and existing organizational structure of the BCTF to build a status-of-women network, provide in-service for teachers, prepare briefs for school boards, and get status-of-women contacts onto local executives. Attempts also were made to integrate women's issues into all the divisions of the federation so that they were not isolated or seen as only of concern to the members of the Status of Women Task Force. By 1977 the task force achieved permanent status as a BCTF cmmittee (Roberts, 1984: 14).

A significant portion of the status-of-women work also focused on the preparation of materials for classroom use. This was a common pattern around the country, but the BCTF was especially active. An array of material, including lesson plans, units of study, and audiovisual kits, was developed and made available to teachers in British Columbia and elsewhere. Workshops and conferences for students and teachers were held, and various sources of funding utilized to develop additional non-sexist curriculum materials and sponsor workshops.

The BCTF was also active in encouraging status-of-women activities across the rest of the country. It initiated the first Canadian Teachers' Federation conference on women's issues (Grove, 1984: 13). Entitled "Challenge '76: Sexism in Schools," the conference brought together delegates from all its member federations to discuss the issues and to develop organizational strategies for action – strategies that were then shared through a series of publications (Canadian Teachers' Federation, 1976; 1977a, b, c).

The success of feminist organizing inside the BCTF stands in stark contrast to the experience in Alberta. There, in the more conservative climate of the Alberta Teachers' Association (ATA) and in a province where union activity and the women's movement were far less prominent, attempts to organize were to run aground.[6] Although a small group of committed women were initially successful in having a Committee on the Status and Role of Women established by motion of the Annual Representative Assembly in 1975, and although the Provincial Executive Council gave support, albeit half-heartedly, to the work of the committee, delegates from the locals to the 1976 Annual Representative Assembly voted against a motion to provide $8,000 for the continuation of the committee's work and thus effectively killed the committee. Another strategy to form a structure within the ATA was devised. An attempt was made to organize a specialist council, similar in structure to existing subject-specialist councils, which would focus on sex-role stereotyping across the curriculum. So as not to threaten anyone, the council was to be called the Human Potential Development Studies Council, and it was to focus on developing and distributing non-sexist materials, compiling inventories of suitable speakers for classroom use, distributing bibliographies and guides, and holding in-service workshops for teachers. The requisite number of charter members were signed up in 1977–78, and the petition requesting the formation of a specialist council was forwarded to the Provincial Executive Council in May 1978. But on a vote of 9 to 7 the motion to approve the new council was defeated. No reasons were given to the petitioners, and no appeal of the decision was possible. Although the Provincial Executive Council authorized the Professional Development Department to pursue the issue of women in leadership, there is little evidence that any further substantive organizing on women's issues occurred for many years, and Alberta remains one of the provinces with the most underdeveloped policy response to gender issues in education (Julien, 1987; Rees, 1990).

The successes in British Columbia and the failures in Alberta are indicative of a number of things. Differences in the cultures of the BCTF and the ATA are an important factor. The BCTF has developed a more consciously social-union perspective on education and societal issues in general. Teachers who have been involved in social movements or left-wing politics also are activists within the BCTF and provide leadership based on a social-justice perspective. The climate within the federation, then, is more open and welcoming, though not without difficulty, to feminist-led organizing. The ATA, on the other hand, until recently adopted the approach of business unionism cloaked in the rhetoric of "professionalism" and was resistant to taking a stand on social issues. The leadership tended to be socially conservative in orientation.

It is also important to recognize the differences between the women who organized in each of the associations. The core of the BCTF women who worked to establish the status-of-women program were more clearly shaped by the contemporary women's movement and operated in a setting where there was an active, lively feminist community. They had organized themselves first as a group of women outside the federation and had engaged in explicitly feminist organizing inside schools. When they came into the BCTF, they brought with them a perspective and skills developed apart from the federation, and the status-of-women program provided them with a base within the organization. In the case of the ATA, the attempt to organize was carried out by a mixed-sex committee composed primarily of association "insiders." Few of the women on the committee identified themselves as feminists or had any experience of feminist or progressive organizing. The weak state of the women's movement in Alberta meant that there was no real feminist community from which to draw for support. Little use was made of local contacts to build a grassroots foundation. The insiders on the committee, some of whom were Provincial Executive Council members, attempted to use the traditional methods of gaining access to power – "playing the boys' game," as it were – without recognizing the hostility and resistance within the association. Most committee members sought to avoid confrontation and in the end were unsuccessful in establishing a women's program.

By the late 1970s most teachers' federations had status-of-women committees, often at the provincial and local levels, and these committees continue their work to this day. Considerable attention has been given to the question of women in administrative positions and to sex bias in the curriculum. This emphasis is certainly why gender-education policies are most developed in these two areas. At the same time, status-of-women committees have become embedded in institutional structures and have lost their radical edge. Many of the federations, especially the Federation of Women Teachers' Associations of Ontario, have produced a wide range of curriculum materials, but these are generally of the "add women and stir" variety and fit easily into existing courses rather than challenging the overall structure of the curriculum in fundamental ways.

As these brief overviews illustrate, the development of gender policies in education in Canada and Sweden occurs primarily through women's organizing initiatives in established institutions. In Sweden, women have been able to organize effectively through the national government. In Canada, while the federal and provincial governments have introduced some broad policy frameworks supportive of gender equality, the real work has been done by feminist educators working through teachers' federations. In both countries, women's organizing strategies have been particularly effective when they utilize and expand upon an existing discourse of equality and when they are seen to meet or match other types of policy objectives. The best example of this can be found in burgeoning efforts to attract more girls and women into the sciences and technology. A closer, more detailed examination of this area reveals a great deal about how a broader policy position is utilized and adapted by women working towards equality.

GIRLS AND WOMEN IN SCIENCE AND TECHNOLOGY

Statistics on the marked sex differentiation in program choice and in employment patterns in the education sector reveal some of the more obvious inequities in education. For this reason, it has been easier for women to argue for policies and programs directed towards correcting the imbalance in numbers since "hard" data or "empirical" studies are readily at hand and the discrepancies are so patently obvious. For example, in both Canada and Sweden a major focus of reform has been on increasing the enrolments of girls and women in science and technology and on encouraging women to take up non-traditional careers, especially in the trades. However, while women argued for these programs on the basis of fairness and social justice, widespread support was more likely generated because of identified needs in the labour market and the economy. As Wernersson (1989) has contended for Sweden, "the power of the labour market and its high visibility tends to turn the whole issue of fairness and equality between the sexes into a matter of educational choice. Economic and other resources for intervention are channelled in one direction only to change the vocational choice patterns" (94–5). Barlow and Robertson (1994) make a similar observation about Canada by noting that getting girls into mathematics and science was popular with all education ministries "because the issue was framed as an employer-and-profit problem rather than as a matter of equity" (128). They wryly observe that high school enrolments in subjects such as advanced politics (65 per cent male) and child development (95 per cent female) show stronger gender differentiation than chemistry but receive virtually no attention from policy-makers.

Of course, women working in the schools have consciously taken up the discourse about education for global competitiveness and schooling for the new economic realities as an integral part of a strategy to draw attention to gender inequality and direct more resources towards girls in schools. There has, in fact, been a shared goal among women, corporations, and the state, although the motivating forces have been different. For this reason, in both Canada and Sweden we see the development and growth of a significant number of programs designed to encourage girls and women to enrol in the sciences and mathematics. In Canada, Julien (1987) discovered "a seemingly constant flow of literature" designed to prepare young women for the new technologies, to broaden their career goals, and to encourage them to consider non-traditional careers (5), and the trend is similar in Sweden. What Berner (1984) notes for that country is true for Canada also. The programs designed to encourage girls and women to enrol in mathematics, science, and technology courses are based on three objectives – to counteract stereotypes, to provide options, and to strengthen self-esteem (233), not at all an agenda to challenge systemic discrimination.

The specificities of women's organizing around mathematics, science, and technology (MST) are very much alike in Canada and Sweden. While we have argued that gender-equality efforts in schools have in Sweden been driven by the support of the woman-friendly state and in Canada by feminist educators working through teachers' federations, the wider interest of industry, business, colleges, and universities in MST issues has encouraged a greater range of activities in education and provided access to more extensive sources of funding. Individual and group initiatives by academics and affirmative-action programs on the part of post-secondary institutions are also common.

One example of an individual initiative in the area of girls and MST developed in Linköping in the early 1980s. To provide role models for young girls, Ingrid Granstam, at the time a university lecturer in technology at the University of Linköping, organized her young female university students of technology to visit schools at different levels from pre-school to secondary school. The main idea was that the technology students would act as living proof that it was possible for girls and women to pursue a career in engineering. The initiative was "private" in the beginning, but soon was funded by the National Board of Education. Similar activities, both locally and centrally initiated, followed at many places.

Another example of an initiative in the same general realm originated in the Ministry of Education. Through the National Board of Education, the ministry funded local projects using single-sex groupings in science education in elementary school. Schools were invited to apply for funding to organize summer computer programs for girls only, to make videos showing women in non-traditional occupations, and so on. A long-term and large-scale project of this kind called BRYT involved all the Nordic countries (Bryt Nytt, 1989).

In Canada, role-modelling programs, career days, summer courses in science for girls, and related initiatives are also widespread and have been supported by funding from governments, school boards, teachers' federations, and the business community. They have been organized by female academics through groups such as WISEST (Women in Scholarship, Engineering, Science and Technology) and by women teachers, and as in Sweden, they often rely on the commitment and dedication of a few individuals who seek the funding and arrange the activities. Often a group of university students will receive funding to provide programs for public school students. Women's directorates or secretariats in the provincial governments produce a wide assortment of posters, workshops, video materials, and bibliographies aimed at encouraging girls to consider careers in science and technology.

As a result of all this activity in both countries, some shifts in enrolment patterns can be observed, but overall change is very slow. In Sweden extra points were given to students who chose non-traditional programs at the university level to help them gain admittance. This incentive program has been unsuccessful (Sweden, 1995). However, at the compulsory school level the 1980 national curriculum stipulated that elective courses must be structured in such a way as to attract an even enrolment distribution of the two sexes (the difference may not be larger than 40:60). According to Härnqvist (1995), this approach has been more successful since extremely sex-typed courses have disappeared from the curriculum. In Canada, government-sponsored scholarship programs and other initiatives to encourage young women to take up engineering and the applied sciences have not been very successful, and in 1991 only 13 per cent of the undergraduate degrees in those fields were awarded to women, (Human Resources Development Canada, 1994). Educators and policy-makers are coming to recognize that the absence of females in certain courses of study may have much to do with the way in which those subjects are structured and taught and with the hostile learning environment that faces women trying to enter fields regarded by men as their domain.

This realization has begun to lead to a reshaping and rethinking of programs in science and technology. In Canada isolated activities, often institution-specific, and a variety of initiatives to improve the learning climate for girls and women in science and technology can be found. For example, many of the technical colleges offer a program called Women Into Trades and Technology (WITT). This is an entry-level, affirmative action program for female students, usually middle-aged women intending to re-enter the paid workforce. Using a feminist pedagogical model, WITT seeks to provide women with basic technical skills as well as enhancing their self-esteem and confidence.

In Sweden one example of independent action to improve learning environments can be found in a group called Women and Mathematics (Kvinnor och Matematik), which brings together as members or supporters a wide range of people, including university mathematicians and primary school teachers interested in gender issues. This organization is not limited to women, and several male mathematicians and mathematics teachers are involved in the work. Since mathematics at the university level is extremely male-dominated (women make up 26 per cent of the students at the undergraduate level, but very few doctoral students or faculty members are female), it is felt that activities to strengthen the visibility of women are important. Women and Mathematics organizes biennial conferences and takes an active part in national and international conferences and networks. A major aim of this group's work is to develop teaching methods that suit girls.

At present in Sweden, women constitute only 20 per cent of the students of technology and 37 per cent of the science students (Statistiska meddelanden, 1995). At the university level, major efforts, financed by the Grundutbildningsrådet (Council of Undergraduate Education), are being made to change pedagogical practices in technological and science subjects in order to recruit and keep women students in these programs. New combinations of subjects (e.g., technology programs that contain humanities or social science courses) are being tried at some universities. Women usually initiate projects of this kind, but many men are active in them, and arguments that "what is good for the girls will also serve the boys" are often used. More women in science and technology is viewed as beneficial for the development of the subjects in the long run because it is felt that women bring the "soft" human aspect into the "hard" technology. In the short run, it is anticipated that the female influence will improve the social atmosphere in the educational setting as well as the quality of knowledge. Women are expected to perceive technological knowledge more in context and less as isolated "things." However, these types of arguments clearly reinforce notions of male and female difference and assign to women the responsibility for "softening" science, for making it more "social" and "humane."

RECENT TRENDS AND DIRECTIONS

Swedish policy on school development has changed considerably since 1970. A model based on carefully researched alternatives leading to a central decision about the best solution, followed by regulations, has given way to an approach that provides for the central support of local initiatives within specific, nationally developed policy frames. As a consequence, the current work at the National Agency of Education is focused on building a network to connect schools and teachers working on different projects to promote equality. Projects are developed on the basis of local initiative and choice of method, and content is also made locally. The major task of the central agency has thus become evaluation rather than initiation.

As mentioned earlier, in both Sweden and Canada the theoretical framework for gender issues has changed – or rather, become more pluralistic. In Sweden, for example, the sex-role socialization paradigm, while still important, shares explanatory ground with several other understandings of the issues. The significance of structural power is increasingly well understood. More important at present in Sweden's policy domain, however, is the argument that men and women each have their specific nature. While "girls and science and technology" is the most common objective of activities in the secondary schools, many gender-equality efforts in elementary schools concentrate on single-sex groupings (Borhagen, 1996). Often the two themes are combined. The idea that girls would profit from single-sex teaching started from an understanding of classroom interaction as resulting from a structural gender system with uneven power distribution. However, currently, a comprehension of direct biological reasons (e.g., brain structure or maturation rates) for differences between the behaviour of boys and girls at school has become a more common justification for single-sex arrangements (Levander, 1993).

In addition, as a response to beliefs about increasing violence among the young, interest has lately been directed towards boys. In Sweden and Canada the lack of (good) male role models in day care, schools, and homes with single mothers has (again) been brought forward as a problem (Coulter and McNay, 1993). But in Sweden, more than in Canada,[7] violence among boys also has been explained as a lack of understanding among female caregivers about the "innate male needs to express aggression" and attributed to the inability of caregivers to channel such behaviour into socially acceptable forms (Kryger, 1988). The conclusions drawn about biological differences and their implications for education or socialization practices are often extremely oversimplified. Unfortunately, biological arguments tend to be attractive because they provide concrete, material explanations and because they reduce individual and social responsibility to a minimum. So, while at present in Sweden there is a fairly strong consensus about gender equality as a desirable goal in education and for society, at the same time the understandings of the causes and character of the sex/gender system are mixed and contradictory.

As in Sweden, the sex-role socialization paradigm is relatively well established in Canada, and ministry, school board, and teachers' federation policies tend to reflect a generalized acceptance of the need to eliminate sex bias in learning materials, to include some material on women in the curriculum, and to encourage girls to take maths and science courses and consider non-traditional occupations. To what extent these beliefs are applied daily in classroom practice is less clear. What is even less evident is how effective current initiatives in schools are. There is a developing sense that analyses of sexism in schooling that emphasize sex-role stereotyping rely on an oversimplified understanding of complex issues and hide the ways in which the gendered nature of education is played out in the content and practice of schooling. Nonetheless, while the discourse on gender relations, power, and male dominance has not been absent in debates about schooling in Canada, it has been muted. Part of the explanation lies with strategic decision-making among feminists striving for change with respect to what would work and what would not, what they could effectively implement and what they could not. Recently, however, educators have shown a renewed interest in understanding the systemic nature of sexism and schooling and in developing anti-sexist, anti-racist pedagogies that focus directly on social transformation (Coulter, 1996).

Also observable in Canada is a trend towards coalition-building, or at least more organized networking among feminists whether they be individual teachers, members of teacher federation status-of-women committees, femocrats, education professors, or students. It is important to note too that increasingly, teachers are joining with community social-justice groups, progressive parents' organizations, and organized labour to protect public education and the possibilities for equity that it affords to the population as a whole.

While women's organizing around education in Canada and Sweden has a long history and there have been many concrete gains, the current economic climate, with its emphasis on the free market and the concomitant growth of the neo-liberal ideology of possessive individualism and private competition, presents new and negative challenges. In Canada the federal and many of the provincial governments, most notably in Alberta and Ontario, are rapidly dismantling the social-welfare state in favour of a neo-liberal one (Brodie, 1995 and 1996).

Economic restructuring, the slashing of social spending, and the emphasis on "self-help" have resulted in major cutbacks to childcare, social services, health, and education, and women and children have been particularly hard hit. Women's programs within the state are either disappearing or have been decimated, and teachers' federations are forced to focus most of their attention on a defence of publicly funded education. In both Canada and Sweden, budget cuts for schooling at all levels mean that individual teachers are confronting increased workloads and class sizes. Teachers also must work with growing numbers of students whose families have been devastated by unemployment. The result is less time and energy to devote to gender issues in the schools. In light of this reality, the future for effective gender work in education in the short term looks bleak.

Women also must confront some of the contradictions and unintended consequences of their organizing work to date. A recent Swedish study, for example, identifies the social stratification that is occurring among girls in different programs in high schools *(Utvärdering av lokala jämställdhetsprojekt inom* JÄMSAMS *nätverk*, 1997). Girls in science programs have begun to look down on those in the social science and humanities programs, thus reinscribing a masculinist devaluation of women's more traditional pursuits. Furthermore, by 1994 the compulsory grade nine school courses in childcare for boys and girls had disappeared from the curriculum, and very little is now said in schools about the importance of the fair division of labour in families as a prerequisite for gender equality. This development is part of a wider pattern where what is seen as "male" is desirable and what perceived as "female" is not. The women regarded as successful are those who have entered male domains and adopted male norms, such as individualism and competitiveness. In an ironic twist, this approach to equality may, in fact, strengthen male hegemony.

Some of the same observations can be made about the middle class in Canada. Many girls listened to the advice to go into non-traditional lines of work, and a new generation of professional women have, in large measure, become very similar to men in the management of their paid work lives, although the double burden of paid and unpaid work is still a reality for all women. But what may be true for the middle class is not so true for the working class. With the disappearance of a significant portion of industrial work as a result of the economic restructuring brought on by the North American Free Trade Agreement, working-class men find themselves increasingly having to take up traditional women's work in the service sector, where wages are low, work is often part-time, and job security is minimal (Armstrong, 1996). Weis (1990) has suggested that these conditions encourage young men to become more violent towards young women and to be susceptible to the blandishments of the New Right and its advocacy of a narrowly defined set of traditional family values; but there is also the possibility that gender solidarity could develop as young men and women are forced to confront similar, and less than satisfactory, employment options. How the schools might contribute to a positive outcome in this regard remains undiscussed. And for working-class women and men alike, the promise of liberal feminism that "you can do whatever you want, you can be whatever you want to be" has proved elusive. It is little wonder that many young women reject feminism. For feminist educators in Canada and Sweden, interesting theoretical and practical dilemmas about gender and employment policies and the role of the education system in creating equality await resolution.

In the past, women organizing for change in education have done so through a variety of institutions. As we have seen, the "friendly Swedish state" has provided substantial support for gender initiatives in schools. In Canada, teachers' federations and governments have supplied funding and other resources to women, especially teachers. However, the deleterious effects of globalization and the growing efforts to dismantle the welfare state in response to demands from international capital are likely to mean that those working for women's equality, whether in Sweden or Canada, will face new difficulties. Changing state forms may well require a more consciously oppositional politics in education than has so far been the case in either country. For historical reasons, and because they are more fully integrated into governance structures, women in Sweden are better situated with respect to sustaining a state commitment to gender equality. In Canada, setbacks to gender-equality policies are already apparent, the loss in 1995 of Ontario's employment-equity plan to encourage the hiring of more female school administrators being but one example (Coulter, 1998). In both countries it is clear that women's organizational efforts will need to intensify, and new strategies must, of necessity, be developed to take account of changing economic and social circumstances.

NOTES

1 Eisenstein (1991) popularized the term "femocrat." It originated in Australia as a way to describe feminists who worked within the government bureaucracy.

2 We have chosen to use the term "gender equality" throughout this paper. However, we must emphasize the fact that there are many different

understandings of equality, and it is by no means clear that the word means exactly the same thing in Sweden and in Canada. In Canada the term "equity" is now more commonly used in education circles as a way to acknowledge that sometimes equality means ignoring differences and treating women and men exactly the same and sometimes it means recognizing differences and treating women and men differently. Equity can also be understood as meaning what is fair under the circumstances and is often used as a synonym for substantive equality. A full discussion of Canadian perspectives can be found in Coulter (1996).

In Sweden during the 1960s and 1970s, gender equality in education was understood as a balance between men and women. "Girls into science and technology" was thus matched by "boys into education and nursing." For example, in 1971 it was decided that men applying for pre-school teacher education would receive extra credit points for admission purposes. To balance this incentive, women applying for specific programs in the technical realm got the same credit. The women did not benefit since they were already able to compete successfully on the basis of the marks that they had earned without the extra consideration, but a few more men at this time were brought into pre-school teaching as a result of this affirmative action (Wernersson and Lander, 1979).

By the late 1970s the perception that obsolete sex roles crippled men and women equally changed to an understanding of gender-based power differentiation and male supremacy. This shift probably was in part a response to the painful experiences of women as they realized that men were not always interested in change and in part the result of an internationalization of the women's movement and research on women which brought more militant political and theoretical analyses of the gender issue to Sweden.

3 While Sweden has until recently had an extremely centralized national system of education, the responsibility for education in Canada falls to the ten provinces and two territories. For the most part, each provincial government controls and manages schooling through a centralized ministry of education while also delegating many school matters to locally elected school boards. Since 1991, school administration in Sweden has been decentralized. The 280 municipalities (with a median population of 16,000) organize and administer their own schools. In order to balance local power and uphold the national aim of equal standards for schooling, goals are set out in the national curriculum (at present, Lpu 94). The primary function of the National Agency of Education is to assess and evaluate how well the municipalities meet the national goals. Also, private schools have to follow national goals and submit to evaluation and assessment (Lander, 1995).

In Canada, schooling is publicly funded through a combination of provincial grants and local property taxation. In Sweden it is supported by the general local tax and a block grant received from the national state. Since 1991 there has been no earmarking of money for education from the block grant, and thus education has to compete locally for its share. There is also a voucher system, meaning that a part of the per student cost follows the individual student who wants to change schools (public or private). Compared to other OECD countries, Canada and Sweden spend the most on education – at least 5 per cent of the gross domestic product in each case (Gendron, 1994).

Compulsory attendance laws require most Canadian and Swedish children to attend school between the ages of six (six or seven in Sweden) and sixteen, although many young people begin kindergarten/pre-school at four or five and complete secondary school at the age of eighteen or nineteen. In 1991, 86 per cent of Canadian citizens between the ages of twenty-five and thirty-four had a high school diploma (Gendron, 1994), and 40 per cent of all adults aged twenty-five to sixty-four had post-secondary qualifications (Human Resources Development Canada, 1994). The comparable figures for Sweden were 85 per cent and 23 per cent respectively (*Utbildningsstatistisk årsbok*, 1995).

4 Despite the development of women's studies programs in Canadian and Swedish universities and the focus on gender equality in schools, teacher-education programs have done little to prepare candidates to address issues of gender and schooling in either country. Given that teaching is seen as a "women's occupation" and that many professors of education and most education students are female, this state of affairs raises many interesting questions. Unfortunately, a thorough analysis is beyond the space limitations of this paper.

5 In Sweden the term "feminist" has had a much more radical or extreme ring about it than in Canada. This view is changing, and the word is used more widely now, but it can still be problematic. One implication is that it cannot be taken for granted that women organizing around gender issues identify themselves as feminists.

6 This brief history of developments in the ATA is based on records held by Rebecca Coulter. To her knowledge, no written history of women's organizing in the ATA since 1970 has been produced.

7 In Canada, while there is concern about the violence of young males, a moral panic about violent girls is developing as a result of a small number of cases that have been intensively profiled in the media. Blame is laid at the door of feminism, and the women's movement is accused of promoting an equality which makes girls think that they have to act like boys. Little consideration is given to the question of why young women might feel anger and rage that erupts in violent acts.

REFERENCES

Ad Hoc Committee Respecting the Status of Women in the North York System. (1975). The rape of children's minds. Unpublished report.

Armstrong, P. (1996). The feminization of the labour force: Harmonization down in a global economy. In I. Bakker (ed.), *Rethinking Restructuring: Gender and Change in Canada*. Toronto: University of Toronto Press.

Bakgrundsmaterial för vuxenutbildning. (1995). Örebro: Statistiska centralbyrån.

Barlow, M., and Robertson, H.-j. (1994). *Class Warfare: The Assault on Canada's Schools*. Toronto: Key Porter Books.

Batcher, E., D. Brackstone, A. Winter, and V. Wright. (1975). *... And Then There Were None*. Toronto: Federation of Women Teachers' Associations of Ontario.

Baude, A. (ed.). (1992). *Visionen om jämställdhet*. Stockholm: SNS Förlag.

Berner, B. (1984). New technology and women's education in Sweden. In S. Acker, J. Megarry, S. Nisbet, and E. Hoyle (eds.), *World Yearbook of Education 1984: Women and Education*. London: Kogan Page.

Borhagen, K. (1996). *"För flickornas skull" – om enkönade undervisningsgrupper i órskur 5 och 9*. Stockholm: Skolverket.

Brodie, J. (1995). *Politics on the Margin: Restructuring and the Canadian Women's Movement*. Halifax: Fernwood Publishing.

– (ed.). (1996). *Women and Canadian Public Policy*. Toronto: Harcourt Brace & Company, Canada.

Bryt Nytt. (1989). *Brytprojektets slutrapport*. Nr 9. Stockholm: Arbetsmarknadsdepartementet.

Canada. (1970). Royal Commission on the Status of Women. *Report of the Royal Commission on the Status of Women*. Ottawa: Queen's Printer.

Canadian Teachers' Federation. (1976). *Challenge '76: Sexism in Schools*. Ottawa: Canadian Teachers' Federation.

– (1977a, b, c). *Challenge '77: Strategies for Action*. January, February, and September. Ottawa: Canadian Teachers' Federation.

Coulter, R.P. (1996). Gender equity and schooling: Linking research and policy. *Canadian Journal of Education* 21: 433–52.

– (1998). "Us guys in suits are back": Women, educational work and the market economy in Canada. In A. Mackinnon, I. Elgqvist-Saltzman, and A. Prentice (eds.), *Education into the 21st Century: Dangerous Terrain for Women?* London: Falmer Press.

– and M. McNay. (1993). Exploring men's experiences as elementary school teachers. *Canadian Journal of Education* 18: 398–413.

Cullen, L. (1972). A study into sex stereotyping in Alberta elementary textbooks. Unpublished paper.

Eisenstein, H. (1991). *Gender Shock*. Boston: Beacon Press.

Ett friare val: Handlingsprogra för jämställdhet i skolan. (1978). Stockholm: LiberLäromedel.

Ett friare val: Jämställdhetsprogram för skolan. (1975). Stockholm: LiberLäromedel.

Fredriksson, I. (1969). *Könsroller i läroböcker.* Stockholm: Arbetsmarknadens kvinnonämnd.

Gendron, F. (1994). Does Canada invest enough in education?: An insight into the cost structure of education in Canada. *Education Quarterly Review* 1: 10–25.

Grove, N. (1984). Challenge '76: Sexism in education. *The B.C. Teacher* 64: 13.

Härnqvist, K. (1960). *Individuella differenser och skoldifferentiering.* 1957 års skolberedning, 2. Stockholm: SOU.

– (1995). *Ett skolsystem med fria studieval: Flickors studieval i 1980-talets grundskola, gymnasieskola och högskola.* Uppsala: Årsböcker i svensk undervisningshistoria.

Human Resources Development Canada. (1994). *Profile of Post-Secondary Education in Canada.* Ottawa: Supply and Services Canada.

Julien, L. (1987). *Women's Issues in Education in Canada: A Survey of Policies and Practices at the Elementary and Secondary Levels.* Toronto: Council of Ministers of Education, Canada.

Kryger, N. (1988). *De skrëppe drenge og den moderne pædagogik.* København: Unga pædagoger.

Kvinnors liv och arbete. (1962). Stockholm: Studieförbundet Näringsliv och samhälle.

Lander, R. (1995). *Evaluation and Governing: The Swedish Background.* Göteborg: Department of Education and Educational Research, University of Göteborg.

Läroplan för grundskolan (Lgr 69). (1969). Stockholm: Liber Förlag.

Levander, S. (1993). Biologiska sillnader i intelligens mellan könen förstärks i den svenska skolan. In *Visst är vi olika!.* Stockholm: Utbildningsdepartementet.

Lpu 94: Lärplaner för det obligatoriska skolväsendet och de frivilliga skolformerna Lpo och Lpf. (1994). Stockholm: Utbildningsdepartementet.

Rees, R. (1990). *Women and Men in Education.* Toronto: Canadian Education Association.

Roberts, P. (1984). Pages from her story. *The B.C. Teacher* 64: 14–15.

Shuto, L. (1974). Background paper on the BCTF status of women program. Unpublished paper.

– (1975). BCTF status of women program. Unpublished paper.

– (1984). If you're not getting enough flack you're not doing your job properly. *The B.C. Teacher* 64: 11–12.

Statistiska meddelanden. (1995). *Universitet och högskolor. Grundutbildning: Nybörjare, registrerade och examina 1993/94*. Örebro: Statistiska centralbyrån.

Svensson, A. (1971). *Relative Achievement: School Performance in Relation to Intelligence, Sex and Home Environment*. Stockholm: Almqvist & Wiksell.

Sweden. (1995). *Shared Power Responsibility: National Report by the Government of Sweden for the Fourth World Conference on Women in Beijing 1995*. Stockholm: Ministry of Health and Social Affairs.

Utbildningsstatistisk årsbok. (1995). Örebro: Statistiska centralbyrån.

Utvärdering av lokala jämställdhetsprojekt inom JÄMSANs nätverk. (1997). Stockholm: Skolverket.

Vi är alla olika: En åtgärdsrapport om jämställdhet i skolan som en pedagogisk fråga och ett kunskapsområde. (1994). Stockholm: Utbildningsdepartementet.

Weis, L. (1990). *Working Class without Work: High School Students in a Deindustrializing Economy*. New York: Routledge.

Wernersson, I. (1977). *Könsdifferentiering i grundskolan*. Göteborg Studies in Educational Sciences, nr 22. Göteborg: Acta Universitatis Gothoburgensis.

– (1989). Gender equality: Ideology and reality. In S.J. Ball and S. Larsson (eds.), *The Struggle for Democratic Education: Equality and Participation in Sweden*. New York/London: Falmer Press.

– and R. Lander. (1979). *Män och kvinnor i barnomsor-gen. En analys av könskvotering, yrkesval och arbetstrivsel*. Stockholm: Jämställdhetskommittån.

Westin, M. (1992). Kvinnligt, manligt och könsroller i hem och yrke. In A. Baude (ed.), *Visionen om jämställdhet*. Stockholm: SNS Förlag.

Women in Teaching. (1975). *Text Book Study*. Vancouver: British Columbia Teachers' Federation.

"Both Wage Earner and Mother": Women's Organizing and Childcare Policy in Sweden and Canada

RIANNE MAHON

ABSTRACT

A comparative analysis of public involvement in childcare arrangements provides a window on the different ways in which the Canadian and Swedish welfare states affect class and gender relations. As this chapter shows, the social democratic Swedish welfare state developed childcare policies that work simultaneously to mitigate gender and class inequalities, while the liberal Canadian welfare state serves to reinforce both forms of inequality. Although the relative strength of "class politics" helps to explain the difference, it is not a sufficient condition. Women's organizing was certainly important to the outcome in social democratic Sweden. Women have organized and struggled for day care in Canada too, but here policy has emerged more as the resultant of bureaucratic politics within the federal government and along the increasingly fragile lines of executive federalism.

Childcare arrangements in Canada and Sweden differ in ways which the comparative literature on welfare states leads one to expect. Sweden's commitment to publicly financed day care, largely provided by (municipal) government, and its generous system of parental-leave insurance[1] are what one would anticipate of a social democratic welfare state where the emphasis is on universal social insurance programs and high-quality public services that appeal to white-collar and blue-collar workers alike. In Canada, childcare arrangements tend to fit the liberal model. Thus the federal government has provided subsidies to low-income families for day-care places on a means-tested basis, while allowing middle- and upper-income parents to deduct a portion of fees from income taxes. Day care comes in very varied forms – from municipal and non-profit centres to unregulated care provided in the child's home or that of an unlicensed caregiver.[2] Federal and provincial leave provisions, until recently for mothers only, have been of limited duration and offer low compensation rates.[3] Those in a better market position have accordingly sought private solutions.

It would be a mistake, however, to stop here, with the "liberal" Canadian and "social democratic" Swedish models frozen in time and space. Childcare arrangements are historical products, and unfinished ones at that. Thus, as we shall see, there was certainly a moment in the 1980s when it looked as if Canada would break the liberal mould, at least with regard to childcare. And unfortunately, the relatively progressive childcare arrangements established in Sweden during the 1960s and 1970s are not immune to the corrosive effects of "globalization" under neo-liberal rules. Moreover, as this chapter will reveal, although childcare arrangements appear to "fit" the models developed by theorists who focus on the relative strength and strategic capacity of national labour movements, women's organizing had an important role to play, especially in framing the universe of political discourse. The latter, in turn, sets limits to the range of conceivable childcare arrangements in a country at a particular historical juncture.[4]

SWEDEN: RENOVATING THE PEOPLE'S HOME FOR WAGE EARNERS OF TWO GENDERS

The Swedish welfare state has stood as the exemplar of the "social democratic" form,[5] that is, one characterized by "decommodification" (policies that confront the *fiction* of labour power as a commodity), universality, and solidarity. These features are understood as institutional embodiments of the values of a labour movement (i.e., the alliance of blue-collar unions and the Social Democratic Party, or SAP). They are seen to reflect the party's capacity for policy innovations which confront the key economic challenges of the day in a way that also helps to create the alliances which provide the necessary political support for such reforms. Thus in the Swedish case, the 1932 "Cow Trade" with the Agrarian Party enabled the minority Social Democratic Party to implement Keynesian economic policies and to develop a comprehensive social-security system offering the same (relatively generous) level of benefits to all. In the 1950s a new alliance of "wage earners" began to be constructed with the burgeoning strata of white-collar workers. The material basis for the alliance was laid by building a second tier of income-related social programs over the original universal, but flat-rate social insurance schemes and by offering high-quality public services which obviated the need for supplementary private solutions of the sort that proliferated in "liberal" welfare states such as the United States.

Contemporary Swedish childcare arrangements fit the social democratic pattern, especially as it came to be construed in the late fifties and early sixties, and this pattern has done much to mitigate gender inequality in the labour market. Yet, as feminist scholars have shown, working mothers were not so well treated when the first floor of the "People's Home"[6] was constructed in the 1930s and 1940s. To be sure, in the 1930s the universe of political discourse included visions of a People's Home that would be characterized by gender, as well as class, equality (Hirdman, 1994). And aspects of these visions were translated into policy. Thus as individual citizens, Swedish women were included in universal social programs such as the *folk* or basic pension. In the 1930s mothers won the right to work after marriage and to one month's maternity leave with some financial compensation (Hobson, 1990; Sundström, 1991). Yet the dominant pattern of policy compromises that emerged from the turmoil of the 1930s focused on the housewife-mother. Universal child allowances, good quality housing, especially for larger families, and various forms of maternity assistance positively supported the modern housewife-mother, who was also to be educated to heed the advice of experts as she went about her tasks of child rearing and housework.

As we shall see, feminist organizing forms an important part of the explanation of why things changed such that the blueprints for renovating the People's Home in the sixties and seventies were based on the recognition that wage earners came in two genders. This change produced what might be called the "social democratic–feminist" model of childcare arrangements. Like the social democratic welfare state onto which it was grafted, it embodies the principles of universality, and it does so in ways that cut across the class or collar line, thus forging the basis for solidarity among wage earners. It is feminist, however, in that it actively recognizes that wage earners come in two genders. The state is thus prepared to provide working mothers with services supportive of economic equality.

To be sure, those who argued for equality of the sexes were aided by favourable economic circumstances. The Swedish economy enjoyed boom conditions well into the 1970s. Tight labour markets, along with the shift from goods to services (a sector that tends to be strongly "feminized" in most OECD countries) and the decision to look to Swedish women, rather than immigrants, to meet labour market needs,[7] certainly made it easier to hear the feminist voices that began to argue for gender equality in the 1960s. The concern over falling fertility rates helps explain why, rather than turning a blind eye to women's mothering role, the Swedish state sought to meet these demands by developing appropriate childcare arrangements.[8] Yet favourable socio-economic circumstances are by no means the whole story: politics, including feminist politics, were necessary to turn these "facts" into signs that new arrangements were needed.

The form that feminist organizing took in Sweden was very much affected by the institutional terrain on which it occurred. Thus feminists chose to work within the established media, unions, and parties, and among the latter, the Social Democrats and the Liberals in particular.[9] Yet that context was not static but itself in flux, and thus created new openings for feminists. The demise of the alliance between the Social Democrats and the Agrarian (now Centre) Party contributed to a new fluidity in party politics and discourse at a time when the SAP, the Liberals, and the Centre Party were discovering the growing strata of white-collar workers.[10] Although the existing party system generally proved capable of absorbing these new social forces, to do so the parties had to open up to new representations of social relations.[11] The growing political salience of white-collar workers, along with a simmering revolt by blue-collar workers,[12] sustained the wave of important policy innovations which came to characterize the Swedish model of social democracy – and also left their stamp on the new childcare arrangements. Thus the Rehn-Meidner version of "Keynes plus" policy was finally implemented, and its promise to maintain full employment was extended to women. The government also erected a new tier of social insurance benefits based on the income-replacement principle and made good on its commitment to provide high-quality public services.[13] With this move the material basis was laid for cross-collar wage-earner solidarity, which stood in marked contrast to the divisive "public-private" arrangements that came to characterize the liberal American welfare state (Esping-Andersen, 1990).

It took feminist mobilizing, however, to make the point that wage earners now came in two sexes. Ginger elements in both the Liberal and Social Democratic parties articulated a feminist-humanist vision which sought not only to free women to participate in the big world of markets and politics but also to free men to be fathers in more than name. In other words, men and women alike could become fully human if it were possible for women to work and for men to care. The publication in 1961 of an important essay by a young Liberal, Eva Moberg, is usually credited with having reignited demand for such a world in which men and women were simultaneously to play two roles, with the assistance of the (social democratic) state. Similar ideas were being raised by young Social Democrats in the party journal *Tiden*, while the 1962 publication *Women's Lives and Work*, written by a group of Nordic social scientists, helped to move the "woman question" from the margins of political life by transforming it into the "sex role debate," which was of concern to all (Baude, 1992: 10).

Although the main proponents of the feminist-humanist vision were divided by party allegiance, an important network of activists that cut across party lines was formed in the mid-1960s. Subsequently known as Group 222, it included women and men who were influential in the trade unions, party circles, and national media. Their agenda included tax reform, educational and labour-market policy reforms, supportive social services, including day care, and a new form of child support that would combine the already generous child allowance with reimbursement for parental home care during the child's first year. Such reforms only became feasible, however, as the activists engaged in a struggle to win over opponents in both the Social Democratic and Liberal parties. And they did so, at least initially, by emphasizing women's "right to choose" between paid work and staying at home.

The notion of "choice," concretely expressed in the feminist-humanists' proposal to establish a care allowance, held a convenient ambivalence that was conducive to the formation of compromises within parties and in Swedish society as a whole. Thus within the Social Democratic Party, "Choice, which became the slogan of the sixties, was a concept susceptible to many different interpretations when it referred to women's freedom to choose between paid work and the life of a housewife. Freedom for married women to choose paid work was seen as very radical by many on the party executive. Unity was achieved despite this, perhaps thanks to the emphasis on choice, which one and all could interpret according to their desires" (Karlsson, 1990: 124). "Choice" also created openings in the wider political debates. Here the convenient ambiguities went beyond the right of women (and eventually "parents") to choose between housework and paid work. It also touched on competing views as to the conditions under which that right to choose was to be exercised. All of this came out in the first debates on the care allowance.

The care allowance was essentially a child bonus system, to be financed by a payroll tax, which would make it feasible for women or parents to choose to stay at home with young children or to work full-time. The proposal appealed to traditionalists within the Social Democratic and Liberal parties. It also made it easier for the Liberals to work out a common family policy with their new allies in the Centre Party, where more traditional views prevailed.[14] Ironically, given later developments, in the 1960s only the Conservative Party opposed the care allowance. For the social conservatives in the party, the allowance was seen as going too far towards meeting the conditions for women to choose paid work. For the laissez-faire elements within the party, a care allowance gave the state too large a role. Instead, the tax system should be adjusted to make it easier for families to choose their preferred solutions (Hinnfors, 1995: passim).

In the mid-sixties, however, the balance tipped in favour of the working mother. One of the forces that helped to shift the balance from "choice" and the care allowance to working mothers and day care was the Swedish union central LO. Since the early 1960s it had been concerned about projected labour shortages and had begun to look to married women to meet these. In the early sixties, LO and SAF, the Swedish employers' organization, agreed to abolish separate women's wages, and by the mid-sixties LO had become a leading advocate for the expansion of public day care. LO staffers connected with Group 222 played an important role in engineering this shift, but to do so they had to learn to cast their arguments in ways that fit with the latter's class-centred identity.[15] This is not to say that LO refused to recognize gender inequality. But it was clearly seen as secondary to the larger question of class inequality (LO, 1969: 11). In fact, during the second half of the sixties, the question of class inequality had taken on a new salience. Thus the feminist-humanist discourse did not so much fall on deaf ears in LO headquarters as it had to struggle to be heard in the unions' reformulated agenda. Both LO and the party did become advocates for day care, and ultimately, parental leave.

The Liberals too moved away from the care allowance to favour public spending on day care. They differed with the Social Democrats, however, on the relative weight to be accorded family home day care and municipally run day-care centres. For the Liberals and their Centre Party allies, family home day care was not only cheaper; it also preserved parental "choice" (now between different forms of day care), and most important, it did so in ways that allowed parents to choose the milieu which most closely approximated the home (Kyle, 1979: 185). For LO, TCO (the Swedish organization of salaried employees), and many Social Democrats, however, public institutions were the best way to provide high-quality childcare to all. Here the pedagogical advantages of public institutions were stressed in a discourse that laid as much emphasis on equal opportunity between classes as between the sexes. Thus like the schools, which were then being expanded to provide all children with at least secondary education, public day care could be justified as a way to erase disadvantages arising out of working-class origins. In fact, both forms of day care rapidly expanded. Between 1965 and 1980 the number of spaces in municipal day-care centres leapt from 11,900 to 136,400, while those in family care grew from 6,000 to 88,500 (Hinnfors, 1995: table 11, 50).

The decision to fund the rapid expansion of day care had not put paid to the notion of a care allowance. The Centre Party continued to seek a kind of "care wage," to be paid to those who chose to stay at home and look after their young children. Like an ordinary wage, it would be subject to taxation. Despite their growing ambivalence towards the whole notion of a care allowance, the Liberals continued to support something closer to Moberg's original ideal: a non-taxable care allowance for all parents to help defray the costs of raising children whether these came in the form of income foregone by the stay-at-home parent or through day-care fees.[16] A third option – parental leave – which clearly favoured a two-earner family norm, began to take shape as the decade came to a close. And here again is found evidence of the effect of struggles within LO and the Social Democratic Party, for it was in LO's 1969 family policy document and the first report of the joint LO-SAP Equality Commission that the idea was first advanced that the state should not only improve maternity leave but also, in the spirit of the feminist-humanist ideal, extend it to fathers as well as mothers. The TCO also embraced the notion of *parental* leave in its 1971 family policy document, setting the stage for the introduction of another element in the policy aimed at consolidating an alliance of wage earners. This addition to the social insurance system, however, explicitly recognized that wage earners came in two genders.

In 1974 the new parental-leave insurance scheme, which originally offered six months of leave to either parent, became law. Like the other parts of the "wage earner" model, the new scheme was based on the income-replacement principle. This focus meant that it not only appealed to both white- and blue-collar women workers but also that it provided an inducement for the often higher-paid fathers to take their share of the leave. In this respect, it marked an important symbolic victory for feminist-humanists: it recognized that fathers too could care for children. Subsequent extensions of the leave period (currently twelve months) have made it even easier, in that fathers, who have not "given birth" and do not nurse infants, can take their share. That it is still women who take most of the "parental" leave (over 90 per cent), however, suggests that more was needed. This Swedish feminists recognized, but as we shall see, they were not successful in sustaining the drive to remodel the People's Home to make room for men and women wage earner–parents who enjoyed full equality.

FEMINIST-HUMANIST REFORM STALLED; CHOICE REAPPEARS WITH A NEO-LIBERAL INFLECTION

It is possible to criticize the feminist-humanist conception of gender relations as it was articulated in the sixties for ignoring the power relations that sustained gender inequality. Such criticism is less valid for the 1970s, when feminists within the Social Democratic Party picked up on the more radical discourse that Group 8 brought to Swedish politics. The radicalism, moreover, fitted the times as the unions and the SAP responded to workplace unrest by raising the banner of industrial and economic democracy. The notion of "women's oppression" did not seem out of place in a context where "class oppression" was again being openly debated. The recognition that women were oppressed, in turn, made it clear that it was not enough to give fathers the choice to assume a greater role in caring for their children. Steps would have to be taken to force them to do so. Among the means for so doing were the introduction of quotas to ensure that leave was shared by both parents and the adoption of the six-hour day as a new norm that would give men and women alike the "time to be human."

Both proposals were placed on the agenda in the 1970s by a radicalized Social Democratic Women in Sweden (SSKF). The demand for a six-hour day was advanced in the document produced by six young social democratic women, *The Family in the Future – A Socialist Family Policy* (1972). The SSKF supported this vision and worked to put the work-time issue on the political agenda by publishing a report on the question, and in 1974, it seemed to have sufficient support in the labour movement to push ahead. An investigation into the issue was set up and the six-hour day included in proposals for the SAP's new party program (Karlsson, 1990: 161). Yet at the SSKF-organized conference in 1974, the unions' ambivalence became apparent. The negotiating secretary for the important metal workers' union made it clear that there were more important demands for LO members, such as a fifth week of vacation and reduced hours for shift workers, while the secretary for LO's family council argued that, rather than trying to adjust the societal (male) norm to women's working day, the unions should focus on securing the rights of part-time workers in collective agreements (Karlsson, 1990: 162–3).

A possible compromise between the SSKF and the unions, along with the first suggestion that a quota should be introduced into the parental-leave legislation, was floated in the 1975 report of the Commission on Family Support. Here it was proposed that parental leave be modified to allow parents of very young children to reduce their work time for up to twenty months while receiving partial compensation for the wages foregone. Although this proposal represented a step back from the idea of a six-hour day for all, the suggestion that a quota be simultaneously introduced sought to assuage SSKF (Baude, 1979). The latter, knowing that in the absence of stronger measures the care burden would fall on mothers, found the notion of a special solution for the "parents" of young children unacceptable. The party managed to defer a decision on the work-time question by passing it on to a family policy committee composed of representatives of the party, the unions, and other movements affiliated with the party. Bold action by a small group of social democratic women MPs, however, secured the party's official commitment to introduce a "father month" as the party went into the 1976 election campaign (Karlsson, 1990: 169–70).

By this time, nevertheless, the radical wave had crested, and the economic crisis which had earlier hit many other OECD economies had reached Sweden. The Social Democrats lost the 1976 election and would not return to office until 1982. The coalition government that followed brought together the Liberal Party, whose conception of the modern family was not far from that of the Social Democrats, and the Centre and Conservative parties, who favoured the "choice" – a care wage for those who stayed home to match the day-care subsidy received by working parents. The compromises that they arrived at served to institutionalize a "one and three-quarters" solution rather than the fully egalitarian vision which inspired the feminist-humanists.

Thus in 1978 parental leave was extended to nine months, the last three at a flat rate that was unlikely to be attractive to the usually higher-paid fathers. The additional three months could be used to reduce the working day for one of the parents; but with no requirement that both parents utilize this option, it has primarily been exercised by mothers. That same year, legislation was introduced which made it illegal to deny parental leave while the child was under eighteen months of age or to refuse a parent's request for a six-hour day until the child started school. The language remained the gender-neutral parlance that the feminist-humanists had introduced into Swedish political discourse, but the institutional supports for turning it into full equality were not forthcoming.

In 1982 the Social Democrats returned to office committed to restoring full employment while simultaneously eliminating the deficit. Although the latter goal meant selective cuts to social programs, money continued to go to public day care, and in 1985 the Social Democrats promised to provide a place for all children over eighteen months. In this respect, the commitment to the feminist-humanist vision, to the extent that it had been institutionalized, remained firm in the 1980s. However, no further steps towards improving the model were to be taken, as feminists in the Social Democratic Party learned when, as economic conditions improved, they renewed their demand for the six-hour day. They thus clashed head on with the LO, which was pushing the party to make a sixth week of vacation part of the

1988 election manifesto. The SAP opted to support LO's demand, while women were offered an extension of parental leave to eighteen months. The question of a six-hour day was handed over to a commission of investigation, which would ultimately conclude that such "standardized" solutions were passé. Flexible work time was now considered to be of greater interest to working parents as well as employers.

Thus instead of the egalitarian family with two earners (and two active parents), the "one and three-quarters" wage-earner family has become the norm, leaving many women economically dependent on their men and on the state. To be sure, public funds continued to be channelled into the expansion of the day-care system throughout the 1980s, and parental leave was extended. Yet in the absence of a quota, it remained to a large extent maternity leave. The legislation passed by the bourgeois coalition government of the late 1970s guaranteed the right of "parents" to reduce their work time to three-quarters until the youngest child reached school age, but this provision only helped to institutionalize the one and three-quarters solution. The drive to realize the feminist-humanist ideal had stalled, and this fact became clear in the late 1980s when the argument for "choice" and the related care allowance were returning to the political agenda, this time with a marked neo-liberal inflection. Thus not only had the reforms stopped short of realizing the dream; the very achievements were not invulnerable.

In fact, the reinsertion of "choice" into the political discourse had begun earlier, initially led, not by the bourgeois parties, but by a newly politicized employers' association increasingly dedicated to dismantling social democratic Sweden. An important part of SAF's campaign was a propaganda drive that celebrated the new individualism, and the associated demand for variety, as the harbinger of a new societal model. Such a model rejects the belief, held by Liberals, feminist-humanists, and Social Democrats alike, that a strong public sector constitutes a vital support for individual development.[17] Rather, markets were presented as the best way to meet the multiplicity of needs and interests found in civil society.[18] SAF was also prepared to challenge the social democratic welfare state more concretely by funding private alternatives. Thus along with private health clinics and private health insurance, SAF and the Swedish Federation of Industry financed the establishment of a private, for-profit day-care company, Pysslingen, named after a character in a popular Swedish children's story.

The Social Democrats answered by the challenge by introducing legislation – Lex Pysslingen – banning private for-profit day care and regulating the growth of other non-public forms (Olsson, 1990: chapter 5). In the parliamentary debate that ensued, "choice" was defended by all three bourgeois parties (and, *sotto voce,* by elements within the SAP itself) in the name of respect for "difference." And the Social Democrats did gradually increase the range of options in the system by making subsidies available to parental cooperatives and day-care centres run by voluntary associations, including churches, while holding fast against the concept of for-profit day care. When the bourgeois parties got another chance to form the government in 1991, however, Lex Pysslingen was abolished and the way opened to for-profit day care.[19]

The bourgeois parties' celebration of "choice" also embraced the old proposal for a care allowance, and with it the opportunity for a "parent" to choose to stay at home with young children beyond the time allotted under the parental-leave legislation. Ironically, the threatened reappearance of the housewife-mother occurred just when the Swedish women's movement was preparing a new push for equality in Swedish society, one which, taking past achievements for granted, would focus on achieving parity representation in political life and pay equity in the labour market.[20] The 1991 election was important in this respect, for it brought a coalition of bourgeois parties to office and thus made it possible for them to legislate "choice." At the same time, the *drop* in women's representation in Parliament led not only to talk about the formation of a new women's party but also to the establishment of an autonomous women's network, the Support Stockings.[21] The legislative enactments of the Bildt government show that feminist mobilization was able to utilize already existing tensions among the governing parties, especially as between the Liberals, who continued to defend their version of the feminist-humanist ideal, and the Centre and Christian Democratic parties, which championed the housewife-mother.[22]

Thus, when in 1992, national subsidies for day care were rolled into a new system of block funding to municipalities – a move that could have made it easier for the local governments to renege on their commitments to provide day care – the egalitarian line was strong enough to insist on legislation that incorporated a national commitment to provide day-care spaces for all children who wanted or needed them. In addition, the Liberals also managed to introduce the first quota into the parental-leave system – a "father month," which could not be traded to the mother. They were, however, unable to resist the introduction of a care allowance.

Both the care allowance and the law rendering commercial day-care centres eligible for public subsidies were rescinded by the Social Democrats when they returned to office in 1994, while the father month was left intact. Yet this development does not mean that the Swedish childcare system is secure. Having accepted financial deregulation in the 1980s and then opted to join the European Union, the Swedish Social Democrats have now to work out their policy options in the circumscribed space permitted by international financial markets and EU convergence requirements. Thus in response to a run against the Swedish currency, the Social Democrats cut the compensation rate for parental leave (and other social insurance programs) to 75 per cent.[23] They also imposed stringent fiscal requirements on the municipalities, thus making it more difficult for the latter to meet their obligations to expand (let alone to maintain) a high-quality day-care system. Although the Persson government raised transfers to municipalities and counties explicitly to improve the quality of education, health, and childcare once the deficit was under control, layoffs continued, and in childcare the child-to-adult employee ratio rose from 4.7 in 1991 to 6.7 in 1996 (*Dagens Nyheter,* 30 April 1998).

The Social Democrats have made some symbolic gestures in the direction of the women's movement, including the appointment of a commission to investigate women's position in the evolving labour market. Yet to the extent that the commission is unable to combat the decline in public day care and the cuts to parental-leave insurance, the foundations of solidarity among women wage earners continue to be vulnerable. Pay and employment equity are important, but they can actually contribute to the growth of class differences among women if they are not accompanied by efforts to strengthen the policies enacted in the name of wage-earner solidarity in the past. Thus men and women who are better situated may well be able to make private arrangements which allow them to continue to live according to the egalitarian model while other women are driven into the contemporary version of the industrial reserve army.[24]

CANADA: SOCIAL LIBERALISM'S PATCHWORK OF CHILDCARE ARRANGEMENTS[25]

While Sweden may be the exemplar of the social democratic welfare state, Canada fits the "liberal" pattern, albeit with important social democratic inflections. In other words, the key reforms of the 1940s and especially the 1960s embodied the principles of universality and solidarity without thereby eradicating the liberal bias towards means-tested programs targeted at the needy.[26] Moreover, levels of compensation have remained low in comparison with Swedish rates, leaving room for the creation of an American-style private social-security network. Canada thus fits the liberal paradigm, although not as well as the United States. The deviations can partly be attributed to the presence of a social democratic party – originally the CCF, now the New Democratic Party (NDP) – in national and provincial politics. Although they have never formed the national government, at various times the social democrats have been able to force the governing Liberal Party to make important concessions.[27] Yet the union-party nexus, which has been so important to Swedish social democracy, has never had much depth in Canada, and while the brokerage politics practised by Canadian parties has affected the course of social policy development, the Canadian welfare state has largely been the outcome of debates conducted within the bureaucracy and the institutions of "executive federalism."[28] As we shall see, this pattern began to change somewhat in the 1970s and 1980s as the federal government adopted a discourse of "equitable access" and began to provide funding for advocacy groups.[29]

Canadian childcare arrangements fit the liberal pattern perhaps better than many other parts of the welfare state. In the earlier period, the features of a liberal breadwinner state were particularly pronounced, especially in the treatment of mothers. The resistance mounted in the inter-war period to the introduction of a "mother's pension" – a right based on one's status as mother with dependent children – is indicative of the difficulty in establishing the principle of the right to assistance against the prevailing liberal preference for volunteer services and means-tested benefits. Instead of mothers' pensions, most provinces opted for means-tested mothers allowances.[30] Canada's first universal program, the 1944 family allowance, put money in the hands of all mothers, but the amount provided has never approached the Swedish level. Nor was the family allowance requested by its potential beneficiaries. Rather, it came from the concern of senior officials to maintain wartime wage controls in the face of the labour movement's campaign to remove at least the controls at the bottom of the pay scale. McTague, whose report first raised the idea, was especially opposed to lifting the controls because many of the low-paid at that time were not male breadwinners (Ursel, 1992: 189). Family allowances were also one of the few reforms contained in the federal government's grand design for post-war Canada to meet with approval at the 1945 Dominon-Provincial Conference.[31]

Working mothers were even more grudgingly acknowledged, and then mainly when they were considered important to the war effort. Thus through a special dominion-provincial cost-sharing arrangement, the federal government covered 50 per cent of the cost of day care for women working in essential industries. Given the concentration of manufacturing in central Canada, the effects were uneven, and only Ontario and Quebec took advantage of this arrangement, which, moreover, ended with the conclusion of the war.[32] In addition, the federal government appears to have introduced special regulations for maternity leave in 1941. Such leave was unpaid, but for awhile after the war, the federal Unemployment Insurance Commission granted unemployment insurance benefits to pregnant women who applied (Burt, 1990: 201). This practice was soon stopped, however, and from 1950 to 1957 married women were ineligible to receive unemployment insurance unless they met special criteria (Ursel, 1992: 235).

The federal government would not become involved in childcare again until the 1960s. Ironically, its first steps better exemplify Gelb's "state feminism" – where the state acts to incorporate a definition of women's concerns into policy without significant pressure or input from women's groups (1989: 5) – than does the Swedish case, to which she applies the term. Like the family allowance program, maternity-leave initiatives and the first federal peacetime subsidies for childcare (included in the Canada Assistance Plan – CAP – of 1966) were largely the product of bureaucratic initiatives. Second-wave feminism, dating from the Royal Commission on the Status of Women (1967–70), appeared mainly after the fact, at least in anglophone Canada.[33] Women were more active in the second phase, when the politics of "equitable access" added an important layer of popular participation to the policy process. This time the women's movement was actively engaged in the struggle to establish a set of childcare arrangements very similar to those already in place in Sweden. Women did not fight alone, however. The struggle for the social democratic–feminist alternative was waged by the women's movement in alliance especially with the unions. This struggle formed part of a broader move to "coalition politics."[34]

As in Sweden, the beginning of the break with the breadwinner model began when labour markets were tight, job growth was increasingly concentrated in the service sector, and women's labour-force participation was on the rise. And in Canada as in Sweden, this was also a time when new political openings appeared. With the merger of the Trades and Labour Congress and the Canadian Congress of Labour to form the Canadian Labour Congress, and the newly formed alliance of the latter with the social democratic party marked by the creation in 1961 of the NDP, the labour movement seemed poised to challenge the old-line parties. The wave of wildcat strikes in the mid-1960s and the struggle of public-sector workers for collective bargaining rights gave class-based issues a new salience. The New Left in anglophone Canada helped to spawn a movement for an independent, socialist Canada (the Waffle), and in Quebec the unions and the women's movement helped to shape, and in turn were shaped by, the new nationalist visions that blossomed during the Quiet Revolution. Towards the end of the decade, aboriginal groups began to mobilize against the government's attempts to redefine the Indian status and to forge their claims as Canada's "First Nations."

The federal Liberal government's first response was a spate of new social policy legislation. As Ursel (1992) notes, "within the years 1963–66, ten new welfare statutes were passed that extended federal cost-sharing in health, education and social welfare, created the first national contributory pension plan and brought in the last universal social programme, Medicare" (272). These initiatives stopped short of the reforms inaugurated by the Swedish state in the name of the emergent figure of the "wage earners." Thus, for instance, the Canada/Quebec Pension Plan may have made the public system somewhat more attractive to higher income earners by introducing the income-replacement principle, but it did so at a rate that failed to obliterate the rationale for private supplements.[35] More important, from the mid-sixties on, social policy reforms took place under the shadow cast by the rediscovery of "poverty," which helped to derail the drive for universality.[36]

The first, and still the most important, ongoing federal program of day-care subsidies came not as a result of feminist organizing but rather as the first shot in Canada's "war on poverty," a war that was fought out less in the sphere of partisan debate than in the trenches of executive federalism. In other words, federal support for day care came as part of the larger package of social assistance reforms, bundled together in the Canada Assistance Plan of 1966. Through CAP, the federal government agreed to share day-care costs with the provinces on a fifty-fifty basis,[37] but the inclusion of the program in CAP did not mean that the federal government was willing to play the kind of leadership role that the Swedish government was preparing to take on at that time. Rather, CAP provided assistance for those "in need, or likely to become in need." It thus established a pattern that has prevailed into the present – means-tested day-care subsidies for low-income parents who meet locally established criteria.

Just as in the case of maternity leave, the initiative that resulted in CAP came from within the bureaucracy, though here consultation and negotiations involving federal and provincial officials had a critical part to play (Haddow, 1993: chapters 2 and 3). Rodney Haddow documents the labour movement's relative invisibility in the debates surrounding the formation of CAP, but his account implicitly provides evidence of the even more glaring absence of women's organizations.[38] Rather, day care seems to have been included under CAP as a by-product of intergovernmental negotiations over other matters. What appears to have happened is this. The decision to include provincial mothers' allowance programs in the new cost-sharing arrangements brought poor mothers into the system of shared federal-provincial concern. Day care, in turn, seems to have been added as a result of federal concerns to thwart the inclusion of provincial workfare schemes by adding a "rehabilitative service" element – training, vocational counselling, job placement, and the like – to existing cost-shared social assistance programs.[39] In this sense, Canada seems to have been quick to follow the pattern than being established in the United States, where the "war on poverty" included an attempt to get single mothers "off the dole" and into the labour force by making federal funds available to states that were prepared to establish the appropriate programs (Michel, 1996). Yet there was a "made in Canada" side to this too in that the demand for day care, such as it was at that time, was articulated primarily by social workers concerned about the lack of support for the growing number of mothers who had to work (Finkel, 1995).

In contrast, the move to establish and fund maternity leave took place under the sign of "universality." In 1971, amendments to the Canada Labour Code granted women the right to seventeen weeks of maternity leave, while modifications to the federal Unemployment Insurance Act provided income replacement for fifteen weeks to those who had worked for twenty weeks over the previous year.[40] Like the Swedish legislation, these reforms were based on the income-replacement principle, but they provided a much lower rate. As the Cook task force on childcare was later to note, "the actual replacement income of all maternity leave claimants is ... below 60 per cent when averaged over the entire leave period. Each claimant must first survive a two week period without benefits" (Canada, 1986: 28). Given the relatively low level at which the maximum insurable earnings are set, many middle-income women got less than 50 per cent. The low replacement rate is typical of Canada's social-liberal welfare state and reflects the relative weakness of the Canadian left, but the failure to consider including fathers demonstrates the still limited influence of second-wave feminism on public policy.

Towards the end of the 1960s, a feminist-humanist discourse that was similar to, but more modest than, its Swedish counterpart began to enter the universe of political discourse. The report of the Royal Commission on the Status of Women constituted the first attempt to codify this new representation of gender relations. In it, as Burt notes, glimmered a vision of a future in which men and women would be able equally to participate in the worlds of paid work and parenting (1986: 117). Yet the royal commission was still rather hesitant to advocate policies designed to produce this new world. Its pages reveal that it listened with greater ease to women whose lives were still being lived according to the housewife-mother model than to the radical young visionaries of the women's liberation movement.

Its hesitancy was reflected in its firm adhesion to a conception of "choice" which, by this time, had been jettisoned by Swedish feminists. Thus in the section on women in the economy, as much attention was devoted to the situation of the middle-class housewife and her volunteer work as to women's participation in the labour market. "Choice" also set its mark on the chapter dealing with women and the family: "Our aim is neither to require women to enter the labour market nor to compel them to stay home with their children. Many women want to undertake the full time care of their children; others prefer outside activities or paid work. They should receive the help they need to make the choice" (Canada, 1970: 262). Thus among other proposals, the commission recommended that women's volunteer work be recognized and that a care allowance be set at a hundred times the existing family allowance, which "is spent on the cost of keeping a child and cannot be regarded as payment for its care" (37). The role envisaged for the state was informed by the principles of social liberalism since the public face of Canadian feminism had yet to be enlivened by dialogue with the generation of feminists schooled in the student movement and the New Left. Nor could it at that time benefit from connections with a strong labour movement able to push a social democratic vision of the welfare state. Although the Canadian labour movement shared that vision with its Swedish counterpart and formed part of the ferment attending the 1960s wave of reforms, it was not in a position to shape these developments. Rather, the governing Liberal Party had established the royal commission, and it was to a Liberal government that the latter would report.

When the royal commission submitted its report, then, the pattern was already established against which it could protest, albeit with limited effect. The commission's preferred system was rather similar to that sketched by Swedish feminist-humanists in the early 1960s. It argued the need to "lift day care out of the context of poverty" and replace it with a universal system designed to appeal to "all families who need and wish to use it" (Canada, 1970: 268, 270). As an alternative means for subsidizing day care, the commission suggested not only capital grants, to be made available under the National Housing Act,[41] but also a care allowance rather similar to that proposed by Moberg and Group 222 in Sweden. Thus in the section on taxation, the commission argued for a childcare allowance to "be paid to all mothers whether the parents themselves care for the children or pay for the substitute" (304).

Former commission member and former minister of health and welfare in the 1970s Monique Begin (1992) later noted that the care allowance and other childcare programs advocated by the commission "were discarded without a word by all the parties concerned, even by the women who appeared to be ashamed to ask for that much money" (30). In fact, the newly empowered "femocrats" in the federal civil service did struggle to take childcare out of CAP and make it a universal program (Mahon, 1997). The commission's report helped bring about the introduction in 1971 of an income tax deduction for childcare, and the terms of CAP applicable to day care were changed to allow subsidies for centres and for a broader income group. In the 1970s, too, several federal programs – notably the short-lived Local Initiatives Programme and Department of Regional Economic Expansion grants, the main instrument of federal regional policy – added modest contributions to Canada's day-care infrastructure (Friendly, 1994).

Yet none of these developments challenged the basic liberal parameters of the model, which offered means-tested subsidies for the poor and tax deductions for the better paid. It was only in the 1980s that an opportunity appeared to remodel this liberal edifice according to a social democratic–feminist blueprint. Unfortunately, these plans came forward just as the state was abandoning "social" for "neo" liberalism. In the growing polarization that followed between the state and civil society, where an emergent "popular sector" challenged the "corporate agenda," the latter would prove strong enough to block the Conservative alternative but too weak to carry its own forward.

A SOCIAL DEMOCRATIC–FEMINIST MODEL OF CHILDCARE FOR CANADA?

In forging a social democratic–feminist vision of childcare arrangements, Canadian feminists were certainly inspired by developments in other countries such as Sweden, but their sense that such an alternative was possible and their political strategy for realizing it were "made in Canada." First, from the 1970s through to the early 1980s, the federal government was guided by a philosophy of "social liberalism plus," and this focus gave activists a sense that more was possible. Thus in economic policy the Trudeau Liberals experimented with "Keynes plus" measures, including incomes policies, and the latter led to further experiments with tripartism whereby the unions were offered a chance to participate in the formation of economic policy in exchange for accepting wage controls.[42] In Canada, moreover, such measures came wrapped in the language of a (liberal) nationalism directed at American control of the economy.[43] Although a liberal emphasis on "poverty" continued to mark Canadian social policy, the emphasis shifted to less-intrusive forms of means testing and to "rehabilitative services" such as training and counselling.[44] In the area of labour-market policy, too, the state began to recognize that women formed an important part of the labour force, but that they, like other "equity" groups, needed pay- and employment-equity measures to achieve equality (Cameron, 1996). The government's embrace of "social liberalism plus" thus created an environment in which it was possible to imagine social democratic–feminist alternatives.

A second factor was that feminists chose to organize for new child-care arrangements through "coalition politics," forged in the trenches of civil society rather than in the stale corridors of party politics. This choice has to be seen in relation to the failure of Canada's conventional parties, schooled in the principles of brokerage politics, adequately to respond to the challenges posed by social movements in the 1970s (Brodie and Jenson, 1988). Thus modern Quebec nationalism quickly escaped Jean Lesage's Liberal Party, finding new, more radical homes among the trade unions, artists, and community groups, all of whom constitute the popular base of the then-new (and social democratic) Parti Québécois. Left nationalism in anglophone Canada initially found a home in the New Democratic Party, but the Waffle caucus was soon ousted, thus widening the gap between the NDP and a whole generation of left intellectuals and activists (Bradford and Jenson, 1992). The CLC-affiliated unions continued officially to support the NDP, but the unions also increasingly turned to mobilization in civil society to advance their aims.[45] Although some First Nations and women's movement activists maintained ties to the mainstream parties, the latter were not as ready as their Swedish counterparts to welcome these new forces. In fact, as Vickers and colleagues (1993) note, while the governing Liberal Party was prepared to establish agencies to represent women within the bureaucratic apparatus, this approach was "not matched by equal efforts on the part of political parties to increase the number of women nominated to run for them in safe ridings" (55).

There was thus a real "thickening" of the representational structure in civil society, with only tenuous ties to the system of partisan representation. The new social movements were not, however, "at a distance" from the state itself in the sense that many came to rely on state financial support. Under the banner of Trudeau's "just society," the Liberal government adopted the principle of "equitable access" and established a variety of programs designed to mitigate the "political poverty" of social assistance recipients, aboriginal peoples, environmentalists, and others. As a result, "By the mid-1970s Canada's post-war regime had come to include both countrywide institutions which addressed citizens as individuals and programmatic acknowledgment of intermediate groups which recognised and represented particular categories of citizenship. This regime recognised both individual and collective rights of citizenship and it accepted the legitimacy of the intermediary associations of civil society to provide the representation of interests" (Jenson and Phillips, 1995: 1).

The Royal Commission on the Status of Women itself had contributed to this situation through the format that it developed to encourage widespread participation in its hearings. Although royal commissions are an often-utilized device in Canada, they are usually elite affairs. This commission, however, sought a wider involvement. For this purpose it developed a special pamphlet that described the commission's mandate and offered advice on how to prepare briefs and so on. The commission also made a point of holding hearings in accessible sites such as church basements, community halls, and shopping malls (Begin, 1992: 33). It was not the only commission to act as a rallying point for popular forces. A few years later the Berger commission of inquiry on the Mackenzie Valley offered aboriginal peoples in Canada's north a similar opportunity (Abele, 1983).

The state's recognition of the right to equitable access may have been guided by a liberal-pluralist conception of policy-making, according to which each group should become involved in its appropriate "policy network" and leave the "interest aggregation" function to parties (and to the bureaucracy). Yet in Canada the groups began to develop mechanisms of cooperation, giving birth to the pattern of coalition politics that in the 1980s would pose a challenge to traditional structures of representation.

Through NAC the Canadian women's movement has developed an institutionalized forum for a wide range of women's groups which facilitates coordination and mutual support across policy areas.[46] Formed in 1972 out of thirty-one member groups, NAC could a decade later boast over two hundred member groups. It also became involved in alliances with other organizations, including unions. NAC's picket-line support for some of the key struggles of union women in the late 1970s and early 1980s helped to give birth to a "working-class feminism" that complemented the stance of the more theoretically inclined socialist–feminists who were coming to form an important element within NAC.[47] On the union side, feminist organizing within unions in turn helped to open up the latter to alliances with the women's movement.[48] These experiences laid the foundation for the coalitions that, *inter alia*, would lead the struggle for social democratic–feminist childcare in the 1980s.

The pattern was already visible in the struggle for maternity or parental leave. In 1979 the common front forged by public-sector unions in Quebec took up the issue and secured twenty weeks of maternity leave at full pay. Given the concentration of women in the social/public-service sector, the agreement affected nearly one-quarter of the female workforce (Canada, 1986: 31). The Canadian Union of Postal Workers (CUPW) made maternity leave the central issue in its 1981 strike, a strategy deliberately designed to build alliances. Other unions have followed suite, such that by 1992 "paid maternity leave had become relatively common, negotiated for almost one-half of the workers covered by major contracts" (White, 1993: 90). The struggle was not confined to the collective bargaining front, however; the women's movement and the unions also supported the demand to extend the right to parental leave to all wage earner–citizens, and they made some important inroads. Thus the 1985 revisions to the Canada Labour Code added the right to an additional twenty-four weeks' leave to "any employee who has the care or custody of a newborn child" (Canada, 1986: 22). This was the first federal move to recognize the rights and responsibilities of both parents to combine paid work and parental care.[49] In 1990, changes to the Unemployment Insurance Act offered *parents* an additional ten weeks of benefits on top of the original fifteen.[50]

Maternity- and parental-leave provisions in Canada, of course, remain less generous than in the Swedish system, even after the latter has been diminished by deficit-reduction initiatives. Nevertheless, the alliance of women's groups and unions did manage to establish a beachhead in the longer struggle for a social democratic–feminist alternative. They have thus far been less successful on the day-care front.

Although the royal commission, whose report set the original agenda for second-wave feminism, had supported the notion of universal day care, it was not until the 1980s that day care became a priority issue and NAC began to work with the labour movement and early childcare advocacy groups towards this end. The first step in forging such an alliance was taken by the Ontario Coalition for Better Child Care, a partnership of groups organized under the aegis of the Ontario Federation of Labour.[51] Throughout the 1980s the coalition remained an important force for universal public day care at both the provincial and the federal levels (Friendly, 1994: 146). An equally important role would be played by a group – the Canadian Day Care Advocacy Association (CDCAA) – formed out of the second Canadian conference on day care.[52] The conference endorsed the demand for universally accessible, comprehensive, high-quality day care, to be provided under the auspices of public or non-profit organizations.[53] It also called for the establishment of a federal committee to look into childcare policy (Friendly, 1994: 151).

In the dying days of social liberalism, the advocates of a new day-care system seemed to have had an impact. The Abella Commission on Equality in Employment stated clearly that equality for women "means acknowledging and accommodating the changing role of women in the care of the family by helping both them and their male partners to function effectively both as labour force participants and as parents" (Abella, 1984: 4). Such recognition meant state support for a universal day-care system of high quality. On the eve of the 1984 election, the minister responsible for the status of women established the Cook task force on childcare, which was charged with developing proposals for "complementary systems of child care and parental leave that are as comprehensive, accessible and competent as our systems of health care and education."[54] Day care remained on the agenda during the 1984 election, where it was one of the key issues in the televised leaders' debate organized by the women's movement.

The Cook task force delivered what the majority of groups had called for. In addition to recommending parental leave, it proposed the establishment of a high-quality, universally accessible day-care system under non-profit auspices, to be funded by a new intergovernmental cost-sharing arrangement. Unfortunately, its advice would be received by quite a different federal government, one determined to complete the break with social liberalism begun in the last years of the Liberal regime, and to embrace a neo-liberal agenda. Moreover, while there were feminists within the Conservative Party, the New Right was also well represented, as was evident in the support for REAL Women in the caucus.

Like that of the Swedish conservative parties, the Conservatives' response included a return to the softer "choice" option. It thus gave several billion dollars in the form of "tax assistance to families *with the express intent of permitting them to choose among different child care options, including the choice of one parent remaining at home*" (Phillips, 1989: 166; emphasis added). To be sure, the strategy also included a research and development fund and a proposed $4 billion Canada Child Care Act, which would replace CAP as a source of federal funding for day care,[55] as well as a modest $60 million for the development of childcare on aboriginal reserves. Although the proposed Child Care Act hinted at a break with CAP's welfare bias, in practice it would have allowed the federal government to put a ceiling on expenditures, something that it could not then do under CAP.[56] Again, like the Swedish bourgeois parties, the Conservatives would have made for-profit day-care centres eligible for government subsidies.

Although the government was able to pass the Canadian version of the care allowance, the women's movement, acting in concert with other members of the emergent popular sector, mobilized effective opposition to the childcare act, which died on the government's order paper when the 1988 election was called. Here NAC worked in close concert with the CLC, the CDCAA, and the Canadian Teachers' Federation, with the support of the National Anti-Poverty Organization and the Canadian Association of Business and Professional Women (Friendly, 1994). Although the 1988 election, in which the Pro-Canada Network played an important role in making the free-trade agreement with the United States (CUFTA) a key issue, an alternative vision of childcare was part of the popular sector's agenda. With opponents of the CUFTA split between the NDP and Liberal parties, the Conservatives were able to form the next government with less than an overall majority.[57] The childcare act was not revived.[58] In 1993, however, the Conservatives were finally able to abolish Canada's first universal program, the family allowance, replacing it with a child tax benefit targeted at low-income families.

During the lead-up to the 1993 election, the CDCAA (now the Child Care Advocacy Association of Canada) mobilized to put the social democratic–feminist alternative back on the agenda. It had the support of NAC, the labour movement, the National Organization of Immigrant and Visible Minority Women of Canada, the Assembly of First Nations, and the Native Women's Association of Canada. The Liberal victory seemed to promise a second chance: the Liberals' "red book" had promised to promote the expansion of childcare through the establishment of a new cost-sharing arrangement with the provinces[59] and offered to devote $720 million to this end over the next three years. The subsequent social security review in 1994 described childcare as central to "work, learning and security," and the follow-up document "Child Care and Development" provided more detail on the Liberals' plans to establish "a national framework of principles to guide and consolidate investment in child care and development" (Friendly, 1995: 2). The 1995 federal budget, however, dashed any hopes that a breakthrough was imminent. It proposed to abolish CAP and other federal transfer programs, replacing them with the Canada Health and Social Transfer (CHST), a block-funding arrangement that would transfer a smaller and declining sum to the provinces and territories with few strings attached.[60]

The Canadian childcare system developed in the 1960s and 1970s was far from ideal, as the struggle to replace it with a Canadian version of the social democratic–feminist alternative has indicated. Yet the elimination of CAP and its replacement with the CHST does not mean that the Canadian system is finally prepared to jettison its liberal orientation. Rather, as the Ontario Coalition for Better Child Care (1995) noted, "with the CHST the federal government has begun a spiral of downloading. Fiscal problems have been passed onto the provinces which, in turn, will pass them onto the municipalities, who will dump them onto service providers and users" (6). In some provinces, such as Quebec, the popular sector may be strong enough to resist such "death by dumping," but in most the CHST is likely to lead, on the one hand, to competition between the various sectors as municipalities, school boards, universities, and hospitals all fight over a shrinking pie and, on the other, to intra-sectoral competition which pits day-care centres against shelters for battered women.

This kind of evolutionary, zero-sum politics also affects labour markets, feeding the growth of non-standard jobs already visible in the 1980s (ECC, 1990). Although men are being thrown into this precarious labour market too, women predominate in the part-time and temporary workforce (Armstrong, 1995). The absence of adequate childcare leaves working mothers particularly vulnerable in this regard. Part-time work or work at irregular hours often becomes the only means for reconciling employment and childcare in an context where few can afford to "choose" between them. Childcare also constitutes part of the feminized labour market, and the failure to institutionalize the social democratic–feminist alternative is likely to mean a reversal of recent efforts to recognize and support the skills of early childhood educators.[61]

CONCLUSIONS

The textbook picture of the "social democratic" Swedish welfare state and its "liberal" Canadian counterpart has been confirmed by this study of the two countries childcare arrangements, but only in part. Thus it is true that Swedish childcare arrangements conform to the model of the high-quality, universal welfare state designed to strengthen wage-earner solidarity, but our story has also shown that the model, especially the childcare wing of the People's Home, was not built overnight. There was little room for the working mother in the original design, and there is no reason to expect that the renovations of the 1960s would have recognized that wage earners come in two sexes had Swedish feminists not organized to press their claims. In addition, the construction stopped before all the features (i.e., the introduction of quotas to the parental-leave system, or the six-hour day for all) could be added. Childcare arrangements in Canada, also established in the 1960s, conformed to the (social) liberal pattern, but there was a serious campaign to remodel these in the 1980s according to a social democratic–feminist design.

Feminist organizing has been important to both stories, but feminists have had to organize in circumstances not of their own choosing. In other words, the ways that they organized were very much affected by the institutional terrain on which they found themselves. In this respect, Gelb (1989) is not wrong to claim that the women's movement has been influenced by the "political opportunity structure" that it faced. Where she errs is in seeing Sweden as a case of "state feminism" – that is, where the state in a sense pre-empted women's organizing by giving them what they needed before they had asked for it. As we have seen, feminists did organize in Sweden, but in a way suited to the context. In other words, they faced a well-established representational system linking organizations in civil society such as unions to the party system and, through corporatist as well as parliamentary channels, to the state. In the 1960s, however, that system was particularly open to new demands, especially those associated with the emergent figure of the wage earner. Swedish feminists therefore formed networks such as Group 222 which allowed them to coordinate across party and union lines in order to advance their feminist-humanist vision of a world in which men and women would be free to be simultaneously wage earners and parents.

Ironically, Canada seems better to fit Gelb's "state feminism," at least in the 1960s, when the foundations of a childcare system were being laid. At that time, the representational structure was one in which the real policy debates took place in the corridors of the bureaucracy and the channels of executive federalism. This state of affairs began to change as second-wave feminism was establishing its organizations, and the Royal Commission on the Status of Women, which set the original agenda, contributed to the forces that led to the recognition of the principle of "equitable access" in federal politics. But the women's movement was also part of the effort to seize the opening thus provided and to develop a zone of "coalition politics" that was only tenuously connected to the parties. This new approach provided an environment conducive to the formation of an alliance of women's groups, trade unions, and childcare experts behind a social democratic–feminist alternative, but it appeared too late. The turn had already begun from "social" to "neo" liberalism. In the polarization between state and civil society that ensued, the day-care coalition had enough strength to block the Conservatives' strategy but not enought to assert its own alternative.

Both countries have felt the turn to neo-liberalism, and in both it has brought the policy associated with the earlier "choice" option – some form of a care allowance – back onto the policy agenda. New Right rhetoric aside, however, the reappearance of the care allowance is not really about increasing parents' ability to choose between paid work and the care of young children. In both countries, families have become increasingly dependent on the paid work of both parents, and neither the Bildt government's care allowance in Sweden nor the Conservatives' child tax credit in Canada was set at a level sufficient to compensate for the lost income. The introduction of care allowances, in combination with cuts to existing childcare supports, is thus not going to fuel the return of mothers to kitchen and child. Rather, these developments are likely to support existing trends to labour-market polarization.[62] Cross-class and cross-gender "wage earner" solidarity could become a historical artefact as men and women with "good" jobs pay other women to look after their children – often for longer hours – while many women (and an increasing number of men) join the new industrial reserve army.

Certainly, these trends are fuelled by new continental and global arrangements that magnify the "cold winds of international competition." These arrangements are contributing to a political climate in which national governments – in both Sweden and Canada – attempt to deal with their budgetary problems by dumping responsibility onto lower levels of government. The resulting decentralization is not being undertaken in such a way as to lead to democratization. Rather, it is simply changing the terrain of struggle in ways that pose a challenge to the women's movement and the left in both countries. For in both the tendency has been to look to national governments to guarantee social programs of high standard. The lesson is not that national politics should not be abandoned, but rather that the women's movement and its allies in the labour movement need to develop new ways to link national politics with struggles connected at the local and international levels.

NOTES

Another version of this chapter appeared in *Social Politics* 4, no. 3 (1997) under the title "Child care in Canada and Sweden: Policy and politics." I would like to acknowledge the financial support provided by the Social Sciences and Humanities Research Council of Canada and to thank Ann Britt Hellmark for her help in collecting information on Sweden and various Canadian colleagues, especially Susan Phillips and Jane Jenson, for leads on good Canadian sources.

1 Until recently, parents had the right to twelve months leave at 90 per cent of pay upon the birth of each child (and an additional period at a flat rate) together with a three-quarter day until the child reached school age.
2 Obviously, it is difficult, if not impossible, to get a clear picture of the range and number of unregulated childcare arrangements, but some interesting work has been done on the position of foreign domestic worker-nannies; see, for example, Arat-Koc (1989). Abbie Bakan and Daiva Stasiulis have been engaged in a major research project in this area. Data are available on the relative preponderance of day-care centres (commercial and non-profit) over licensed family day care. In the four largest provinces, day-care centres account for the clear majority of spaces (over 80 per cent) in all but British Columbia, where as many as one-third are in family homes. Non-profit day care is the dominant form in British Columbia, Ontario, and Quebec, but in Alberta nearly three-quarters of the spaces are classified as commercial. See White (1995).
3 Since 1971, new mothers have been eligible to claim approximately 65 per cent, with no pay for the first two of the seventeen weeks, from the federal Unemployment Insurance fund. In 1990 the rules were amended to allow eligible *parents* to obtain another ten weeks of benefits, to be shared or taken by either parent (White, 1993b: 90).
4 The concept of a "universe of political discourse" was developed by Jane Jenson in the early 1980s. For a more recent version, see Jenson (1993).

Class-centred theorists such as Esping-Andersen are not the only ones who overlook the importance of women's organizing, especially in Sweden, where it has not fit the Anglo-American paradigm of autonomous women's organizing. For example, Gelb (1989) goes so far as to say that "Swedish women (the 'daughters of the welfare state') ... appear to have many of the demands of their feminist sisters elsewhere taken care of by the state and the political system, yet their concerns seem to be almost obscured by the efforts to reach equality that are, in the main, not the result of their own efforts" (173). As we shall see, Swedish women did organize for change, although in a manner that fit the circumstances in which they made their choices.

The "agency" question is also interesting with regard to what theory leads one to expect in Canada. Thus the class-centred analysis provided by Esping-Andersen and colleagues would suggest that liberal childcare arrangements would result in a political division between middle- and working-class women. This certainly appears to be the case in the United States (Michel, 1996), but as we shall see, it has not been so in Canada precisely because of the form that women's organizing took, especially in the 1980s and early 1990s.

5 Esping-Andersen (1985; 1990). But this writer's work needs be viewed as a development of earlier contributions by Marshall and Titmuss. Insights drawn from the latter were woven together with the political analyses developed by the so-called power resource theorists. These include Scandinavians such as Korpi (1978) as well as Americans such as Martin (1978). Some feminists have found a modified version useful, while others would opt for a classification scheme based on the way in which welfare states institutionalize particular patterns of gender relations. Both views are represented in the Sainsbury (1994) volume. As should be clear by now, my own approach aims to combine gender and class.

6 The "People's Home" is a powerful metaphor for the Swedish welfare state, credited to former leader of the Social Democrats and prime minister in the 1930s Per Albin Hansson. Feminist critiques of the Swedish welfare state include Baude (1979), Scott (1983), Holter (1984), Eduards (1991), Hirdman (1992; 1994), Acker (1992), and more recently, Sainsbury (1994). See also Jenson and Mahon (1993).

7 On the choice between immigrants and Swedish women, see Kyle (1979) and Knocke and Ng in this volume.

8 See Näsman (1990: 5) for data on fertility rates in the 1950s and 1960s. Fertility rates also fell in Canada, reaching a low of 1.5 by 1991, but with the partial exception of Quebec, this development has not given rise to the same concerns, a result that seems to be linked to the weakness of natalist elements in the anglophone Canadian version of the nation myth. The latter focuses primarily on language (English and French as Canada's two official languages) as modes of integrating new generations of immigrants. It is an issue that I hope to explore in the future.

9 There is also the Fredrika Bremer Association, a "bourgeois" women's organization formed in the late 1800s, but it did not play a major role. The small women's liberation Group 8, which appeared in the late 1960s, was more influential. Like its counterparts in other countries, it brought to second-wave feminism an understanding that gender inequality is rooted in power relations. Yet whereas in Canada the young militants effected a change in the feminist discourse of the National Action Committee on the Status of Women, in Sweden the challenge was felt and responded to by the women's branches of existing political parties, especially the Social Democrats (Karlsson, 1990). The small, but influential Euro-Communist VPK, which does not have a women's league as such, has also been one of the carriers of a socialist-feminist discourse.

10 The Agrarian Party changed its name to the Centre Party in the 1960s as it moved to forge an alliance of farmers and white-collar workers concerned with quality-of-life issues. Interestingly, the alliance with the Social Democrats had broken down in 1958 over the new earnings-related pension scheme from which Esping-Andersen and others date the Social Democrats' efforts to forge an alliance of white- and blue-collar workers.

11 One might also mention the system of corporatist representation, a system of representation and policy formation involving employers, unions, and, where applicable, farmers' organizations, which has proved must less open to women (Bergqvist, 1994). See also Bergqvist and Findlay in this volume.

12 The parties were certainly discovering the importance of white-collar workers, whose unions, whether affiliated with the TCO or the SACO, eschewed official partisan ties. Yet there were also signs that the Social Democrats could not afford to take their traditional blue-collar constituency for granted. This became especially clear with the outbreak of wildcat strikes launched by that of the Kiruna miners in 1969. For the latter, it was important to challenge not only employers' power in the workplace but also the special privileges that helped to mark off the collar line.

13 See Martin (1978) and Esping-Andersen (1985) for more on these policy innovations. For a broader picture of the Swedish political system that includes discussion of the system's response to the new social movements, see Pontusson (1992).

As we shall see, these same principles were applied in renovating the childcare wing of the People's Home. However, the unions, especially LO, resisted the extension of the next step towards wage-earner solidarity – the industrial policy and industrial relations reforms undertaken in the name of industrial and economic democracy for wage earners – to women wage earners. In other words, while they were prepared to accept state intervention in collective bargaining in the name of industrial democracy, they were unwilling to accept it as a means of promoting equal opportunity (*jämställdhet*).

14 From 1965 to 1973 the Liberals and the Centre Party had an official alliance that left the Conservatives isolated on the right of the political spectrum (Hinnfors, 1995: chapter 3).

15 See, for example, the interview with Gertrud Sigurdsen and Anita Gradin in Baude (1992: 40–1). LO's 1969 family policy document bears witness to the difficulties that it had in incorporating gender equality into its class-centred discourse. LO openly complained that the sex-role debate had hitherto been shaped by the concerns of professional women rather than LO members (LO, 1969: 13).

16 See Hinnfors (1995: 20–1) for a discussion of the different care options and their implications.

17 For more on SAF's propaganda campaign, see Hansson and Lodenius (1988) and Pestoff (1991). I do not wish to suggest that the rise of individualism traced by Pettersson and Geyer (1992) is simply the effect of SAF's propaganda, but rather that SAF has worked to neutralize the radical potential of such "reflexive individualism," detaching it from the demands for economic democracy and turning it into a force supportive of its own neo-liberal project.

18 In fact, the term "civil society" came to be reinserted into Swedish discourse by the neo-liberals, who look to voluntary work and the family to supplement the market. This discourse has been picked up by the Conservative Party in particular.

19 In turn, the Social Democrats reintroduced a version of Lex Pysslingen when they got back into office in 1994.

20 A key moment here is the report of the Commission of Inquiry on Women's Representation (1987). See Bergqvist (1994: chapter 3) for more on this commission. As Bergqvist argues, the report made visible the *absence* of women from the channels of corporatist representation. It helped to create an opening for feminists not only in the parties but also in such very "masculine" bodies as the LO. The involvement of union women in turn added the issue of pay equity to the commission's concern with parity. See Mahon (1995) for more on the rise of wage-earner feminism within LO.

21 This network deliberately remained rather nebulous. Although its leading representatives are publicly identified – people such as economist Agneta Stark and journalist Maria-Pia Boethius – the membership is not.

22 The latter is a small party formed when a socially conservative faction split from the Conservative Party in the 1960s. Until the 1991 election, it had never received enough votes to enter Parliament on its own, although the Centre Party had allowed the Christian Democratic leader to take one of its own seats in the 1985 election.

23 The two quota months – the mother's and the father's – are to be kept at 85 per cent, and the new prime minister (and former finance minister) has promised to restore the 85 per cent rate "when economic conditions permit," a proviso that was not mentioned when the cut was made, thus giving rise to fears that the burgeoning alliance of the SAP and the Centre Party would mean the dismantling of the wage-earner floor and a return to the old People's Home built on flat-rate programs.

24 I am here thinking of the increasingly popular argument that one of the best ways to tackle the problem of unemployment is to remove the tax-based disincentives to job creation in the private service sector, including *domestic* services. The Bildt government's initial moves in this direction

were rescinded by the Social Democrats, but some of the latter are certainly drawn to the idea.

25 "Social liberalism" is actually a Swedish term designed to distinguish between laissez-faire and the more social democratic versions of liberalism. I have decided to apply it to Canada's welfare state – at least as the latter developed in the 1960s and 1970s – because it helps to capture the blend of liberalism and social democracy adopted by the federal Liberals (and, to a lesser extent, the Conservatives) at that time. To this approach was added in the 1970s a more activist stance vis-à-vis the economy which I label "social liberalism plus."

26 Family allowances and the old age security of the immediate post-war years were universal programs based on a flat-rate payment. Some of the main reforms of the 1960s and 1970s moved in the direction of universality and solidarity – the expansion of public education, including the post-secondary level; medicare; the Canada and Quebec Pension Plans; and changes to unemployment insurance. On Canada's welfare state from a comparative perspective, see Myles (1998, 1995), O'Connor (1989), and Haddow (1993).

27 They have governed in the provinces of Saskatchewan, Manitoba, British Columbia, and most recently Ontario. They are very weak in the Atlantic provinces, Quebec, and Alberta. In Quebec the banner of social democracy has been most effectively borne by the independentist Parti Québécois.

28 See Jenson (1989) on the broader argument. "Executive federalism" is the term coined by Smiley (1976) to refer to the channels of intergovernmental bargaining that mushroomed in the post-war years. They usually involve senior bureaucrats and cabinet ministers from the federal, provincial, and territorial governments.

29 See Phillips (1991) and Jenson and Phillips (1995). As the latter note, "the rationale for such funding was a belief in a pluralistic society and state, a presumption that strong organizations of citizens were of intrinsic value to a healthy society, and the notion that the state has a responsibility in facilitating access. Thus if some interests were disadvantaged in a way which made their collective action difficult, then government support (including funding) was necessary" (23).

30 Interestingly, Guest points to the important role played by the state-funded Canadian Council on Child and Family Welfare. Founded in 1920, the council became an important voice for selective, means-tested measures. Charlotte Whitton, long-time director of the council, was also one of the leading opponents of the universal system of family allowances introduced in 1944 (Guest, 1980: 52–6 and chapter on post-war reconstruction planning).

31 Old age security had to wait another six years, and the Canada Health Act until the 1960s. The broad programme of housing support for low-income families urged in the Curtis report never came to pass. Instead, the National Housing Act of 1944 resulted in the creation of some housing for returning veterans, but it focused primarily on securing low-interest mortgage rates for middle-income families (Ursel, 1992: 222).

32 For a wonderfully detailed analysis of the wartime policy and what happened in Ontario after the wartime supports were terminated, see Prentice (1993).

33 The Fédération des Femmes du Québec, an organization similar in structure to NAC, was formed in 1964, eight years before NAC. The Quebec women's movement was very involved in redesigning Quebec society, a process unleashed by the Quiet Revolution (Begin, 1992). Thus, as with the labour movement, where Quebec has developed its distinct associational system, the Canadian women's movement has two separate, but related histories, one in Quebec, for which the provincial government and politics constitute the paramount focus, and the other in the rest of Canada, where there are also local associations but where, for the left, the tendency is to look to the national level to guarantee certain standards. I follow others – Burt (1986), Vickers et al. (1993) – in recognizing that much of what I have to say applies only to the latter.

34 During the 1970s there were an increasingly number of examples of such coalition politics, forged in civil society. Nevertheless, the emergence of a "popular sector" is perhaps best dated from the Royal Commission on the Economic Union and Development Prospects for Canada (Macdonald Commission, 1982–95). The effort by Cameron and Drache to assemble the alternative voices in *The Other Macdonald Report* helped to make visible the "lines of demarcation between a neoconservative corporate vision of Canada and a 'popular sector' perspective" (Bleyer, 1992: 105).

35 Myles (1995) notes that, in combination, public retirement-income schemes in Canada offer a replacement rate of 60 per cent as opposed to closer to 85 per cent in the Nordic systems (10).

36 Haddow (1993) details the emergence of a liberal, poverty-centred perspective on welfare reforms. My own understanding has been shaped by numerous discussions with John Myles and Wendy McKeen as the latter wrote her MA thesis, which began to explore why the women's movement never posed an effective challenge to the family-centred discourse (McKeen, 1991). McKeen is taking the analysis deeper in her doctoral dissertation at Carleton University.

37 Provinces such as Ontario, in turn, shared their 50 per cent with municipal governments. The original provisions seem, moreover, to have been

quite restrictive. The royal commission noted that by the end of January 1969 only Ontario and Alberta had bothered to apply for funds, and then only for a limited amount (Canada, 1970: 269). While CAP moved from an income-based to a broader "needs-based" test (Haddow, 1993: 23), the latter seems to have been too narrowly interpreted to incorporate many low-income families with two wage earners. The rules seem to have been loosened somewhat, allowing subsidies to go to a larger number of "low-income" families (Abella, 1984: 186).

38 Haddow, of course, used a theoretical framework which required him to look for evidence of *class* mobilization but remained blind to *gender*. It is thus possible that he simply failed to see the latter. I have, however, been unable to find evidence of the involvement of women's organizations even in the work of feminist scholars on day care.

39 To this interpretation might be added Ontario's insistence that child services also be included (Haddow, 1993: 28). Later Haddow documents the resistance that officials from the federal Department of Health and Welfare encountered from the department charged with labour-market policy (Labour until 1966; thereafter Manpower and Immigration).

40 The impetus for these reforms came mainly from the wave of wildcat strikes that occurred earlier in Canada (1964–66) than in Sweden (1969–74). Interestingly, the government task force established to interpret the strikes evoked the image of the "new worker," who was better educated and thus no longer prepared to put up with authoritarian management styles. In other words, there was a hint of the same figure that stood behind the industrial democracy reforms in Sweden in the 1970s. The Canadian reforms, however, stopped well short of those undertaken in Sweden.

It should be noted that the Canada Labour Code only applies to workers in federally regulated industries. The major part of the workforce is governed by provincial legislation. Federal legislation has, however, often acted as something of a pace-setter. Unemployment insurance (UI) is a federal scheme that applies to all workers. Burt (1990) argues that the government chose to implement maternity-leave insurance through UI because it has exclusive jurisdiction in this field and thus could circumvent the still-reluctant provinces (203).

41 They also recommended that day-care centres be included in housing developments, "including university buildings" (where young feminists were organizing for day care); that Health and Welfare establish an advisory service to aid the provinces and territories; and that these jurisdictions establish childcare boards to plan, regulate, and support the development of a network of day-care centres. Ontario had already established a regulatory and advisory branch, but most other provinces still lack such a mechanism for enforcing standards.

42 By "Keynes plus" I mean the whole plethora of "post-Keynesian" policy instruments that add a supply-side activism to the original focus on macroeconomic demand management. These measures were not without their limitations, nor were they by any means unambiguously progressive. Nevertheless this form of liberalism did accept an active role for the state in the economy and hence gave more radical demands a certain legitimacy.

The offer of tripartite consultations gave rise to important debates within the labour movement, with the more radical elements firmly opposed to the CLC's proposed "social corporatism." Later, the left within the unions would fashion its own alternative, "social bargaining." For more on the 1970s, see Mahon (1984: chapters 1 and 8). On social bargaining, see Jenson and Mahon (1993a; 1995).

43 Again, I do not wish to suggest that liberal nationalism posed a serious challenge to foreign control. Yet the presence of a nationalist element within the federal government helped to make the left-nationalist project seem less utopian. This fact appears particularly clear today, when the hegemony of a continentalist neo-liberalism seems difficult to shake. See Cameron and Gonäs in this volume for insight into the Pro-Canada Network's important efforts to challenge this hegemony.

44 For example, the guaranteed income supplement (GIS), which relies simply on income tax data to determine eligibility for supplementary old age transfers. The key idea in the social policy review is a guaranteed annual income, supplemented by rehabilitative measures to "modernize the periphery." On the GAI and the GIS, see Myles (1988, 1995). On the social security review, see Haddow (1993).

45 The reasons for this trend are complex. Union-party ties have never been strong, and as Yates (1993) notes, unions such as the United Auto Workers (now CAW) retained a strong syndicalist tradition even after the formation of the NDP. The public-sector unions, which became an increasingly important part of the labour movement after they gained bargaining rights in the 1960s, have their own reasons for keeping their distance from the party, especially in provinces where NDP governments have instituted income policies and other disciplinary measures. Finally, there are generational reasons: the Waffle had an impact on a whole generation not only of left academics but also of trade union activists, who thus remained sceptical of the NDP.

46 In the first major study of NAC, Vickers and colleagues (1993) describe it as an "institutionalised parliament of women." Phillips (1991) also provides insight into the structure of linkages among the groups that constitute the Canadian women's movement.

47 On working-class feminism, see Maroney (1987) . On NAC support for the strikes at Fleck and elsewhere, as well as on the rise of socialist-feminists within NAC, see Vickers et al. (1993) and Cohen (1992).

48 As Briskin (in this volume) argues, feminist organizing within unions clearly helped to begin to transform a masculine trade union culture but the task was made easier by the strength of the "social unionism" tradition, especially in unions such as CUPW. See, for example, White (1993a) for an analysis of the postal workers' union and its support for part-time workers, as well as its adoption of a bargaining strategy very similar to the Swedish unions' "solidaristic wage" policy.

49 Parents were given the right to share the additional leave if both were employed under the jurisdiction of the Canada Labour Code – a pretty big "if" – and they also had the right to reinstatement in their former jobs or equivalent ones, upon return to work.

50 The way for the introduction of parental leave was smoothed by the Abella Commission on Equality in Employment in 1984, the Parliamentary Committee on Equality Rights in 1985, and the Forget Inquiry on Unemployment Insurance in 1986. See Phillips (1989: 170).

51 For a useful description of the history of the struggle for day care in Ontario, see Lero and Kyle (1991). A comprehensive history of the development of support for a social democratic–feminist day-care system would have to bring such provincial, and even local, histories into the picture.

52 The first conference had taken place in 1971 (Tyyska, 1994). The second was sponsored by Health and Welfare Canada, and the latter went on to provide financial support for the other group, the Canadian Child Care Federation, which arose out of the debates over whether state support should also be extended to commercial, for-profit day care. The CDCAA was funded by the more feminist-oriented Women's Program in the Department of the Secretary of State. See Findlay (1987) and Bergqvist and Findlay in this volume for more on the latter.

53 The term "comprehensive" means recognition of a diversity of needs. In other words, the policy should support a range of options, to be worked out at the local level (Friendly, 1994: 163). Both the Abella and the Cook reports recognized the different needs with particular reference to First Nations, "visible minorities," and the disabled, as well as those living in rural areas. In this sense, the Canadian version of the social democratic–feminist ideal is more "postmodern" in spirit than the Swedish system, which was essentially based on the notion of the same (high-quality) service to all.

54 Minister Judy Erola; cited in Friendly (1994: 153).

55 In the version tabled in the House of Commons, provinces were given the option of staying with CAP or moving to the new program, which did not restrict funding to subsidized spaces for low-income families. It was intended, however, that funding through the new program would diminish as day-care capacity expanded. In other words, it was not an

open-ended program in which the federal government had to match every dollar spent by the lower levels of government.

56 In 1990 the Conservatives did put a cap on CAP for the three richest provinces.

57 In fact, of the opposition parties, it was the Liberals who paraded the banner of nationalist opposition to the CUFTA, while the NDP played to a bland view of what it thought "ordinary Canadians" wanted.

58 According to Friendly (1994), the government's own advisory council on social policy was quite critical of the act, suggesting that it constituted a second-rate alternative (178).

59 Forty-forty, with parental fees covering the remaining 20 per cent. This approach would have left parents responsible for a larger share than in Sweden (10 per cent), but nonetheless represented a major breakthrough.

60 The federal government seemed to hear the protests, and in October it reiterated its intention to set up a $720 million fund. It also intervened when the neo-liberal Ontario government threatened to gut the day-care system (White, 1995). However, the sense of victory snatched from the jaws of defeat proved to be short-lived. In February 1996 the federal government announced that it was cancelling its childcare program "due to insufficient provincial interest."

61 A part of the social democratic–feminist alternative which I have not discussed treats the staff side of the "high-quality" objective. As Friendly (1994) notes, "training and education, turnover (or consistency), working conditions, and wages are all key predictors of quality" (219). Thus the struggle has included such questions as pay equity for workers in the "broader public sector" including day care, recognition of qualifications, the establishment of standards ranging from health and safety to staff-child ratios, and unionization. See also Lero and Kyle (1991) for a discussion of these issues in the debates over childcare in Ontario.

62 Polarization has gone further in Canada than in Sweden because the welfare state and the industrial relations reforms of the 1970s have strengthened the unions' capacity to resist, but changes to this structure of rights, as well as developments within the Swedish unions themselves, are opening the way to the model of polarized growth pioneered by the United States.

REFERENCES

Abele, Frances. (1993). Political transformation in the Mackenzie Valley, 1968–1980. Doctoral dissertation, York University.

Abella, Rosalie S. (1984). *Report of the Commission on Equality in Employment*. Ottawa: Government of Canada.

Acker, Joan. (1992). Reformer och kvinnor i den framtida välfärds-staten. In *Kvinnors och mäns liv och arbete*, edited by Joan Acker and et al. Stockholm.

Arat-Koc, Sedef. (1989). In the privacy of our own home: Foreign domestic workers as solution to the crisis of the domestic sphere in Canada. *Studies in Political Economy*, no. 28.

Armstrong, Pat. (1995). The feminization of the labour force: Harmonizing down in a global economy. In *Invisible Lines*, edited by B. Neis, L. Dumas, and K. Messing. Charlottetown: Gynergy.

Baude, Annika. (1992). Inledning. In *Visionen om jämställdhet*, edited by A. Baude. Stockholm: SNS.

– (1979). Public policy and changing family patterns in Sweden, 1930–1977. In *Sex Roles and Social Policy: A Complex Social Science Equation*, edited by J. Lipman-Blumen and J. Bernard. London.

Bergqvist, Christina. (1994). *Mäns makt och kvinnors intressen*. Uppsala: Acta Universitatis Uppsala.

Begin, Monique. (1992). The Royal Commission on the Status of Women in Canada: Twenty years later. In *Challenging Times: The Women's Movement in Canada and the United States*, edited by C. Backhouse and D. Flaherty. Montreal: McGill-Queen's University Press.

Bleyer, Peter. (1992). Coalitions of social movements as agencies for social change: The Action Canada Network. In *Organizing Dissent: Contemporary Social Movements in Theory and Practice*, edited by William Carroll. Toronto: Garamond Press.

Bradford, Neil, and Jane Jenson. (1992). The roots of social democratic populism in Canada. In *Labor Parties in Post-Industrial Societies*, edited by Frances Fox Piven. London: Polity.

Briskin, Linda, and Patricia McDermott. (1993). *Women Challenging Unions: Feminism, Democracy and Militancy*. Toronto: University of Toronto Press.

Brodie, Janine, and Jane Jenson. (1998). *Crisis, Challenge and Change: Party and Class in Canada Revisited*. Ottawa: Carleton University Press.

Burt, Sandra. (1990). Organised women's groups and the state. In *Policy Communities and Public Policy in Canada: A Structural Approach*, edited by William and Grace Skogstad Coleman. Mississauga, Ont.: Copp Clark Pitman.

Burt, Sandra. (1986). Women's issues and the women's movement in Canada since 1970. In *The Politics of Gender, Ethnicity and Language in Canada*, edited by Alan Cairns and Cynthia Williams. Toronto: University of Toronto Press.

Cameron, Barbara. (1996). From equal opportunity to symbolic equality: Three decades of federal training policy. In *Changing Spaces: Gender and State Responses to Economic Restructuring in Canada*, edited by Isabella Bakker. Toronto: University of Toronto Press.

Cameron, Duncan, and Daniel Drache. (1985). *The Other Macdonald Report.* Toronto: Lorimer.

Canada. (1970). Royal Commission on the Status of Women. *Report of the Royal Commission on the Status of Women in Canada.* Ottawa: Government of Canada.

– (1986). Task Force on Child Care (Cook task force). *Report of the Task Force on Child Care.* Ottawa: Status of Women Canada.

Clement, Wallace, and John Myles. (1994). *Relations of Ruling: Class and Gender in Postindustrial Societies.* Montreal: McGill-Queen's University Press.

Cohen, Marjorie Griffin. (1992). The Canadian women's movement and its efforts to influence the Canadian economy. In *Challenging Times: The Women's Movement in Canada and the United States*, edited by C. Backhouse and D. Flaherty. Montreal: McGill-Queen's University Press.

Daune-Richard, Anne Marie, and Rianne Mahon. (1996). Only a parenthesis? Swedish family policy in crisis. Paper presented at the Tenth International Conference of Europeanists, Chicago.

Economic Council of Canada (ECC). (1990). *Good Jobs, Bad Jobs: Employment in the Service Economy.* Ottawa: Supply and Services Canada.

Eduards, M.L. (1991). Toward a third way: Women's politics and welfare policies in Sweden. *Social Research* 58, no. 3.

Esping-Andersen, Gösta. (1990). *The Three Worlds of Welfare Capitalism.* Princeton, NJ: Princeton University Press.

– (1985). *Politics against Markets: The Social Democratic Road to Power.* Princeton, NJ: Princeton University Press.

Findlay, Suzanne. (1987). Facing the state: The politics of the women's movement reconsidered. In *Feminism and Political Economy: Women's Work, Women's Struggles*, edited by Heather Jon and Meg Luxton Maroney. Toronto: Methuen.

Finkel, Alvin. (1995). Even the little children cooperated: Family strategies, child care discourse and social welfare debates, 1945–1975. *Labour/Le Travail* 36: 91–118.

Friendly, Martha. (1994). *Child Care Policy in Canada: Putting the Pieces Together.* Don Mills, Ont.: Addison-Wesley Publishers.

– (1995). So you say you want a devolution ...? Child care and the federal budget of 1995. Presentation to the House of Commons Finance Committee Hearings on Bill C-75. Ottawa.

Gelb, Joyce. (1989). *Feminism and Politics: A Comparative Perspective.* Berkeley: University of California Press.

Gonäs, Lena. (1989). *En fråga om kön. Kvinnor och män i strukturomvandlingens spår.* Stockholm: Arbetslivscentrum.

Guest, Dennis. (1980). *The Emergence of Social Security in Canada.* Vancouver: University of British Columbia Press.

Gustafsson, Siv. (1994). Childcare and types of welfare states. In *Gendering Welfare States*, edited by Diane Sainsbury. London: Sage.
– (1984). Equal opportunity policies in Sweden. In *Sex Discrimination and Equal Opportunity: The Labour Market and Employment Policy*, edited by Gunther and Renate Weitzel Schmid. New York: St Martins.
Haddow, Rodney. (1993). *Poverty Reform in Canada, 1958–1978*. Montreal: McGill-Queen's University Press.
Hansson, S.-O., and A.-L. Lodenius. (1988). *Operation högervridning*. Stockholm: Tiden.
Hinnfors, Jonas. (1995). *Familjepolitk, samhällsförändringar och partistrategier, 1960–1990*. Stockholm: Almquist and Wiksell.
Hirdman, Yvonne. (1994). Social engineering and the woman question: Sweden in the 1930s. In *Swedish Social Democracy: A Model in Transition*, edited by Wallace Clement and Rianne Mahon. Toronto: Canadian Scholars' Press.
– (1992). Utopia in the home. *International Journal of Political Economy* 22, no. 2.
Hobson, Barbara. (1990). No exit, no voice: Woman's economic dependency and the welfare state. *Acta Sociologica* 33.
Holter, Harriet. (1984). *Patriarchy in a Welfare Society*. Oslo.
Jenson, Jane. (1993). All the world's a stage: Ideas, spaces and times in Canadian political economy. In *Production, Space, Identity*, edited by J. Jenson, R. Mahon, and F. Bienefeld. Toronto: Canadian Scholars' Press.
– (1989). "Different" but not "exceptional": Canada's permeable Fordism. *Canadian Review of Sociology and Anthropology* 26, no. 1: 69–94.
– and Rianne Mahon. (1995). From "Premier Bob" to "Rae Days": The impasse of the Ontario New Democrats. In *La social-démocratie en cette fin de siècle/Late Twentieth-Century Social Democracy*, edited by Jean-Pierre and Jean-Guy Prevost Beaud. Presses de l'Université du Québec.
– (1993a). Representing solidarity: Class, gender and the crisis of social democratic Sweden. *New Left Review* 201: 76–100.
– (1993b). Legacies for Canadian labour of two decades of crisis. In *The Challenge of Restructuring: North American Labor Responds*, edited by Jane Jenson and Rianne Mahon. Philadelphia: Temple University Press.
– and Susan Phillips. (1995). Redesigning the citizenship regime: The roots of the current reconfiguration in Canada. Paper presented at the Intégration Continentale, Recomposition Territoriale et Protection Sociale, Université de Montréal, 25–27 October.
Karlsson, G. (1990). *Manssamhället till behag?* Stockholm.
Korpi, Walter. (1978). *The Working Class in Welfare Capitalism*. London.
Kyle, G. (1979). *Gästarbeterska i manssamhället*. Lund.

Lero, Donna, and Irene Kyle. (1991). Work, families and child care in Ontario. In *Children, Families and Public Policy in the 1990s*, edited by Laura C. and Dick Barnhorst Johnson. Toronto: Thompson Educational Publishing.

LO. (1969). *Fackföreningsrörelsen och familjepolitiken*. Stockholm: Prisma.

McKeen, Wendy. (1991). Social policy and the women's movement in Canada: Why the women's movement has not been able to place the issue of family-based social programs on the political agenda. MA thesis, Carleton University.

Mahon, Rianne. (1997). The never-ending story, Part I: Feminist struggles to reshape Canadian day care policy in the 1970s. Paper presented at the workshop of the Research Network on Gender, State and Society, held in conjunction with the Social Science History Association meetings, Washington, DC, 16 October.

– (1995). Swedish unions in new times: Women workers as the basis for renewal? Paper presented at the annual meetings of the APSA, Chicago.

– (1984). *The Politics of Industrial Restructuring: Canadian Textiles*. Toronto: University of Toronto Press.

Maroney, Heather Jon. (1987). Feminism at work. In *Feminism and Political Economy*, edited by Heather Jon and Meg Luxton Maroney. Toronto: Methuen.

Martin, Andrew. (1978). Dynamics of change in Keynesian political economy. In *State and Economy in Contemporary Capitalism*, edited by C. Crouch. London: Crown Helm.

Michel, Sonya. (1996). A tale of two states: Gender and public/private welfare provision. Paper presented at the Tenth International Conference of Europeanists, Chicago, March.

Myles, John. (1998). Decline or impasse? The current state of the welfare state. *Studies in Public Economy* 26.

– (1995). Why markets fail: Social welfare in Canada and the United States. United Nations Research Institute for Social Development discussion paper, no. 68. June.

Näsman, Elisabet. (1990). Models of population policy – The Swedish conception. Paper presented at the conference on Population, Society and Demography: Policies for Europe, Turin.

Nätti, Juoko. (1992). Atypical employment in the Nordic countries: Toward marginalisation or normalisation? In *Scandinavia in a New Europe*, edited by T.P. Boje and Sven Olsson-Hort. Oslo: Norwegian University Press.

O'Connor, Julie. (1989). Welfare expenditure and policy orientation in Canada in comparative perspective. *Canadian Review of Sociology and Anthropology* 26: 127–50.

Olsson, S. (1990). *Social Policy and the Welfare State in Sweden*. Lund: Arkiv.

Ontario Coalition for Better Child Care. (1995). Burying a national child care program. Brief to the House of Commons Standing Committee on Finance. Ottawa.

Pestoff, Victor. (1991). The Demise of the Swedish model and the rise of organized business as a major political actor. Paper presented at the Society for the Advancement of Socio-Economics, Stockholm.

Pettersson, Thorleif, and Kalle Geyer. (1992). *Värderingsförändringar i Sverige: Den svenska modellen, individualismen och rättvisa*. Samtal om rättvisa nr 4. Stockholm: LO.

Phillips, Susan. (1991). Meaning and structure in social movements: Mapping the network of national Canadian women's organizations. *Canadian Journal of Political Science* 24: 755–82.

– (1989). Rock a bye Brian: The national strategy on child care. In *How Ottawa Spends, 1990–91*, edited by Katherine Graham. Ottawa: Carleton University Press.

Pontusson, Jonas. (1992). Sweden. In *European Politics in Transition*, edited by M. Kesselman and J. Krieger. Lexington, Mass.: Heath.

Prentice, Susan L. (1993). Militant mothers in domestic times: Toronto's postwar childcare struggle. Ph.D. dissertation, York University.

Qvist, Gunnar, Joan Acker, and Val R. Lorwin. (1984). Sweden. In *Women and Trade Unions in Eleven Industrialized Countries*, edited by Val Lorwin, Arlene Kaplan-Daniels, and Alice Cook. Philadelphia: Temple University Press.

Sainsbury, Diane. (1994). *Gendering Welfare States*. London: Sage.

Scott, H. (1983). *Sweden's "Right to be Human"; Sex Role Equality: The Goal and the Reality*. Armonk, NY: M.E. Sharpe.

Smiley, Donald. (1976). *Canada in Question: Federalism in the Seventies*. 2d ed. Toronto: University of Toronto Press.

Sundin, Elisabeth. (1988). *Omåttliga önskningar – måttliga framsteg: Kvinnor i dagens och morgondagens samhälle*. Stockholm: FRN – Framtidsstudier.

Sundström, Marianne. (1991). Sweden: Supporting work, family and gender equality. In *Child Care, Parental Leave and the Under Threes: Policy Innovation in Europe*, edited by Sheila and Alfred Kahn Kamerman. New York: Auburn House.

Tyyska, Vappu. (1994). Women facing the state: Childcare policy process in Canada and Finland, 1960–90. *NORA* 2.

Ursel, Jane. (1992). *Private Lives, Public Policy: One Hundred Years of State Intervention in the Family*. Toronto: Women's Press.

Vickers, Jill. (1992). The intellectual origins of the women's movements in Canada. In *Challenging Times: The Women's Movement in Canada and the United States*, edited by C. Backhouse and D. Flaherty. Montreal: McGill-Queen's University Press.

– Pauline Rankin, and C. Appelle. (1993). *Politics as if Women Mattered: A Political Analysis of the National Action Committee on the Status of Women*. Toronto: University of Toronto Press.

White, Julie. (1993a). One union responds: The case of the Canadian Union of Postal Workers. In *The Challenge of Restructuring: North American Unions Respond*, edited by Jane Jenson and Rianne Mahon. Philadelphia: Temple University Press.

White, Julie. (1993a). *Sisters and Solidarity: Women and Unions in Canada*. Toronto: Thompson Educational Publishers.

White, Linda. (1995). Partisanship or politics of austerity? Child care policy development in Ontario and Alberta, 1980–1995. Unpublished manuscript.

Yates, Charlotte. (1993). Curtains or encore: Possibilities for restructuring in the Canadian auto industry. In *The Challenge of Restructuring: North American Labor Movements Respond*, edited by Jane Jenson and Rianne Mahon. Philadelphia: Temple University Press.

Organizing to Stop Violence against Women in Canada and Sweden

MONA ELIASSON AND COLLEEN LUNDY

ABSTRACT

This chapter traces women's organizing in Canada and Sweden in response to male violence against women. An examination of the movements in both countries contrasts levels of awareness of the nature and extent of violence and women's organizing strategies to respond to the problem. A comparison of the strategies and outcomes indicates that, while approaches to organizing have differed, achievements in these areas over the past twenty years have been impressive. The reaction of the state in both countries in relation to, and independent from, women's lobbying for change is also discussed. The challenges now facing the women's movement, particularly in the current economic climate of globalization, privatization, and reduced social spending, are outlined. The chapter closes by offering some thoughts for future organizing strategies.

In most countries, violence against women has elicited strong reactions among women and has been recognized as a barometer of their unequal position in society. In response, women activists have mobilized to raise public awareness, set up services for abused women, and lobby the state for legal, social, and economic changes that would benefit women. Overall, the achievements in these areas in countries such as Canada and Sweden over the past twenty years have been impressive, considering that in the early 1970s woman assault was not an issue within the women's movement, let alone in the larger society.[1] However, the current economic climate of globalization, restructuring, privatization, and withdrawal of support for social-welfare programs marginalizes the needs of women and is threatening many of the gains made by the women's movement, including progress in the area of violence. This chapter traces the Canadian and Swedish activities to address the violence that women experience in their intimate relationships with men.[2]

AWARENESS OF THE PROBLEM

The governments of both Canada and Sweden have declared a commitment to gender equity, including the right of women to be free from violence. However, in reality, women remain subordinate to men in social and economic terms, and they continue to be verbally, sexually, and physically assaulted by them. In fact, the extensive nature of the violence, sometimes with permanent and lethal outcomes, in both countries has prompted many women to view it as a national crisis in urgent need of attention.

Understanding of the reasons behind gender inequity differs in Canada and Sweden and influences the interpretation of violence in the two countries as well as the responses. Based on a political analysis from the 1960s and 1970s, the Swedish state made a commitment to gender equity and equal opportunities for both men and women to participate in working life, family life, and public service. It is ironic that the centrality of gender equity as a philosophy also contributes to the denial of gender differences and conflict in that country and thereby masks the need for separate organizing by women. Feminism has been resisted because it would polarize women and men. Therefore gender conflicts, or conflicts of interest between women and men, have not been recognized in the official gender discourse in Sweden until very recently (Eduards, 1992), and violence did not become part of this agenda until the mid-1980s.[3] This ideology of equity is not as widely entrenched in Canadian society, and women's unequal position relative to men has been the spark of the women's movement. The social, political, and economic gains that Canadian women have achieved and the current visibility of gender violence have not come easily and have been the result of women's organized struggle.

Women, particularly those in the shelter movement, have consistently spoken out about the brutality that women face at the hands of men. In Canada the Violence against Women survey of 1993, the first national study of its kind in the world, offered confirmation on the degree of violence in women's day-to-day lives (Statistics Canada, 1993). For example, the majority (60 per cent) of Canadian women said that they were afraid to walk alone after dark in their neighbourhoods. One-half (51 per cent) of all women had experienced at least one incident of violence since the age of sixteen, and of the women who had ever lived with a male partner, 29 per cent had been physically or sexually assaulted by him at some time in the relationship. For those women assaulted, a weapon was used in 44 per cent of the cases, and 45 per cent of the women assaulted were physically injured. Despite the seriousness of the violence and the fact that 34 per cent of the women feared for their lives, 22 per cent did not mention the violent incidents to anyone.

Another recent survey focused specifically on the Canadian university population and found that one in five undergraduate women was physically abused, while one in eight was pressured into intercourse during campus dating (DeKeseredy and Kelly, 1993). It is not surprising, then, to find that university women protect themselves from potential violence by restricting their activities on campus and therefore often miss opportunities for study and work (Harris, 1991; Klodawsky and Lundy, 1994).

National statistics or broader community surveys are not yet available in Sweden. While the current reliance on police, hospital, and shelter statistics results in the under-reporting of violence against women, these statistics do offer a glimpse into the degree of violence that they are experiencing and the legal response to that violence. According to public statistics in 1994, 14,629 instances of male assaults against women were reported to the police. This figure represents an increase of 100 per cent since 1981, but it is believed to be more a reflection of a readiness to report such crimes than an actual rise in the number of attacks on women. Of the assaults against women reported to the police, 27 per cent resulted in formally charged cases.[4]

In 1994 there were 40,000 contacts from women seeking help at the women's shelters in Sweden, which handle all kinds of abuse of women, including battering, rape, and incest (Lindmark, 1995). Canadian women and children who entered shelters for victims of domestic abuse in the twelve months ending in May 1995 totalled 85,000, 3,000 more than in 1992–93.[5] While it is difficult to present a direct statistical comparison between the two countries, the findings of various studies do reveal that violence against women in both Canada and Sweden is a troubling reality and that women are reaching out for help.

AMBIVALENCE IN ADDRESSING MALE VIOLENCE

Even though violence against women has become recognized and is well documented, the ongoing struggle of women's groups has been to advance the understanding of male violence as a political problem that is based on women's inequality and rooted in the social structures of society. During the early years in Canada, the struggle centred on language, and the women's movement actively opposed terms such as "family violence" and "domestic assault," which detracted from the reality of men abusing women. More recently, feminist language has been incorporated into the government lexicon, and women are concerned that "feminist claims have been subsumed within and used to legitimize governmental actors' own agendas" (Gotell, 1998: 40).

Explanations for male violence that deny or minimize men's responsibility and blame women also detract from the political nature of the problem. One popular argument is that male violence is due to the over-consumption of alcohol. Given the tradition among Swedish men of drinking hard liquor until one is senseless, it is understandable that many violent acts are committed under the influence of alcohol. At the same time there is a widespread opinion that what one does when inebriated is to be forgiven – but only if one is a man. Women's excessive use of alcohol has even been presented as a risk factor for *male* violence (Bergman and Brismar, 1992). Swedish men in general tend to subscribe to official statements about gender equity and are expected to contribute to housework. Blaming alcohol intoxication can conveniently hide their ambivalence and be an excuse for violence without a deviation from the principle of gender equality, at least in private relations.

Male alcohol use is felt to be a precipitating factor in only one-third of violent situations (Johnson, 1996). Although alcohol reduces inhibitions and impairs judgment, not all men who drink are violent; nor are violent men necessarily drinkers. Women's groups have argued that alcohol does not in itself cause violence and have emphasized that such a conclusion removes responsibility from the perpetrator. For example, in Canada a recent Supreme Court ruling supporting a man who used drunkenness as a defence against an assault charge was withdrawn only after a protest by women's groups. The Criminal Code was amended in 1995 to prevent anyone who had harmed another person from using a defence of intoxication.

The Role of the Media

The media also play an important role in portraying social problems such as violence against women, and in their reporting they can cloak the unequal status of women and divert responsibility from the men who perpetrate the abuse. In Canada the most intensive and controversial reporting by newspapers and television occurred during the coverage of the "Montreal Massacre" of 6 December 1989. On that date a man named Marc Lépine shot and killed fourteen women, wounded thirteen others, and then killed himself at the Ecole Polytechnique de Montréal. He targeted these women because he saw them as feminists who had chosen engineering, a traditionally male profession. His suicide letter included "a hit list" of nineteen women – "radical feminists" with important achievements whom he had been unable to kill because of "lack of time."[6]

The initial response of the media was to detract from the political nature of the act and to focus on the killer as a "sick man" or "mad man," to speak of the women as "students" and the massacre as "an unexplainable act" (Berard, 1991). In the weeks that followed, women across the country raised the issues of male misogyny, feminist backlash, the degree of violence against women in society, and the need for social and political change. However, the media filtered these voices: "Feminists could express acceptance of the emotional consequences of the massacre, but were not permitted to rail against it. Feminists were honoured as victims, but not respected as politicized participants who could constructively shape the event's meaning. There was some exploration of the environment of violence against women that produced Lepine, but no examination of the anti-feminist climate that created a political assassination" (Lakeman, 1990: 23).

In many ways, 6 December, now a national day of remembrance and action on violence against women marked by vigils and demonstrations, has heightened general awareness and has constituted a turning point in general recognition of the stark reality of violence against women.

Initially, it was the work of the shelter movement that increased public awareness in Sweden and brought the problem to the attention of the media as anything but a rare, individual, and vociferous conflict (Eduards, 1992). However, the Swedish media continue to take a very ambivalent stance which detracts from the reality of male violence against women while at the same time unfavourably targeting feminist initiatives. In the 1990s, as more publicly known women identify themselves as feminists and as feminism is recognized as a significant modern movement, the resistance to it is increasing in the conservative sections of Swedish society, which for the most part are uneasy with the principles of gender equality.[7] Although violence is identified as a severe social problem by the public, the media have not seriously covered situations where women have been abused by their male partners. The daily drama of women fighting for their lives gets media attention only occasionally. The main focus has been on the spectacular violence perpetrated by young men and aimed primarily at other men or mixed groups in public places.[8] When violence becomes associated primarily with public acts between males, private violence directed at women in their homes by men whom they love(d) and live(d) with is easily forgotten (Eduards, 1992).

The tendency of the media to construe violence against immigrant women as a problem of "culture" emerged clearly during the winter of 1996–97 when three tragic cases of extreme assault against young women from the Middle East occurred and two of them died. All three women had chosen to live like Swedish women rather than following the traditions that the male members of their families advocated. The media discussed cultural differences emphasizing Sweden as a land of freedom for women where male violence does not exist. When the manifestations of Swedish men's violence are presented, culture or society is not included.

The most popular explanation by the Swedish media has focused on biologism (violence is conferred by nature and not easily controlled), simplified Freudianism that blames mothers (they have not met their sons' needs, thus shaping the sons' reactions to other women),[9] and individual psychological aberrations (temporary mental confusion) as explanations for male violence. It is also argued that single-parent mothers are unable to control growing sons, who, lacking male models in their search for masculinity, become violent (see, for example, *Dagens Nyheter*, 1995).[10] The exclusion of any deeper gender analysis of male violence absolves men of individual responsibility and even displaces it to women – that is, mothers.

Efforts to promote books attacking feminism – for example, those by Camille Paglia and Katie Roiphe – while ignoring feminist publications, are paired in the conservative press with resistance to new laws regarding violence against women. Assaults on the group called the Support Stockings[11] are also common in these newspapers. Many liberal male academics are united in the conviction that this group is not representative of all Swedish women and thus not worthy of being listened to. Furthermore, they repeatedly tell the Support Stockings what they should be doing, without any awareness that such a patronizing attitude is offensive and illustrates the very need for women to organize separately.[12]

STATE RESPONSE: CONSULT AND STUDY

While this ambivalence to acknowledge fully and respond to the problem is evident in both countries, it is manifested differently as a result of their divergent political histories, economic structures, and geography. In Canada the three levels of government (federal, provincial, and municipal), the relative political autonomy of the provinces, the racial and ethnic diversity of the population, and the regional differences and size of the country all contribute to diverging views, positions, and responses. Although various levels of government espouse a commitment to end violence against women, this commitment is seldom reflected in practice. With the current shift away from state regulation, the responsibility for funding shelters and other programs has been downloaded by the central government to the provinces, while at the same time federal transfer payments have been substantially reduced. In turn, many provinces in Canada are responding by cutting these programs because "we can no longer afford them."

State responses have been motivated for the most part by an increase in public awareness of violence and the mounting pressure from women activists for state intervention. While the first mention of male violence against women in a federal document occurred in 1979 and the first national study was undertaken in 1980,[13] it has been only in the past eight years that the state has become particularly active and visible in its response. This involvement has mainly consisted in commissioning studies of the problem and in "consultation" with women's groups. While these enquiries have offered insight and direction, there has been little in the way of action. Unfortunately, at the same time funding to those very groups that are working to end violence has been reduced.

In 1989 the federal Conservative government invited four hundred researchers, practitioners, and policy-makers in the areas of child abuse, elder abuse, and wife assault to attend a four-day national consultation called "Working Together: National Forum on Family Violence."[14] The stated goal was to advise the government in its development of a national strategy on family violence. As is is the usual practice, a number of federal ministers addressed the gathering and expressed concern and support. However, along with congratulatory speeches came silence about forthcoming funding and backing to implement a national strategy to combat violence against women.

Instead, the 1989 federal budget severely reduced funding to women's organizations, revealing the true level of commitment to end violence. The already meagre Women's Program in the Department of the Secretary of State was targeted for a series of cuts that would affect women's publications and eighty women's centres across the country. This downsizing did not occur without resistance from women, particularly grassroots activists. In the spring of 1990, women in St John's, Halifax, and Vancouver occupied offices of the Secretary of State to protest the elimination of operational funding to women's centres. Police removed women in Halifax and Vancouver, but the St John's occupation lasted five days. This organized resistance resulted in the reinstatement of funding to all centres.

The federal government's next show of concern was to set up a parliamentary committee to study the problem. In 1991 the Standing Committee on Health and Welfare, Social Affairs, Seniors and the Status of Women issued its report, *The War against Women*, which contained twenty-five recommendations. Although the report strongly supported action on a number of fronts, including a royal commission on violence against women, the federal government decided to appoint a panel to study the problem further and to develop a national action plan.

The Canadian Panel on Violence against Women, formed in August 1991 for this task, was seen by some to be "just another in a long series of consultations and reports the state had used to contain protest while appearing to be responsive" (Levan, 1996: 319). In July and August the following year five national women's organizations withdrew their support from the panel.[15] The feminist opposition centred on the panel membership – eight members, all government-appointed, who lacked formal links to a variety of women's organizations.

The final report, released in 1993, was entitled *Changing the Landscape: Ending Violence – Achieving Equality*. The massive document was a compilation of eight hundred submissions from individuals and groups in 139 communities across Canada, and it verified, yet again, the extent and scope of violence against women in Canada. It also included a national action plan, which was accompanied by 497 recommendations. However, it was presented without a timetable for implementation, plans for funding, or an organizational structure to put the recommendations into action.

On the heels of the panel report came the 1993 nation-wide survey on Violence against Women, also initiated and funded by the federal government. Twelve thousand women across the country were interviewed by telephone regarding the degree of violence in their lives. Although the nature of the survey excluded certain categories of women, the findings provide comprehensive statistics on the degree and nature of violence against women and their attempts to reach help.

There has been no action as a result of this state-sponsored research, and all indications are that the panel report and the plans for a national strategy have already been consigned to the dustbin. The current Liberal government has continued the practice of its Conservative predecessor in that it has been engaging women in a "consult, brief, and lobby" process without a commitment to implement much needed changes.

Similarly, in Sweden in 1991 Bengt Westerberg, vice prime minister, minister for gender equity, and the chair of the Liberal Party, appointed the Committee on Violence against Women to study questions concerning such violence from a "woman's perspective" and propose a suitable course of action to deal with the problem. The aim of this program is to improve responses in the judicial system, social services, and health-care agencies, as well as looking into the inclusion of violence in the education of professionals. Recommendations have taken account of criticisms from women's groups and the shelter movement. A radical proposal is that stalking men should be fitted with an electronic bracelet connected to an alarm at a police station which would be activated if the man came too close to the home of the woman who had obtained the restraining order.[16] More-strict views on emotional abuse and the controlling behaviour of violent men are other innovations. Despite some hopeful first signs, there has been a delay in Parliament, apparently as a result of the fact that most of the consulted legal bodies do not recognize the problem and reject the proposals. Others – for example, the medical profession and the church – do approve and have recommended swift passing of the bill.[17] The response of the minister of justice that the proposals were not adapted to Swedish law and therefore needed to be reworked was perhaps more revealing than she realized. Like the Canadian example, a timetable or action plan for the implementation of the proposed changes has not been presented.[18]

It is likely that women's groups will continue to be invited to "consult," and it is imperative that women rethink the importance and usefulness of such forums. State-sponsored forums and consultations draw women away from grassroots organizing and mobilization into a bureaucratic direction that can have a deradicalizing and demobilizing effect. The state sets the agenda, with funding for activities that tend to contain and undercut the potential for more radical and independent action on the part of women. A clarity of purpose and expectations, as well as a means to press for greater state accountability and commitment, are needed. In particular, a monitoring process to ensure that recommendations are implemented by the state is crucial.

WOMEN'S ORGANIZING EFFORTS

The very distinct paths taken by Canadian and Swedish feminists in the work to stop violence against women largely reflect historical differences in the struggle for gender equality and the social condition of women in each country. Perhaps the most salient differences between Canada and Sweden in addressing male violence can be found in the location of the struggle, the role of the women's movement, and the centrality of feminism in relation to the state.

Women's organizing efforts in both countries are currently taking place in a conservative climate in which women's issues are increasingly met with resistance, denial, and minimization. Social change and advancement of the position of women are particularly difficult in times of economic restraint and recession. In the context of "debts and deficits," neo-liberal responses unfortunately focus on reducing government spending by scrapping the social programs on which women and children depend. Such agendas contribute to the backlash against the gains that women have achieved, while at the same time creating social and economic conditions of hardship for many women and the organizations that represent them.

Social problems in Sweden are generally perceived to be the responsibility of the welfare state, and until recent cuts to social programs, Swedes could depend on compensation when they found themselves in socially and economically precarious situations. With women's traditional economic dependency on men lessened and to some degree transferred to the state (Hernes, 1987), the need for special organizing was not seen as pressing, and change was perceived as more readily achieved through existing political channels. In the 1990s, proposals for changes to Swedish state policy regarding violence emanated mainly from women in political parties, who frequently also involved themselves in the shelter movement. As well, many were also acting in response to lobbying from the Swedish Organization of Emergency Shelters for Battered Women (SOES).[19]

The women's sections of political parties led the way in getting the government to admit that sexual violence was an extreme form of male oppression and also of gender inequity (Eduards, 1992). Declarations against male violence, as well as action programs, have emerged from all the political parties, largely through the work of women in politics. However, the explanations for this violence differ depending on the political position on a left-to-right spectrum, with the more conservative parties leaning towards individual explanations and the socialist parties focusing on patriarchy (Eliasson, 1994).[20]

In comparison, Canadian women activists have been less likely to have their concerns represented by elected women politicians or to find them on the agenda of political parties. Instead, women's organizing efforts started from a conscious feminist perspective and have focused on setting up structures, both formal and informal, at community, regional, provincial, and national levels and lobbying the state to create laws to protect women and to fund much-needed services.

While a great deal has been accomplished, there are regional differences in the services available to women, and in some provinces the gains won are now being eroded. In Ontario and Alberta, for example, the social-welfare system has been dismantled at a rapid and brutal rate, and much-needed services for women are disappearing. Such forms of assistance as shelters, programs for abusive men, day care, affordable housing, and supportive counselling all depend on the provincial and municipal funding that is being drastically reduced. This situation is creating hardship for those who rely on these programs, as well as for those working towards social change. Many women's groups and service agencies are struggling to keep their doors open and continue much-needed organizing activities.

In Sweden the struggle to stop violence against women has received support from elected politicians, but formal women's groups, with the exception of SOES, are less visible. Until recently, most women's organizations have chosen the "mainstreaming," instead of the "disengagement," strategy (Briskin, 1991). However, at the start it was not obvious to those adopting disengagement, where alternative social practices are envisioned, that shelters for abused women could and should be a task for the women's movement (Bolin, 1984; Mral and Ericsson, 1986) even when society did not offer any appropriate help. Instead, it was argued, sheltering was the responsibility of the society that had created the problem in the first place. This sentiment, though muted, is echoed by the president of SOES, Ebon Kram, when she says that shelters should only be a complement to the state, not do its work. One major obstacle that she mentioned – that state agencies do not recognize the oppression of women and compartmentalize the problem by viewing it as totally separate from gender inequity – is being removed in recent laws. State agencies have no obligation to alter established social practices, while shelters controlled by the women's movement are committed both to helping women and to changing society in order to eliminate the problem. Ebon Kram states that SOES now has attained a position of influence as a result of its work during more than a decade of lobbying political women and the government agencies on issues bearing on woman battering, rape, and other forms of violence.[21]

The other aspect of the dilemma that the commitment of professionals in state agencies is not identical to those of shelter women who work both to help women and to change society is being addressed in the new laws of 1998. The controversial aspect of the law is the perception that that violence emanates from gender inequality. In the future, professionals (nurses, physicians, lawyers, psychologists, and social workers) will be required to have taken compulsory education about violence and gender inequality in order to graduate. The frequent consultations by the government with SOES on violence-related issues have in all probability contributed to this significant change.

Feminist Research

Ongoing research by feminists is vital in order to advance the theoretical understanding of violence, to assess organizing efforts, and to contribute to social change. Unfortunately, Swedish feminist research has not placed violence against women high on its agenda. There are two possible and interrelated reasons for this state of affairs. The resistance to areas of study and research that do not easily fit into the established academic disciplines, with their strictly observed and defended borders, is exceedingly strong. The violence-against-women theme challenges both official gender discourse and this academic tradition.[22] An academic career has to be planned carefully, especially by women. Further, academic research and teaching, including women's studies, are not considered to be connected to the general women's movement in Sweden. On the contrary, care has been taken by feminist academics to avoid such "contamination."[23]

One exception to this situation is the opening of a special centre for services to battered and raped women in 1995. The centre is attached to a major teaching hospital, with the additional mission to educate professional hospital staff about the problem, develop innovative practice responses, and spearhead new research.[24]

This approach contrasts strongly with the research focus of Canadian feminists, where enquiry in the area of violence against women is viewed as important and legitimate and is highly encouraged. In 1991 the federal government's Family Violence Prevention Division and the Social Sciences and Humanities Research Council of Canada funded three (two more were added later) Centres for Research on Family Violence and Violence against Women. These "centres of excellence" were designed to bring academic women and women activists together in order to integrate research with community needs.

However, developing and maintaining academic-community partnerships has proven to be a difficult task in at least one centre. Community women felt that the partnership was university-based and unequal and that it resulted in research which did little to contribute to social change (Barnsley, 1995). On the other hand, the academic women felt misjudged as "unreliable and self-serving" and then "scapegoated for the general failings of the institutions" that they represented (Strong-Boag, 1994: 111). The difficulty in forming working relationships of trust between women in the academy and those in the community may in part be due to the fact that the need for these partnerships did not emerge from the women and their organizations but was imposed by the government. Also, the economic and political context likely contributed to the tension and conflict. The formation of these partnerships occurred while cynicism among community activists was growing. Federal monies were being diverted away from services to the survivors of violence just as $10 million was provided for the Panel on Violence against Women and funding to much-needed women's shelters and other resources was cut.

Common Initiatives

Four initiatives of women's organizing that have received considerable attention both in Canada and in Sweden are the campaign for more-responsive policing and criminal justice approaches to violence against women, the growth of shelter and support services available to women, the efforts to re-educate abusive men, and the attempts to provide education and to coordinate activities. Although developments in these areas represent significant accomplishments, they also demonstrate the necessity for ongoing change.

Policing and the Criminal Justice System Women organized long and hard to have assault within relationships recognized as a crime and for a more responsive criminal justice system. There has been an outcry for more policing and laws to protect women and harsher punishment for perpetrators. Legislative victories in the past ten years in Canada include the following: the mandatory charging of the man in wife-abuse cases (1982 in Ontario), making rape of the woman partner a crime (1983), a broadening of the sexual-assault law with regard to what is required for a woman to consent to sex (1992),[25] and most recently an anti-harassment law that deals with stalking (1993).

Similarly, Swedish legislation in the area of violence against women by men in intimate relationships has been developed. Laws against rape in marriage were instituted in 1965 and since 1982, violence in heterosexual relationships falls under public prosecution, together with a policy of an automatic charge. Restraining orders were introduced in 1988, transgressions being punishable by up to six months in jail.

Mandatory-charging laws are important in shifting violence against women into the public sphere. However, despite the changes to the Criminal Code, men who have assaulted their partners are not always charged with the offence, and of those who are charged, few are convicted. For example, in the Canadian Violence against Women survey, police were called to only 26 per cent of the cases of violence, and of these only 28 per cent resulted in criminal charges.[26] The effectiveness of the anti-stalking legislation is also in question. A recent study of 601 stalking cases found that, for the 35 per cent accused who were found guilty, 58 per cent of the stalking charges were withdrawn before the men reached trial or were stayed by crown attorneys.

Since restraining orders have proven to be inadequate to protect women from being stalked by violent men, other attempts have been initiated. In both countries alarm kits have been made available to women who were being stalked or felt threatened. Pressing a button, we are told, will have a police patrol available within minutes. It appears that these measures have been somewhat successful in keeping the stalker at a distance. For example, in Sweden few women with alarms have been attacked and none have been hurt (Rikspolisstyrelsen, 1993). Another effective option available to Swedish women is a twenty-four-hour-a-day bodyguard at public expense.[27]

Unfortunately, reliance on more policing and the involvement of the criminal justice system has not begun to solve the problem. Cooperation with the police is still essential for building a case, and even more important for conviction. In Sweden, official police statistics indicate that the number of calls is increasing, while at the same time the number of charges is decreasing, as compared to ten years ago. In 1983, 71 per cent of reported cases led to the man being charged; by 1993 the proportion had declined to 65 per cent, and only 10 per cent lead to a conviction. Lack of solid evidence is the official explanation (Statistics Sweden, 1994). Recent news reports indicate that, increasingly, women are too frightened to cooperate with the police in cases of battering.

Also, overt police racism against visible-minority men and women deters some women who must decide whether or not to seek help. Rozena Maart, in her submission to the Canadian Panel on Violence against Women, speaks to the dilemma for minority women: "Black women and other racial minorities have long perceived elements in the police forces and social service agencies as dangerous to their communities. They know, that by calling the police, they risk getting their men maimed, psychologically humiliated and often times killed" (Canada, 1993a: 81).

Other critics of the criminal justice system and the current policy directives argue that an automatic charging policy leaves women with little control over the legal process that is set in motion, a process that often revictimizes the woman (Goyette, 1990). Since women are acutely aware of the economic, emotional, and social consequences of their partner being charged, automatic charging keeps some from seeking help (Currie, 1989). Canadian working-class women and children often experience negative economic repercussions as a result of men's arrest. Realization of the potential costs of an arrest (fines and incarceration) can become a deterrent from calling the police for help.

An additional concern in both countries is the long waiting period between the time the charge is laid and the court date, a period that can place women in a difficult and dangerous situation. Men who are charged often pressure women to drop the charges (if possible) or threaten them if they testify against them. In 1993, when knowledge of procedures and support services was at a peak in Sweden, only 41 per cent of all women who called shelters reported this violence to the police. Escalation of violence and death threats are among the most common reasons why women do not notify the police (Elman and Eduards, 1990). Also, if a woman agrees to testify, she will have no direct representation in the courts. The crown attorney represents the state, while the woman is considered only a witness for the prosecution. Since 1982, Swedish law has allowed a woman to bring her own counsel with her to court, but only in exceptional cases of extreme brutality and other difficult circumstances. Legal assistance is provided during the preliminary investigations, as well as during the trial(s).

Often, Canadian women are not given clear and consistent information about what charges can be laid, what court procedures will follow, the conditions of any probation for the man, and the support and advocacy services available to guide her through the process. While protocols for both the police and the Crown have been established to assist in responding to wife assault,[28] the practice often falls short of serving women.

There have been some successful initiatives that respond directly to these problems in the criminal justice system. In Winnipeg the Women's Advocacy Program, established in 1986, provides a service for women whose partners have been charged with wife abuse. Women are offered support and legal information about their partners' charges and the procedures of the criminal justice system. Following this development, the specialized Family Violence Court was created in 1990 to handle cases of wife assault, child abuse, and elder abuse. The court has been successful in reducing delays, with an average processing time of three months, and in providing more consistent sentencing (Ursel, 1994).[29]

Similarly, the Ontario government has turned to specialized domestic-assault courts and a coordinated community response to create a more effective criminal justice process. The features of this approach include a specialized court for all domestic-assault cases; designated crown attorneys assigned to the court who have a commitment to more vigorous prosecution of cases; police officers trained in collection of evidence; programs for offenders after sentencing; support to women after the assault and throughout the court process; probation officers knowledgeable about domestic violence; and the collaboration of all participating agencies and services during the process. In 1997 two courts began operation in Metropolitan Toronto, and the apparent success of the initial experiences led to the decision to create additional domestic-violence courts in six Ontario cities, along with an intensive evaluation program. While these developments may contribute to significant change in the criminal justice system, a "law and order" agenda must be balanced with adequate and accessible community services for all women who experience violence.

The Shelter Movement The shelter movement has been primary to the struggle to end violence in both Sweden and Canada, but its beginnings and paths have been very different. The opposing strategies of self-help and professional services (Schechter, 1982) have taken different directions in the two countries. In Sweden, women's shelters have maintained a self-help orientation, over time becoming progressively more openly feminist, while in Canada there has been a movement from grassroots self-help towards professional support.

Currently in Sweden there are women's shelters or hotlines in 133 locations financed through local subsidies (Lindmark, 1995) and supplemented with state funds for specific projects, such as educational programs in schools or at military bases. Most of the shelters initially organized in Sweden conformed more to the "philanthropy model," in that the emphasis was mostly on helping without any conscious feminist emphasis (Dobash and Dobash, 1991). The lack of a widespread and deliberate movement or commitment to respond to violence in the shelters at that time probably contributed to the resistance from radical feminists. A recent survey of shelters indicates that, over time, most have taken on a more consciously feminist-activist orientation (Eliasson, 1994). Many shelters have made a point of resisting the professionalization of shelter work and allow only limited appointments of paid workers.

The assistance offered by shelters under the motto of "women helping other women" includes advising them of their rights, but never proposing a solution for them; accompanying women to court; and educating the public about battering. It is primarily carried out by nonpaid volunteers – ordinary women with very ordinary jobs who are using their free time to help other women in their community.[30] In addition, some shelters have a professional psychologist or counsellor with whom the workers can consult and unburden themselves. Few shelter workers have experienced intimate violence themselves. All volunteers, as well as the paid staff members, have to go through a short study program about violence against women, the legal aspects, and the shelter routine before they are allowed to meet with women seeking help in the shelters. Later this preparation can be supplemented with education and training organized by SOES.

The same limitations with regard to the self-help approach as are indicated by Schechter (1982) in the United States appear in Swedish shelters. Women in acute mental distress and those with drug problems cannot be accommodated and have to seek help from professional agencies, which are frequently less able to deal with the problems of violence. In effect, these women are often excluded from needed services. All shelters in Sweden and Canada are dependent on public funds. They are obliged to have a formal structure and to have their books audited regularly. The shelter movement differs from most other organizations in that it emphasizes a grassroots perspective and takes on a formalized structure with reluctance.

Since the formation of SOES in 1984, the Swedish shelter movement has been at the forefront both in terms of helping women and in formulating the problem in more explicitly feminist terms. The organization has definitely taken the lead with regard to issues pertaining to aid for abused women. It has also contributed to a move away from the official avoidance of issues of power difference and gender conflicts in the greater women's movement. The non-professional position of SOES is ambivalent, however. When its president claims that state authorities and institutions resist important social change when they disregard knowledge about male violence against women developed in the shelter movement through practical work and feminist analysis, her statement is certainly based on expertise in the field.[31]

The history of the Canadian sheltering movement is somewhat different in that the initial responsibility and impetus came explicitly from the women's movement with "the grassroots commitment of women helping women" (Gilman, 1988: 9). The first women's shelters emerged during the early 1970s, and the latest count, not considering recent closures as a result of funding cuts, reports approximately 319 refuges for women – 248 transition houses, 22 second-stage houses, and 48 safe-home networks (Canada, 1992). Funding comes primarily from the provincial ministries of social services, which provide between 50 and 75 per cent; fund-raising and donations account for the remainder.

Although shelters were initially organized at the grassroots level and often had collective structures, more and more now have the hierarchical structures found in most service agencies. There has also been a shift from volunteer or grassroots workers to those who are university educated, and in most cases unionized. The involvement of the state in funding shelters has come with a high price, according to Andrea Currie (1989), since it has meant "the dilution of the feminist vision of transition houses as part of a social movement, and the growth of a 'professional' model of transition houses as social service agencies" (22). There is concern that the move towards more professionalized and institutionalized services creates greater distance between shelter workers and the women coming for help (Ahrens, 1980). Early in the shelter movement, abused women were sisters in the struggle, but with the increased professionalization and bureaucratization of services, they are now more likely to be subjects of study and program clients (Morgan, 1981).

Feminists in Sweden and Canada clearly have different views of the state, and the shelter movements started from divergent positions. However, it remains to be seen whether Sweden will follow the developments in Canada. The opportunities for education with a feminist perspective are increasing, attracting many young women to a distinctly feminist practice in the shelter movement. At the same time, the state's greater commitment to helping abused women with more public facilities[32] will likely increase the numbers of professionals involved.

In both Canada and Sweden one of the most difficult tasks is to give adequate support and aid to immigrant and refugee women. In Sweden they constitute one of the fastest growing groups to seek help at the shelters. Almost 60 per cent of the women staying in shelters in Stockholm come from this category (Kerpner, 1995). The language barrier is considerable, even if interpreters are available.

When they seek help from mainstream agencies, aboriginal and immigrant women in Canada often face racism from service providers who have a limited understanding of their culture and history. For these reasons, aboriginal women have organized to provide shelters and healing lodges that are culturally relevant and responsive to the needs of First Nations women and their children.[33] Likewise, specific services for immigrant and refugee women have been developed in both Canada and Sweden.

In Stockholm special initiatives for immigrant women being organized by other immigrant women are affiliated with the largest shelter in the metropolitan area. For some immigrant women, leaving their husbands and seeking assistance at the shelter constitutes a betrayal of their community and culture. The problem of protecting these women from irate men – husbands, fathers, or brothers – seeking restitution for the perceived offence to themselves and their culture can be demanding, but all tendencies to blame their different cultures have to be resisted. Similarly, totally misguided proposals to regard violence against women by men from non-European cultures more leniently within the law, as an allowance for their different culture, cannot be accepted (Banakar, 1990).

While women in the shelter movement in both Canada and Sweden have placed responsibility on the state to fund much-needed services, responses to the dilemma of the self-help worker or volunteer versus the professional have been different. In Sweden the emphasis on generating volunteers from the community has meant few permanent paid positions and a reliance on women's unpaid work. However, it has also resulted in the mobilization, education, and politicization of a diverse number of women. On the other hand, the focus in Canada has been on ensuring that women get paid for their work and on the recruitment of more professionally educated women. The importance of unions for shelter workers has also surfaced. During conflicts with the board, workers have realized that "not all women have the same interests, and as women increasingly take up the practice of management there will be more and more times when they will oppress (other) women" (MacDonald, 1995: 17). While there has been state involvement in both movements, the shape of services has been dissimilar. Nevertheless, it is clear that Canadian and Swedish women share a vision and struggle for the well-being of the women who come to them for help.

Programs for Abusive Men Programs for abusive men have become part of the movement to end violence against women. These programs, which began in the late 1970s in North America, have increased dramatically in the last ten years. Currently there are approximately 125 such programs in Canada (Canada, 1993b). Of these, 2 have been designed solely for aboriginal men, 2 are culturally sensitive to the needs of aboriginal men, and 1 has been set up explicitly for Indo-Canadian men. The move to mandatory charging of wife batterers in the early 1980s was partly responsible for the increase in men's programs during that period. While the majority of such programs have been separate from services for women, several are attached to and controlled by shelters. More recently, private practitioners are specializing in the treatment of abusive men by offering individual and group counselling.

Unlike in Canada, attention to abusive men by way of organized programs is recent in the Swedish shelter movement, and there is great ambivalence regarding such programs. The position of SOES is that women's safety comes first, and since a woman cannot under any circumstances live safely with a violent man, separation and punishment for his transgression are the only efficient alternatives available. However, the majority of women do not want the relationship to end. They desire the violence to stop and would like facilities for men, as do some shelter workers. The question is how the shelters and SOES should be involved. Service-oriented women, especially professionals involved in the two shelters initiated and sponsored by the cities of Stockholm and Göteborg, feel that men are entitled to treatment and have developed such programs. Unfortunately, these services have followed traditional psychiatric thinking in sympathizing with the men while urging battered women to change their ways as a solution to the problem (Lenneer-Axelson, 1989). This is also the approach taken by another individual therapy program for violent men with prison sentences for battering or rape, which is conducted in a prison (Göransson, Järvholm-Andersson, and Kwarnmark, 1988). None of these programs makes an attempt to locate the problem in a broader perspective, and all fail to recognize that individual therapy for men gives no priority to, and has little consequence for, the protection of women. The difference in concerns as compared to SOES is striking.

In 1994 a modest movement towards a pro-feminist approach started in the city of Norrköping, inspired by the Domestic Abuse Intervention Project in Duluth, Minnesota, a model for many of the programs in Canada. The "Frideborg-project" is an alternative to a jail sentence and is directed at both women and men through group sessions. Provided with information from police reports on domestic violence, male counsellors contact the men, and female counsellors call the women. The emphasis is on men taking responsibility for their violence, and the objective is to help them to stop using violence altogether through group sessions with other men who have similar problems. There are also tentative plans to offer the program in a local prison. A preliminary report indicates that the men who have completed the mandatory sixteen sessions have expressed the need to continue (Kuntscher and Jonsson, 1994). However, this program has not been evaluated with respect to its long-term impact on women in the relationship and their safety. SOES claims that input of the local shelter has been reduced to a babysitting service for the women in the program.[34] So far, the accountability issue has not been addressed.

In Canada the recent focus has been on the accountability of programs to the women's community and to women partners, and it draws on the work of Barbara Hart (1988). The safety of women and active partner outreach, while considered essential by shelter workers and the staff in pro-feminist men's programs, is absent from some programs for abusive men. In response to lobbying by women's groups, several provinces now have accountability guidelines for men's programs and have made government funding contingent on compliance with these requirements.[35] Along with partner outreach, the guidelines include limits on confidentiality for male participants, thus allowing women partners to have access to reports on their attendance and progress. Also, in order to ensure that attendance in a program does not become a way of avoiding police charges, accountability guidelines suggest that men not be accepted into a program if they have pleaded not guilty to an assault charge.

There is some indication that programs for men do reduce violence and lead to behavioural changes. A unique evaluation of a pro-feminist twenty-four-week program for men conducted intensive interviews with the women partners over a one-year period. According to the overall accounts of the women, all forms of abuse decreased and women themselves felt more empowered (Lundy et al., 1996). Nonetheless, programs for violent men ought to be closely monitored by those working in the shelter movement to ensure accountability to women survivors, and the women's community is central to the mandate.

Education and Coordination Organizing activities have also resulted in educational programs on violence against women in order to increase the knowledge and awareness of professionals, particularly those involved in violence work. In 1991 the Swedish non-socialist government initiated a two-tier educational program on violence against women for agencies encountering this problem in the course of their regular work. The Swedish National Police Board started out with a two-day seminar in 1992 attended by higher-echelon members of the police and prosecution forces from all over the country, who were expected to go home and organize similar training for their subordinates. Regional programs aimed at educating senior police officers, public prosecutors, social workers, and health-care and hospital staff and networks for further training and cooperation have been implemented. Feminist speakers and feminist analyses have been a part of this process. Almost twenty thousand people have attended these programs, according to government figures, and they are to continue as part of a broader government program for the better care of survivors of male violence (Sweden, 1998). Along with changing attitudes and improving knowledge, one task of these programs is to facilitate cooperation between different agencies that deal with battering in order to build networks. A primary focus is to build solid court cases against violent men, while providing support and care for the women and their children.[36]

Similar education and coordination strategies have been adopted in Canada. Women and men working in the area of violence offer voluntary public education and training to hospital staff, schools, police officers, and crown attorneys. Although the final reports from both the Standing Committee and the Canadian Panel on Violence against Women recommended mandatory training for all judges, this has not happened. Certificate programs for workers in the area of violence against women are now available at some universities.

In a number of communities, committees or networks have been formed to coordinate the work, while service-oriented agencies are also connected by provincial networks such as the Ontario Association of Interval and Transition Houses. There are also national women's organizations which have been formed to address the general problems facing women, but which also have subcommittees devoted to the issue of violence.[37] Many communities have set up committees to ensure clear communication and to build a common understanding among those involved in anti-violence work.

LOOKING FORWARD

The process of cross-country study, as one of the project participants in this volume stated, offers an opportunity "to go away and to come back home again." An awareness of another's experience provides a renewed understanding of our own and illuminates the possibilities for change. In reviewing the Canadian and Swedish organizing activities that respond to the problem of gender violence, we are encouraged to see accomplishments by changes to the law, new policies, and the provision of services. The diligent labour of women has transformed a hidden "personal" concern into a public "political" problem in both countries.

However, while both Canadian and Swedish governments have commissioned national studies of gender violence, concrete action on specific recommendations has not been forthcoming. On the contrary, the social-welfare structures that have buttressed the programs important to women in Canada are disappearing at a rapid rate, and Sweden is not far behind. It is disheartening to realize that for women the violence has been unabated and that long-fought-for gains are being taken away. As Adamson, Briskin, and McPhail (1988) remind us, "The funding practices of the state, on which so many women's organizations depend; the establishment of advisory commissions and women's councils that demonstrate change through bureaucracy; and the language of legislation, which often limits the actual benefits accruing to women, have all moulded and to some extent undermined the struggle of women to make change" (153–4).

The impact of the state on women's organizing has prompted some feminists to view all state involvement as co-opting and depoliticizing, since "state-initiated, funded and supported organizations of any hue necessarily carry out state aims" (Carty and Brand, 1993: 22). Others, such as Jane Ursel (1994), see the possibility of a convergence of state and women's interests; Ursel suggests, "The policy implications of this alternative approach are to approach the state strategically, to select issues in which potential for convergence of interests does exist, and then to involve the state as much as possible in working toward those changes" (91). Her position is supported by a historical and statistical overview of the changes to the criminal justice system in Manitoba that resulted in increased options and support services to battered women.

To return to the work of Adamson, Briskin, and McPhail, the task facing women's organizing against violence is to ensure a tension between the "politics of disengagement" and the "politics of mainstreaming" – that is, to develop and maintain a critique of existing economic and social structures, while at the same time developing new strategies for social action and mobilizing an extensive network of women's groups around concrete issues.

This act of working "in and against the state" requires both integration and segregation, and it has differing implications for women in Canada and Sweden. As we have mentioned, although there has been more study and perhaps more program development in response to women's organizing in Canada, official recognition of, and advocacy for, women's concerns by elected politicians and political parties is not common. The Swedish state has been seen as friendly to women's concerns, a view that has probably delayed the radicalization of shelter women. The experience of working with and for abused women, paired with the educational efforts by SOES and the local study groups, has brought a great many women into an important social movement. On the other hand, although acknowledgment of gender conflict, such as violence against women, has occurred only recently in Sweden, the long history of social democracy has provided greater social and economic gains for women than is the case in Canada. However, within both countries there is now a tide of conservatism which has created a serious backlash against women's accomplishments in achieving equality.

The struggle ahead for women is to mount a unified resistance, a return to organizing at the grassroots level based on accumulated experience, and a refined analysis of the problem and the response of the state. Such a mobilization of women can emerge out of and build on the existing structures that are already in place. The extensive network of women's organizations and the shelter movement, with the large numbers of women who work and volunteer in local shelters, can provide direction and leadership.

NOTES

1 For example, in 1969 there was little comment within the U.S. women's movement about violence against women, despite the fact that Betty Friedan, one of the leaders, was fighting for women's equality with a blackened eye carefully covered with make-up. See Marcia Cohen, *The Sisterhood* (New York: Ballantine Books, 1988). Also, there was no mention of violence in the Royal Commission on the Status of Women

in Canada, Report (Ottawa: Queen's Printer, 1970. Nor was violence alluded to in the first Canadian anthology of women's issues, *Women Unite!* (Toronto: Canadian Women's Educational Press, 1972). The pattern was the same in Sweden. Neither Anna-Greta Leijon nor Brigitta Wistrand, who were both commissioned by the Swedish government to write overviews on women and equality, mentioned violence in the family or woman abuse. Their books, *Swedish Women, Swedish Men* (1966) and *Swedish Women on the Move* (1981) respectively (both published by the Swedish Institute, Stockholm), were distributed by Swedish embassies in foreign countries and could be assumed to be representative of official government policy. American feminist scholar and activist Cheri Register observed with surprise that no Swedish women's groups had violence against women on their agendas in the mid-1970s (Cheri Register, *Feminist Ideology and Literary Criticism*, 1977).

2 We are not addressing violence in lesbian relationships or women's organizing work within the rape movement.

3 There is in many quarters a remarkable blindness regarding male violence against women which is difficult to change. In 1976 a Swedish government commission proposed that "rape" be eliminated from the law books and replaced with the milder designation "sexual assault" (SOU, 1976: 9). This proposal was withdrawn only after protests from women's organizations. Another important element in official Sweden, the Swedish Academy, which monitors language change and decides what is officially recognized as "good" or not, does not include the term "woman battering" in its latest edition of the official dictionary (1986).

4 The reported instances include repeated offences by the same person, while cases correspond to individuals.

5 More women, children using shelters, *Globe and Mail*, 12 December 1995.

6 The complete text of Marc Lepine's suicide letter is printed in Malette and Chalouh (1991). Among the women named on his list were a feminist journalist, the president of a teachers' union, the first woman firefighter in Quebec, the first woman police captain in the province, a transition-house worker, a bank manager, a sportscaster, a television host, and the Canadian champion in the chartered accountancy exams.

7 For example, women and men associated with the small Christian Democratic Party are increasingly speaking out against women's employment and independent incomes in favour of family wages, a concept that would have previously been unheard of. In the weekly radio news and commentary program *God Morgon Världen* on 17 September 1995, Karin Stenström from the Christian newspaper *Dagen* claimed that women's employment was behind the current economic situation, unemployment, and other problems.

8 The so-called Stureplan murders, in which four innocent people waiting to enter a nightclub were shot to death and many others injured, have been covered by all the media from every angle. Initially, the explanations for this horrific crime bordered on racism, because one of the suspected perpetrators turned out to be foreign-born. When it was clear that the main culprit had a more ordinary national background, the search for reasons shifted towards blaming mothers.

9 A Canadian woman senator, speaking at an event honouring International Women's Day, reflected this position when she said, "Behind every abusing husband is an abusing mother."

10 An emphasis on the value of fathers and men is typical of Swedish analysis of social problems; it does not contradict the understanding of gender conflicts as not relevant for gender equity.

11 The major threat from the Support Stockings, an informal network of mostly professional women mobilizing against the temporary decline in the parliamentary representation of women after the 1991 election, was the idea of a woman's party. The general public supported the concept to a surprising degree. See Agneta Stark, Combatting the backlash: How Swedish women won the war, in Ann Oakley and Juliet Mitchell (eds.), *Who's Afraid of Feminism?: Seeing Through the Backlash* (London: Hamish Hamilton, 1997).

12 For example, *Svenska Dagbladet*, 2 February 1995.

13 Violence was mentioned for the first time in the report *Towards Equality for Women* (Ottawa: Minister of Supply and Services, 1979). The first national study was prompted by the Canadian Advisory Council on the Status of Women, an organization whose mandate was to inform and advise the federal government. The findings of the study conducted by Linda MacLeod were published in *Wife Battering in Canada: The Vicious Circle* (Ottawa: Canadian Advisory Council on the Status of Women, 1980).

14 The national forum was part of a four-year (1988–92) $40 million family-violence initiative.

15 The five groups were the National Action Committee on the Status of Women, the Canadian Association of Sexual Assault Centres, the Dis-Abled Women's Network, the National Organization of Immigrant and Visible Minority Women, and the Congress of Black Women of Canada.

16 This method has been tried on men sentenced to prison but allowed to live at home, continuing to work, and not permitted to stray beyond these areas.

17 Madeleine Leijonhufvud, Stoppa kvinnomorden! *Dagens Nyheter*, 12 February 1997.

18 In the aftermath of the commission's report, state research agencies, such as the Swedish Council for Crime Prevention, have initiated more-

specific studies of violence against women, primarily of a statistical nature. Statistics Canada's 1993 survey has been an important inspiration for this work.

19 The shelter movement differs from most other women's organizations in Sweden in its position on men. The question of men's responsibility has also caused problems within this movement. In 1994 the annual meeting of SOES was a stormy one, when some shelters objected to SOES's position that "all men are potential batterers" and that "all [married/cohabiting] women have been raped" since they have had sex with their husbands/male partners against their will (*Dagens Nyheter*, 2 December 1994). Two years later a group of 16 shelters out of about 130 left SOES and formed a national organization of their own (Press release, November 1996). This group does not deviate from a strong feminist commitment, however. Many shelters, which want to include men in their work against male violence but not in actual shelter work, are known not to be comfortable with SOES positions like those described above.

20 Social Democratic Women in Sweden has publicly claimed to be a feminist association. The Left Party has no separate women's organization.

21 Telephone interview with Ebon Kram, 18 September 1995.

22 In the early 1990s the government, in response to lobbying from the shelter movement, created a position devoted to studies of violence against women, a designation that did not fit existing categories. The university concerned transformed it into a professorship of sociology in women's studies, with violence against women as the second special field. This change meant that applicants had to be qualified in sociology first, women's studies second, and the study of violence against women last.

23 An illustration: an internationally well-known and respected feminist scholar observed, after one semester and visits to all the universities in Sweden, that she had never visited a country where feminist scholars were so worried about not being academic enough in their work. This attitude is more an expression of Swedish academic culture than of feminism in the university.

24 A major reason behind the location of the centre was the success of a special project to create new routines for the care of abused women at the hospital and to teach the staff about violence against women, which was initiated by a group of committed feminist staff members in collaboration with the local shelter. A probably unique feature of the centre is a twenty-four-hour-a-day on-call list with only female gynecologists, who volunteer their services beyond their regular schedules, to ensure that women coming to the hospital will always be seen by a female physician.

25 The new law states that, when a woman says no, she means no. There is no consent if a man abuses a position of power (i.e., a physician and a

patient; a professor and a student) or if the woman is under the influence of alcohol or other mood-altering drugs.

26 Statistics Canada (1993).

27 This protection is available only under conditions of extreme and well-documented threats and persecution. The Bangladesh feminist and writer Taslima Nasrin, who had to flee from her own country, has been living in Sweden at the invitation of the government since 1993, protected by bodyguards twenty-four hours a day.

28 See, for example, Canada, Ministry of the Solicitor General and Correctional Services, *The Model Protocol on Police Response to Wife Assault* (Toronto: Steering Committee on Wife Assault); and Ontario, Ministry of the Attorney General, *Crown Policy Manual*, 15 January 1994.

29 Of the cases in the Family Violence Court, 64 per cent proceeded to sentence, compared with 53 per cent before the court was established.

30 Although unpaid labour is the norm, Ebon Kram, chair of SOES, states that the tasks preformed at the shelters would not be of lesser quality if workers were paid. A great problem in a tightening economy is that the shelters cannot always reimburse workers for time lost at work; thus possibly over time the grassroots movement may become one of women who can afford to work for free.

31 Telephone interview with Ebon Kram, 18 September 1995.

32 In Stockholm an eighteenth-century palace is being converted by the city into a women's house, which will include a shelter for battered women.

33 See, for example, Aboriginal Women's Support Program Ltd, A community needs assessment Aboriginal Women's Support Program (submitted to the Ontario Ministry of Community and Social Services, April 1993).

34 Telephone interview with Ebon Kram, 18 September 1995.

35 See, for example, Interministerial Working Group, *Interim Accountability and Accessibility Requirement for Male Batterers Programs*, February 1994.

36 Altogether there are thirteen county organizations in Sweden.

37 Examples of these are the National Action Committee on the Status of Women, the largest coalition of women's groups in Canada; the Canadian Research Institute for the Advancement of Women, which has been fostering funding and supporting research on women since 1976; and the National Organization of Immigrant and Visible Minority Women of Canada, which has been working towards equality for immigrant and visible-minority women since 1985.

REFERENCES

Adamson, Nancy, Linda Briskin, and Margaret McPhail. (1988). *Feminist Organizing for Change: The Contemporary Women's Movement in Canada*. Toronto: Oxford University Press.

Ahrens, Lois. (1980). Battered women's refuges: Feminist cooperatives vs. social service institutions. *Radical America,* summer, 41–9.

Andrews, Caroline, Fran Klodawsky, and Colleen Lundy. (1994). Women's safety and the politics of transformation. *Women and Environments,* 14 (1): 23–6.

Banakar, Reza. (1990). Lagens dilemma. *Invandrare & Minoriteter,* 3: 2–9.

Barnsley, Jan. (1995). Co-operation or co-optation? The partnership trend of the nineties." In Leslie Timmins (ed.), *Listening to the Thunder Advocates Talk About the Battered Women's Movement.* Vancouver: Women's Research Centre.

Berard, Sylvie. (1991). Words and deeds. In Louise Malette and Marie Chalouh (eds.), *The Montreal Massacre.* Charlottetown: Gynergy Books.

Bergman, B., and B. Brismar. (1992). Offer och gärningsman – Misshandel sedd ur akutsjukvårdens perspektiv. *Läkartidningen* 89: 3371–5.

Bolin, Elsa. (1984). *Kampen mot kvinnomisshandel.* Stockholm: Brevskolan.

Briskin, Linda. (1991). A new approach to evaluating feminist strategy. In Jeri Dawn Wine and Janice L. Ristock (eds.), *Women and Social Change: Feminist Activism in Canada.* Toronto: James Lorimer and Company Publishers.

Canada. (1991). House of Commons. *The War against Women.* Ottawa: Standing Committee on Health and Welfare, Social Affairs, Seniors and the Status of Women.

– (1992). Health and Welfare. *Transition Houses and Shelters for Battered Women in Canada.* National Clearinghouse on Family Violence.

– (1993a). Canadian Panel on Violence against Women. *Changing the Landscape: Ending Violence – Achieving Equality.*

– (1993b). Health Canada. *Canada's Treatment Programs For Men Who Abuse Their Partners.* Ottawa.

Carty, Linda, and Dionne Brand. (1993). Visible minority women a creation of the Canadian state. In Himani Bannerji (ed.), *Returning the Gaze: Essays on Racism, Feminism and Politics.* Toronto: Sister Vision Press.

Currie, Andrea. (1989). A roof is not enough: Feminism, transition houses and the battle against abuse. *New Maritimes* 8 (1): 16–29.

Dagens Nyheter, 5 April 1995.

DeKeseredy, Walter, and Katherine Kelly. (1993). *The Incidence and Prevalence of Woman Abuse in Canadian University and College Dating Relationships: Results from a National Survey.* Ottawa: Health and Welfare Canada.

Dobash, R.E., and R.P. Dobash. (1991). *Violence against Wives: A Case against the Patriarchy.* London: Open University Books.

Eduards, Maud Landby. (1992). Against the rules of the game: On the importance of women's collective actions. In Eduards et al., *Rethinking Change: Current Swedish Feminist Research.* Stockholm: HSFR.

Eliasson, Mona. (1994). The name of the game: Struggling with violent men in Sweden. Paper presented at WISE meeting, Vienna NGO-Forum, 14 October 1994.

Elman, R. Amy, and Maud L. Eduards. (1991). Unprotected by the Swedish welfare state: A survey of battered women and the assistance they received. *Women's Studies International Forum* 14: 413–21.

Gilman, Susan Thomas. (1988). A history of the sheltering movement for battered women in Canada. *Canadian Journal of Community Mental Health* 7 (2): 9–21.

Globe and Mail. (1994). End sought to mandatory wife-abuse cases. 27 January.

Göransson, Birgitta, Inga Järvholm-Andersson, and Elizabeth Kwarnmark. (1988). *Mannen bakom kvinnovaldet.* Stockholm: Prisma.

Gotell, Lise. (1998). A critical look at state discourse on violence against women: Some implications for feminist politics and women's citizenship. In Manon Tremblay and Caroline Andrew (eds.), *Women and Political Representation in Canada.* Ottawa: University of Ottawa Press.

Goyette, Chantal. (1990). The patchwork policy. *Vis à Vis* (Canadian Council on Social Development) 8 (1): 4–6.

Harris, Debbie Wise. (1991). Keeping women in our place: Violence at Canadian universities. *Canadian Women Studies* 11 (4): 37–41.

Hart, Barbara. (1988). *Safety for Women: Monitoring Batterer's Programs.* Harrisburg: Pennsylvania Coalition against Domestic Violence.

Hernes, Helga. (1987). *Welfare State and Woman Power: Essays in State Feminism.* Oslo: Norwegian University Press.

Jacobsson, Ranveig, and Karin Alfredsson. (1993). *Equal Worth: The Status of Men and Women in Sweden.* Stockholm: The Swedish Institute.

Johnson, Holly. (1996). *Dangerous Domains: Violence against Women in Canada.* Scarborough: Nelson Canada.

Kerpner, Christina. (1995). Misshandeln som "inte finns." *Uppsala Nya Tidning,* 10 November.

Klodawsky, Fran, and Colleen Lundy. (1994). Women's safety in the university environment. *Journal of Architecture and Planning Research* 11 (2): 128–36.

Kuntscher, Helga, and Lars Jonsson. (1994). *Projekt Frideborg Delrapport II.* Norrköping: Kriminalvården och Norrköpings kommun, Kvinnovaldsprojektet Frideborg.

Lakeman, Lee. (1990). Women, violence and the Montreal massacre. *This Magazine* 20, no. 7 (March): 20–3.

Lenneer-Axelson, Barbro. (1989). *Mannens röster i kris och förändring.* Stockholm: Prisma.

Levan, Andrea. (1996). Violence against women. In Janine Brodie (ed.), *Women and Canadian Public Policy.* Toronto: Harcourt Brace.

Lindmark, Barbro. (1995). Mans väld mot kvinnor: Intervju med Ebon Kram, ordförande i ROKS. *Kvinnobulletinen* 2: 30–3.

Lundy, Colleen, et al. (1996). Re-education for men abusive to women: An evaluation of effectiveness. *Canadian Social Work Review* 13 (2): 157–70.

MacDonald, Maureen. (1995). Chalk one up for sisterhood! *New Maritimes* 8 (6): 4–17.

Malette, Louise, and Marie Chalouh (eds.). (1991). *The Montreal Massacre*. Charlottetown: Gynergy Books.

Morgan, Patricia. (1981). From battered wife to program client: the state's shaping of social problems. *Kapitalistate* 9: 17–39.

Mral, Brigitte, and Ann-Charlotte Ericsson. (1986). *Uppsala kvinnojour 1980–1985: En dokumentation*. Uppsala: Uppsala kvinnojour.

Rikspolisstyrelsen. (1993). *Försöksverksamhet med livvaktsskydd för hotade kvinnor mm*. RPS rapport 6. Stockholm.

Schechter, Susan. (1982). *Women and Male Violence: The Visions and Struggles of the Battered Women's Movement*. Boston: South End Press.

Schuler, Margaret (ed.). (1992). *Freedom from Violence: Women's Strategies around the World*. New York: UNIFEM WIDBOOKS.

SOU. (1976). *Sexuella övergrepp*, 9.

– (1995). *Kvinnofrid*, 60.

Statistics Canada. (1993). The Violence against Women survey. *The Daily*, 18 November.

Statistics Sweden (SCB). (1994). *Krinfo*, 4.

Strong-Boag, Veronica. (1994). Too much and not enough: The paradox of power for feminist academics working with community feminists on issues related to violence. In Cannie Stark-Adamec (ed.), *Violence a Collective Responsibility*. Proceedings of the 1994 symposium on violence. Ottawa: Social Science Federation of Canada.

Sweden. (1998). Fact sheet (summary of the government proposal, 1997–98): 55.

Ursel, Jane. (1994). Eliminating violence against women: Reform or co-optation in state insitutions. In Les Samuelson (ed.), *Power and Resistance*. Halifax: Fernwood Publishing.

Walker, Gillian. (1990). The conceptual politics of struggle: Wife battering, the women's movement and the state. *Studies in Political Economy* 33: 63–90.

Normalization versus Diversity: Lesbian Identity and Organizing in Sweden and Canada

BECKI L. ROSS AND CATHARINA LANDSTRÖM

ABSTRACT

In both Canada and Sweden, lesbians experience heterosexism and invisibility, and they have confronted discrimination in ways that are similar and also different. Social, educational, and cultural initiatives such as coming-out groups, music festivals, support for lesbian mothers, recreation clubs, publishing, visual arts, and peer counselling are common to both countries and underscore the significance of identity formation and community development. With respect to the differences, Swedish lesbians active in anti-discrimination work have chosen RFSL (Riksförbundet for Sexuellt Likaberättigande), the national organization for gay and lesbian rights, to lobby all levels of government. In contrast to RFSL's comprehensive intervention in Sweden's mainstream political culture, Canadian lesbians have sustained a more ambivalent relationship with the Canadian state and a more sceptical view of its role in effecting social change. They have, however, more recently turned to a number of mixed-gender organizations, such as EGALE, the Coalition for Lesbian and Gay Rights in Ontario, and the Campaign for Equal Families, to lobby governments for equality rights on the basis of sexual orientation. In this chapter we analyse the strategies mobilized in each country over the past twenty-five years of activism. Specifically, we examine political and legal contests over the meanings of "family" and "spouse"/ "domestic partner" as they relate to hegemonic conceptions of normative gender and sexuality. From this analysis, we compare and contrast the prominence of a discourse of normalization in Sweden and a discourse of diversity in Canada as they are deployed by lesbian and gay activists in the respective countries.

In both Sweden and Canada, practices and ideologies of heterosexism continue to oppress lesbians and gay men. Today assumptions about normative gender and sexuality are embedded in all societal institutions

– organized religion and sport, the school system, law, medicine, the mass media, counselling services, the military, police forces, and others. Though each of us is an "out" lesbian activist in our respective country, we recognize that only a small percentage of Canadian and Swedish lesbians are actively involved in struggles against heterosexism and homophobia. The majority negotiates the limits of the closet, fearful of what disclosure might mean in terms of jobs, friends, family, and children. Internalized homophobia remains a real and painful experience for many and is often expressed through self-hate, depression, alcoholism, and suicide. Lesbians of colour and older, disabled, and working-class lesbians are especially vulnerable to the hobbling effect of multiple oppressions.

In Sweden there is a generally accepting attitude towards homosexuality; however, although quite free of homophobia, Swedish society is thoroughly infused with heterosexism. Homophobia is very marginal (expressed by fringe groups such as religious fundamentalists and the political far right), but heterosexism has not been eradicated by legal reforms. And it has severe consequences for the life of lesbians in Sweden, who experience invisibility as a major problem. When one of the country's most famous pop stars, Eva Dahlgren, registered her partnership with her girlfriend, Elva Attling, Swedish lesbians were tremendously excited by the public visibility of this event. In Canada, heterosexuality is hegemonic in similar ways; in addition, homophobia is expressed through lesbian and gay bashing, covert harassment at the workplace, child-custody rulings that declare lesbian mothers "unfit," and a well-organized right-wing opposition led by coalitions of Christian churches and joined by neo-Nazi groups.

Courageous lesbian activists in Canada and Sweden have confronted discrimination in ways that are both similar and different. The strategies and tactics chosen reflect certain traditions in the history of radical social movements in each country, specifically the relationship forged between the lesbian-gay movement and the state. Law reform has served as an ongoing preoccupation of lesbian and gay movements, though Canadian lesbians have also been involved *as lesbians* in struggles against HIV/AIDS, breast cancer, workplace discrimination, and violence against women. Lesbian activists *as feminists* in Canada have also played pivotal leadership roles in the women's movement (e.g., in day care, reproductive choice, health care, and publishing) and other social movements (labour, disability, anti-racism, youth, and sex workers), where they have systematically raised consciousness around issues of sexualities. Swedish lesbians, by contrast, have devoted the bulk of their energy in organizing *as lesbians* to working collectively with gay men for legal reforms.[1]

In the first half of this chapter we analyse the social, educational, and cultural efforts made by lesbian organizers that are common to both countries, such as coming out groups, support for lesbian mothers, recreation clubs, publishing, visual art, and peer counselling. We offer a brief descriptive and comparative summary of these activities with a focus on membership composition, internal structure, size, group objectives, funding sources, and lifespan. Inspired by "new social movement theory" that refuses to reduce "the political" to exclusively state-centred practices (see Carroll, 1992: 16), we reflect on the role of these groups in contesting heterosexism, ending the invisibility of lesbian (and gay) lives, and breaking the silence that has traditionally surrounded us.

We recognize that lesbian sexuality in both Canada and Sweden has seldom been addressed explicitly in legislation (see Kinsman, 1996; M. Smith, 1998), in contrast to the direct targeting and policing of gay male sexuality via criminal codes in some countries. This does not mean, however, that Swedish and Canadian lesbians in the contemporary context are exempt from discrimination in law and social policy. Swedish lesbians have worked in RFSL (Riksförbundet for Sexuellt Likaberättigande), the national organization for gay and lesbian rights, to lobby all levels of government to advance the discourse of equality and accommodation. In Canada no organization matches the scope and power of RFSL; nor has there been consensus among lesbian (and gay) activists about the role of the state in securing lesbian and gay liberation. Therefore discourses of equality and diversity have coexisted, and they reflect an ongoing ambivalence among lesbian activists towards the state as a partner in social change. In the second half of this chapter, we examine the current status of lesbian and gay equality rights with reference to the gains and losses registered in Sweden and in Canada. We explore the ways in which definitions and meanings of reproduction, relationships, family, and biological/social parenting have been raised as primary questions and concerns. Indeed, campaigns by lesbians and gays for law reform have served as lightning rods for political debate and practice in the respective countries.

PART ONE: MAKING LESBIAN IDENTITIES AND COMMUNITIES

Social and Cultural Activities in Canada

After more than twenty-five years of social and cultural initiatives in Canada, there is a wealth and diversity of lesbian, gay, and bisexual activity, albeit regionally specific and concentrated in large urban centres. In ways that affirm "queer" identities and communities, these developments have built upon the history of secretive urban networks established by gay women and men through house parties, bar culture, costume balls, and after-hours clubs from the 1910s to the 1960s.[2] Today, decades later, when we scan the social horizon, we find lesbian and gay bars and assorted Dyke Nites at heterosexual clubs, lesbian and gay Pride Day committees, choirs, potluck dinner groups, opera appreciation clubs, "fuckerware" (lingerie and sex toys) parties, and lesbian and gay softball, soccer, golf, swimming, bowling, water polo, and curling leagues. Sporting enthusiasts join recreation clubs such as Toronto's Out and Out and Vancouver's Out and About for regular weekend sprees of cycling, camping, hiking, and birdwatching. Vancouver hosted the 1990 Gay Games amid right-wing fundamentalist hysteria that the city would be transformed into "Sodom of the North." Gay- and lesbian-owned businesses often specialize in social and leisure activities. Wild Women Expeditions in northern Ontario is a lesbian-run outfit that guides canoe and camping excursions. More than six hundred entries for bed-and-breakfast inns, bars and clubs, and restaurants and bookstores are listed in travel sources such as the *Bent Guide to Gay/Lesbian Canada*. At the same time, residential and commercial enclaves (also known as "fruit belts") in large cities such as Vancouver, Montreal, Toronto, and Winnipeg offer lesbians and gays a sense of comfort and home, an oasis in a sometimes unsafe world (see Bouthiellette, 1997).

Founded to enhance both spiritual and social connections, the Metropolitan Community Church (MCC) ministers to a lesbian, gay, and bisexual congregation and has branches across Canada. In Toronto, spiritual leaders at MCC and Crystos regularly perform holy union ceremonies ("marriages") for lesbian and gay couples (Turner, 1994). As well, there are lesbian and gay Buddhist associations, and groups of lesbians and gay men who maintain affiliations to the Jewish, Catholic, Anglican, and United Church faiths. The United Church of Canada, the country's single largest Protestant denomination, performs "covenanting" unions for lesbian and gay couples that are recognized by the church and the congregation but not by law (Philip, 1995). In all, these social and religious activities afford their lesbian and gay participants access to symbolic and actual spaces, and opportunities in which to strengthen and consolidate their identities and communities.

The largely white, middle-class, able-bodied character of Canadian lesbian activism in the 1970s has been challenged on many fronts.[3] Today contributions to lesbian/bi/gay culture and community formation are made by queers of colour and working-class, older, and disabled queers. Bisexual men and women have also begun to build their own support networks and their own agendas (see Bisexual Women's Anthology Collective, 1995). There are currently over eighty lesbian, gay, and bisexual social, political, and support groups in British Columbia's lower mainland, a metropolitan territory with a population of close to four million people (Steele, 1994).

Groups such as Lesbian Youth Peer Support, Nice Jewish Girls, and Two-Spirit Peoples of the First Nations were founded and continue to operate on a volunteer basis, and typically embrace a collective, consensus decision-making model. Along with the political lobby groups, none of these organizations receive state funding. To raise money for operating costs, dances, cabarets, and special events are held and promotional goods such as buttons and T-shirts are sold. In addition, the Lesbian and Gay Community Appeal is a unique organization, now over fifteen years old, whose mandate is to raise funds, which are then allocated annually in the form of grants to lesbian and gay groups and individuals to further community and arts development in Toronto.

Across Canada, social services run by and for lesbians and gay men abound in both urban and rural settings. Counselling centres, AIDS/HIV hospices, lending libraries, and peer-run coming-out groups offer assistance to those coping with internalized self-hate and shame, confusion about sexual identity, addictions, HIV infection, abusive relationships, lesbian and gay parenting and more (see O'Brien, Travers, and Bell, 1994).[4] Community venues such as the Vancouver Gay and Lesbian Centre, the Vancouver Lesbian Centre, the 519 Church Street Community Centre in Toronto, the Gay and Lesbian Community Centre of Edmonton, and the Lesbian and Gay Community Centre in Montreal provide low or no-cost meeting rooms for all kinds of group assemblies. Because coming out of the closet continues to be a major event in the life of a lesbian or gay person, the availability of cultural and social resources is critical to facilitating the transition.

Social and Cultural Activities in Sweden

Swedish lesbians have a history of socializing in networks not visible to the general public. In the earlier half of the twentieth century they met at each others' homes or around particular tables in restaurants or cafés: the first known lesbian club, Diana, was formed in Stockholm in 1954. In the 1970s a lesbian feminist movement emerged alongside and in tension with heterosexual feminist activity.[5] Several lesbian feminist groups in the country engaged in direct action to affect laws and social policies and to create social and cultural space for lesbians. This activity died out during the early 1980s, and there are no longer groups that base their activities on lesbian feminist analyses.

Today, in the 1990s, it is important to point out that most Swedish lesbians never organize *as lesbians*. They join with other people who share their interests regardless of gender or sexual identity. However, when they do organize as lesbians, their focus is often on what could be called "confirmation of identity" – that is, making lesbianism visible in order to see and communicate with other lesbians. In Sweden it is difficult to signify lesbian identity; every woman can look like a lesbian, but none is expected to be one. Swedish lesbians have occasionally picked up signifiers popular in North America, such as haircuts, jewellery, and fashion, but these are not generally interpreted as lesbian among the straight population.

Lesbian organizing in the 1990s (as in the 1970s and 1980s) in Sweden has focused on counteracting marginalization and invisibility. Many initiatives have been taken to create social and cultural space where lesbians become visible to each other and to a larger public. For example, LN! (Lesbisk Nu!) is the largest lesbian-only organization and is located in Stockholm. (Backström, 1991). It got started because lesbians were angry over being marginalized by the male-dominated RFSL, an organization that claimed to work for lesbian rights. LN! quickly managed to get public funding and put a lot of energy into creating a nice meeting place for all lesbians and producing and distributing a newsletter, *Pinglan*, for members.[6] LN!'s main aim is to provide a milieu for all lesbians; the organization arranges cafés and pubs, sometimes with music or theatrical performances.

Large, formal lesbian organizations such as LN! are very unusual. Typically, lesbians meet in smaller groups to pursue common interests. Over the past ten years, there have been local lesbian groups that have covered every interest which anybody could possibly think of – for instance, theatre, rock music, academic studies, motorcycling, mothering, sports, study groups, spiritualism, and so on. There have also been groups that focus on arranging events for other lesbians, such as discos and theme parties. The groups tend to have a limited lifespan and dissolve when the most engaged members quit. To a newcomer the lesbian groups in Sweden often appear closed because they are based on the efforts of a few individuals; it can be difficult to join when one is not personally acquainted with any of the members. This characteristic is reinforced when groups gather in spaces not open to the public, such as the homes of members, or in public places, where lesbians are difficult to identify, such as cafés or restaurants.

In Sweden there is almost no tradition of fund-raising for or donations made to lesbian groups, since they have access to a stable inflow of communal and state funding, which is extended to a variety of non-profit organizations. This has not been the case in Canada, where lesbians have had no comparable history of claims to state-supplied monies. In Sweden, state funding has always been linked to accountability, and thus it requires formal structures that ensure full legal responsibility for how the money is spent. These conditions in practice place a limit on group size; a group has to be large enough to acquire a board, members, and accountants (though unlike funding to immigrant women's groups, state funding to lesbian and gay groups is not conditional on the number of members). Requirements of legal responsibility also affect the activity of a group because there has to be a certain degree of formality and administration when public funding is received.

As well, securing a financial base takes a lot of time and effort since grant applications have to be written. Five lesbians who wanted to play badminton once a week would probably refrain from entering the granting process and instead would try to ally themselves with some organization that already had financing. While the funding tradition in Sweden does not favour small, independent groups, it does create a certain degree of stability in the larger organizations such as RFSL, which can function as providers to the small groups. Women active in RFSL also initiate lesbian group activitites. For instance, a few lesbian activists in RFSL Göteborg have made an effort to start their own groups. They arranged for an open-to-all discussion in order to find out what topics the interested women would like to engage in. So far this initiative has resulted in six groups: lesbians over forty, bridge, culture, literature, hiking, and indoor ball hockey.[7]

In general terms, the social and cultural activities of lesbian activists in small, local groups in Sweden and Canada have been of paramount import to the emergence of lesbian consciousness and visibility. Lesbian groups and individuals connect, do things, and become visible to each other and sometimes to a larger public. In both countries, non-profit, volunteer work is the backbone of this self-sufficient lesbian culture.

Lesbians Communicating Knowledge in Canada

Across Canada the expansion, visibility, and maturing of lesbian and gay communities is reflected in the veritable explosion of queer cultural expression: fiction and non-fiction, video, photography, dance, performance art, theatre, and comedy.[8] Film or video, poetry, and theatre festivals from St John's to Victoria showcase the work of independent lesbian and gay artists. The National Film Board has ended its historic avoidance of overtly queer themes to finance several dazzling feature documentaries.[9] Community and university-based radio stations program regular weekly shows with lesbian and gay content such as *Pink Antenna* on CKLN and *Gay Wire* on CIUT in Toronto and *Reading*

Out Loud on CJSF and *The Lesbian Show* on CO-OP Radio in Vancouver. Gradually, arts councils and film funding institutes have begun to recognize some queer applicants and queer content, though class and racial barriers stubbornly persist, and the funding is periodically refused or revoked on moral grounds.[10] Nourishing our own indigenous popular culture stands as a testament to our hunger for oppositional images. Indeed, image-making by and for queers is a priority in the 1990s. How we are represented, why we are represented, and if we are represented are central issues of contemporary homosexual politics and identity in North America.

Lesbian and gay fiction and non-fiction are being published by the Women's Press, Sister Vision Press, Press Gang, Ragweed, and Queer Press. The University of British Columbia Press launched a series entitled "Critical Sexuality Studies" in 1998. Local magazines include *Khush: A Newsletter of South Asian Lesbians and Gays* (Toronto), *X-tra!* (Toronto), *Capital X-Tra!* (Ottawa), *X-Tra West!* (Vancouver), *Sami Yoni, for Lesbians of South Asian Descent* (Toronto), *Angles* (Vancouver), *Lesbianews* (Vancouver Island), *Gaezette* (Halifax), *Labrys* (Ottawa), CLUE! *Magazine* (Calgary), *Swerve: Winnipeg's Lesbian and Gay Rag* (Winnipeg), *Perceptions* (Regina), *Lezzie Smut* (Vancouver), and *Lickerish: Polymorphous Queer Candy.* Over the years, fanzines with a gay, lesbian, or queer focus have been published under the names *Q.T.*, *Bimbox*, *Dr. Smith*, *S.M.A.C.K.S*, *J.Ds*, and *Pussy Grazer.* Lesbian, gay, and queer issues have been put out by the magazines *Undercurrents*, *This Magazine*, *Fireweed*, and *Fuse*. Print resources, particularly in small towns such as Sioux Lookout in Ontario, Grand Falls in Newfoundland, and Moose Jaw in Saskatchewan constitute a lifeline for lesbians and gay men who have limited access to other lesbian or gay people, places, and communities (see Stone, 1997: 187–8). Increasingly, lesbians, bisexuals, and gay men of colour are challenging the dominance of white representational narratives and icons.

An ironic counterpart to the blossoming of lesbian and gay representation, which includes making overtly sexual images, is the long, nasty history of state censorship in Canada, which has no Swedish parallel. Newly retooled federal obscenity legislation – the Butler decision (1992) – has been deployed to trap, detain, and/or destroy offending materials such as the American lesbian sex magazine *Bad Attitude* (see Ross, 1997). And at the Canada-U.S. border the Prohibited Importations Unit continues to instruct the seizure and confiscation of "obscene" lesbian and gay materials under Memorandum D 9-1-1.[11] Artists, sex workers, and anti-censorship feminists and booksellers have decried recent rulings as reactionary, moralistic, and discriminatory (see Fuller and Blackley, 1995, Dixon, 1998). As matters stand, Canadian obscenity rulings legally enshrine sexual ignorance and the fear of sexual difference, and they serve only to reinforce the painful condition of lesbian and gay invisibility and marginalization.

Lesbians Communicating Knowledge in Sweden

Sweden is a small language community, but there have been successful attempts to create lesbian and gay cultural expresssion and to communicate experiences. In the larger cities, theatre groups have been engaged in staging plays with lesbian or gay content on a non-profit basis. Lesbians also sing in choirs; in Stockholm and Göteborg there are lesbian choirs with nation-wide reputations. Film and video festivals held each year screen mostly English-language material. Lesbians are also active in the production of the visual arts. Printed material can be found in bookshops run by the local chapters of RFSL. Of particular interest is Medusa, a women's bookshop in Stockholm with a large selection of lesbian fiction and non-fiction.

Lesbian groups can make their existence known to others via the gay media and through women's communication channels. As in Canada, the mainstream media in Sweden have not been particularly interested in writing about lesbians for lesbians. Journalists are mainly content to write about lesbians in order to sell copies to non-lesbians. The gay media in Sweden consist of one national magazine, several local information newsletters, and some local radio stations.[12] The national magazine is *Kom Ut!*, the official voice of RFSL. It is distributed to all the members in the organization, and it is also available in libraries, RFSL bookshops, and lesbian and gay establishments, where it can be picked up free of charge. Another magazine, *Reporter*, covering Scandinavia in both content and distribution, was a commercial publication, issued on a monthly basis to subscribers and for sale on larger newsstands; however, it went bankrupt in 1995, and the last issue was printed in July that year. *Kom Ut!*, issued bi-monthly, is mainly based on volunteer work. It reports lesbian activities and initiatives so any group with ambition to let others know about its existence can be seen there. *Kom Ut!* also has lesbian reporters. The RFSL bookshops and Medusa carry the full inventory of Swedish-language lesbian materials and complement their stock with English-language publications. Everything by lesbian (and gay) authors printed in English or other languages is available in stock or by order. There are no censorship practices comparable to the state and social censorship carried out in Canada.

At the local level, many RFSL sections produce and distribute newsletters to their members, also offered free of charge in selected locations. As well, there are newsletters from other gay and lesbian groups such as the Christian group EKHO (Eukumeniska Gruppen för Kristna Homosexuella). Another method used to reach the lesbian public, especially those who do not visit lesbian or gay places, is the local radio. Several RFSL sections broadcast regularly, and some even have women's programs. In these broadcasts, information about lesbian activities is provided, and lesbians are also active in the production of programs that are non-lesbian-specific.

Since 1989 there have been no lesbian magazines, but during much of the 1980s the most visible expression of lesbian feminist activities was a magazine published by a group that called itself Stina Line.[13] The group was based in Göteborg, but the magazine was circulated throughout the whole country. It covered a range of issues concerning lesbians in Sweden and carried debates, reports from various events, reviews, cartoons, photographs, poetry, and advertisements for upcoming events. The last issue appeared in 1989.

Canadian Educational Initiatives

Since the early 1970s, lesbian and gay male activists across Canada have identified curriculum reform at all levels of schooling as a major priority. They have targeted elementary and secondary schools in an effort to dislodge heterosexist assumptions that structure courses in family studies, sex education, and history among others. Increasingly, lesbian and gay youth, who suffer invisibility and humiliation in school settings, have assumed a leadership role on the education front. For the most part, local school boards across Canada – powerful, tax-financed institutions – obstruct the inclusion of lesbian- and gay-positive curricula. In 1992 the Toronto Board of Education published *Sexual Orientation: Focus on Homosexuality, Lesbianism and Homophobia*, a resource guide for teachers of health education in Ontario secondary schools.[14] In response, a loose coalition of parents' groups named CURE (Citizens United for Responsible Education) was formed that year to fight this curriculum guide at the municipal level. Along with fundamentalist religious and anti-abortion groups, it seeks to publicize the view that homosexuals mock family values, "promote homosexuality," endorse promiscuity, spread HIV/AIDS, and molest children. (CURE members have also expanded their campaign beyond the education front. They have pressured city councillers to ban the explicit safe-sex pamphlets directed at youth and produced by the publicly funded AIDS Committee of Toronto.) At the same time, the sexual orientation guide has been widely dispersed across Ontario and throughout the country. In September 1993 over a thousand people gathered at a conference to support the Toronto board's gay/lesbian-positive policies and the rights of queer youth. In other regions across the country, the struggle continues to be acrimonious. In June 1995 Nicki Hokazono, the chair of the Central Okanagan School Board, was overthrown by conservative members who rejected her attempts to eliminate anti-homosexual bias from the curriculum that reaches 21,000 students in the interior of British Columbia. Hokazono, who lost a non-confidence vote, pointed to the power of the evangelical churches in the Kelowna district and the bigotry that "is alive and well" (Johnson, 1995: 11). Three years later, in July 1998, Gay and Lesbian Educators Everywhere (GALE) in Vancouver challenged the Surrey school board's decision to ban three "children's books" with lesbian and gay content (Bolan, 1998a, 1998b). The case, heard for two weeks in the provincial court, was the culmination of two years of preparation and fund-raising by GALE, with the support of the British Columbia Teachers' Federation.[15]

At the university level in Canada, lesbian and gay studies exist in an emergent form and seem to be gaining some ground, though there remains little agreement about the effects of this trend towards "institutionalization." Within women's studies programs, which exist in the majority of colleges and universities across Canada, lesbian content and courses were first introduced. Canadian academic ventures include the Toronto Centre for Lesbian and Gay Studies and its newsletter, *Centre/Fold*, a smattering of credit and non-credit courses in colleges and universities, and assorted campus-based lesbian and gay groups, conferences, and seminars. Beginning in 1989, Ryerson Polytechnic University pioneered a small progam of non-credit lesbian and gay studies courses. Between 1995 and 1998 the Toronto Centre for Lesbian and Gay Studies offered a new model, the "queer exchange," through which two-month-long courses in lesbian and gay literature, film, organizing, and theory are taught (and receive rave reviews) for a nominal fee. Within the university, however, few lesbian or gay courses have permanent status; most are clustered (and rendered invisible) under the rubric of "special topics" and are subject to the whims and budgetary constraints of deans and department chairs. The exception is the University of Toronto which inaugurated a program in "sexuality diversity studies" at University College in May 1998. In addition, the Lesbian and Gay Studies Association was founded at the Learned Societies meeting in Calgary in 1994, and within the Canadian

Historical Association, the Canadian Committee on the History of Sexuality was officially formed in Montreal the following year. To date, the majority of academics and theorists are also community-based activists whose research and writing is informed by links to both sites.

Swedish Educational Initiatives

The school curriculum in Sweden demands that teenagers become educated in sexuality and relationships, including homosexuality. Over the last decade, the local sections of RFSL have developed expertise in presenting information about lesbian and gay lifestyles to pupils. A tradition has developed in which schools engage speakers from RFSL to ensure that knowledge about lesbian and gay life is made available to all students. During the budget cuts of the 1990s this activity has been threatened, and although teachers are required to treat homosexuality as a normal expression of love and desire, the quality of education varies.

Lesbians interested in studying with other lesbians can find space in women-only facilities. In Göteborg there is Kvinnofolkhögskolan, an adult-education facility, state-funded since 1985. The school offers specially designed courses aimed at deepening the understanding of a particular area. In 1995 one such course was Women's Studies and Video Documentation.[16] Besides full-year or term-long courses, there are weekend programs and guest lectures spanning all possible subjects, academic, political, and practical.[17] Some of the courses address lesbian themes, and lesbians are visible in many aspects of the school's work. As one of the few women-only spaces in Sweden, it has a certain attraction for lesbians, especially those with a feminist political outlook, and they are to be found among both students and teachers. The policy of the school is to create space for all women to be empowered by increasing their knowledge and by communicating with one another. This activity includes lesbians as well as Muslims; working-class women as well as academics.

Another study facility for women that also provides space for lesbians is Kvinnohöjden, located in Storsund outside Borlänge in central Sweden. It is owned by a non-profit foundation and has been organizing camps and courses since 1981.[18] Inside this women-only space, there are activities for lesbians, they take part in running the facility, and they are active in program planning for the non-profit organization. Though this is not a lesbian organization, lesbians feel comfortable in the women-only facility and benefit from the educational aim of empowering women.

Swedish universities have not been particularly eager to accommodate lesbian and gay studies, with the exception of the Unit for Interdiciplinary Women's Studies at Göteborg (recently turned into the Department of Feminist Studies), which has offered a series of open seminars that discuss the social construction of sexuality. In effect, women's studies as an interdisciplinary academic enterprise has not developed in Sweden in the same way as it has in Canada. The University of Göteborg was also the location for the first Swedish conference on lesbian and gay studies, held in October 1995. There have been a few individual efforts by people working in the university to research lesbian and gay themes, but not much organized work so far. In Sweden, mainstream feminist reseach (e.g., Eduards, 1992; Jonasdottir. 1991; Hirdman, 1988) is often overtly heterosexist, treating heterosexual desire as a given fact of human nature.

In attempting to educate people about lesbian and gay lifestyles – for example, through the high school curriculum – Canadian efforts have been severely hampered by Christian fundamentalist resistance, particularly in small towns and rural communities. In Sweden there is no equivalent resistance, but lesbian and gay issues have still not been fully integrated into the required curriculum at any level of schooling. Because the state has not sanctioned this integration, RFSL has stepped in to play a significant role in diffusing lesbian and gay information to teenagers through schools. Education by and for lesbians has found space in Canadian universities, whereas in Sweden the long, rich Nordic tradition of adult education has afforded some room for the production of lesbian-specific knowledge.

To summarize, there are significant similarities in the ways that Canadian and Swedish lesbians have pursued social, cultural, and educational activities. The objectives of coming out and encouraging visibility work to motivate individuals to find others like themselves and form groups. In Canada, with a population of nearly 30 million people scattered across ten provinces and two territories, there is a vast number of lesbian resources, primarily concentrated in large urban centres. In Sweden a population of 8.7 million means that there are fewer lesbians groups, but we find a similar concentration in the larger cities. The high level of visibility of Canadian lesbians (and gay men) is reflected in the concerted targeting of "pink" consumers by companies such as IKEA, Volvo, Absolut Vodka, Banana Republic, and Calvin Klein (Maynard, 1994; Giese, 1994; Jacobs, 1994). In Sweden, comparable targeting directly connected to the lower level of lesbian (and gay) visibility does not exist. In other words, "identity" does not sell.

The major difference between the two countries is that the discourse of diversity is highly developed and sophisticated in Canada – in the

1990s, identity-based culture and politics are expressed through groups of lesbians (as well as bisexuals and transgenders) who organize along lines of class, age, sexual practice, language, region, race, ethnicity, and disability. Indeed, the flourishing of identity-based lesbian groups in Canada over the past twenty-five years has occurred in the context of loud and organized discursive contests about difference and diversity, manifest in the broader struggles for women's liberation, disability rights, Quebec sovereignty, First Nations self-determination, and "multiculturalism."

Lesbian social, cultural, and educational initiatives in Sweden have been created in a spirit of social need. Because the country has a strong tradition of gay-lesbian (and gender) friendly state policies and explicit prohibitions against public homophobia, visibility becomes an issue of informing and enlightening the public about lesbian and gay lifestyles. Identity has not served as a basis for diversifying lesbian social and cultural developments in Sweden in the same way it has in Canada. Rather, Swedish activists have emphasized the sameness of lesbians with different backgrounds.

PART TWO: LEGAL REFORMS

One major strategy used in both Sweden and Canada to increase the visibility of lesbians and gay men has been to lobby all levels of government for legal reforms that enshrine anti-discrimination directives. In response to years of pressure by Swedish and Canadian activists, gains have been made and losses registered in the area known as "lesbian and gay rights." Significant numbers of lesbians in both countries have made law reform a political priority. They have worked inside equality-rights organizations such as RFSL in Sweden and in a range of rights-oriented groups in Canada, including Equality for Gays and Lesbians Everywhere, the Coalition for Gay Rights in Ontario (now the Coalition for Lesbian and Gay Rights in Ontario), and the Campaign for Equal Families. It is important to note that the significant differences in the political and legal structures of Sweden and Canada have shaped the struggle for lesbian rights in contrasting ways. Sweden is one nation and has a single legislative body, the Riksdag, which is entrusted with making all laws and national policies. Canada has three levels of law and policy formation – municipal, provincial, and federal. Decision-making at these levels has often had a contradictory character and has been inconsistent across provinces and regions.

In both countries the heterosexual nuclear family (including common-law couples) has been and continues to be held in higher esteem than all other familial arrangements. In addition, the long-standing medico-social equation of homosexuality with pedophilia, combined with the fear that homosexual parents *produce* homosexual children, lies behind claims to refortify the heterosexist status quo. These assumptions inform legislation in both countries.

Sweden: RFSL*'s Policy-Making and Law-Reform Activity*

In Sweden, homosexual relationships were decriminalized in 1944, and the age of consent (fifteen years) has been the same for homosexual and heterosexual relationships since 1978. The National Board of Health removed homosexuality from the category of disease a year later. In 1987 the law against unlawful discrimination was extended to cover homosexuals, and on 1 January 1995 the law that permitted homosexual registered partnerships came into effect.[19]

Years of persistent law-reform activity have been supported by a strong Swedish lesbian and gay rights movement. As a result, there is a "lesbian/gay friendliness" expressed in the legislative framework that structures everyday life. The major actor in this movement has been RFSL, but other, smaller groups have also taken part at times. With a history reaching back to 1951, RFSL is today a large and stable mixed-gender group that has gained an important position as the organization representing gay men and lesbians. To have one large lesbian and gay rights organization is a tradition in Scandinavia, where the emphasis is put on the common interests of lesbians and gay men and on political and legal reform.[20]

RFSL has about six thousand members; a third are women. It is organized in two levels: a National Board and local sections, of which there were twenty-nine in 1995, according to the magazine *Kom Ut!* The local sections vary in size from fifteen to around a thousand members (figures from RFSL, 1995). The governing power in RFSL lies with the local sections, which meet at the yearly congresses where representatives decide on activities and strategies. At the congresses a National Board of executives is elected for the year.

The organization has received public funding since the late 1970s; in the mid 1980s there was a large increase in its funding because the state chose to channel money for HIV/AIDS prevention among gay men through RFSL. This increase enabled it to expand its work in this area by employing professional staff and by starting up advice centres. The HIV/AIDS-related funding increase occurred at both the national and the local levels. At the national level "HIV-kansliet" was created to function as a resource for the local sections and to prepare the policy agenda, which further strengthened the influence of the organization.

Over the years, RFSL has worked intensively on improving the rights of homosexuals in Swedish society. It functions as a lobby organization, with calls and visits to politicians and civil servants, but members also arrange events that are intended to attract media attention, such as marches, public meetings, and direct action, and to make visible inadequacies in the laws. Over time a relationship has been formed between RFSL and the media, so that when reporters are interested in issues related to homosexuality, they turn to the organization for information.

The relationship between RFSL and the state can be examined by analysing two parliamentary commissions appointed by the Riksdag to study and suggest changes in legislation concerning homosexuals. The first commission was called Homosexutredningen (HU), and it presented its report in 1984.[21] The original directives for HU stated that it was to "clear away remaining discrimination." The main focus was on anti-discrimination incentives, and it was in this spirit that the commission suggested that cohabiting homosexual couples be included in the legal paragraphs addressing heterosexuals in "marriage-like" relationships. Such a measure was relevant to social insurance, an area in which the commission also argued that homosexual spouses were to be treated as next of kin and thus be able to benefit from the rules governing economic compensation for caretaking of a sick spouse (up to thirty days). However, if the relationship ended, homosexual spouses were not to be entitled to the social security granted to heterosexual couples (Holmberg, 1993). The commission also put forth suggestions on legal reforms to protect homosexual men and women in their relationship with state employers and business owners.

Already in 1977, RFSL's National Board had been in contact with politicians and civil servants, who had discussed with its members the directives for HU.[22] Between 1977 and 1985 HU was the main issue for RFSL; lesbians and gay men from the National Board met several times with representatives from the appropriate government department. The National Board also diffused information about the commission to its local sections by arranging regional study weekends, lectures, study groups, debate panels, and so on. In 1980 RFSL distributed a questionnaire from P.A. Håkansson, the social scientist appointed by the commission to carry out an empirical study of the living conditions of homosexuals in Sweden.[23] In the years that followed, RFSL's National Board monitored developments, informed its members, and talked to the commission. When the report was completed in 1985, RFSL wrote an official response and tried to influence other agencies that were appointed to give their own official comments:

for instance, the National Board of Health and Welfare.[24] In its report, RFSL was critical of many aspects of the commission's work, especially the recommendations that downplayed constitutional protection for homosexuals and the right of same-sex couples to marry.[25]

The second commission, Partnerskapskommitten (PK), was appointed in 1991 as a response to a suggestion from the National Board of Social Welfare that homosexual couples be allowed to legalize their relationships. The task of the commission was to evaluate a law from 1987 that equated homosexual couples with heterosexual (but not married) couples without children and regulated how the common property was divided if the relationship ended,[26] and to consider the need to legislate registered partnerships. The commission arrived at the conclusion that homosexual couples should be given the possibility of formalizing their relationships in a way that resembled civil marriage for heterosexual couples: that is, a registered partnership. Homosexual couples who entered into partnership would then be legally equal to heterosexual married couples, with the exception of the rights to adopt children and to assistance for artificial insemination. PK took up the issue after years of intense lobbying by RFSL and some politicians in the Riksdag. Its only task was to investigate the legal feasibility of registered partnership and to formulate a legal position. RFSL monitored its every move and rejoiced when the Riksdag voted in favour of the legal reform in June 1994.

In the years between the two commissions, RFSL had become larger and better financed, and its policy-related activities were more extensive than had been the case ten years earlier. From the organization's annual reports, it is obvious that lobbying had become established as the major means to advance social change. In 1993 alone, fifty-eight meetings and visits with politicians and civil servants were held. The topics of these meetings covered much ground, from the European Security Conference and the human rights of homosexuals to "Grupplivförsäkringar för AMU-elever, doktorander och värnpliktiga" (special collective life insurance that groups such as trade unions can get for their members). Several visits concerned registered partnership and homosexual parents. RFSL also provided official commentary on reports from various governmental commissions. As well, the organization was concerned with international issues, and it arranged demonstrations at the embassies of countries that harassed homosexuals; it also tried to influence discussion of Swedish refugee policy (see Knocke and Ng in this volume).

Although RFSL counts both lesbians and gay men among its leaders, it has often been perceived as male-biased. It made gains through state commissions, but both HU and PK perpetuated lesbian invisiblity. One of the major drawbacks of the research upon which HU based its recommendations was the low representation of lesbians in the surveys and interviews. In Håkansson's study, only 16 per cent (205 of 1,305) of the respondents were women. He claimed that the imbalance was compensated for by personal interviews with a proportionally larger group of women (43 per cent), and he also stated that, according to the Kinsey report (1953) in the United States, there are fewer lesbian women in the population than gay men. Some Swedish lesbian critics at the time viewed the invisibility of lesbians in public debate as a problem which was reinforced by the report, and they opposed the treatment of gay men and lesbians as equivalent entities. The absence of lesbians, the critics pointed out, had to do with the refusal of many lesbian groups to participate in the research. Lesbiska Feminister, a group of lesbians who had broken away from the sexist RFSL, tore up the questionnaires. RFSL members, who were heavily involved in shaping the consciousness of commission members and the recommendations governing HU, were upbraided for not addressing how gender structures the lives of gay men and lesbians differently, and how these differences influence the discussion of "legal rights."

According to a former activist in RFSL interviewed by Catharina Landström in the late 1970s and early 1980s, RFSL perceived a need to emphasize the sameness of all homosexual people. The political logic stated that it was acceptable to grant equal rights to homosexuals because they were in the end really like heterosexuals, apart from their desire for same-sex partners. In line with this position, all homosexuals had to be alike; to say that lesbians and gay men differed would have questioned the underlying logic. In RFSL there was also a certain hostility towards homosexuals who challenged the norm of sameness: for example, drag queens, promiscuous men, and butch women. Today politically active lesbians also organize in RFSL, but there has been no autonomous lesbian feminist organizing since the mid-1980s. In the period discussed here, RFSL has not articulated any specific lesbian issues, and lesbians, though increasingly numerous in the organization, have not been very visible as spokespersons or leaders.

In the early 1990s, gender entered the RFSL agenda as a question of lesbian representation, and as demands increased for lesbian-run events. Representation was brought up at the congresses of 1991 and 1992 in the form of bills requesting that the organization name two chairpersons, one man and one woman. (These positions would replicate the organization of the International Lesbian and Gay Association, which has two general secretaries: one woman and one man.) In both years the request was turned down; it was considered unnecessary because the chair and the vice-chair already had to be of different sexes, and members felt that the issue was unnecessarily divisive. The launching of activities especially for lesbians seems to have been much less controversial, and "lesbian issues" had become an annual agenda item both for RFSL and HIV-kansliet. Notwithstanding attempts to address gender concerns, RFSL has not articulated any lesbian-specific political issues and has only briefly addressed the Insemination Act of 1983, the one piece of legislation where lesbians are explicitly excluded. The Insemination Act is a result of another government commission, this one on artificial insemination – Inseminationsutredningen (IU). The act asserts that only heterosexual women in relationships are granted the right to assisted insemination; lesbians and single women are disqualified.

This decision was interpreted by lesbians and feminists as highly problematic, especially in light of studies that show the value of lesbian parenting. In the IU report, research on children growing up in lesbian relationships was reviewed, and it was stated that these children did not display any "negative effects" (Tiby, 1985). That children were well cared for in lesbian relationships did not lead the investigators to conclude that lesbians in stable relationships would make good parents. Instead, the IU explained its rationale for the exclusion on the grounds that artificial insemination was to be viewed as a technological aid to compensate for male infertility.[27] This interpretation makes it clear that insemination is not to be used by women who do not want to live in a heterosexual relationship. It was further underlined when the commission stated that the heterosexual couple is a family constellation which should be favoured and that other family forms, such as those led by single mothers or lesbians, should be avoided. Parenting in Sweden is perceived as a joint endeavour best carried out by a mother and a father who cohabit. In the discussion of registered partnership to date, RFSL has kept a low profile with regard to all issues pertaining to children and childcare. It has framed adoption and insemination as questions of equality; however, the existing legislation explicitly states that it is an exclusively heterosexual privilege to become parents with the aid of society's resources. Given the pressing question of parenting by homosexuals, whether through adoption/fostering or insemination, the heterosexuality (and the "opposite gender") of the parents can no longer be assumed. In its efforts to remedy the overt heterosexism of the law, RFSL will need to highlight lesbians (as women and mothers) who are most negatively impacted by laws that regulate parenting. Thus it will be forced to acknowledge the limitations of "homosexual" as a purportedly gender-neutral term.

Canada: Policy-Making and Law Reform

In Canada since the early 1970s, the lesbian and gay movement has contained individuals and organizations determined to fight for social change through law reform.[28] What Didi Herman (1994) calls "the modern day lesbian and gay rights movement" has demanded legal protection "primarily through inclusion within anti-discriminatory statutes and the extension of social benefits to lesbian and gay couples" (3). Canadian laws that govern bereavement leave, pensions, adoption, alternative insemination, prison and hospital visitation, immigration policy, inheritance, and the right to marry remain steeped in heterosexist assumptions that buttress the categories of "spouse" and "family." In Canada, though the body of judicial and quasi-judicial rulings recognizing the rights of lesbians and gays is growing, the process is expensive and time-consuming, and it deals ineffectively with discrimination on a case-by-case basis.[29]

The premise underlying campaigns for equality rights in both Canada and Sweden has been that lesbians and gay men deserve the same economic and social benefits as heterosexuals. Says Canadian gay rights campaigner Brian Mossop (1993), "Trying to legally distinguish a gay couple from a common-law heterosexual couple with no children is simply not possible without an irrational appeal to homophobia" (13). Mossop argues that the struggle for rights is growing in popularity among lesbians and gays for economic, rather than ideological, reasons, hence its pragmatic and strategic nature. Herman (1994) adds that lesbian and gay struggles for equal rights are not about rights per se, but about what rights are seen to signify – public and official recognition, social citizenship, and identification (19).

On the Canadian lesbian and gay civil rights front in the 1980s and 1990s, we find Equality for Gays and Lesbians Everywhere (EGALE, Ottawa), the Coalition for Lesbian and Gay Rights in Ontario (CLGRO, Toronto), the Foundation for Equal Families (Toronto), the December 9th Coalition (Vancouver), AIDS Action Now! (Toronto), the Same Sex Benefits Committee (Vancouver), the Lesbian and Gay Immigration Task Force (LEGIT, Vancouver), the Action Network for Gay and Lesbian Rights (Montreal), Censorstop (Toronto), SansCensure (Montreal), and lesbian and gay caucuses in unions such as the Canadian Union of Educational Workers, the Public Service Alliance of Canada, and the Canadian Union of Public Employees. For twenty-five years, CLGRO, an umbrella organization with member groups that have voting rights, has consistently pressured the Ontario government to expand definitions of "spouse" and "family" to include lesbian and gay relationships and families. The groups mentioned above have small, but loyal members, rarely numbering more than twenty unpaid volunteers. Increasingly, lesbians have become involved in these mixed-gender groups upon discovering that certain sex-related laws have a direct impact on their own lives. Questions of same-sex spousal benefits, parenting (including fostering, adoption, and alternative insemination), and access to lesbian erotic literature have kindled the interest and energy of Canadian lesbians in ways that previous legal battles over criminal laws and the policing of anal intercourse/sodomy, intergenerational sex, bawdy houses, and (gay men's) public sex did not.

Most of the groups use lobbying tactics to influence politicians; they engineer sophisticated promotional campaigns employing fax machines and direct mail, present briefs to provincial parties, hold press conferences, publish brochures and pamphlets, and pressure the mainstream media to take issues of lesbian and gay rights seriously. In virtually all cases, these Canadian lobby groups are not, unlike Sweden's RFSL, state funded.[30] Indeed, in 1988 the secretary of state responsible for promoting and financing the achievement of gender equality through the Women's Program, declared the ineligibility of all lesbian individuals and groups seeking money to fund anti-heterosexist projects.[31] For over twenty years in Canada, while feminist concerns have received some state-administered financial support, first through the secretary of state's Women's Program, and later through the Court Challenges Program, lesbian and gay concerns for the most part have not. In contrast to developments in Sweden, there has never been an expectation of state funding among grassroots lesbian and gay political leaders in Canada. Such funding for this kind of work has never been offered, a fact that reflects the antagonism which has persistently shaped the relationship between the movement and the Canadian state. Too, activists have not wanted to compromise their own agendas to fit state stipulations on how the money was to be spent. In other words, dependence on state funding in Canada has always signified the inevitability of "selling out" – bargaining away radical proposals in exchange for state approval. However, the absence of state funds has not prevented activist lesbians (and gays) from forwarding demands for a slate of equality-based rights. Indeed, the entrenchment in the constitution of the Canadian Charter of Rights and Freedoms (specifically section 15) in 1982 has greatly enabled litigation, though in Quebec, nationalist lesbians and gays have been noticeably disinterested in engaging the charter (see Smith, 1998). Increasingly, anglo-Canadian lesbian, gay, and gay-positive lawyers have assumed leadership roles as consultants and legal experts in equal-rights cases.

In Canada, gains have been made in two major areas: individual complaints based on existing grounds of discrimination (e.g., sex) and statutory reform campaigns based on asserting sexual orientation as a protected category. Most of the lobbying has happened at municipal or provincial levels, with some challenges made at the federal level but without the coordination and legitimacy of Sweden's RFSL. At the provincial level the Ontario legislature passed legislation to prohibit discrimination on the basis of sexual orientation in 1986, joining Quebec (1977), Manitoba (1987), the Yukon (1988), Nova Scotia (1991), New Brunswick (1992), British Columbia (1993), Saskatchewan (1993), Newfoundland (1996), and Alberta (1998).[32] The only remaining provinces and territories that do not have anti-discrimination statutes are Prince Edward Island and the Northwest Territories. The Canadian Human Rights Commission alone is currently faced with over eighty cases of discrimination, harassment, and employment benefits launched by lesbians and gay men in Canada.

Canadian lesbian and gay rights activists have long argued for the need to expand traditional notions of the family, and they have done so with the support of feminists, disabled activists, and civil libertarians. As a result of decades of tenacious protest, a number of courtroom victories have been achieved. In December 1990 the New Democratic government in Ontario extended job benefits – including health, dental, and leave time – to same-sex couples in the civil service. In 1991 the Michelle Douglas decision, made at the Supreme Court level, determined that homosexuality is no longer grounds for discrimination in the Canadian Armed Forces (Brown, 1992). In 1992, in what is known as the "Leshner decision," a human-rights tribunal ordered the Ontario government to change its definition of marital status so that partners of lesbian or gay employees could receive spousal benefits, including survivor or pension benefits. And since the 1993 Supreme Court decision in *Canada (A.G.) v. Ward*, a small number of lesbian and gay refugees have been permitted entrance to Canada on the basis of "a well-founded fear of persecution" in their home countries because of their so-called "immutable" sexual orientation (Laviolette, 1997: 3).

In May 1995, almost one year after the defeat of Bill 167 (see below), Judge David Nevins granted adoption orders to four lesbian couples in Ontario, ruling that a law preventing gay and lesbian couples from applying to adopt cannot be justified in a free and democratic society (Galt, 1995; Fine, 1995).[33] Prior to this decision, gays and lesbians who act as parents to their partners' biological children were not legally recognized as parents (this remains the case in every province in Canada except British Columbia and Ontario). It is not clear whether the ruling can be extended to lesbians and gays who apply to adopt or act as foster parents to the children of strangers.

Moreover, a ruling by Madame Justice Epstein of the Ontario provincial court in 1996 expanded the definition of spouse to include same-sex couples for the purposes of provincial legislation on spousal support. The ruling, known as *M v. H*, permits lesbians and gay men in conjugal relationships of three or more years to claim financial support from one another, in accordance with need and ability to pay (see Claridge, 1996; Boyd, 1996: 322–3). Though there is disagreement about the ramifications of these two verdicts, they mark a dramatic shift in the definition of "family" and "spouse" in Canadian law. Also in 1996, the federal government amended the Canadian Human Rights Act to include sexual orientation as protected grounds against discrimination (see Delacourt, 1996a, 1996b). The implications of this initiative for legalized domestic partnership or same-sex marriage, the income tax act, and other issues in Canada remain uncertain.[34] In 1998 the Canadian Union of Public Employees won the legal challenge that it had posed to the federal Income Tax Act in the Rosenberg case. Judges in the Ontario Court (General Division) ruled that provisions in the act that defined spouses as of the opposite sex were unconstitutional under section 15 of the Canadian Charter of Rights and Freedoms. In the spring of 1998 both Nova Scotia and British Columbia introduced legislation to extend pension benefits to the same-sex partners of public employees, the first provinces in Canada to take this step (Cox and Campbell, 1998; Hunter, 1998; Culbert, 1998). Finally, also in 1998 the Supreme Court of Canada ruled that Delwin Vriend, a gay male teacher fired from a private college in Alberta, was wrongfully discriminated against; the judges stated that the Alberta government must amend its Human Rights Code to include protection for sexual orientation.[35]

Defeats paradoxically coexist with victories. On 9 June 1994 the second reading of Bill 167 in the Ontario legislature was defeated by a margin of 68 to 59 after a charged, emotional debate. This sweeping bill was the result of a four-year pressure campaign mounted by the Coalition for Lesbian and Gay Rights in Ontario; it proposed seventy-nine amendments to scores of provincial statutes in order to eliminate discrimination against same-sex couples, including issues of adoption, spousal pension benefits upon the death of a partner, and tax benefits.[36] While thousands of lesbians, gays, bisexuals, and supporters participated in an angry demonstration in downtown Toronto, fundamentalist leaders such as Ken Campbell hailed the quashing of the bill as a victory for the "majority of the province" (McInnes, 1994a).[37] Over the course of several months of heated skirmishes, these fiercely competing positions took on the character of an informal national referendum on homosexuality, sexual liberation, and the family, with all the properties of a full-scale moral panic (see J. Smith, 1994). Interestingly, Bill 167 was defeated at the same time as domestic partnership reform was being debated, and passed, in Sweden. A year later, in May 1995, the Canadian Supreme Court denied Jim Egan and Jack Nesbitt, an elderly gay couple in a forty-six-year relationship, access to low-income security payments in the ruling *Egan and Nesbitt v. Canada* (Fine and Philip, 1995). In this instance, the judges refused to redefine "spouse" to include same-sex partnerships, a decision that was a cruel blow to Egan and Nesbitt. In all, though legal reforms in Canada over the past thirty years have been impressive, deep-seated resistance to the full acceptance of lesbian and gay lives persists within municipal, provincial, and national legislatures and among "ordinary" heterosexual Canadians.

CONCLUDING THOUGHTS

In both Canada and Sweden the majority of lesbians are not out and politically active, in part because the risks of being socially and economically marginalized are greater than the benefits to be accrued by being militant and vocal. Unlike women of colour, who cannot "pass" for white in racist cultures, lesbians for the most part can pass for heterosexual; they can "choose" the safety of the closet, though often at substantial personal cost (see Khayatt, 1992). Nonetheless, in both Canada and Sweden there is a history of lesbian energy directed at forming strong cultural, social identities and networks – an empowering, post-Stonewall development born out of frustration with the heterosexism of straight feminists, the sexism of gay men, and the (sometimes subtle) homophobia of mainstream culture.[38] It is also clear that lesbians have long played key leadership roles in all facets of women's organizing in both countries. Indeed, their commitment and political reach has been largely under-documented. We conclude that there are discernable similarities in what Swedish and Canadian lesbians do *as lesbians* together, such as form support groups, provide services, attend potluck dinners and film festivals, play soccer, dance, and listen to and create music. Here goals of belonging to community, affirmation, and visibility are expressed. However, when we assess the involvement of lesbians in policy and law reform, the differences in approach and strategy can be conceptualized as a discourse of diversity versus one of normalization.

In Canada the discourse of diversity has flourished in social and cultural realms to heighten lesbian visibility and strengthen identity formation, but it has not translated easily into traditional political arenas. (It is also true that postmodern, theoretical critiques of "lesbian" as a stable identity category have flourished alongside the popular proliferation of women-desiring drag kings, daddies, butches, femmes, bisexuals, queers, and transgenders.) Disunity among Canadian lesbians, rooted in differences of identity and/or ideology and aggravated by variable degrees of commitment to working with gay male allies, has limited the effectiveness of equality-rights campaigns. Not only do activist lesbians (and other sex radicals) in Canada harbour suspicion of government operations, but they disagree about the value of pressing for reforms that privilege "families" and "couples" and potentially exclude those who are not white, monogamous, middle-class professionals (see Allen, 1993; Cossman, 1997).[39] According to Canadian legal scholar Susan Boyd (1994), "Adopting family law as a means of regulating our relationships may not constitute a 'benefit' or a radical advance when the lives of all lesbians and gay men are taken into account. Indeed some would argue that poor lesbians and gay men in relationships might be better off under the current regime of exclusion" (555). Boyd and others add that the liberal pluralist incorporation of same-sex couples into law leaves intact the normative family form of heterosexual marriage (Boyd, 1994: 556; Robson, 1994; O'Brien and Weir, 1995; Gavigan, 1993; Robson, 1994; Brodsky, 1994; Cossman, 1996, 1997). In addition, lesbian activists in English-speaking Canada have embraced feminism, and feminist critiques of gay men's sexism, in ways that have produced complicated, vexed relationships with their gay "brothers." In Sweden, by contrast, lesbians have joined together with gay men to gain political clout via the discourse of normalization. (This approach is in keeping with the Swedish tradition of women and men working together for the common good.) Lesbians and gay men in RFSL have argued that the sole basis for differentiating homosexuals from heterosexuals is the gender of one's partner. As a political strategy, this position has been very successful in accomplishing the goals of redressing legal and political discrimination, but the assimilationist thrust has thwarted attempts to further the development of lesbian social space and visibility. Thus the emphasis on unifying homosexuals has made it exceedingly difficult to argue for the specificity of lesbian identity and experience.

It seems clear that law reform and "rights talk" (M. Smith, 1998: 3) initiated by lesbian and gay activists in Canada and Sweden over the past thirty years have translated into a series of important victories. There is considerable symbolic and material purchase in aiming to achieve formal legal equality. In Canada this goal is especially urgent in the face of rising right-wing virulence that names lesbians and gays as anti-family and un-Canadian. At the same time, reformist strategies are contingent on proving some sort of state-adjudicated family status wherein the law is afforded power to constitute and regulate familial and sexual identities (Foucault, 1980). In both Canada and Sweden the emphasis on conjugality lived out by same-sex spouses or registered partners legitimates certain lesbian and gay familial arrangements over others; in effect, political lobbying on this front seems less radical than campaigns for entitlement to universal social benefits regardless of familial status (see Eichler, 1988). Moreover, in the broad context of the contraction of the welfare state and the dismantlement of universal social programs, large numbers of lesbians (including mothers) who work and live as women independent of a male wage stand to suffer considerable economic hardship, especially in Canada. So questions of resources and their distribution in late-capitalist nations remain as salient as ever.

In the short term, the legal arena, however insufficient, offers Swedish and Canadian lesbian, gay, and bisexual activists one significant avenue – "a political opportunity structure" – in which to contest publicly the legacy of invisibility compounded by heterosexist and homophobic policies and practices (Jenkins and Klandermans, 1995: 3; Peterson, 1995). We recognize that this kind of strategic focus, like the challenge to racist immigration policy (see Knocke and Ng in this volume), must continue to exist alongside a comprehensive range of non-legal initiatives – social, cultural, educational – that seek to advance class, sexual, gender, and racial equality.

In Canada the appeal to normalization (or assimilation) recently articulated through challenges to state definitions of "family" and "spouse" appears to mirror strategies developed in Sweden for over forty years. Here we note a convergence in the priorities of (some) lesbian, gay, and bisexual activists across national borders. This convergence complicates the view that Canadian activists have tended to work "outside" or in opposition to the state apparatus; it also underscores the shrewd pragmatism of Swedish lesbian "insiders," who nonetheless continue to find themselves positioned on the "outside" by heterosexist state policies, such as those regarding fostering/adoption and alternative insemination. Contradictions abound. In the end, we predict ongoing discursive scuffles in both countries around what it means to be a lesbian, gay, or bisexual citizen; what it means to reconfigure "family" (for example, conceiving and raising children in non-heteronormative contexts); and what it means to effect genuine social and sexual transformation in the face of conservatizing, corporatizing, and individualizing shifts worldwide.

NOTES

We would like to thank Linda Briskin and Mona Eliasson, the project directors, for inviting us to participate in this joint Canada-Sweden research project. Each provided valuable editorial comments. And we acknowledge our spirited co-participants in both countries for their stimulating, valuable insight and debate over the past three years. Catharina wants to thank the Swedish women who were willing to be interviewed for this project, and Becki is grateful for ongoing conversations with Gary Kinsman, Susan Boyd, and Cynthia Wright. Together, we want to recognize the generous financial contributions made by the Social Sciences and Humanities Research Council of Canada and the Swedish government.

1 Research on Swedish lesbian organizing was done by Catharina Landström in 1995.

2 For a sampling of sources in the expanding field of Canadian lesbian and gay history, see Lesbians Making History (1989); Chamberland (1993); Higgins and Chamberland (1992); Rob Champagne, Canada's pioneer gay activist: Jim Egan, *Rites,* December 1986/January 1987, 12–14; Grube (1986); and Becki Ross (ed.), *Forbidden Love: The Unashamed Stories of Postwar Canadian Lesbians* (Vancouver, in press). For American sources, see Newton (1985, 1994); Nestle (1992); Duberman, Vicinus, and Chauncey (1989); Kennedy and Davis (1993); Berubé (1991); Chauncey (1994); Penn (1994); *Radical History Review* (1995); and Lewin (1996).

3 The shifts in lesbian feminist ideology and membership in Toronto from the 1970s to the 1990s are mapped out in Ross (1995). On recent initiatives by lesbians of colour and on the integration of anti-racist politics and ideas in lesbian organizing, see Decter (1993). Specific groups around Canada include Lesbians of Colour (Toronto), the Vancouver Island Support Group (Victoria), Da Poonani Posse (Toronto), Gays and Lesbians Aging (GALA) (Toronto), Lesbian Youth Peer Support (Toronto), Pink Triangle Youth (Ottawa), Hola, for Gay Latinos, and No Me Digas Qu No Sabias for Latin American Lesbians (Toronto), the Lesbian Youth Group (Vancouver), the Femme Support Group (Vancouver), Khush, for Gay South Asians (Toronto), Black Socialist Dykes (Toronto), Gays and Lesbians at the University of Manitoba (Winnipeg), Fredericton Lesbians and Gays, Nice Jewish Girls (Toronto), the Truro Lesbian Support Group (Truro, Nova Scotia), Asian Lesbians of Toronto, Atish, for "Lesbigays" of South Asian Heritage (Vancouver), Two-Spirit Peoples of the First Nations (Toronto, Vancouver), the lesbian caucus of the Disabled Women's Network, Outrageous, Wiser Lesbians (OWLS) (Toronto), and SAGE (Ottawa), among others.

4 On the issue of lesbians and HIV/AIDS, see Gaynor (1993).

5 Lesbian feminists in Göteborg documented their existence in a publication called *Gotas Kanal: Internbulletin for Lesbiska Feminister* (Göteborg), spring 1981.

6 *Pinglan: Newsletter for Föreningen Lesbisk Nu!* (Stockholm). The statement of purpose is printed in every issue.
7 RFSL Göteborg (1995).
8 Most larger Canadian cities offer lesbian and gay film festivals, performance art evenings, art gallery shows, theatre companies such as Buddies in Bad Times in Toronto and the Out West Performance Society in Vancouver. Notable are the following: cartoons by Noreen Stevens; prose by Dionne Brand, Peter McGehee, Jane Rule, and Beth Follett; poetry by Brenda Brooks, Leleti Tamu, Jim Nason, Daphne Marlatt, Betsy Warland, Stuart Blackley, Carolyn Gammon, Tamai Kobayashi, and Mona Oikawa; music by Faith Nolan, Seven Cent Posse, Sugar and Spice, k.d. lang, David Sereda, Ingrid Stitt, and Women With Horns; the films and videos of Midi Onodera, Michelle Mohabeer, Lorna Boschman, Richard Fung, Shanni Mootoo, Rose Gutierrez, Ian Rashid, and Gitanjali; and the visual art of Stephanie Martin, Stephen Andrews, Buseje Bailey, Grace Channer, Daniel Collins, Kiss 'n Tell, Courtnay McFarlane, Karen Augustine, Anna Camilleri, River Sui, and Shonagh Adelman. Theatrically, lesbian and gay playwrights, actors, and technicians – Bryden MacDonald, Ann-Marie MacDonald, Brad Fraser, Alisa Palmer, Ahdri Zhina Mandiela, Sky Gilbert, Robert Lepage, and others – hone their craft through assocation with companies such as Buddies in Bad Times (Toronto) and the Out West Theatre (Vancouver). And Toronto's annual Desh Pardesh (home away from home) festival of diasporic South Asian artists and activists consistently integrates work by and for lesbians, gays, and bisexuals.
9 The National Film Board produced its first full-length documentary, *Forbidden Love* by Lynne Fernie and Aerlyn Weissman, in 1992. The NFB has since been involved in financing *Out: Stories of Lesbian and Gay Youth* (1993) and *Stolen Moments* (1997) and has co-produced the drama *Skin Deep* (1995) by Midi Onodera. David Adkin independently produced and directed his most recent documentary, *Jim Loves Jack: The Jim Egan Story* (1995), and Lynne Fernie and Aerlyn Weissman released an independent documentary, *Truth and Other Fictions: The Jane Rule Story* (1995).
10 On the refusal of funds by the management committee of Metropolitan Toronto's Council, see Czach (1993) and Brown (1993).
11 A major site of lesbian and gay law-reform activity that is not related directly to equality-rights debates about "family" and "spouse" is obscenity law and the successive prosecutions of lesbian or gay publications and bookshops. For example, the American lesbian sex magazine *Bad Attitude* was seized from Glad Day Bookshop in Toronto and later deemed to be obscene and "likely to harm and degrade women" by Judge Claude Paris. On the *Bad Attitude* trial (*R. v. Scythes*), see Ross (1997). And for a trenchant discussion of the seizure and confiscation of

lesbian and gay materials by Customs Canada officials at the Canada-U.S. border, see Fuller and Blackley (1995).

12 According to *Kom Ut!* 2 (1995), there are six RFSL radio stations.

13 Föreningen Stina Line: *Extremistnytt, Stina Line,* and *Gun Powder* in 1983; *Offen Siv* and *Julia* in 1984; *Aqua Vera* and *Normella* in 1985; *Majvår* and *Sån'ja* in 1986; *Gråtrut* and *Doris Gay* in 1987, and *Åtgerd* in 1988.

14 This curriculum guide is in direct contrast to Saskatchewan's Teen-Aid program designed by the province's Pro-Life Association and taught yearly to more than 20,000 students in 203 primary and secondary schools. The program extolls chastity or abstinence, the sanctity of marriage, and negative views on homosexuality. See Mitchell (1993).

15 The three children's books banned by the Surrey school board were *Asha's Moms, Belinda's Bouquet,* and *One Dad, Two Dads, Brown Dads, Blue Dads.* Joseph Arvay, legal counsel representing the Gay and Lesbian Educators of British Columbia, argued in provincial court that the board's vote to ban the materials "is tantamount to a wholesale indictment of all gay and lesbian professional resources" (cited in Bolan, 1998b).

16 *Kvinnofolkhögskolan 95/96* (Göteborg: Kvinnofolkhögskolan, 1995).

17 See *Kortkurser och förelasningar våren 1995* (Göteborg: Kvinnofolkhögskolan, 1995).

18 See *Kvinnohöjden-feministisk kurs-och gästgård, Kurser april-oktober 1994* (information brochure) and *Kvinnohöjden-feministisk kurs-och gästgard, Kurser november 1994 – februari 1995* (information brochure).

19 This information can be found in *Homosexuellas rättigheter* (Socialstyrelsen, 1991), a small booklet that provides a summary of the laws affecting lesbians and gay men.

20 RFSL in Sweden, LBL in Denmark, and LLH in Norway are the large lesbian-gay organizations. SETA in Finland has not been as successful in influencing public policy.

21 SOU (1984): 63.

22 Förbundsstyrelseprotokoll, RFSL, 22 Septermber 1977.

23 Ingående skrivelser 1980, RFSL Göteborg avdelning 2.

24 Förbundsstyrelseprotokoll, RFSL, 14 April 1985.

25 RFSL Remissyttrande, 14 April 1985.

26 Lagen om homosexuella sambor, SFS 1987: 813; Socialstyrelsen (1991).

27 The use of the term "artificial" instead of "alternative" reflects the language of Swedish policy. It is likely that the emphasis is on the "strangeness" of the procedure, a view that is consistent with state efforts to regulate this and all other forms of assisted reproduction.

28 Many organizations flourished in Canada that attempted to formulate a civil rights platform for lesbian and gay equality in the 1970s and

1980s, including Gay Alliance Towards Equality, the National Coalition for Gay Rights, the John Damien Defense Committee, the Right to Privacy Committee, the *Body Politic* Defense Fund, Lesbians against the Budget, the Canadian Commitee against Customs Censorship, and many more. See Kinsman (1996) and Rayside (1998).

29 Four cases in the 1970s and early 1980s were very important in the development of a civil rights strategy among gay and lesbian activists: Doug Wilson versus the University of Sasketchewan (1975), John Damien versus the Ontario Racing Commission (1975), the Gay Alliance Towards Equality in Vancouver versus the *Vancouver Sun* (1974), and Vogel versus Manitoba Health Care (1983).

30 EGALE did obtain a small amount of money to act as an intervenor in the Mossop (bereavement leave) case in 1985 and 1990 through the now-disbanded Court Challenges Program.

31 Prior to 1987, the secretary of state's Women's Program did provide small grants to a handful of lesbian organizations to promote lesbian feminism and visibility – for example, several lesbian conferences, the Calgary Lesbian Mothers Defense Fund, and several "lesbian issues" of feminist periodicals. After 1987, however, all funding was stopped. See Ross (1988).

32 In Canada, "out" politicians have helped to articulate a lesbian and gay agenda at the provincial and national levels through their stature as democratically elected political representatives. Svend Robinson is an openly gay member of the federal New Democratic Party for Burnaby, British Columbia, who recently lost his bid for the party leadership. André Boulerice, an openly gay Parti Québécois member of the Assemblée nationale, represents Montreal's east-end riding of Ste-Marie/St-Jacques. Betty Baxter ran (unsuccessfully) for the federal NDP in Vancouver in 1993. As well, a smattering of publicly identified gay and lesbian municipal politicians, school board trustees, and alderpersons across the country have endeavoured to engineer challenges to heterosexist social policies. See Fulton (1994); see also Rayside (1998): 105–211.

33 Many do not agree that the decision marked a victory. In response to Judge Nevins' ruling, Edward Field (1995) wrote in a letter to the *Globe and Mail*: "It is one thing to permit consenting homosexuals their own choice of lifestyle; it is quite another for society to legally create what nature itself will never create: same-sex human parents. By what twisted logic can we justify the adoption and guidance of children by people who reject the very means by which those children were created?"

34 For a thoughtful exploration of the implications of Canadian taxation policy on lesbians and gay men, see Young (1994).

35 The Supreme Court's decision to amend the Alberta Human Rights Code to include protection for lesbians and gay men was met with province-

wide fury, particularly on the part of conservative Christians. For in-depth coverage, see Laghi (1998a, 1998b).

36 Two days prior to the second reading of Bill 167, Attorney General Marion Boyd elected to remove a provision that would have given same-sex couples the right to apply for child adoption. She also agreed not to change the current legal definition of "spouse" or "marital status." Lesbian and gay activists expressed outrage and disappointment that the amendments weakened the initial bill and capitulated to the right wing; see McInnes (1994b). For a critical analysis of the defeat of Bill C-167, see Munter (1997).

37 In 1993 an Unemployment Insurance Commission appeals board ruled that two women were spouses. The ruling argued that one of the women had "just cause" to quit her job (in order to relocate to be with her lover) and should receive unemployment benefits. The commission is appealing the decision to a federal court judge. See Brown (1994).

38 The riots at the Stonewall Inn in New York City in June 1969 are commonly invoked in North America as the catalyst for modern-day gay and lesbian liberation. In Sweden, as in other Scandinavian countries, Britain, and part of western Europe also, "Stonewall" has accumulated considerable iconic meaning over the past three decades.

39 In her article "Who gets to be family," Carol Allen (1993) makes the valuable point that poor lesbians on social assistance might suffer economically when the definition of "spouse" changes in the Family Benefits Act. It is possible, she argues, that one woman might then be considered financially dependent on her (female) spouse, which would make the couple vulnerable to cutbacks in family benefits (105). For additional sources on lesbian mothering in Canada, see Coalition of Lesbian and Gay Rights of Ontario (1993); Ursel (1995); Andrews (1995); Arnup and Boyd (1995); Gavigan (1995); and Nelson (1996).

REFERENCES

Allen, Carol. (1993). Who gets to be family: Some thoughts on the lesbian and gay fight for equality. In Linda Carty (ed.), *And Still We Rise: Feminist Political Mobilizing in Contemporary Canada*. Toronto: Women's Press.

Andrews, Karen. (1995). Ancient affections: Gays, lesbians and family status. In Katherine Arnup (ed.), *Lesbian Parenting: Living with Pride and Prejudice*. Charlottetown: Gynergy Press. 358–377.

Arnup, Katherine. (1995). Living in the margins: Lesbian families and the law. In K. Arnup (ed.), *Lesbian Parenting: Living with Pride and Prejudice*. Charlottetown: Gynergy Press.

– and Susan Boyd. (1995). Familial disputes? Sperm donors, lesbian mothers and legal parenthood. In Didi Herman and Carl Stychin (eds.), *Legal Inversions: Lesbians, Gay Men and the Politics of Law.* Philadelphia: Temple University Press.

Backström, Malin. (1991). Tjejer har alltid behovt traffas. *Kom Ut!* 1: 10.

Bell, Laurie. (1991). *On Our Own Terms: A Practical Guide for Lesbian and Gay Relationships*, Toronto: Coalition for Lesbian and Gay Rights in Ontario.

Bent Guide to Gay/Lesbian Canada. (1994). Toronto: Bent Books, ECW Press.

Berubé, Alan. (1991). *Coming Out under Fire: The History of Gay Men and Women in World War II.* New York: Penguin Books.

Bisexual Women's Anthology Collective. (1995). *Plural Desires: Writing Bisexual Women's Realities.* Toronto: Sister Vision Press.

Bolan, Kim. (1998a). Surrey book case likened to old U.S. policy on segregation. *Vancouver Sun,* 2 July, B1, B2.

– (1998b). Banned books aimed at "inculcating." *Vancouver Sun*, 11 July, A3.

Bouthillette, Anne-Marie. (1997). Queer and gendered housing: A tale of two neighbourhoods in Vancouver. In G.B. Ingram, A.M. Bouthillette, and Y. Retter (eds.), *Queers in Space: Communities/Public Spaces/Sites of Resistance.* Seattle, Wash.: Bay Press.

Boyd, Susan. (1994) Expanding the "family" in family law: Recent Ontario proposals on same sex relationships. *Canadian Journal of Women and the Law* 7: 545–63.

– (1996). Best friends or spouses? Privatization and the recognition of lesbian relationships in *M. v. H.*, *revue canadienne de droit familial/ Canadian Family Law Review* 13: 321–41.

Brodsky, Gwen. (1994). Out of the closet and into a wedding dress? Struggles for lesbian and gay legal equality. *Canadian Journal of Women and the Law* 7 (2): 523–35.

Brown, Eleanor. (1992). Canadian Forces surrender: Court decision opens gates for lesbian and gay soldiers, *X-Tra!* 30 October, 15.

– (1993). Inside/Out loses funding, *X-tra!* 23 July, 11.

– (1994). These two women are spouses, *X-tra!* 7 January, 1.

Carroll, William. (1992). Introduction: Social movements and counter hegemony in a Canadian context. In W. Carroll (ed.), *Organizing Dissent: Contemporary Social Movements in Theory and Practice.* Toronto: Garamond.

Chamberland, Line. (1993). Remembering lesbian bars: Montréal, 1955–1975. *Journal of Homosexuality* 25 (3): 231–69.

Champagne, Robert. (1986). An interview with Jim Egan, and Alfred Taylor, A perfect beginner: Jim Egan and the tabloids. *Canadian Lesbian and Gay History Newsletter*, 2 September, 11–18.

Chauncey, George. (1994). *Gay New York: Gender, Urban Culture and the Making of the Gay Male World, 1890–1940*. New York: Basic Books.

Claridge, Thomas. (1996). Same-sex couples win support rights. *Globe and Mail*, 10 February, A1, A2.

Coalition of Lesbian and Gay Rights of Ontario. (1993). *Happy Families: The Recognition of Same-Sex Spousal Relationships*. Toronto.

Cossman, Brenda. (1996). Same-sex couples and the politics of family status. In Janine Brodie (ed.), *Women and Canadian Public Policy*. Toronto: Harcourt Brace and Company.

– (1997). Family inside/out. In Meg Luxton (ed.), *Feminism and Families: Critical Policies and Changing Practices*. Halifax: Fernwood Publishing.

Cox, Kevin, and Murray Campbell. (1998). N.S. extends same-sex rights. *Globe and Mail*, 26 May, A1, A3.

Culbert, Lori. (1998). Province to extend pension benefits to same-sex couples. *Vancouver Sun*, 22 June, A1, A2.

Czach, Liz. (1993). Bigot busting: Fighting the right at city Hall, *X-tra!* 23 July, 13.

Decter, Ann (ed.). (1993). Different places we are building: Lesbians discuss politics and organizing. In Linda Carty (ed.), *And Still We Rise: Feminist Political Mobilizing in Contemporary Canada*. Toronto: Women's Press.

Delacourt, Susan. (1996a). Liberals could renege on promises to homosexuals. *Globe and Mail*, 21 February, A1, A4.

– (1996b). Putting gay rights on back burner may apply heat to PM. *Globe and Mail*, 22 February, A3.

Dixon, John. (1998). Freedom-of-speech challenge likely to go to country's top court. *Vancouver Sun*, 8 July, A15.

Duberman, Martin B., Martha Vicinus, and George Chauncey (eds.). (1989). *Hidden from History: Reclaiming the Lesbian and Gay Past*. New York: Penguin Books.

Eduards, Maud. (1992). Against the rules of the game. In *Rethinking Change: Current Swedish Feminist Research*. Stockholm: HSFR.

Eichler, Margrit. (1988). *Families in Canada Today: Recent Changes and Their Policy Consequences*. Toronto: Gage.

Field, Edward. (1995). The natural order. *Globe and Mail*, 24 May, A23.

Fine, Sean. (1995) Courts lead politicians on gay rights, *Globe and Mail*, 12 May, A6.

– and Margaret Philip. (1995). Divorced mothers, gay couples lose in court. *Globe and Mail*, 26 May, A1.

Foucault, Michel. (1980). *The History of Sexuality*. Vol. 1. New York: Vintage Books.

Fuller, Janine, and Stuart Blackley. (1995). *Restricted Entry: Censorship on Trial*. Vancouver: Press Gang Publishers.

Fulton, E. Kaye. (1994). Gay and proud: Canada's only publicly gay MP tells his story. *Maclean's,* 16 May, 36–9.

Galt, Virginia. (1995). Lesbian pairs allowed to adopt. *Globe and Mail,* 11 May, A1, A6.

Gavigan, Shelley. (1993) Paradise lost, paradox revisited: The implications of familial ideology for feminist, lesbian and gay engagement to law. *Osgoode Hall Law Journal* 31: 598–624.

– (1995). A parent(ly) knot: Can Heather have two mommies? In Didi Herman and Carl Stychin (eds.), *Legal Inversions: Lesbians, Gay Men and the Politics of Law.* Philadelphia: Temple University Press.

Gaynor, Lesli. (1993). Are lesbians at risk of getting AIDS? The damned sex debate. *Herizons,* 6 (4): 16–20.

Gebhardt, Gunilla, and Abby Peterson. (1985). Homosexutredningen. *Kvinnovetenskaplig tidskrift* 6 (4): 44–66.

Giese, Rachel. (1994). I feel pretty and witty and gay. *Border/Lines* 32: 26–9.

Globe and Mail. (1995). Rethinking the traditional family. 12 May. A20.

– (1996). Justice delayed for homosexuals. 22 February, A22.

Götas Kanal. (1981). Internbulletin for Lesbiska Feminister, Göteborg, Spring.

Grube, John. (1986). Queens and flaming virgins: Towards a sense of gay community. *Rites*, March, 15.

Håkansson, Per Arne. (1987). *Längtan och livsform: Homosexuellas situation i ett heterosexuellt samhälle.* Lund: Lunds universitet.

Herman, Didi. (1994). *Rights of Passage: Struggle for Lesbian and Gay Legal Equality.* Toronto: University of Toronto Press.

Higgins, Ross, and Line Chamberland. (1992). Mixed messages: Lesbians, gay men and the yellow press in Quebec and Ontario during the 1950s and 1960s. In Ian MacKay (ed.), *The Challenge of Modernity.* Toronto: McGraw-Hill Ryerson.

Hirdman, Yvonne. (1988). *Genussystemet: Teoretiska funderingar kring kvinnors sociala underordning.* Uppsala.

Holmberg, Carin. (1993). Välfärdsstaten och den obligatoriska hetrosexualiteten. *Sociologisk Forskning* 4: 56–67.

Hunter, Justine. (1998). Ottawa chided on gay spouses issue. *Vancouver Sun*, 23 June, A3c.

Jacobs, Andrew. (1994). Advertisers discover the gay dollar, *Globe and Mail*, 28 June, A17.

Jenkins, J. Craig, and Bert Klandermans. (1995). The politics of social protest. In J.C. Jenkins and B. Klandermans (eds.), *The Politics of Social Protest.* Minneapolis: University of Minnesota Press.

Johnson, Pat. (1995). Kelowna bigots victorious: Family life debate causes school board upheaval. *X-tra West* 50 13 July, 11.

Jonasdottir, Anna G. (1991). *Love, Power and Political Interests.* Örebro Studies, 7. Orebro: University of Orebro.
Kennedy, Elizabeth Lapovsky, and Madeline Davis. (1993). *Boots of Leather, Slippers of Gold: The History of a Lesbian Community.* New York and London: Routledge.
Khayatt, Didi. (1990). Legalized invisibility: The effect of Bill 7 on lesbian teachers. *Women's Studies International Forum* 13 (3): 185–93.
– (1992). *Lesbian Teachers: An Invisible Presence.* New York: SUNY Press.
Kinsman, Gary. (1996). *The Regulation of Desire: Sexuality in Canada.* 2d ed. Montreal: Black Rose Books.
Laghi, Brian. (1998a). Gay rights fight gets ugly. *Globe and Mail,* 9 April, A1, A6.
– (1998b). Rage finds its voice in Alberta. *Globe and Mail,* 11 April, A1, A4.
Laviolette, Nicole. (1997). The immutable refugees: Sexual orientation in *Canada (A.G.) v. Ward. University of Toronto Faculty of Law Review* 55 (1): 1–41.
Lesbians Making History. (1989). People think this didn't happen in Canada. *Fireweed, Lesbiantics II* 28: 81–94.
Lewin, Ellen (ed.). (1996). *Inventing Lesbian Cultures in America.* Boston: Beacon Press.
McInnes, Craig. (1994a). To homosexual parents, a family is a family. *Globe and Mail,* 2 June, A1, A4.
– (1994b). Boyd backs off on gay spouses. *Globe and Mail,* 9 June, A1, A10.
– Martin Mittelstaedt, and James Rusk. (1994). Ontario bill on gay rights defeated. *Globe and Mail,* 10 June, A1, A10.
Maynard, Steven. (1994). What colour is your underwear? Class, whiteness and homoerotic advertising. *Border/Lines* 32: 4–9.
Mitchell, Alanna. (1993). Faith, hope and chastity. *Globe and Mail,* 18 February, A1.
Mossop, Brian. (1993). Equal rights for gay families. *Canadian Dimension,* August, 13.
Munter, Alex. (1997). Fighting for our families: The challenge of mobilizing Ontario's lesbian, gay and bisexual communities. A paper presented at the Queer Nation? Conference, York University.
Nelson, Fiona. (1996). *Lesbian Motherhood in Canada: An Exploration.* Toronto: University of Toronto Press.
Nestle, Joan (ed.). (1992). *Persistent Desire: A Femme-Butch Reader.* Boston: Alyson Publications.
Newton, Esther. (1985). The mythic, mannish lesbian. *Signs, the Lesbian Issue,* 7–26. Chicago: University of Chicago Press.
– (1994). *Cherry Grove, Fire Island: America's First Gay and Lesbian Town.* New York: Routledge.

O'Brien, Carol-Anne, Robb Travers, and Laurie Bell. (1994). *No Safe Bed: Lesbian, Gay and Bisexual Youth in Residential Services*. Toronto: Central Toronto Youth Serices.

O'Brien, Carol-Anne, and Lorna Weir. (1995). Lesbians and gay men inside and outside families. In Nancy Mandell and Ann Duffy (eds.), *Canadian Families: Diversity, Conflict and Change*. Toronto: Harcourt Brace and Co.

Oldham, Jim. (1993). Spreading the word: CURE founder travels to Ottawa to sow new seeds. *X-tra!* 30 April, 11.

Pegis, Jessica. A sick body of evidence: CURE scrapes bottom for find "scientific" support for its homophobic agenda. *X-Tra!* 3 September, 17.

Penn, Donna. (1994) The lesbian, the prostitute, and the containment of female sexuality in postwar America. In Joanne Meyerowitz (ed.), *Not June Cleaver: Women and Gender in Postwar America 1945–1960*. Philadelphia: Temple University Press.

Peterson, Cynthia. (1995). Envisioning a lesbian equality jurisprudence. In Didi Herman and Carl Stychin (eds.), *Legal Inversions: Lesbians, Gay Men and the Politics of Law*. Philadelphia: Temple University Press.

Philip, Margaret. (1995). More churches blessing gay unions. *Globe and Mail*, 27 May, A6.

Radical History Review. (1995). "The Queer Issue."

Rayside, David. (1998). *On the Fringe: Gays and Lesbians in the Political Process*. Ithaca and London: Cornell University Press.

RFSL. (1995). Kongresshandlingar. Unpublished archival material.

RFSL Göteborg avdelning 2. (1995). *Verksamhetsberattelse, verksamhetsaret 1994*. Göteborg.

Robson, Ruthann. (1994). Resisting the family: Repositioning lesbians in legal theory. *Signs* 19 (4): 975–96.

Ross, Becki. (1988). Heterosexuals only need apply: The secretary of state's regulation of lesbian existence. *Resources for Feminist Research* 17 (3): 35–9.

– (1995). *The House that Jill Built: A Lesbian Nation in Formation*. Toronto: University of Toronto Press.

– (1997). "It's merely designed for sexual arousal": Interrogating the indefensibility of lesbian smut. In Brenda Cossman, Shannon Bell, Lise Gotell, and Becki Ross, *Bad Attitudes: Pornography, Feminism, and the Butler Decision*. Toronto: University of Toronto Press.

Smith, Julie. (1994). Archbishop assails same-sex benefits. *Globe and Mail*, 30 May, A5.

Smith, Miriam. (1998). Social movements and equality-seeking: Lesbian and gay rights in Canada, 1971–1995. Unpublished manuscript, Carleton University, Ottawa.

Socialstyrelsen. (1991). *Homosexuellas rättigheter*. Stockholm.

SOU. (1984). *Homosexuella och samhället: Betänkande av utredningen om homosexuellas situation i samhället.* Stockholm.

Steele, Scott. (1994). Coming out. *Maclean's*, 16 May, 40–3.

Stone, Sharon Dale. (1997). From stereotypes to visible diversity: Lesbian political organizing. In William Carroll (ed.), *Organizing Dissent: Social Movements and Social Theory.* 2d ed. Toronto: Garamond Press.

Tiby, Eva. (1985). Inseminationsutredningen. *Kvinnovetenskaplig tidskrift* 4: 66–8.

Turner, Janice. (1994). State of the union. *Toronto Star,* 23 April, H1, H9.

Ursel, Susan. (1995). Bill 167 and full human rights. In Katherine Arnup (ed.), *Lesbian Parenting: Living with Pride and Prejudice.* Charlottetown: Gynergy Press.

Young, Claire. (1994). Taxing times for lesbians and gay men: Equality at what cost? *Dalhousie Law Journal* 17: 534–59.

Organized for Health: Women's Activism in Canada and Sweden

GEORGINA FELDBERG AND MARIANNE CARLSSON

ABSTRACT

Women's health activism provides an example of the tenuous and fragile relationships between women's organizing and public policy. Our chapter begins with a brief overview of women's organizing for health and the different Canadian and Swedish approaches to this subject. It then examines the ways in which Canadian and Swedish women have also formed their own organizations to respond to the limitations of institutional efforts by drawing on two case studies: first, the state-driven or top-down transformations of health care that attempt to contain costs and redefine health and care, and second, bottom-up or popular and voluntary movements to support women with breast cancer and fibromyalgia. We examine women's roles in effecting governmental and policy transformations, and we look briefly at the alternatives that their grassroots organizing has provided. In conclusion, we assess the ways in which the different portraits of women's organizing that we have constructed reflect our own national and disciplinary backgrounds together with the very different relationships that Canadian and Swedish women have to the authorities of science and the state. We suggest that the importance of diversity issues and the critique of science as masculine shape Canadian women's organizing around health, while in Sweden the influence of labour organizing is more critical.

Women's health activism provides an example of the tenuous and fragile relationships between women's organizing and public policy. As historians and sociologists in both North America and western Europe have demonstrated, health has long been a fundamental pivot for women's mobilization, association, and interaction with the state.

Women have rallied at various historical moments to ensure their access to safe contraception, maternity, and working conditions. They have sought food and care for themselves and their families. Yet the relationships between women's concerted activity and policy change remain unclear.

Anglo-American feminist scholarship suggests significant international commonalities in women's organizing for health which are true of Canada and Sweden. In both countries they struggled to preserve women's distinctive forms of healing and curing, such as midwifery and herbalism (Ehrenreich and English, 1979; Apple, 1992; Lewenhak, 1992; Carlsson and Holmdahl, 1992; Wendt, 1984). In both countries, women worked to ensure that children were adequately fed (Arnup et al., 1990; Arnup, 1994; Davidsson, 1986). In both they fought to ensure access to safe abortions and effective contraceptives (Callersten-Brunell and Lidholm, 1985; SOU, 1994). Canadian birth-control advocates Elizabeth Bagshaw, Helen MacMurchy, and Mary Hawkins find their Swedish counterpart in Elise Ottesen Jensen, a pioneer in the field of sexual education who founded the organization RFSU (Association of Sexual Education).

But despite such historical similarities, the task of looking at intersections between women's organizing and health policy in Canada and Sweden poses significant conceptual and methodological problems. The first relates to documentation. Health work in both Canada and Sweden is primarily women's work. However, historiographical and analytical traditions that privilege medicine over other health-related activities have rendered much of what women do virtually invisible. Second, in both countries, women who engage in activism and activities designed to change health policy attach greater importance to getting their work done than to record-keeping and historical documentation. Hence we cannot accurately gauge the impact that women's organizing has had on policy without going beyond written reports and texts to oral histories, interviews, and other primary research that is mostly outside the scope of this article. Third, comparisons are difficult to make and differences difficult to assess when viewed out of context. How does one meaningfully interpret differences between the following: large, fragmented Canada and the much smaller and more homogeneous Sweden; old and established Swedish society and the much newer Canadian society; the differential impacts of globalization and trade as they are mediated by the European Union and the North American Free Trade Agreement; different social relationships to class and labour movements; and citizens' very different expectations of the state?

These questions proved particularly challenging to the authors of this chapter because, incidentally but significantly, we approached the task of mapping relationships between gender, health policy, and women's organizing very differently. Our distinct approaches reflect both the more fundamental differences in Canadian and Swedish traditions of organizing, which are elaborated upon in the introduction to this volume and built upon here, and definitions, structures, and concerns that are unique to women's health activism. But they also reflect our very different disciplinary backgrounds – one of us is a psychologist who teaches in a health sciences program, the other is an interdisciplinary social scientist who teaches within a faculty of arts. Hence this article, in addition to describing and assessing national differences in women's organizing around health policy, also reflects the difficulties of cross-disciplinary, cross-national research.

Our chapter begins with a brief overview of women's organizing for health and the different Canadian and Swedish approaches to this subject. It then uses two case studies – health reform and activism around the diseases of fibromyalgia and breast cancer – to explore specific Canadian-Swedish differences: in the relationship between the state and women's organizing, in types of organizing, and in voluntarism and women's organizing. In Canada, women's struggles to influence policy on their health exemplify a familiar contest with the institutions of a middle-class state (Bashevkin, 1993; Adamson et al., 1988; Vickers et al., 1993). Although there is a strong professional component to Canadian women's health reform, most of what is "recognized" as women's organizing around health policy shares much with other grassroots activism. Canadian women's organizing falls outside the domain of established politics, is extra-governmental, and stands apart from the major interest groups and lobbies that have gained the ear of government. It is isolated from the standard sources of political power. Women's struggles to change health policy are consequently mediated by their constrained economic and political power and their limited access to the institutions of government. In Canada, women's grassroots mobilization around health also stands outside the major institutions of medicine. Thus grassroots women's health organizations such as the Montreal Health Press, the Healthsharing Collective, DES Action, the Toronto and Canadian Women's Health Networks, and the Winnipeg Women's Health Clinic are known for their critical perspectives on medicine as well as on government. The Swedish author of this article did not recognize these kinds of women's activism. In her experience, women's organizing around health took place in more institutional settings, such as unions and "disease organizations." Both of these had established and accepted links to state funding and state authority.

Women's distinct relationships to the state offer one explanation for the differences seen in Canadian and Swedish health activism. So do differences in women's relationships to labour, economic and ethnic diversity, voluntarism, and the authority of science. The case studies of health reform, fibromyalgia, and breast cancer expose the interconnections between women's organizing around health and the authorities of science and unions. We examine women's roles in effecting governmental and policy transformations, and we look briefly at the alternatives that women's grassroots organizing has provided.

WHAT IS WOMEN'S ORGANIZING?

Recent Canadian scholarly and academic traditions acknowledge the ways in which women have acted, at a variety of sites both inside and outside the institutions of government and medicine, to transform policy. They note that in every province and virtually every major city, Canadian women have worked formally and informally, at both institutional and grassroots levels, to change the delivery of services and to create conditions that promote health. Scholars recognize that organizing has occurred in cities across the country and at a range of sites, which include women's "clubs," feminist collectives, workplaces, educational and health-care institutions, community centres, and a myriad of voluntary agencies. Hence, though much of women's organizing is invisible, the concept of organizing for change is familiar to Canadian feminists and academics, who struggle to find the gaps in our knowledge of women's action and to fill them.

Neither the concept of women's organizing nor the frameworks that Canadian scholars have used to study it were shared by our Swedish colleagues. Whether for disciplinary or national reasons, the central questions of whether and how women appeal to the state that marked the starting point for the Canadian author of this chapter had little meaning for the Swede. To the Swedish author, women's organizing was synonymous with women's organizations – groups structured to support and act as advocate for women with a range of medical conditions. However, in Sweden these organizations are fewer and of very different kinds from those that exist in Canada. Moreover, they are markedly different from Canadian organizations in that they resemble unions in the way they work for the interests of members. Our discussions of these very different perceptions and approaches led us to conclude that Canadian and Swedish women have different patterns of understanding and participating in organizing around health; they have played, and continue to play, different roles in shaping health policy.

The literature that exists suggests that Canadian women's efforts to transform health policy have taken at least three different forms: they have been part of general statist efforts to improve the population; they have attempted to use the power of the professions to "mainstream" women's health issues; and they have challenged the authorities of existing institutions. Creating a healthy population was one of the principal goals of the nineteenth-century nation state. Hence in Britain, Germany, the United States, and other Western democracies, statist interests in population growth led, at the turn of the twentieth century, to top-down efforts to improve the health of mothers, if not of women (McLaren and McLaren, 1986; Gordon, 1976; Arnup, 1994). As the Canadian nation came of age, it too identified the need for a healthy population. Both provincial and federal governments implemented laws, institutions, and practices to safeguard mothers and children (Dodd, 1991; Valverde, 1991). During the 1920s, elite Canadian women – women privileged with education and money – worked reciprocally and reflexively and sometimes even as agents of the state. Through voluntary endeavours such as mothers and children's clubs, rallies, and written treatises, they lobbied for improvements in maternal and child health (Strong-Boag, 1979, 1982). Health concerns mobilized women and became a powerful and persistent focus of Canadian women's organizing. In turn, women's organizing around health issues, such as birth control and reproduction, united and consolidated their political activity. In Sweden the same tendencies can be identified in the work of Alva Myrdahl. She was a Swedish social democratic politician and social psychologist who was the best-known advocate for feminism in Sweden and between 1920 and 1940 who fought for health care and social rights for mothers and children (Hirdman, 1988).

Since the 1920s, Canadian feminists have attempted to "mainstream" women's health issues by using the law, the bureaucracy, and medicine to legitimate women's concerns and give them equal status. They have fought to open the system to women and to make it more inclusive. Many of the women who engaged in this kind of organizing belonged to the medical professions. Their issues have included equal opportunity for women physicians in education and training or more recently the inclusion of women subjects in clinical trials. These tendencies can also be identified in Sweden among some women physicians and feminist researchers. The claim for including more women in medical research and clinical trials in order to achieve more equality has been expressed in a report from the Swedish parliament (SOU, 1996a).

By the 1960s, however, Canadian women had also begun to work concertedly outside the state. Through university-based, student-run birth-control clinics or populist movements such as the Abortion

Caravan, they not only demanded inclusive services but also played a part in ensuring that those services – such as safe and effective contraception and abortion – were delivered. The women engaged in this organizing were not content with measures that extended and broadened existing state and medical institutions to make them more inclusive. A critique of existing medical practices and state policies, concerted calls for change, and demands for new and different institutions exemplified their efforts. The Montreal Health Press, the Healthsharing Collective, and other feminist health-care collectives underscored the need for new kinds of health information and services. DES Action, INFACT, and other advocacy groups challenged production standards and they led campaigns to restrict, more fully assess the risks of, and more accurately report the hazards of "medications" that ranged from infant formula to the controversial birth-control agents Depo-provera and Norplant. A vast range of voluntary and community-based agencies emerged to provide information and support on issues of general health and for specific conditions, such as PMS, AIDS, infertility, and breast cancer.

The challenge to health care has also involved broadening the definition of women's health to include the many physical, social, and economic conditions that adversely affect them. Women within universities and the labour movement have challenged provincial and federal ministries of labour to pay greater heed to women's work-related diseases. Within labour unions they have also lobbied for greater attention to childcare and pay and the ways in which these basic social services affect women's health. Canadian women are in a way struggling to achieve an understanding of health and social equality that Swedish women already seem to have. In Sweden, legislation already exists to provide some of what Canadian women want. For example, Swedish women (and men) already have the right to twelve months' parental leave and sixty days of sick leave per child per year, with compensation from the social insurance system. Swedish health care is more comprehensive than the Canadian system, and its goals are broader. It seeks to secure, preserve, and improve the health of the whole Swedish population by working through prevention, health promotion, education, treatment and cure, and chronic care.

During the past decade there have been efforts, with varying degrees of success, to create a rapprochement between these diverse and sometimes incompatible Canadian approaches to women's health reform – between those who want to add women to existing health structures and those who want to create new ones. The Canadian Coalition for a Royal Commission on New Reproductive Technologies successfully mobilized a national investigation into new reproductive technologies that, while it had familiar institutional structures, included research and testimonials from women whose perspectives were critical of the system. In late 1993, scientists, clinicians, pharmaceutical manufacturers, women with breast cancer and their families, and breast cancer advocates met in Montreal at the National Forum on Breast Cancer. Their aim was to increase awareness of the disease, redress imbalances in research funding, and promote a new kind of research, one jointly directed by patients and practitioners.

Such activities have created a political profile for women's health. When the federal Liberal government was elected in 1993, it made women's health a campaign priority; it affirmed this commitment in its "redbook" and throne speech and through a financial commitment to the Centres of Excellence for Research in Women's Health program. In response to women's calls for variety in health-care services, the government of Ontario legalized midwifery and implemented strong new legislation to prevent sexual abuse of clients by health-care providers. The Medical Research Council of Canada also recognized the importance of women's health issues by constituting an Advisory Committee on Women's Health. Thus governmental institutions at a variety of levels have seemed to respond to women's organizing around health.

Canadians have come to recognize the many and diverse ways in which women have mobilized to transform health policy. Some of their awareness relates to the degree of activity, but some of it also relates to scholarly traditions. In Canada, because voluntarism is an important analytic category, at least some of women's organizing around health is captured in broader studies of the voluntarism that has so characterized women's health work and activism (e.g., Valverde, 1991). The work of unpaid political activists and of charitable volunteers alike is captured, if not focused on, in the literature that explores elite women's relationships to the state and science (Ainley, 1990; Dodd and Gorham, 1994).

Voluntarism is less well studied and accepted in Sweden. Most Swedes think that necessary services should be provided by paid workers and not by volunteers and that voluntarism is the same as charity. Although international organizations such as the Salvation Army and the Red Cross may rely on volunteers to offer support and help to the elderly (Swedish Institute, 1996a), neither Swedish social policy nor social research pays significant attention to voluntarism. However, a growing interest in voluntary work can be seen to be emerging in Swedish debate (SOU, 1993). One study has indicated that almost 50 per cent of Swedes are members of at least one voluntary organization. However, the central theme in voluntary work was to gain influence rather than help others. Only 6 per cent of voluntary work was done in direct social support, and two-thirds of that was carried out by women. Though Swedes are willing to engage further in voluntary work, they do not see voluntarism as an alternative to the public provision of services (SOU, 1993).

WOMEN AND THE STATE: THE TRANSFORMATION OF STATE-FUNDED HEALTH CARE

Different relationships between women and the state, as exemplified in attitudes towards public health care and health-care reform, offer one possible explanation for Canadian-Swedish differences. In structure and design the Canadian and Swedish health-care systems can be seen as remarkably similar. Both systems are administered locally and nationally.[1] Both are universal, ensuring that care is accessible in all geographic areas and without prejudice to linguistic, ethnic, or age differences (SFS, 1982; SOSFS, 1993a, 1993b). Both systems are primarily publicly funded, although the Swedish system is more decentralized than the Canadian. Both are committed to providing comprehensive care. Moreover, Canadians, like Swedes, are extremely satisfied with their health-care system (Armstrong and Armstrong, 1996). However, Swedes, unlike Canadians, view the state as benevolent and believe that it takes good care of citizens and their health. Thus in Canada and Sweden different attitudes towards state authority, unions, and voluntarism exist.

These differences can be seen in women's participation in health-care reform. Both Canada and Sweden are currently participating in the international effort to restructure health care. Proposals for reform include the reduction of health-care spending, the reallocation and restructuring of health care so that a significant proportion of work is transferred to the community, and the redefinition of health care and essential health services. In both Canada and Sweden, political debate focuses on claims that the costs for public health care are much too high and must be reduced. In both countries, reducing spending and redefining care present two options for change (Armstrong et al., 1994a; SOU, 1995; Armstrong and Armstrong, 1996). On both sides of the Atlantic one hears frequent laments about the "crisis" in costs, which has served as an impetus to limit funding to particular kinds of care, most particularly hospital care.

The efforts to cut costs, transfer care to the community, and redefine health have significant implications for women in Canada and Sweden. In both countries, changes in funding and delivery are contributing to gendered health inequalities.[2] Another implication is that services "for women" and services used preferentially by women, such as abortions, prolonged hospitalization after operations and childbirth, and new reproductive technologies, are assigned lower priority, provided less comprehensively, and privatized so that patients pay a larger part of the costs (SOU, 1995).

The "funding crisis" has also supplied the rationale for providing different kinds of care, most often in homes and communities. As care for the elderly, the chronically ill, and the disabled is moved from the institution into the home, work falls primarily to women, who serve as either paid and formal or unpaid and informal care providers. In both Canada and Sweden elder care – the services required by frail, elderly patients – poses a major economic and political challenge. Much of this care remains informal and in both countries is provided by relatives and friends. Prior to the Ädel reforms of 1992, Sweden had the highest percentage of elderly persons among Nordic populations, but a low ratio of nursing-home beds (Ribbe and Ljunggren, 1997). Because the elderly and frail elderly are mainly women, and because daughters assume the greatest burdens of care, health-care reform poses significant economic challenges to women (Jansson et al., 1997; Johansson et al., 1992). It also creates social and psychological challenges. Swedish research suggests that relationships are important to quality-of-life issues for women; that women and men define and value health in different ways; that women define their own health in a broader sense than men do, including physical, psychological, social, and existential concerns in their assessments; and that for women, the health of their husbands and children is often more highly valued than their own. As a result, both the economic and the psycho-social burdens of caregiving fall disproportionately on women. A growing number of Swedish women who are daughters, wives, mothers, or sisters have to stay at home to take care of their sick relatives (Kangasniemi, 1997). This is a new phenomenon that will, in a few years' time, pose an obstacle for many women who want to work full-time outside the home.

In Canada much of the critique of health restructuring has come from outside of government. Despite the economic and psycho-social burdens that it imposes upon women, they and their issues were not central to the formal restructuring process initiated in either Canada or Sweden. Despite calls for gender-sensitive planning, for example, only in the last month of its three-year consultative process did the Metropolitan Toronto District Health Council hold a focus group on women's health (MTDHC, 1995). Diverse groups of Canadian women – health-care workers, advocacy groups, and mothers – have formulated critiques of the argument that current levels of spending on health must be reduced. They have responded formally and informally to the debates over health-care restructuring, and they have challenged the definition of health used to justify restructuring. Women physicians and patients have lobbied to preserve services that women use. The Canadian and Ontario Health Coalitions have addressed the impact of hospital closures on paid and unpaid care providers, the majority of whom are women.

As in Canada, Swedish unions, especially those representing auxiliary nurses, have most vociferously challenged the legitimacy of cost-cutting. They have protested the loss of jobs that are largely women's and addressed traditional union issues, such as pay scales, job security, and employment conditions. Sweden, as part of a Nordic community, has engaged in a planned-market approach to delivering health care. In 1973 it was among the first countries to note the limitations of hospital-based delivery systems and advocate greater roles for primary and preventative services (Chaulk, 1994; Kohler and Jakobsen, 1987). However, this early restructuring reaffirmed commitments to social values and public access. Public ownership and access and public operation and accountability of financing and delivery, rather than privatization, were the key vehicles and objectives (Saltman, 1990, 1992). The critique of health restructuring in Sweden has come from inside as well as outside the government. The Swedish prime minister in 1998 gave an oral promise that, within the next two or three years, more money would be allocated to the health-care sector.

Attitudes within and towards unions exemplify some of the differences in Canadian and Swedish women's organizing around health. In Sweden, for example, unions such as the nurses' association that entered bargaining in 1995 have focused on raising wage levels for their own members and not on global issues, such as the definition of health care or the health consequences of unemployment. Raising the wage level and improving working conditions were the key organizing issues, and nurses were criticized during the strike of 1995 for being too "self-interested." Like their Swedish union sisters, Canadian nurses have faced charges of isolation and self-interest, but in Canada, where professionalism, unionism, and activism are less synonymous, they find themselves divided as well along lines of class and feminism. Hence tensions between nurses and other hospital workers, particularly housekeepers, have emerged when nurses failed to extend their bargaining tactics to ensure that all women's work is appropriately remunerated or to broaden their definitions to include housekeeping and other kinds of women's work (Armstrong et al., 1994c). And tensions between nurses, other health-care workers, and women at large have emerged as Canadians debate the consequences of transferring work to the home.

The focus on the interests of the bargaining unit is consistent with the dominant form of Swedish organizing, which is closely connected to labour activism. In Canada, where labour is less strong, workers such as nurses less clearly situated within unions, and unions less clearly identified as key institutions for social change, union activism is further constrained by political agendas of health and social reform. As hospitals have closed, nurses have addressed changes in the quality of care, but they have focused on the loss of medical services and not the broader implications for paid and unpaid female caregivers of hospital closure.

WHAT IS HEALTH? WHAT IS HEALTH CARE? THE ROLES OF GRASSROOTS AND ELITE WOMEN IN CHANGING PRACTICES AND DEFINITIONS

If the restructuring of health care in both Sweden and Canada is about saving money and redistributing work, it also reflects a fundamental debate over definitions of health and health care. In both countries, diverse groups of women have participated in transforming social, medical, and policy understandings of health and health care. Definitions of health span the spectrum from focused biomechanical and biochemical assessments of disease to more holistic discussions of quality of life, health promotion, and population health. Once again, national practices reflect international trends. Since the mid-1970s both national and international agencies have modified the definitions of health. This redefinition is not simply semantic; it has involved a major reconceptualization of what health is and how it is achieved. Once defined as the absence of disease, it is now seen to be a constellation of conditions that create individual and population-wide physical and psycho-social well-being (UN, 1985; WHO, 1995; Carlsson and Holmdahl, 1992; Padilla et al., 1991; Nordenfelt, 1995). The determinants of health include such diverse factors as food, water, shelter, clothing, personal security, education, and economic security. From this perspective, health is an outcome of social and economic experience, and women's health is shaped by their shared social experience. What most sharply distinguishes Canadian and Swedish women's activism around health, then, is the significant differences in social-welfare policy, women's access to a broad spectrum of social services, the "politics of difference," and Swedish women's justified faith that the state will intervene to protect their interests (cf. Eliasson and Lundy in this volume).

In both Canada and Sweden, women have organized to ensure that their health is defined broadly and holistically. In Canada this organizing first took place at the grassroots level and is exemplified in the work of *Healthsharing*. A magazine that reflected the work of a women's collective, it attempted to reflect the radical roots of feminist health activism and broaden the traditional concept of health. For *Healthsharing,* women's health issues were not just reproductive ones, not just about diseases that affect women more than men. For the magazine, feminist health activism was about looking at women's lives as a whole, about the impact of oppression, poverty, racism, class bias, ableism, and ageism on our lives; it was about making fundamental changes to our medical system so that it addressed all of who we were (Gottlieb, 1994). Hence for a significant group of Canadian women, women's health reform seemed inextricably tied to issues of poverty and social justice.

The broader understanding of health that emerged from grassroots activism has come, in both Canada and Sweden, to enjoy a more elite status. During the past two decades, academic social scientists, nurses, and other health researchers have championed new and still broader approaches to women's health research which recognize caring and caregiving as work and interpret it as such (Armstrong et al., 1993b; Bentling, 1992; McPherson, 1996). They broaden medical practice and research to include women's experiences, and they use participatory and qualitative methods and develop theory that begins from female perspectives and experiences (Walters, 1991, 1992, 1993; Charles and Walters, 1994; Messing, 1995; Öster, 1997). A new rhetoric of medical research extols the importance of "women's emotional, social, cultural, spiritual and physical well-being," recognizes that "it is determined by the social, political and economic context of women's lives as well as by biology," and acknowledges "the validity of women's life experiences and women's own beliefs about the experiences of health" (Phillips, 1995). Similarly, policy documents and programs promote a population-health approach to women's health. For example, the recently funded Canadian Centres of Excellence in Women's Health program specifically adopts the parameters and principles of the approach that recognizes the social determinants of health.

New definitions of health and new approaches to health research also make links between knowledge and lived experience with the affirmation that "every woman should be provided with the opportunity to achieve, sustain and maintain health, as defined by that woman herself, to her full potential" (Phillips, 1995). In Canada such affirmations of the interconnections between health and social services have raised concerns about women's employment, economic status, and social position. They have illuminated the ways in which race, ethnicity, age, ability and sexual orientation affect not only women's perceptions of health but also their access to health and health services. And they have exposed the health implications of violence against women.

Canadian women, then, working primarily at the grassroots level, are moving towards the equation of health with social justice and economic well-being that prevails in Sweden. Yet significant differences exist. In Canada, research and rhetoric are stronger than reality. Though definitions of what constitutes health have broadened, and discussions of the social determinants of health have become more pervasive, health-care practice has not actually changed significantly. In some ways, the gap between rhetoric and practice has actually grown. The need to promote health rather than treat disease is one justification given for hospital closures, but no funding is provided to health promotion initiatives. Discussions of environmental causes of breast cancer have become common, but funding for their exploration has not increased.

Swedes, in contrast, less openly equate health reform with social-justice issues. At least at the rhetorical level, the debate over the transformation of care has remained with the professional elites. During the last fifteen years, an ongoing discussion of the meaning of good care has occurred in part because the law (SFS, 1982) states that care should be provided in consultation with the patient. Swedish studies suggest that staff and patients sometimes do not share the same perceptions about what is good caring (Essen, 1994). While staff tend to stress the importance of emotionally oriented caring, patients, especially in somatic care, emphasize task-oriented caring and information. Precisely the opposite could be argued for Canada, where women's organizing around issues of mental health reform and obstetrics, in particular, can be seen to emphasize the importance of more sympathetic or "emotionally oriented" care. In Ontario, for example, women led the struggles for the implementation of legislation that sets standards for professional conduct; this legislation emphasizes patient-practitioner interactions and not technical standards of care.

These varied debates over care reflect broader and more significant differences in Canadian and Swedish feminism that are themselves located in politics of difference. Canadian women, like their Swedish sisters, commonly struggle for "adequate health care," but various groups of Canadian women have perceived the challenge of assuring quality or adequate care differently. As Canadian women witness both the broadening of definitions of health to include healthy public policy and health promotion, and a concomitant increase in technological and medical approaches to health care, the questions "What is women's health?" and "What is good health care" have generated both action and dissension. The needs of diverse groups of women – First Nations, immigrant, disabled, elderly, and lesbian among them – demarcate one line of debate. Organization along lines of diversity is less common in Sweden. The situation for elderly women who need medical care in the home has grown more and more difficult as a result of economic cutbacks. And according to Swedish research, although immigrant women in Sweden think that their health is just as good as that of Swedish women, their perceived quality of life is worse and their rate of unemployment higher, compared with Swedish women. Immigrant women have also reported that they did not receive the warmth and understanding from Swedish health-care personnel as they had expected (Belmar, 1997; Carlsson and Lindquist, 1997).

Population diversity, economic conditions, and limitations to the social-welfare net in Canada highlight interconnections between poverty, social justice, and health that in Sweden are, if not non-existent, virtually invisible. As a Canadian federal policy document indicated, "social and economic variables in women's lives can strongly influence their health and make their health care needs quite different from those of men" (Conference of Deputy Ministers of Health, 1990: 3). At both grassroots and institutional levels, Canadian women have responded to these challenges by allying their crusades for health with broader campaigns for social justice. They acknowledge interconnections between health promotion and disease prevention and environmental, economic, and social reform. For example, when the Federal/Provincial/Territorial Working Group on Women's Health issued its report in 1990, it concluded that "all sectors which influence women's physical and mental health – health, housing, employment, social services, justice and education – must work together to create healthy public policies" (Conference of Deputy Ministers of Health, 1990: v). Women's organizing around health intersects with labour organizing, environmental activism, advocacy for those of minority status, and other broad initiatives for social reform. Efforts to improve working conditions are also attempts to protect health; appeals for better access to education, day care, food, or housing are "health-related." Concern for the environment is also concern for health. So are issues of poverty and the economic constraints that minority women face.

These interconnections are also understood in Sweden, which has long pioneered in social justice and primary health reform. But most Swedes expect the state to attend to any problems. The struggle to make these interconnections is far less important and meaningful to Swedes, who live in a much more homogenous society, with minimal poverty and no food banks (organizations that dispense food to families who are hungry and cannot afford to buy food themselves), and who have much greater access to social services. Diversity issues are paramount to Canadian women (cf. Ross and Landström in this volume), but the special needs of immigrant and minority women, cultural sensitivity, and diversity in definitions of health needs that are critical to Canadians are currently of less consequence to Swedes. Struggles of great importance to Canadians, such as access to childcare or breastfeeding rooms within the workplace, are not important to Swedish women because they are guaranteed parental leave during the breastfeeding period. Struggles about access to culturally specific health care that are important to Canadians are non-existent in Sweden because such diversity is as yet unrecognized.

THE ORGANIZING POWERS OF FEMINISM, SCIENCE, AND VOLUNTARISM: FIBROMYALGIA AND BREAST CANCER

The section above suggests that the different social and economic positions of Canadian and Swedish women and their distinct relationships to labour and the state have given rise to divergent agendas and strategies for health activism. So have distinct relationships with science, feminism, and voluntarism. These factors have multiple and distinctive meanings for Canadian women health activists. While some seek to expand the presence and influence of women within orthodox medicine, others vilify physicians and science for moving slowly to meet women's medical needs and failing to act in their women patients' best interests. They cast female patients as victims of orthodox medicine and demand alternative and oppositional health movements. Swedish women are less committed to the critique of biomedicine for conceptual, political, and economic reasons. In Sweden, science and technology still represent progress, and feminist critiques of science are mostly limited to equality and access issues. The focus by a social democratic government on measures to promote sexual equality has similarly minimized the debate over women's differences: to invoke biological sex differences is, in Sweden, to promote inequality. The links between science and health care appear to be less tightly forged, and traditional and modern medicines are less commonly viewed as incompatible opposites. Despite the dominance of biomedicine, midwifery and other women-centred practices prevail (Benoit, 1998; Benoit and Heitlinger, 1998). These tensions and contradictions create some fundamental Canadian-Swedish differences in women's organizing for health which can be seen in the examples of women's efforts to cope with experiences of fibromyalgia and breast cancer.

Fibromyalgia: The Science and Societies of Woman's Disease

Primary fibromyalgia is defined as a rheumatic disease. It affects between 1 and 3 per cent of the Swedish population; of these, 85–90 per cent are women. The prevalence is about the same in all Western countries (McCain and Scudds, 1988). Because fibromyalgia is less well recognized in Canada, its prevalence is more difficult to estimate; however, the disease is similarly known to affect a disproportionate number of women. As with candidiasis or chronic fatigue, the symptoms of fibromyalgia include a range of physical and mental concerns: trouble sleeping, with concomitant depression and inability to work (Henriksson, 1995). Until recently, fibromyalgia was regarded as a vague psychological illness with no identifiable cause and dubious legitimacy (University of Toronto, 1994) and virtually ignored by medical professionals in both Canada and Sweden. It was not considered a "real" disease, and most treatments for fibromyalgia were not thought to be medically credible.

In both countries, women have struggled to achieve medical legitimacy for fibromyalgia, and in doing so they have sought the assistance of voluntary agencies. These agencies are a typical form of organizing; in both Canada and Sweden some women's organizing around health has taken shape in organizations created to meet women's special interests.

However, there are significant differences in the structure and mandates of Canadian and Swedish voluntary associations. Support groups for women with premenstrual syndrome (PMS), seasonal affective disorder (SAD), infertility, cancer, disabilities, and a range of psychological and chronic conditions proliferated in Canada after the 1960s. The vast majority of these are voluntary. They rely primarily on women's unpaid labour to generate information, support, and funding. More recently, organizations that provide funding or lobby for research into diseases which disproportionately affect women, such as lupus or breast cancer, have emerged. Swedish organizations similarly exist to meet the needs of people with rheumatic diseases, cancer, heart and lung ailments, neurological diseases, or asthma and allergic conditions. These organizations are more formal and nationally structured than their Canadian counterparts. They are also publicly funded and rely on financial support from the state. Moreover, their structure, mandate, and impact are different. Despite their women-centred focus, they are often not considered feminist organizations. They are typical of Swedish organizations mobilized not just around health issues but also in the areas of temperance, religion, and labour. Their function and structure are much like those of Swedish unions; apart from lobbying, they also create boards and approach governments.

Two specific types of patient organizations – the association for patients with primary fibromyalgia and the association for women with breast cancer – exemplify Canadian-Swedish differences. The national dissimilarities in associations established to serve women with these diseases point in particular to differences in the relationships between women's organizing, voluntarism, and the power of science.

In Sweden, despite the medical murkiness surrounding fibromyalgia, the diagnosis is probably more legitimate than in Canada. Women with the disease are organized in the Arthritis Society. A special Fibromyalgia Association was formed in 1992 to look after the interests of women with the disease; two years later it had four thousand members. Both the membership and the management structure of the Fibromyalgia Association are dominated by women. Though neither of these organizations has any gender-specific consciousness or feminist imperative, both could be classified as "women's organizations" because the majority of their members are women. Their primary objectives have been to follow international research, make that research more commonly available, and increase awareness of the disease. The Fibromyalgia Association aims to include information and/or education about fibromyalgia in all health education programs and to make public health, medical, and social-service authorities, employment offices, the public, and the media more knowledgeable about the disease. The association plays an important role in educating and disseminating information to patients, the health-care system, and society. Its most important functions are to offer personal support and to help women with primary fibromyalgia give and get support and comfort and to learn to cope both psychologically and practically with the disease.

Another important function is to protect the rights of members. Despite the emphasis placed on providing support and comfort to members, the Fibromyalgia Association recently shifted its energies towards the protection of rights, and it is likely that in the future this will become the most important function. As part of the climate of health-care restructuring and reform, Sweden has reduced compensation for sickness and social benefits. Those with low incomes and chronic diseases – such as fibromyalgia patients, who have difficulty working because they suffer chronic pain and associated fatigue – are the most affected. Hence the association has worked to ensure that women's economic interests are protected. More specifically, it has lobbied the government to try to ensure that the Swedish health and social-services sectors provide sick pay, accommodate reductions in workload, compensate for the costs of disease, and provide the equipment that fibromyalgia patients need in order to function (Söderlund, 1995).

Canadian women's activism around fibromyalgia is both greater and less visible than that in Sweden. There are more Canadian associations to serve women with fibromyalgia, yet the disease is less widely recognized by Canadians. The organizations that serve Canadian women with fibromyalgia include the Arthritis Society; but in large measure because the diagnosis of fibromyalgia is so ambiguous, affected Canadian women also belong to the Chronic Fatigue Association, the Fibromyalgia Association, and the Fibrositis Association. Yet, though this disease disproportionately affects females, it is not widely publicized, and it has far less status than PMS, breast cancer, and reproductive issues.

The Canadian associations that serve women with fibromyalgia provide information about the symptoms of the disease, lobby for improved treatment, and offer counselling and support. Canadian campaigns to ensure that women with fibromyalgia are covered by insurance policies, that fibromyalgia is listed as a compensable disease (under worker's compensation), or that women with fibromyalgia receive disability allowances are limited. Whereas in Sweden, labour is organized and work issues of relevance to women with fibromyalgia are emphasized, in Canada most activity has focused on the importance of treatment. Two distinct approaches to securing treatment exist. First, Canadians have promoted alternative approaches and treatments for fibromyalgia that include homeopathy, acupuncture, and nutritional therapies. Second, Canadian organizations have struggled, with some measure of success, to obtain medical legitimacy for fibromyalgia and to promote scientific research on the disease. Women have fought this battle by providing testimonials, gathering collective experiences, and using their individual and collective experiences to challenge prevailing assumptions about the nature of fibromyalgia. Their efforts have been successful. *Health News,* a publication of the University of Toronto's Faculty of Medicine, acknowledged that fibromyalgia is a "perplexing pain syndrome ... yet standard laboratory tests find no underlying organic abnormalities to explain the demoralizing symptoms." But the journal nonetheless gave the disease front-page billing and reviewed its medical management (University of Toronto, 1994).

While such medical recognition may be a first and necessary step towards making appeals for disability and unemployment insurance, these employment issues have not been a focus. Instead, activism has involved efforts to convince orthodox medical practitioners of the existence of the condition and to gain medical acceptance of treatment regimens.

The success of Canadian women's organizing around fibromyalgia can in many ways be seen as the outcome of a grassroots initiative in which women who suffered from the disease campaigned successfully from outside the standard political and medical establishments. However, to achieve their goals, fibromyalgia societies in Canada as well as in Sweden have enlisted medical authorities. Now it is physicians, primarily males, who lead the campaign to have fibromyalgia recognized. It is their publications that are reviewed and considered as the debate over fibromyalgia continues. And as the medical profession has come to recognize the condition, some of the battles over alternative and critical status that women were fighting fell by the wayside. As a result, it becomes difficult to assess the extent to which the Canadian and the Swedish fibromyalgia associations are actually successful examples of women's organizing. The societies and organizations that have lobbied around fibromyalgia serve a population which is predominately women, and through them women have presented their individual cases; but the legitimization of fibromyalgia may owe more to the work of male physicians who have published articles on the subject.

Breast Cancer Activism: Science, Industry, and the State

Women's organizing around breast cancer provides an even more compelling example of the difficulties inherent in evaluating women's efforts to organize for change in health care and health policy, and it illustrates the ways in which differing expectations of the links between science and industry distinguish women's organizing for health in Canada and Sweden. Unlike fibromyalgia, which is among the least publicized and recognized diseases, breast cancer is the most common and feared tumour disease of women. In Sweden about 4,700 women a year are diagnosed with breast cancer; about 1,500 die. Canadian prevalence and mortality statistics are comparable.

As is the case with fibromyalgia, a national organization exists in Sweden for women with breast cancer, the BRO. Founded in 1982, it is part of an international network called "Reach to Recovery." By the mid-1990s the BRO had grown significantly. Local organizations for women with breast cancer, such as the BCF, supplement the work of the BRO. The primary functions of the BRO are to rehabilitate patients and assist in the development of aids and prostheses. The BCF provides personal support, information, and education to both health-care professionals and the public. It works with the medical system to improve access to rehabilitation and care. As is the case for members of the Fibromyalgia Association, patients who use the BRO and the BCF stress the importance of support services. The diagnosis of breast cancer evokes grief, anger, and intense fear in most women. The patient organization assists women in their efforts to deal with these emotions, and it specializes in providing social support. In contrast to the Fibromyalgia Association, neither the BRO nor the BCF has attempted to reform the benefits provided to or the working conditions for women with breast cancer.

In Canada, organizing around breast cancer has only recently assumed a status that is independent of the Canadian Cancer Society. The National Forum on Breast Cancer, held in Montreal in 1993, provided a unique and important testimony to women's activism. A response to the pleas of breast cancer survivors, victims, and their families – who wanted to know why there is still no cure for this disease and why, after so many years, early detection has made little difference to survival – the forum sought to give legitimacy to a range of women's concerns. It provided the opportunity for survivors, the families of victims, health care providers, biomedical researchers, and sociologists and anthropologists of health to meet together, define a research strategy that would give women a greater voice in the research that was being undertaken on breast cancer, and address factors – among these, environmental causes of disease and the impact of stress – that were not adequately understood.

This emphasis on research funding and priorities and the appeal for investigations into the environmental and dietary causes of disease distinguishes Canadian and Swedish women's organizing around breast cancer. Again, these different focuses reflect fundamental dissimilarities in Canadian and Swedish women's experiences. In Sweden the Cancer Society is a rich organization, strongly supported with private donations, and breast cancer, as the most common type of cancer in women in the country, gets significant attention. Because the state imposes strict controls on agriculture, concerns about PCBs, organochlorines, and other environmental and dietary toxins are minimal.

Discussions at the Canadian forum also indicated that in Canada, unlike in Sweden, breast cancer activism and women's health more generally reflect a struggle by women to define and control their own health care that is further encumbered by divisions among them. Now, as in the past, these divisions are based on ethnicity, race, and class, but they are also located in women's disparate access to the power and authority of science. In a very fundamental way, the National Forum on Breast Cancer reflected the long-standing and fraught relationships among Canadian women, and between women and the biomedical establishment, that constrain women's grassroots organizing around health.

The National Forum and subsequent battles within the "breast cancer reform community" demonstrate that three communities of women, as outlined below, which have mobilized around women's health can have very different expectations of health policy and health-care reform policy. For some, the preservation and re-creation of women's special and distinct experiences of health and healing are paramount. For others, equity for and equality of women within medicine are more important than critiques of science or masculine science. For still others, women's distinct experiences of health reflect their political, economic, and social roles and their differential access to the modes of production, rather than any inherent biological sex differences.

The National Forum crystallized these different expectations and commitments. In some ways, it appeared remarkably successful in that it reshaped both medical research and health policy. Following the forum, the Medical Research Council of Canada devoted special funds to research on breast cancer that would move beyond standard approaches. It also set aside funds for investigations of treatment. Provincial agencies and Health Canada provided funding for breast cancer support and resource centres, among these, Ontario's Willows, which had its launch in June 1995. But though the forum effectively moulded policy, recent controversy over breast cancer resource centres suggests that it compromised many of its original aims and objectives. It succeeded in placing breast cancer on the research map, but breast cancer genes and heritable forms of breast cancer – rather than stress, environment, and other factors that survivors themselves identify – have taken the limelight. Hence, by translating their issues into the traditional language of biomedicine, women legitimized their concerns, but they lost some of the substance of those concerns. As the Medical Research Council declares the need for research on women and dedicates funds to finding "cures for breast cancer" or studying hormone therapy for menopausal women, social services and grassroots agencies that serve women with breast cancer are cut. For some Canadian women, these health-policy successes occurred because women found ways in which to ally themselves with the institutions of science and translate their concerns into the language of science, and that alliance compromised some women while silencing others.

In Sweden the alliances and compromises are less clear. Scientists other than traditional biomedical staff have taken an interest in research into breast cancer; this is especially true of researchers in nursing and psychology, who stress the importance of the psychosocial and existential aspects of living with the disease (Hamrin et al., 1996). The legitimacy accorded this research is difficult to measure, but it provokes less-heated conflict among women, perhaps because of the status that Swedes accord to women's work. Though occupational segregation by sex is great in Sweden and other Nordic countries – with women concentrated in midwifery, nursing, and other helping professions – the economic and social value of this work is less contested. Moreover, between 1970 and 1990 the "feminization gap" between high- and low-status medical employment narrowed significantly in Sweden, and this change was largely the result of the increased number of women entering medicine (Melkas and Anker, 1997).

Canadian women seem particularly preoccupied with the "mainstreaming of women's health" – with questions of the proper domain of women's health initiatives and their relationship to science. As indicated above, much of the recent Canadian women's grassroots organizing around health has been predicated upon a critique of biomedicine. This critique has successfully united women of varied backgrounds who share no more than that they are women and that they do not accept a traditional Western faith in the power of science. Their issues are diverse and encompass concerns about the environment, alternative forms of healing, and disability.

Finally, in Sweden, critiques of science, particularly feminist critiques, are less concerned with economic or market issues. In Canada the power of science is perceived to be both ideological and economic. In the era of the North American Free Trade Agreement, the health industry is growing, and women's health is emerging as big business. Both Western biomedicine and more traditional or holistic forms of medicine are capitalizing on women as markets. *Prevention Magazine*, which advocates nutritional approaches to the prevention of disease, has had an increasing impact on policies pertaining to research on menopause, osteoporosis, and other women's health concerns as vitamin products and supplementation have become increasingly lucrative. Older women have similarly come to influence health policy when their market share, or the costs of caring for them, is calculated. But Native women, disabled women, and other women with less clear access to the market have not been as successful in making their voices heard. In Sweden, though there is growing commercial interest in health magazines that stress the importance of healthy food, vitamins, and natural products, women's health has not yet become an industry, driven by biotechnology.

CONCLUSION

The divergent patterns of women's organizing for health found in Canada and Sweden reflect differences in the socio-economic conditions of women, their different patterns of organizing, and more fundamental differences in women's relationships to labour, the state, economic inequity and the authority of science. In comparison with their Canadian counterparts, Swedish women identify more strongly with labour, have greater confidence that the state will intervene appropriately, and have relatively little experience with poverty. In debates over health-care restructuring, they have been more accepting of the need for costs than have Canadian women. In North America, where access to science supersedes class as a dividing force, women's organizing around health has been less accepting of the authority of science, more circumspect about interconnections between science and industry, and more sensitive to issues of population diversity.

As the above discussion indicates, globalization and new trade alliances are transforming the delivery of health care in both Canada and Sweden. As debate focuses on the costs of care and the need to reduce spending, women in both countries will notice threats to and compromises in what they believed to be human rights. In Sweden, when this development becomes more obvious, Carlsson predicts that the motivation to organize, demand, and look after rights will be much greater, and that women's organizations in relation to the health care system will grow during the next several years. As the Swedish population becomes increasingly diverse and new health markets are created, women may also become more concerned about the intellectual and economic authorities of science. In Canada the erosion of services has already created new campaigns for social justice and closer alliances among women's health activists and unions. There is much that we can learn from each other.

NOTES

The authors wish to thank Fataneh Farahani and Tracy Shannon for the research assistance that they provided.

1 The geographical base of the Swedish health-care system is twenty-three county councils and three big city regions (Stockholm, the capital; Göteborg on the west coast; and Malmö in the south. These county councils and city regions are organized into six hospital regions (from south to north), with a university hospital and a training program for medical doctors in every region. In Canada, health care is governed by the Canada Health Act. Administration of the act and ultimate responsibility for health is shared among three different levels of government: federal, provincial, and local. Technically, health care falls within the jurisdiction of the provinces, but though they have ostensible authority, they pay for their individual health-care systems through funds that are "transferred" from the federal government. In order for provinces to

receive funding for health, they must comply with the provisions of the Canada Health Act. These include universality, accessibility, and portability. As a result, there is no single health-care system but a series of provincial ones (Armstrong et al., 1994; Vayda and Deber, 1992).

2 In Sweden marked differences in health between different social groups, especially men and women, are growing. Women from the working class and lower middle class have had a negative health development since 1980 (Swedish Institute, 1996b; SOU, 1994). A comparison between Sweden and other countries in western Europe showed that for Swedish women the level of perceived general health by level of education demonstrated greater inequality than in the other countries (Mackenbach et al., 1997).

REFERENCES

Adamson, Nancy, Linda Briskin, and Margaret McPhail. (1988). *Feminist Organizing for Change: The Contemporary Women's Movement in Canada*. Don Mills, Ont.: Oxford University Press.

Ainley, Marianne Gosztonyi. (1990). *Despite the Odds: Essays on Canadian Women and Science*. Montreal: Vehicule Press.

Apple, Rima D. (1992). *Women, Health and Medicine in America*. New Brunswick, NJ: Rutgers University Press.

Armstrong, Pat, and Hugh Armstrong. (1996). *Wasting Away: The Undermining of Canadian Healthcare*. Toronto/Oxford: Oxford.

Armstrong, Pat, et al. (1993a). *Take Care: Warning Signals for Canada's Health System*. Toronto: Garamond.

– (1993b). *Vital Signs: Nursing in Transition*. Toronto: Garamond.

– (1993c). Vital signs: Voices from the ward. In Armstrong et al., *Take Care*.

Arnup, Katherine. (1994). *Education for Motherhood: Advice for Mothers in Twentieth-Century Canada*. Toronto: University of Toronto Press.

– Andrée Lévesque, and Ruth Roach Pearson. (1990). *Delivering Motherhood: Maternal Ideologies and Practices in the 19th and 20th Centuries*. London: Routledge.

Bashevkin, Sylvia. (1993). *Toeing the Line: Women and Party Politics n English Canada*. Don Mills, Ont.: Oxford University Press.

Benoit, Cecilia. (1998). Midwives' identity and practice: Canada and Sweden in comparative perspective. In V. Olgiati, L. Orzack, and M. Saks (eds.), *Professions, Identity and Order in Comparative Perspective*. Onati, Spain: Onati International Institute.

– and A. Heitlinger. (1998). Women's health caring work in comparative perspective: Canada, Sweden and Czechoslovakia/Czech Republic as case examples. *Social Science and Medicine* 47 (8): 1101–11.

Belmar, F. (1997). Att vara gravid och föda barn i en främmande miljö. Paper delivered at the Conference for Swedish Health Care Personnel, Stockholm.

Bentling, S. (1992). I idéernas värld. Dissertation, University of Uppsala.

Callersten-Brunell, M., and M. Lidholm. (1985). *Abort: Erfarenheter och teorier.* Stockholm: Liber Förlag

Carlsson, M., and B. Holmdahl. (1992). *Psykologiska utgångspunkter för vård och omvårdnad.* Stockholm: Almqvist & Wiksell.

Carlsson, M., and R. Lindquist. (1997). Perceived health and quality of life in women and men in Sweden. Unpublished data.

Charles, N., and V. Walters. (1994). Women's health: women's voice. *Journal of Health and Social Care in the Community* 2: 329–38.

Chaulk, C. Patrick. (1994). Preventive healthcare in six countries: Models for reform? *Health Care Financing Review* 15 (4): 7–21.

Conference of Deputy Ministers of Health (Canada). (1990). Federal/Provincial/Territorial Working Group on Women's Health. *Working together for Women's Health: A Framework for the Development of Policies and Programs.* [Toronto?]: The Working Group.

Davidsson, J. (1986). *Primärvård: Hälso- och sjukvården i primärvårdens regi.* Lund: Studentlitteratur.

Dodd, Dianne. (1991). Advice to parents: The blue books, Helen MacMurchy, M.D., and the federal Department of Health, 1920–34. *Canadian Bulletin of Medical History* 8: 203–30.

– and D. Gorham. (1994). *Caring and Curing: Historical Perspectives on Women and Healing in Canada.* Ottawa: University of Ottawa Press.

Ehrenreich, Barbara, and Dierdre English. (1979). *For Her Own Good: 150 Years of the Experts' Advice to Women.* New York: Anchor Doubleday.

Essen, L. von. (1994). What is good caring? Dissertation, University of Uppsala.

Gordon, Linda. (1976). *Woman's Body, Woman's Right: A Social History of Birth Control in America.* New York: Grossman.

Gotlieb, Amy. (1994). Saying goodbye to healthsharing. *Canadian Women's Studies* 14 (3): 117–18.

Hamrin, E., M. Carlsson, C. Häggmark, A. Langius, and A. Wahlström. (1996). *Utvärdering av bröstcancerpatienters livssituation utifrån olika vårdperspektiv: Rapport från förstudier.* Omvårdnadsforskning vid Hälsouniversitetet i Linköping, nr 9. Linköping: Faculty of Health Sciences, University of Linköping.

Henriksson C. (1995). *Living with Fibromyalgia A Study of the Consequences for Daily Activities.* Linköping: Department of Caring Sciences and Department of Rheumatology, Faculty of Health Sciences, Linköping University, and Department of Health and Society, Institute of Tema Research, Linköping University.

Hirdman Y. (1988). Alva Myrdahl – en studie i feminism. *Kvinnovetenskaplig Tidskrift* 4: 15–30.

Jansson, W., M. Grafström, and B. Winblad. (1997). Daughters and sons as caregivers for their demented and non-demented elderly parents. A part of a population-based study carried out in Sweden. *Scandinavian Journal of Social Medicine* 4: 289–95.

Johansson, L., and M. Thorslund. (1992). Care needs and sources of support in a nationwide sample of elderly in Sweden. *Z Gerontology* 25 (1): 57–62.

Kangasniemi, S. (1997). *Den okända anhörigvårdaren*. Uppsala: Magisteruppsats Centrum för Omvårdnadsvetenskap, Uppsala Universitet.

Kohler, L., and G. Jakobsen. (1987). *Children's Health and Wellbeing in the Nordic Countries*. Oxford: McKeith.

– (1991). *Children's Health in Sweden*. Stockholm: socialstyrelse.

Lewenhak, S. (1982). *Kvinnoverk*. Stockholm: Wahlstroöm.

McCain, G.A., and R.A. Scudds. (1988). The concepts of primary Fibromyalgia (fibrositis): Clinical value, relation and significance to other chronic musculosceletal pain syndromes. *Pain* 33: 272–87.

Mackenbach. J.P., A.E. Kunst, A.E.J.M. Cavelaars, F. Groenhof, J.J. Geurts, and the EU Working Group on Socioeconomic Inequalities in Health. (1977). Socioeconomic inequalities in morbidity and mortality in western Europe. *The Lancet* 349: 1655–9.

McLaren, Angus, and Arlene Tiger McLaren. (1986). *The Bedroom and the State: Changing Practices and Politics of Contraception and Abortion in Canada, 1880–1980*. Toronto: McClelland and Stewart.

McPherson, Katherine. (1996). *Bedside Matters: The Transformation of Canadian Nursing*. Don Mills, Ont.: Oxford University Press.

Melkas, Helina, and Richard Anker. (1997). Occupational segregation by sex in Nordic Countries: An empirical investigation. *International Labour Review* 136: 341–63.

Messing, Karen. (1995). Don't use a wrench to peel potatoes: Biological science constructed on male model systems is a risk to women workers' health. In S. Burt and L. Code (eds.), *Changing Methods: Feminists Transforming Practice*. Toronto: Broadview.

Metropolitan Toronto District Health Council (MTDHC), Hospital Restructuring Project. (1995). *Report on Women's Health*. Toronto.

Nordenfelt, L. (1995). On chronic illness and quality of life: A conceptual framework. *Health Care Analysis* 3: 290–8.

Öster, I. (1997). Könsteoretiskt perspektiv på hälsa. Paper delivered at the Conference for Swedish Health Care Personnel, Stockholm.

Padilla, G.D., B. Ferrell, M. Grant, and M. Rhiner. (1991). Defining the content of quality of life for cancer patients with pain. *Cancer Nursing* 13 (2): 108–15.

Phillips, Susan. (1995). The social context of women's health: Goals and objectives for medical education. *Canadian Medical Association Journal* 152: 507.

Ribbe, Miel W., and Gonnar Ljunggren. (1997). Nursing homes in ten nations: A comparison between countries and settings. *Age and Aging* 26: 3–12.

Romlid, C. (in press). Swedish midwives and their instruments in the the eighteenth and nineteenth centuries. In H. Marland and A.M. Raaferty (eds.), *Midwives, Society, and Childbirth. Debates and Controversies in the Modern Period.*

Saltman, Richard B. (1990). Competition and reform in the Swedish health system. *Milbank Quarterly* 68 (4): 397–618.

– (1992). Recent health policy initiatives in Nordic countries. *Health Care Financing Review* 13 (4): 157–68.

SFS. (1982). *Hälso- och sjukvårdslagen.* 1982: 763. Uppsala: Författningshandboken, Almqvist & Wiksell.

Söderlund, M. (1995). The Swedish Fibromyalgia Association. Personal communication.

SOSFS. (1990). In K. Wilow, *Författningshandbok för personal inom hälso- och sjukvård.* 1990: 22. Stockholm, 1997.

– (1993a). *Socialstyrelsens allmänna råd. Omvårdnad inom hälso- och sjukvården.* 1993: 17. Stockholm: Socialstyrelsens författningssamling.

– (1993b). *Socialstyrelsens föreskrifter. Kvalitetssäkring i hälso- och sjukvård inklusive tandvård.* 1993: 9. Stockholm: Socialstyrelsens författningssamling.

– (1996). *Barnmorskans förskrivningsrätt.* 1996: 21. Stockholm: Socialstyrelsens författningssamling.

SOU. (1993). *Frivilligt socialt arbete: Kartläggning och kunskapsöversikt.* Rapport av socialtjänstkommittén. 1993: 82. Stockholm.

– (1994). *Folkhälsorapport.* 1994: 9. Stockholm.

– (1995). *Priorities in Health Care: Ethics, Economy, Implementation.* 1995: 5. Final report by the Swedish Parliament Priorities Commission, Stockholm.

– (1996a). *Jämställd vård: Olika vård på lika villkor.* Huvudbetänkande. 1966: 133. Stockholm: Utredningen om bemötande av kvinnor och män inom hälso- och sjukvården.

– (1996b). *Ny behörighetsreglering på hälso- och sjukvårdens område.* Betänkande av 1994 års behörighetskommitté. 1996: 138. Stockholm.

Strong-Boag, Veronica. (1979). Canada women doctors: Feminism constrained. In Linda Kealy (ed.), *A Not Unreasonable Claim: Women and Reform in Canada, 1880–1920.* Toronto: Women's Press.

– (1982). Wages for housework: Mothers' allowances and the beginnings of social security in Canada. *Journal of Canadian Studies* 14: 24–34.

Swedish Institute. (1996a). *Swedish Institute's Fact Sheets on Sweden: The Care of the Elderly in Sweden.* FS 8.

– (1996b). *Swedish Institute's Fact Sheets on Sweden: The Health Care System in Sweden.* FS 76.

United Nations (UN). (1985). *Nairobi: Forward-Looking Strategies for the Advancement of Women.* Geneva.

University of Toronto, Faculty of Medicine. (1994). Probing the mystery of fibromyalgia. *Health News,* October, 1.

Valverde, Mariana. (1991). *The Age of Light, Soap and Water: Moral Reform in English Canada, 1885–1925.* Toronto: McClelland and Stewart.

Vayda, Eugene, and Raisa Deber. (1992). The Canadian health-care system: A developmental overview. In C. David Naylor (ed.), *Canadian Health Care and the State.* Montreal and Kingston: McGill-Queen's University Press.

Vickers, Jill, et al. (1993). *Politics as If Women Mattered.* Toronto: University of Toronto Press.

Walters, Vivienne. (1991). Beyond medical and academic agendas: Lay perspectives and priorities. *Atlantis* 17: 28–35.

– (1992). Women's views of their main health problems. *Canadian Journal of Public Health* 83: 371–4.

– (1993). Stress, anxiety and depression: Women's accounts of their health problems. *Social Science and Medicine* 36: 393–402.

Wendt, R. (1984). *Självständighet eller underordning: Kvinnoperspektiv på vårdarbete.* Stockholm: Debatt-SHSTF, Studentlitteratur.

Wilson, D.M. (ed.). (1995). *The Canadian Health Care System.* Edmonton: D.M. Wilson.

World Health Organization (WHO) (1995). *Declaration on Women and Health Security.* Geneva.

Index